A MILITARY HISTORY
OF MODERN CHINA
1924-1949

A Military History
of Modern China
1924·1949

By F. F. LIU

PRINCETON, NEW JERSEY

PRINCETON UNIVERSITY PRESS

1956

F. F. Liu was formerly an officer in the Chinese Nationalist forces in both staff and combat assignments. He was wounded twice during World War II, and decorated "for conspicuous gallantry in action." He came to the United States and received his doctorate at Princeton University. His military experience and his training as a scholar have given him an unusual background for the writing of this book. He has used German, French, Russian, and Japanese sources, as well as Chinese and English.

Professionally, Dr. Liu has continued his work in engineering and science. Until recently he has been engaged full-time as an electronics and rocket instrumentation specialist at the Forrestal Research Center in Princeton and is now a senior research scientist with a leading aviation company in California, doing important research in advanced measurements and high-speed aerodynamics.

❖

The title-page design was drawn by the author. The flag is the military banner of Whampoa Academy; the soldier's ballad on the left reflects the realization that learning and wisdom are ultimately more powerful than swords and fighting courage.

Printed in the United States of America
by Princeton University Press, Princeton, New Jersey

TO
MY PARENTS
IN
MEMORIAM

PREFACE

MANY statesmen and scholars have shown a keen interest in the overwhelming changes and tragic upheavals which have torn China asunder in recent years. In search for a key to the causes and significance of these turbulent decades, they have turned to the military history of modern China, which unfortunately is still inadequately recorded and often poorly analyzed. This book has been written in an attempt to offer a clearer statement of the chief events and their true significance.

Six years were spent in research and four in the preparation of the present study. Once the work had started, a man trained primarily as an engineering scientist found the labor of writing it both enormous and challenging, and it did not leave the author's hands until Mr. Leonard R. N. Ashley had collaborated with him for two years, reorganizing and rewriting many parts of the book. I am most indebted to him for his scholarly suggestions and improvements. Many eminent scholars and scientists have lent assistance and encouragement either directly or indirectly. Sir Hugh Taylor, Dean K. H. Condit, and Professors C. D. Perkins and Luigi Crocco, all of Princeton University, did much to make it possible for the author to continue his writing concurrently with research in the instrumentation field of aeronautical electronics. To Professors George A. Graham, Harold H. Sprout, Jacob Viner, A. T. Mason, William Ebenstein, H. L. Childs, and Edward S. Corwin my debt is great. Professor W. W. Lockwood and my classmate at Princeton, Colonel A. J. Goodpaster, were the first to suggest the necessity for the study and to inspire its inception. A number of others have read the manuscript in its entirety or in part and have contributed invaluable suggestions and constructive counsel. Among these must be mentioned Field Marshal General Alexander von Falkenhausen; Mr. Herbert S. Bailey, Jr., Director of the Princeton University Press; and, particularly, Miss Miriam Brokaw, also of that organization; Dr. Hu Shih, the eminent Chinese scholar; Dr. George R. Loehr; and my friend, Professor K. W. So. To my neighbors Monsieur and Madame Henry G. F. Jacqz and to Mr. Shih-kang Tung, Librarian of the Gest Oriental Library at Princeton, I am indebted for much kind assistance. Mrs. Zoe L. Belth and Mrs. Mary Riker have typed parts of the manuscript. Catherine

R. Johnson compiled the index. Dr. James Thorpe, Assistant Dean of the Graduate School at Princeton, was instrumental in obtaining a generous grant from Princeton University to help with the final revision of the manuscript and the preparation of the index. My wife Lily rendered unfailing assistance in typing, proofreading, and many aspects of the preparation. To her goes the credit of encouraging me through a long-drawn-out battle of research and writing over the years until the book was completed.

Finally, to Princeton University's scholarly atmosphere, to its stimulus and great tradition, the author gratefully acknowledges his indebtedness.

F.F.L.

Princeton, New Jersey
June 1955

CONTENTS

CONTENTS

CONTENTS

CONTENTS

The map on page 28 was drawn by
R. S. Snedeker, the charts by
the author.

A MILITARY HISTORY
OF MODERN CHINA
1924-1949

1 · PARTNERS IN REVOLUTION. SOVIET MILITARY POLICY AND ADVISERS IN CHINA

THE spirit of revolution was abroad in China in the 1920's. The warlords who controlled the government at Peking had suppressed the country and laid her open to the rapacious colonialism of Britain and Japan. The youth of China, stirred by the news of the October Revolution in Russia, were ready to rise in revolt. Largely disappointed in the powers of the West, they turned to the example of the Russian Soviet for inspiration.

In the midst of China's unrest there came to leadership a figure to whom the educated class gave substantial support: Dr. Sun Yat-sen, founder of the Chinese republic. But, without an effective army, Dr. Sun found himself ill-equipped to battle in the arena of Chinese politics with the warlords who backed their desires and demands with guns. As far back as 1913, when the feuding warlords of the north had balked at Sun's constitutional proposals, he had been forced to recognize the salient role of military force in Chinese politics. He noted then that ". . . [now] the Parliament engages merely in tongue-lashing and the constitutional law itself has no power to curb their influence; the *tuchun* [military governors during the rule of warlords] mostly belong to the private faction of Yuan Shih-k'ai. Unless we appeal to the force of arms there is no way to settle the present national crisis."[1]

But to create and equip an army was no easy task for Dr. Sun and his Kuomintang. The mission of the revolution seemed doomed to delay or destruction in the hands of undependable forces subject to the whims of the warlords of South China. Soviet Russia, however, saw both China's plight and her potentialities. Lenin, an astute observer of China's revolution, perceived the importance of China to Russia's plan. In the tenth anniversary issue of *Pravda*, he wrote: "China and India are seething. These two nations have a population of more than seven hundred millions. Add to them their Asian neighbors who are in like condition and they comprise over half the popu-

[1] "Dr. Sun Yat-sen's manifesto to the nation on *yueh-fa* in 1913," *Chung-shan ch'uan-shu* (The Complete Works of Dr. Sun Yat-sen), I, Ch. 4.

lation of the earth."[2] Lenin went on to mention the growing revolutionary movements of China and India and their key roles in communism's international plan.

Lenin added action to words. To China he sent some of the Soviet's best diplomats, shrewd men like G. Maring, Adolf Joffe, L. M. Karakhan. Some of the best minds in the Politburo and the Comintern planned for the Chinese revolution. Stalin and Trotsky kept their fingers on the pulse of events in China. Some of the most brilliant minds of the Red Army studied the Chinese military picture. Trotsky, Sklyansky, Yegorov, Bluecher, Bubnov, and others kept themselves constantly informed on developments in the Far East. A policy of Soviet-Chinese friendship was formed in an attempt to foster a spirit of cooperation and a concept of common purpose. Meanwhile the British were still posting notices on the gates to the park in Shanghai which read: "Chinese and dogs not admitted."

The Kremlin's policy paid off. In the vigorous communist activities of Berlin and Paris such men as Chou En-lai, Li Li-san, and Chu Teh took an active part. On the campuses of Shanghai and Peking, Ch'en Tu-hsiu, Li Ta-chao, Mao Tse-tung, and others established the Chinese Communist Party. In Moscow the Sun Yat-sen and Eastern Universities were founded to train the revolutionary core. At the Eastern University, in a lecture to a group of Chinese students, Stalin said: "Formerly, in the eighteenth and nineteenth centuries, revolutions began when the people rose, largely unarmed or poorly armed, to encounter the army of the old regime, trying to demoralize it or at least draw part of it over to their side. . . . In China matters have gone differently. . . . In China an armed revolutionary force is fighting against an armed counter-revolutionary force. Herein lies one of the special features and one of the advantages of the Chinese revolution. Here is the special importance of the Revolutionary Army of China."[3]

Even the Kremlin's timing of its proffer of friendship and help was perfect. Lenin's representative contacted Dr. Sun Yat-sen at the lowest point of the latter's career, after he had been betrayed and forced out of Canton by the army of a treacherous warlord, Ch'en Ch'iung-ming. For sixty days Dr. Sun and his naval force fought Chen from the Pearl River base at Whampoa. A loyal officer joined

[2] "Lenin on China," *Pravda, Tenth Anniversary Issue,* 1922.
[3] Stalin, J. V., *Sochinenya* (Moscow, 1946), VIII, p. 363.

Sun and stayed at his side while he spent his days on a gunboat: Chiang Kai-shek, whose faithfulness and ability endeared him to the elder statesman; he became one of Sun's trusted military advisers.

Another man came to offer Sun assistance—Lenin's personal representative, Maring. At Sun's request a Soviet military representative went to Shanghai to confer with Chiang Kai-shek, whom Sun had delegated to work out a scheme of Canton-Moscow military cooperation. In October 1923 Chiang headed for Moscow, bearing despatches from Sun Yat-sen to Lenin. That mission started the hitherto-unknown officer on his meteoric rise.

While Sun waited for the results of his embassy to Moscow he conferred with Mikhail Borodin on the possibilities of an entente with Soviet Russia that, without subjecting the Chinese to excessive ideological affiliation with the Kremlin, might provide needed support for the Kuomintang. Borodin was able to extend promises of support that would be to China's military and political advantage.

Meanwhile, in Moscow, Lenin was seriously ill. Chiang was received by Trotsky and Stalin and turned over to Sklyansky, then Trotsky's right-hand man in the Commissariat. Arrangements were made for assistance to the Kuomintang and material aid was assured by the Kremlin. The first step was taken with the sending of a small mission of selected military advisers to Canton. Chiang was conducted on extensive tours of various Soviet military establishments, including naval and air bases, in order to acquaint him with the activities of the Red armed forces. In December 1923, passing through Vladivostok on his way back to China, Chiang met the famous Russian commander Vasily K. Bluecher, who, as General Galen (his *nom de guerre*), was later to be the Kuomintang's chief military consultant.

Bluecher was one of the Soviet's most celebrated commanders, exceptionally gifted in organizing and training troops. After the October Revolution he whipped a conglomerate mass of raw recruits into a crack army and led them to victory after victory over the White Russian forces. Bluecher combined the forcefulness of a successful field commander with the shrewdness of a diplomat and the suavity of an experienced public speaker; he was to prove a distinct gain to the conference tables of the Kuomintang.

At about the same time another famous Red Army commander, Marshal A. I. Yegorov, was sent to Peking as the Kremlin's military attaché. His function was to supervise and coordinate all the Soviet's military activities in China. Soviet Russia's interest in Chinese affairs at this period may be judged by the caliber of the men she placed in key positions there. Bluecher's importance has already been noted. Yegorov was later to become chief of the Red Army's general staff and to command important battle fronts in Russia's civil wars. Both Bluecher and Yegorov were among the first five marshals of the Red Army created by Russia in 1933. The others were Tuchehavsky, Voroshilov, and Budyenny.

To assist Bluecher, a skillful military administrator, General Victor Rogacheff, was appointed chief of staff to the Soviet military mission in China, a mission of which Marshal Georgi K. Zhukov, who later gained fame as a Red Army commander in World War II, was reported to have been a member. The size of the mission has been variously reported. During 1925, it was estimated that about a thousand military and political personnel represented the Soviet in China. In that year a nucleus of twenty-four key military advisers was stationed in Canton to assist the Kuomintang.

No other foreign organization can be credited with as much influence in the rise of the Nationalist Army in China as General Galen's (Bluecher's) military mission. Aside from its obvious political functions, the task of this mission was formally stated as follows:

"1. To organize and instruct a National Revolutionary Army in the South of China for national liberation from the yoke of imperialism and for the unification into one independent democratic republic.

"2. To give every assistance to the government [at Canton] by working in the army and among the population in order to promote its democratic principles.

"3. To make popular the doctrine of Communism and of Sovietism and to work toward bringing about complete rapprochement and [mutual] support between China and the U.S.S.R. and to create in the Army, in the labor organizations, and in the peasantry the desire for a further revolutionary movement."[4]

The first move of the Soviet political and military missions under Borodin and Galen was to effect reorganization in the Kuomintang. According to Dallin, Borodin's first task was reorganization rather than revolution. Galen's work, however, was concentrated in assisting

[4] The Metropolitan Police Headquarters of Peking, Official Document, *Soviet Plot in China* (Peking, 1927), p. 56. "Document Supplement," *Chinese Social and Political Science Review*, XI (1927), p. 131.

the Kuomintang to create a basic military force for revolutionary purposes.[5]

In January 1924 the First National Congress of the Kuomintang accepted Chiang Kai-shek's proposal of reorganizing the army, resolving on immediate reorganization, presumably along Russian lines. As the first step it decided upon the establishment of the Whampoa Military Academy. The influence of Chiang Kai-shek loomed large in the reorganization, for, as a rising military figure and the leading Chinese expert on Soviet systems, he was the figure in whom the influences of the Kuomintang and the Soviet combined. Chiang found support on all sides: as the trusted friend of the ailing party leader, Sun Yat-sen; as the closest tie with the Soviet advisers; as the respected model of all the young military men of China. He enjoyed the growing allegiance of the young graduates of the Paoting Military Academy and the Shikan Gakko, the Japanese military school, and eventually the loyalty of the cadets and graduates of the Whampoa Academy, which he himself had helped to found. Chiang's role was succinctly stated in a report to Moscow from the Soviet military representative in China dated May 11, 1925: "The first step in the reorganization of the army was the creation of the Kuomintang military school as chief of which General Chiang Kai-shek, a faithful friend of Dr. Sun Yat-sen, was appointed. His task was to supply the army with junior officers of political understanding. . . ."[6]

The Kuomintang instituted other changes in addition to its establishment of a training-ground for new officers. It created a political and military council along the lines of the Russian model (Revoyen Soviet), the supreme military authority set up by Trotsky after September 1918. But the chief move in the Kuomintang's extensive reorganizational program, the chief work of Chiang, and the chief evidence of Soviet influence, was the establishment of the Whampoa Military Academy.

[5] Dallin, D. J., *The Rise of Russia in Asia* (New Haven: Yale University Press, 1949), p. 212.

[6] "Report of Soviet Military Attaché at Peking, May 11, 1925," quoted in Great Britain, Foreign Office, *Documents Illustrating the Hostile Activities of the Soviet Government and the Third International against Great Britain* (London, 1927), pp. 20-31. Kawakami, K. K., *Japan in China* (London: John Murray, 1938), p. 8.

2 · THE ASCENDANCE OF WHAMPOA AND CHIANG KAI-SHEK

I. THE FOUNDATION OF THE MILITARY ACADEMY: ITS POLICIES. II. EARLY WHAMPOA VICTORIES. CHIANG'S LEADERSHIP ASSURED. III. *CHENG-CHI-PU*: POLITICAL ADMINISTRATION OF THE ARMY. IV. GALEN AND THE ESTABLISHMENT OF SOVIET DOMINANCE. V. CHIANG KAI-SHEK RISES TO POWER.

I

THE birth of the Whampoa Military Academy was one of the greatest single events in the early history of the Kuomintang. The school was a novel departure, for it was the first time in the modern military annals of China that a professional military school was created with an indubitable revolutionary purpose. Said Dr. Sun Yat-sen in his address at the opening exercises:

"It was the lessons of the revolutions of Soviet Russia that have led us today to inaugurate this academy. When the revolution began in Russia, the party members formed the vanguard, but immediately afterwards a revolutionary army was organized to support them. Because of this support the party members were able to overcome great obstacles and accomplished the revolution in a short time.

"In our own revolution we had the spirit and the martyrdom of the revolutionaries . . . but we had only the struggle of the party, without the struggle of a revolutionary army. Because of this the republic today is still in the hands of militarists and bureaucrats.

"We have established this academy in the hope that the revolutionary movement may be revitalized. Therefore you, the cadets of this academy, must dedicate yourselves to forming the backbone of the revolutionary army. Otherwise, failing to achieve this armed might, the Chinese revolution will be foredoomed from its beginning. This academy, therefore, has the sole purpose of creating a new revolutionary army for the salvation of China."[1]

[1] "Dr. Sun Yat-sen's address on the Inauguration Day of the Whampoa Military Academy," *Whampoa chiēn-chün shih-hua* (Historical Notes on Whampoa and Its

The founding of Whampoa was felicitous in its timing, coinciding as it did with the growing youth movement of the 1920's. Following the May 4th and May 30th movements, zealous young patriots flocked to Canton from many sections of China. Many of them were enrolled at Whampoa, and the academy gained much of its driving force from their determined dedication to national salvation. Out of 3,000 applicants, an initial cadet corps of 499 was formed in May 1924.

The faculty of the academy was particularly fortunate. General Chiang Kai-shek, the youthful and extremely zealous president of the school, was aided by a capable administrator, Liao Chung-k'ai. Together they formed perhaps the best military-civil team the Kuomintang could offer at the time: Chiang was universally popular as military leader, and Liao was likewise familiar with the military aspects of revolution. During the previous spring Liao had negotiated with Adolf Joffe, Soviet representative in China, and was therefore, like Chiang, well acquainted with Soviet methods, a knowledge which was a distinct necessity for the administrator of an academy where the faculty numbered among its members such men as General Galen and the Soviet military expert Cherapanoff.

The Chinese members of the faculty were either graduates of the Shikan Gakko (Japanese Military Academy) and the Paoting and Yunnan military schools or political advisers recently returned from study abroad. The present premier of the Chinese communist regime, Chou En-lai, then recently returned from France, was among their number. The Whampoa cadets were sure to get substantial political indoctrination along with their more strictly military training.

The double purpose of the academy—political and military—led to some friction between Chiang Kai-shek and the Soviet consultants. Before the academy actually opened its doors to the cadets, a preparatory committee met on February 6, 1924. At this meeting Chiang and the Soviet advisers differed substantially on important points concerning the curriculum and management of the academy. Indignant at Soviet objections to his plans, Chiang submitted to Sun Yat-sen his resignation as superintendent of the academy, protesting Soviet dominance of the planning. Chiang returned to his home, and the work of the committee came to an abrupt stop. The central executive com-

Founding of the Army), (Chungking, 1939), p. 28; Also in *Whampoa chi-k'an* (The Whampoa Quarterly), I, No. 3.

mittee of the Kuomintang was alarmed at this disruption of the plans for the academy and, through the efforts of Liao Chung-k'ai (who thereby gave ample promise of his future success in coordinating the three principal elements of Whampoa's faculty: the military instructors, the political commissars, and the Soviet advisers) managed to placate Chiang, reduce the Soviet demands, and restore order to the committee. Chiang returned to Canton almost in triumph, and the Russians, impressed by Chiang's assertiveness, and under orders from Galen and Borodin, temporarily limited their demands. Liao had been successful in repairing the breach and realizing the initial objective of the Kuomintang's policy: a working relationship between the Chinese and Soviet advisers.

Indeed, prior to Liao's untimely death, the Kuomintang's military power was securely under the authority of non-military experts such as Liao. Even in his address at the opening of the Whampoa Academy, Dr. Sun had voiced the idea that the military was to be regarded as the strong right arm of the party, but under the guidance of the non-military, political head. Apparently Sun's plan was to balance Chiang's military leadership with the civil-political authority of Liao, who helped formulate the policies, managed the finances, and coordinated the disparate purposes of the various members of the faculty.

From the first, Chiang, as superintendent of Whampoa, strove to instill an *esprit de corps* in the cadets under his command. It was at Whampoa that he coined the phrase *ch'in-ai ching-ch'eng*—"Love your comrades with the utmost sincerity."[2] He united the student body by appeals to their patriotism, to their militant party feeling, and to their common devotion to the Kuomintang's principles and revolutionary discipline. A study of Chiang's speeches during this period reveals no particular political wisdom nor any of Sun Yat-sen's eloquence and fire. The force Chiang used, the secret of his leadership, was some indefinable force of personal magnetism, a presence which inspired confidence, and a justice in all details of discipline which produced unflinching loyalty and respect for him among many cadets. He combined a knowledge of Leninism with dedication to the cause of the Kuomintang and, in small details and great issues, pursued his aim with fortitude, confidence, and complete singleness of purpose.

[2] This is the motto of the Whampoa Military Academy. Chiang's concept of this motto is best exemplified by his statement in the "Foreword of the Whampoa alumni book," quoted in *Chiang Kai-shek ti ke-ming kŭng-tsò* (The Revolutionary Activities and Selected Works of Chiang Kai-shek) (Shanghai, 1929), pp. 38-46.

Supported by a competent and faithful faculty and with an admiring and zealous student body, he could not but be successful at Whampoa.

The Whampoa Military Academy's early policy was to train as many junior officers as possible for front-line duty, and as quickly as possible. Chiang Kai-shek initially had suggested a three-month training course for the Whampoa cadets, but the faculty argued for a minimum of one and a half years of instruction. A compromise in the form of a course of six months' duration was dictated by the exigencies of time. The Kuomintang was anxious to put trained officers into the field as quickly as was practicable. Liao Chung-k'ai was once heard to remark, "If the revolution cannot be accomplished within three years the future of the nation would indeed seem to be very dim."[3] As the need for more training came to outweigh the necessity for haste, the period of instruction was increased. With Whampoa's fourth class the course was extended to one year. Later it was increased to two years.

Being designed for revolutionary expediency, Whampoa's training program was by no means a balanced education, one which would equip future officers with intellectual development as well as military proficiency. The early graduates were trained in a hurry, like the officers of the Red Army during the Russian Revolution. As General D. A. Petrovskii, director of training of the Red Army, said: "The Red Army commanders promoted during the civil war were, for all practical purposes, merely well-trained soldiers with a well-developed sense of duty."[4] China, engaged in civil war, could hope to do no better than to meet similar goals.

The basic policy infusing all Whampoa's training was, in essence, the application of Leninism to the solution of politico-military problems. The curriculum of the academy, modeled along the lines laid down by Trotsky for the Red Army training after the October Revolution, was calculated to apply these principles in every phase. Chiang considered the ideological indoctrination of men the most important single task of the academy, and there was a special emphasis placed on "spiritual and ideological training," or what the Chinese call *ching-shen chiao-yü*. Through this indoctrination the academy hoped to foster political consciousness, revolutionary ideals, and discipline in

[3] *Whampoa chiēn-chün shih-hua* (Chungking: Ti-pah Press, 1944), pp. 28-40.
[4] White, F. D., *The Growth of the Red Army* (Princeton, 1943), p. 58.

the future officers and, through them, in the rank and file of the army.

General Cheng Chi-cheng, formerly superintendent of the Central Military Academy, summed up the Whampoa training under five points. First, emphasis was placed on the ideological indoctrination mentioned above. Second, there was a strict enforcing of military discipline. Third, stress was placed on the practical application of military skills and the importance of a realistic approach to the problems of warfare. Chiang Kai-shek had this to say: "During peacetime adjust yourself to wartime conditions; under wartime conditions keep up to the peacetime standard." Fourth, Cheng emphasized the need for flexibility. "Principles must be applied," he said. But he continued, "There are but few military principles, and the skill of applying them rests within your own heart."[5] Last, the training was to be as thorough as possible, with minute attention to the details of each cadet's daily life.

In shaping the Whampoa program Chiang had blended a knowledge of modern techniques with the traditional philosophies of Chinese warfare. His military thought was strongly influenced by the great Chinese scholars, Sun-tzu, Ts'eng Kuo-fan, Ch'i Chi-kuang, and Hu Ning-yi. Chiang's annotations of these famous works of the past enjoyed wide circulation.

If the military training was to be classical and Chinese, however, the political training was to be modern and Soviet. According to General Wang Pei-ling, one of the early senior faculty members, this training was given by the group conference (*hsiao-tsu hui-i*) technique, a method of instruction which Wang called "the soul of Whampoa's training and the life-blood of the academy's success."[6] The seminar method served not only to convey information to the class but to provide a showcase for leadership and various other talents. These discussion periods were the chief tools with which General Teng Yen-ta's department of political education at the academy operated. General Teng's deputy was Chou En-lai, later one of the most powerful Chinese communist leaders and currently the premier of the communist government in China.

In addition to inculcating a certain political discipline, the academy sought to establish the mental habit of military discipline. The system

[5] Cheng Chi-cheng, "T'an Whampoa chiāo-yü" (On Whampoa Education), *Whampoa chiēn-chün shih-hua, op.cit.,* p. 63.
[6] Wang Pei-ling, "Ts'uan-hsiào-hui-ì" (Reminiscence of the Founding of the Academy), *Whampoa chiēn-chün shih-hua, op.cit.,* pp. 28-40.

used to enforce responsibility was of ancient Chinese origin. In January 1925, shortly before the Whampoa cadets entered their first campaign, Chiang Kai-shek put into operation *nien-tso-fa* (military law of collective responsibility). This ruthless system had been devised by the famous Chinese general Ch'i Chi-kuan, who defeated the piratical Japanese invaders in the sixteenth century. Its nature may be seen by the following extract:

"If the platoon leader retreated with his platoon without orders, he must be executed. If the company commander retreated with his entire company without orders, the company commander must be executed . . . and so forth, the same death penalty must apply to commanders of battalions, regiments, divisions, who retreated without orders.

"When, however, the commander of an army corps did not retreat but the officers and men did so without orders, then all his subordinate divisional commanders must be executed. . . . When the squad leader did not retreat, but his entire squad retreated without orders, thus causing the death of the squad leader, then all the privates of the squad must be executed."[7]

This iron discipline was maintained in the ranks of the Whampoa cadets and among the forces they eventually led into battle. With the threat of the death penalty rigidly enforced, the system ensured strict responsibility upwards and downwards throughout the entire chain of command and demanded responsible coordination and cooperation on the part of commanders in battle.

With equally matched forces, a device such as this would prove of undeniable effectiveness for the side employing it. Its enforcement when the enemy had a preponderant superiority in equipment and firepower led only to excessive sacrifice of men and materials. Its rigid application cost the early Whampoa graduates dearly in human lives.

During the early years, as we have mentioned, the administration of Whampoa Academy was planned and carried out jointly by the Chinese and the Soviets. There was also a strong Japanese influence. The principal members of the Chinese faculty were graduates of the Japanese military academy, Shikan Gakko: Chiang Kai-shek himself;

[7] "Ke-ming-chün Nien-tso-fa" (The Inter-locking Military Law of Punishment of the Revolutionary Army) quoted in *Chiang Kai-shek tī ke-ming kūng-tsò, op.cit.*, II, pp. 112-115.

his commandant of cadets, General Ho Ying-ch'in; and two important officials mentioned earlier, Generals Wang Pei-ling and Chien Ta-chung. Three of the four department heads at Whampoa were Japanese-trained.

The rest of the Chinese faculty was Chinese-trained. The intermediate level was occupied mainly by graduates of the Paoting Military Academy, chief of whom were Generals Ch'en Ch'eng and Chang Chih-chung, later to become well-known as Kuomintang military "brass." The lower stratum of Whampoa's faculty was composed in large part of graduates of the Yunnan Military Academy. According to General Wang Pei-ling, sometime academic dean of Whampoa, 60 per cent of the academy's faculty came from the Yunnan school and 20 per cent from Paoting.[8] The two schools together have produced some of the most celebrated military leaders of the Chinese Communist Army: Chu Teh, Yeh Chien-ying, Lin Piao, Chou En-lai, Hsu Hsiang-ch'ien, and others. Yunnan Academy was founded by the revolutionary general Ts'ai Sung-po, a graduate of the Japanese military academy, and was staffed at one time by a number of Japanese-trained officers. Paoting Academy likewise received a strong Japanese influence from its foreign-trained staff. Even the graduates of Chinese military schools, therefore, had been brought up by Japanese-influenced methods. They continued to exert this influence at Whampoa, and many of Whampoa's instructional materials were obtained from the Japanese through Japan's assistant military attaché at Canton. Later, when the army of the Kuomintang, spearheaded by Whampoa cadets, began to score victories in South China, the Japanese press took considerable delight in playing up the role of Japanese military training in the Kuomintang's successes.

The Soviet influence played an important part in Whampoa's early life. The academy had been founded essentially to accomplish the same ends as the Soviet's own military schools: to create the military cadre of the revolution. We have noted what interest the Soviet government took in its establishment and the men it sent as consultants. The importance of Whampoa's Soviet advisers became particularly significant after the first Russian shipment of war material to Canton on October 7, 1924. On that date a Soviet vessel slipped into Whampoa to deliver 8,000 rifles with 500 rounds of ammunition for each.[9] Up to this time the hostile attitude of the warlord-controlled arsenals of

[8] Wang Pei-ling, *op.cit.*, p. 40.   [9] *Ibid.*, p. 166.

Canton had deprived the infant academy of the crudest kind of military equipment, and Whampoa had at its disposal only 30 rifles.[10] After this first shipment Whampoa was able to get on its feet. Later, another 15,000 rifles, machine guns, and pieces of artillery were obtained from the Soviets through cash purchase or other transactions. The number and power of the Soviet advisers increased. The cadet corps grew in size and their training became more extensive. Whampoa Academy began to train specialists in artillery, engineering, supply, and infantry for the revolutionary army.

II

With the arrival of the first shipment of Russian arms, the Whampoa Academy began to expand. By October 1924, a cadet detachment and two training regiments were equipped and put into operation. A month later this force, led by the 490 graduates of Whampoa's first class and totaling 3,000 officers and men, was established. Sun Yat-sen christened it "The Party Army" (*tang-chün*). On his last inspection tour at the academy, the ailing Sun had said, "Now that we have Whampoa I may die peacefully."[11] Sun died in Peking on the eve of the first victory of the new Party Army, Whampoa's first achievement. The first major victory was at Mien-hu, Kwangtung, where the superior discipline of the Whampoa cadets proved sufficient to rout Ch'en Chiung-ming and his larger force.

Chiang Kai-shek, advised by General Galen, directed the strategy at Mien-hu, placing the brunt of the attack on Ho Ying-ch'in's First Training Regiment. The importance of this victory to Chiang and the Kuomintang might well be compared to that of Tsaritsin (later called Stalingrad) to Stalin and his party. The historians of the Kuomintang have always regarded this action as the turning-point of their party's fortunes.

Although much credit is due Chiang, the importance of the Soviet adviser Galen in this battle cannot be neglected. He himself barely escaped death in the skirmish, and emerged from the fighting with a new confidence in the Chinese troops and their courage which could

---

[10] According to Chiang's biographer, Professor Chang Chi-yuen, before the arrival of the Russian shipment, the Whampoa Military Academy had only 500 rifles. Even these were allocated secretly to the academy from the stock of the Canton arsenal at the personal order of Dr. Sun Yat-sen. Chang Chi-yuen, *Tang-shih kai-yao* (Taipeh, 1951), II, p. 464.

[11] *Ibid.*, I, p. 368.

not but affect future Sino-Soviet dealings. He presented his own sword to the unit commander as a token of his appreciation and, on March 16, 1925, addressed Whampoa's First Training Regiment in these words: "Seeing the fighting valor of your unit—a kind of spirit not only rarely seen among Chinese troops but comparable to that of any of the best fighting forces in the world—I see evidence that the Chinese revolution definitely will succeed. You, the men of the Training Regiment, assured it through your superb fighting spirit."[12]

Chiang and his Whampoa troops had achieved not only the confidence of the Russians but also the esteem of his own party. On May 13, 1925, the Central Executive Committee of the Kuomintang, meeting in Swatow, resolved to name Chiang commanding general of the Kuomintang's Party Army.

Whampoa's trained soldiers went on from one victory to another in the face of superior numbers. Wherever the army went, the local population enthusiastically supported it. Throughout the province of Kwangtung the army was thought of as invincible. And, as it grew in reputation, it grew in size. In the first fourteen months, the Whampoa brigade expanded into an army division. In another half year it had become the most powerful army corps of the Kuomintang —the best-known, best-led, best-trained, and best-equipped fighting force in South China.

Following the initial victories of the Whampoa force, the National Government was established in July 1925. Using the Whampoa group as its nucleus, the new government set about the establishment of a national revolutionary army (*kuo-min ke-ming-chün*), forging a unified force out of the disparate elements of the various provincial units then existing in South China. By political and military means the provincial units of Canton, Hunnan, Kwangsi, etc., were wrested from the control of warlords and forced to yield their separate identities to a unified command. The forces were standardized and indoctrinated with the new political and military credos of the new government. The central military council assumed all control over military supplies, whether procured from Soviet Russia or manufactured in local arsenals, and paid all military salaries. This unification was by no means facile, and the six turbulent weeks between August 20 and

[12] "General Galen's Speech to the Training Regiment of the Whampoa Military Academy at Ho-po on March 16, 1925," *Whampoa chiën-chün shih-hua, op.cit.*, p. 180.

October 3 were critical days for the new government. From the struggle the National Government emerged with new vigor; its chief forces, the National Revolutionary Army and Chiang Kai-shek's Whampoa group, had met the test and gained new strength. The conflict had succeeded in establishing Chiang's military leadership and political importance on a new and firmer foundation.

III

The reliance of the government on the strength of its armed forces was sufficiently obvious, but the party gave a great deal of effort to setting up a political structure within which the army would be subjected to various civil and political checks. The government operated under a strict party rule, and its care was to ensure that the army also remained under the direction and supervision of the Kuomintang. The three branches of the national government in 1925 cooperated thus to prevent the emergence of strong military men as politically dominant figures. The most powerful group was the political council, with a membership of both civilian and military leaders and an auxiliary group of Soviet advisers; it coordinated the efforts of two subsidiary groups, the military council and the government committee. The whole operation of the system of government until 1927 was based entirely upon the Soviet principle of so-called "democratic centralism." This familiar communist pattern may be summarized in a few points: (1) The application of the elective principle from the lowest to the highest level. (2) The periodic accountability of the operating bodies to their respective superiors. (3) Strict discipline in the majority's rule of the minority. (4) The absolute binding nature of the decisions of higher bodies upon lower bodies.

The political council, at least between October 1925 and June 1926 (when all the civil, military, and financial affairs of the state were centralized in that body), made all policy decisions of major military importance as well as all of a purely civil or political nature. The dictates of the council were put into operation by a military council, which was modeled after Soviet Russia's Revolutionary Military Council (Revoyen Soviet) and was entrusted simply with military administration on routine and purely technical levels. Like its Soviet counterpart, it coordinated military activities and the services of supply. It advised the political council on military decisions but was at most the lesser collaborator in the formation of policy.

Through all the levels of administration the Soviet advisers exerted their profound influence. The Kuomintang's very plan in introducing all the changes into its army system came from the original design of the Bolshevik Party. The political commissar (or party representative), the party cell system, the political control and indoctrination of the armed forces—all owed their existence to Russian models.

When Chiang visited Soviet Russia in 1923, one of the most conspicuous events he recorded in his diary was his meeting with General D. A. Petrovskii, director of military training for the Red Army.[18] With him Chiang discussed the methods of the Soviet system, and upon his return to China he joined the Soviet advisers in Canton in their plea for the immediate adoption of these methods by the Kuomintang. Sun Yat-sen provided the Chinese with a home-grown version of the system the Soviet advisers were advocating when he divided *neng* (technical proficiency) and *ch'uen* (authority) between the professional military officers and the party representatives in the army. The whole plan was to place the control of the armed forces securely in the hands of the party and prevent it from falling into the hands of the warlords who had caused so much difficulty in the past. All men, said Sun, are party members, be they generals or privates and, just as the privates are responsible to their officers, so the whole army, officers and men, is subservient to the ends of the party.

Liao Chung-k'ai, at Whampoa and later in the party army, put the politico-military system into practice. Party members, appointed to serve as liaison officers with the army, were empowered to countersign and even to countermand the orders of military commanders. The political administration of the army (*cheng-chih-pu*) was managed by a group of political commissars who thoroughly organized and controlled the army in a system of party cells. Each of these party representatives in an army corps had about 100 political workers assisting him, so that there was approximately one "political soldier" to every 100 fighting men. There was, of course, an appreciable amount of friction between the political advisers and the military commanders whenever divergent aims arose, and these clashes were credited with having an undeniably important role in effecting the final split between the Kuomintang and the Soviet Communist Party.

[18] The Chinese Ministry of National Defense, *Wei-tà-ti Chiang chu-hsi* (The Great President Chiang), (Nanking, 1946), see "Chiang's chronology by his confidential aide Chiang Hsi-teh."

IV

The problem in Kwangtung during the years 1923-1927 was one of fusing a number of disparate elements into a reliable and loyal army and of creating a unified force around which other forces might be encouraged to rally. Politically, there were the various influences of the Kuomintang, the warlords, the Russian and Chinese communists, the nearby British in their colony of Hong Kong. There was also the problem of molding the armies of Kwangtung, Hunan, Yunnan, Kwangsi, and Chekiang into a single, harmonious force.

As a means of achieving unity, a council of various military leaders was formed. The council provided a workable common ground and solved the ticklish problem of equal rank for the Kuomintang members, the various warlords, and the Soviet advisers. The Chinese military men were pacified with high office and equal responsibility; the Russians, seeing the opportunities for guidance in the inherent inertia of committees and the inexperience of the Chinese, considered themselves well provided for and rested content. All the groups involved, moreover, were aware of the necessity for unity in this, as in any other, revolutionary venture; the committee system seemed to guarantee this unity.

The need for exerting political control and spreading political ideology in the army was another point of agreement. All factions accepted, with confidence in its correctness and efficiency, the institution of the political commissar system. It was easier for the Kuomintang to indoctrinate a youthful group of students than to train and equip several armies, and so they adopted a plan of gathering armed forces by every conceivable means and then inserting trained political commissars at the various levels of the newly absorbed groups. These commissars took up the task of organizing the soldiers into party cells, educating them politically, teaching them to read and write, and acting as guardians and spokesmen for the underprivileged soldiers. Once these methods had succeeded in winning the soldiers to the commissar's side, a political party could mobilize their collective strength to influence the military commanders. Thus the Kuomintang could afford to swell its ranks with heterogeneous groups of men, in full confidence that they would eventually be won over to the party.

The political commissars were also spokesmen for the grievances of the soldiers and, through advocating to the party that measures be taken or dealing directly with the military commanders, were instrumental in correcting such defects as irregularities in military spending, favoritism, and nepotism. Their duties were all part of their dual purpose of reforming the army through bettering its morale and of strengthening party loyalty. At the same time they won the reputation of keeping the soldier's welfare at heart.

In peace the commissars were in charge of army public relations; in war they waged the political battle of propaganda and organized a fifth column behind enemy lines. The new spirit of cooperation between the soldiers and the party, and between both of them and the populace, was as valuable to the cause of the Kuomintang in peacetime as their quite different tasks in war.

General Galen was a capable soldier, strategist, and diplomat. His reputation as a Russian commander and his apparent enthusiasm for all things Chinese endeared him to the leaders at Whampoa. Attired in Chinese military uniform and reputed to be a connoisseur of Chinese cuisine, he was accepted by the Chinese more as a colleague in arms than as a foreign counselor. With a more original mind than Borodin, he balked at too much Soviet dogma and often spoke of the "impractical" emphasis on ideology—*le fatra doctrinal*, doctrinal rubbish, as he called it.[14] Trotsky described him as "no bureaucratic functionary," but branded him as a theatrical figure who was, as a Marxist, only a "dilettante" in politics.[15] In practical matters of running an army, however, Galen's common sense and "brass-tacks" approach was unquestionably effective. In the early days of the Soviet-Kuomintang entente, when radical and irresponsible communists at Canton were agitating for coups and demanding wild revolutionary measures, Galen warned that "revolution is not so simple."[16] It was he, with Borodin, who helped the Kuomintang to meet the exigencies of the struggle with a practical and realistic approach.

Galen's methods were put into practice at Whampoa by the Soviet adviser he assigned to the academy—Cherapanoff, an experienced soldier and seasoned diplomat. So well did Cherapanoff manage to get along with Chiang Kai-shek that in 1938 the Kremlin sent him back to China, this time accompanied by the famous Marshal Georgi Zhukov, at the head of the Soviet military mission.

[14] Trotsky, Leon, *Problems of the Chinese Revolution* (N.Y.: Pioneer, 1932), p. 248.
[15] *Ibid.*   [16] *Ibid.*, p. 255f.

Before Galen took his first leave of China he had accomplished the initial phase of his mission, which was to assist the Chinese in the organization and training of the Kuomintang army. This objective reached, the Soviet General Rogacheff took over, his goal, the secure entrenchment of the Russians in the Chinese military administration. Rogacheff, a product of the Soviet general staff training, made it a point to attend nearly every meeting of the military and political council. His views on organization, supply, military appropriations, general staff planning—indeed almost every phase of the army operations—were clearly outlined and generally very influential. He pursued the conscious and determined goal of carrying out the master plan of the Russians, which was, as the charter of the Soviet mission put it, to be "all embracing" in their concerns and to achieve the "penetration of its workers" into every branch of the operations at every level.[17] Under the direction of a chief adviser and a political commissar, a small army of Russians labored to infiltrate and influence every administrative echelon from that of the Chinese commander-in-chief even to the divisional or regimental level.

The Russians, anxious to bend every effort toward reaching their goal, gradually engendered feelings of menace and antagonism in the Chinese. They gave ever clearer evidence of their intentions to overreach the bounds of simple counseling, and the Chinese commenced to suspect that, if it had not been politically inexpedient, the Russians might well have attempted to seize the reins of power outright. The Chinese, grateful for Soviet arms and assistance, yet unfamiliar with the new Soviet organization and largely unprepared to match the Soviet advisers with their own equally competent officials, had fallen prey to Russian dominance.

V

By the early days of 1926 the Soviet advisers were working to carry on political activities in the army on a large scale. The Chinese reaction to the aggressive but still somewhat immature actions of such communist organizers as Chou En-lai and the resolute and incisive actions of Borodin (by then nicknamed "The Emperor of Canton") grew stronger. The Kuomintang members of the academy at Whampoa moved to check or contain communist activity in the academy and countered it with a Sun Yat-sen Society, founded on the principles of

---

[17] *Soviet Plot in China, op.cit.*, pp. 41-43.

Sun and Tai Chi-t'ao's nationalistic writings. Borodin retaliated with an order which created the Marxist-Leninist Union of (Communist) Youth in January 1926. The repercussions of friction were beginning to be felt in the army and naval units as Whampoa's graduates poured into the Kuomintang forces.

Chiang Kai-shek, with his sympathies on the side of the Kuomintang, strove to keep peace between the rival organizations but was obdurate in refusing to let any of the new communist influence seep into his own First Army Corps. He took steps to prevent the members of the new movement from assuming control on the general staff, in the finance bureau, or at the arsenals.

The assassination of Liao Chung-kai on August 19, 1925, removed the chief pivot of Kuomintang-Soviet coordination and left the door open for the rise of certain nationalistic Chinese factions, such as the Hsi-shan-hui-yi P'ai (Western Hill Conference Group), which drew their membership largely from the young and aggressive officers trained at Paoting or the Japanese military schools.[18] The Soviet plan for expanding control was met with a firm front of nationalistic resistance.

Chiang Kai-shek, with the disciplined force of the Whampoa cadets and the party's crack fighting units at his disposal, was in a position to command the loyalties of the Paoting and Japanese-trained groups. With this solid backing, reinforced by the right-wing elements of the Kuomintang, Chiang emerged as the undoubted leader opposing the leftist front. On March 20, 1926, as military commander at Canton, he struck a sudden blow, arresting a number of communist commissars, including a number of Russian advisers at the Whampoa Academy, and disarming the semi-military Workers' Guard, actually a thinly veiled military cadre of the Chinese Communist Party.

The coup caught the Russians off guard. Galen and Borodin were not in Canton at the time and Rogacheff, then acting head of the Soviet military mission there, fled to Peking to reorganize. The Russian report on the affair reflected the bitterness of their attitude; the senior military adviser, Stepanoff, wrote this to Moscow: "On March 20, 1926, the Labor Union at Canton called for a strike, and organized a strike committee. At that time the influence of Russian advisers and political workers was great, and there were communist members within

---

[18] The assassination was said to have been traced to a right-wing Kuomintang conspiracy; Hu Han-ming, a senior leader of Kuomintang, and General Hsu Ch'ung-chih, commander of the Cantonese army, were allegedly involved.

the Kuomintang. Chiang Kai-shek, without consulting the Kuomintang central headquarters, suddenly disarmed the strikers and obstructed the labor movements. Henceforth, the Russians are beginning to realize that they are not using Chiang, but are actually being used by him."[19]

The Kuomintang's version of the incident was quite different. They called it "the incident of the warship *Chung-shan*" and alleged that the communist commander of the gunboat had been directed by the Soviet naval adviser to move into Canton in order to render support to incipient communist uprisings in that area. The plot, it was stated, was revealed to Chiang at the last minute and he had lost no time in quashing it.[20] The communists charged that Chiang's move had been aimed solely at seizing the control of Whampoa from Wang Ching-wei, the communist representative at the academy.

Shortly before this incident a group of important Soviet emissaries had arrived in Canton from Moscow. Heading the group had been Andrey S. Bubnov, then known as an important member of the Stalinist faction in the Bolshevik Party. Certain rumors were circulated that in the Kremlin's Politiburo a struggle was being waged between the Stalinists and the Trotskyites, but the connection (if any) of the March 20 incident remains obscure. Chiang was reported to have told General Wang Pei-ling, an important figure at Whampoa, that the entire story could never be told until his own diary revealed the facts after his death.[21]

After they had been presented with Chiang's *fait accompli*, both Borodin and Bubnov sided with the Chinese commander and praised him for his action against those who were, so the Soviet advisers said, "too far to the left." Bubnov assumed the name Kisanka to mask his identity and took over the post of chief military adviser to the Kuomintang. Strictly speaking, he was not a military man, having been director of propaganda and later chief of the political administration of the Red Army, but his command of politics would have earned him the envy of any politician. Under Kisanka Soviet activities did not diminish; rather, they became more numerous and more subtle. To these activities Kisanka devoted himself wholeheartedly, for he realized the prize Russia could win in China. Ad-

[19] *Wei-tà-ti Chiang chu-hsi*, *op.cit.*, p. 86.
[20] "Chiang's letter to the cadets of Whampoa military academy," *Chiang Kai-shek ti ke-ming kŭng-tsò*, *op.cit.*, III, pp. 58-65; also consult Chang, *op.cit.*, II, pp. 507-10.
[21] Wang Pei-ling, *op.cit.*, pp. 164-168.

dressing the annual meeting of the Bolshevik Party in Moscow, shortly before his departure for Canton, he said: "The nationalist movement in the Far East, awakened by us in 1925, has reached its climax. . . . The organization of the colonial revolution has consequently become the chief task of the Soviet government. . . . On this point no divergence of opinion is possible. Everything must be consecrated to the development of the revolutionary movement in the Far East."[22]

The Soviet advisers, however, had discovered by this time—as Stepanoff had reported to the Kremlin—"that they are not using Chiang, but are actually being used by him." Having asserted his power in the matter of the gunboat *Chung-shan*, Chiang went on to check the spread of Soviet dominance. On April 30, 1926, he called a joint conference of the central executive committee of the Kuomintang and the supervisory committee. He laid on the line a policy of removing Soviet advisers from administrative and executive posts and stressed the advisability of clearly demarcating the limits of Soviet authority. The central executive committee at its second plenary session adopted all of Chiang's proposals. Stepanoff had been even more correct than he had known.

[22] *Current History*, XXIII (Oct. 1925 to Mar. 1926), p. 852.

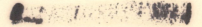

3 · LAUNCHING THE NORTHERN EXPEDITION: REASONS AND RESULTS

༺༺༺༺༺༺༺༺༺༺༺༺༺༺༺༺༺༺༺༺༺༺༺༺༺༺༺༺༺༺༺༺༺

I. A DIFFICULT PROBLEM: THE EXPANSION OF THE NA-
TIONAL REVOLUTIONARY ARMY. II. THE BOLD SOLUTION:
PREPARATIONS FOR THE NORTHERN EXPEDITION. III.
CROSS PURPOSES: CHIANG AND THE NORTHERN CAM-
PAIGN—AND THE COMMUNISTS.

༺༺༺༺༺༺༺༺༺༺༺༺༺༺༺༺༺༺༺༺༺༺༺༺༺༺༺༺༺༺༺༺༺

I

THE National Government at Canton was an administration whose ideology and purpose seemed to the youth of China to offer new hope for their homeland. In its idealism and dedication it appealed to their aspirations, and in its organization it professed to offer, particularly in its rapidly expanding army, every opportunity to youthful courage and initiative. The young men of China swelled its ranks, and some idea of its phenomenal growth may be conveyed by the following table dealing with the growth of its nucleus, the Whampoa-officered army:[1]

Period	Strength: Officers and Men
May 1924	960
Jan. 1925	1,500
April 1925	3,000
July 1925	9,000
Sept. 1925	13,000
Nov. 1925	30,000

The following figures may be taken as an accurate report on the strength of the National Revolutionary Army:[2]

Period	Total Strength (Number of army corps)
July-Aug. 1925	3
Sept.-Oct. 1925	5
Dec. 1925	6 (85,000 men)
Feb. 1926	7
July 1926	8
Aug. 1926	10

[1] Data collected and correlated from numerous original sources.
[2] Data collected and correlated from numerous original sources.

[25]

In about February 1926 the National Revolutionary Army was joined by the hard-fighting armies of Kwangsi under the command of Generals Li Tsung-jen, Pai Chung-hsi, and Huang Shao-hsiung. The latter formed the new Seventh Army Corps of the National Revolutionary Army. The government then had three crack fighting armies. Chiang Kai-shek himself commanded the First Army Corps, evolved from the Whampoa force. The Fourth Army Corps (Cantonese) was under the successive commands of Li Chi-shen, Ch'en Ming-shu, and Chang Fa-kuei. The Seventh Army Corps (Kwangsi) was commanded by Li Tsung-jen. Of the combined military force, Chiang Kai-shek could report to the Kuomintang in December 1925: "At present the Revolutionary Army is entirely under the control of the government. It can be completely mobilized at a single order. Numerically, the army is 85,000 strong. There is a budget system for military expenditure and the standard of living of the soldiers has been materially improved. Besides, there are 6,000 cadets in various military schools—enough to comprise a division. With adequate attention to further military reforms and with the power of our Party [Kuomintang] the unification of all of China will not be a difficult task for us."[3]

The military power of the National Government meant great expenditures. The party's own army and the schools under Chiang's personal command, for example, had a monthly budget of 510,000 dollars (Chinese).[4] Each of the other army corps spent 250,000 dollars (Chinese) every month. At the time that the army of the Kwangsi became the government's Seventh Army Corps, the National Government was facing an outlay of 3 million dollars (Chinese) each month for military expenses. This was already too much of a drain on the resources of the government, whose revenues came principally from a single province, Kwangtung. By the spring of 1926 the government was spending more each month on military expenditures than its total receipts. A new source of money and matériel had to be found if the armed forces were not to be cut.

Since the *coup d'état* of March 1926, Russia had become a more careful and less openhanded benefactor. She began to find it advisable to reserve material and financial aid as a useful method of coercion in the plan of forcing the Kuomintang to meet Soviet terms. Russian

---

[3] Chiang Kai-shek, "Report on Military Affairs of the Kuomintang Second National Congress," *Chiang Kai-shek tī ke-ming kŭng-tsò, op.cit.*, III, p. 13.
[4] "Minute of Meeting," Document No. 5, *Soviet Plot in China, op.cit.*, pp. 45-53.

aid was not, moreover, as generous as it was reported to be. Its quantity was meager, its quality low. Many obsolete German and Japanese arms were unloaded on the Chinese and charged to the Nationalist Government at high cash prices. All these supplies came to China via the long land route of the Trans-Siberian Railway as far as Vladivostok before they were loaded on ships for Canton. When they arrived at their destination the Soviet advisers favored the more leftish military units, such as the Fourth Army Corps, in large measure composed of "Workers' Guards," and were more anxious to "invest" in Chinese communist than in Kuomintang party members.

The over-taxing of their financial resources and the Soviet policy caused a good deal of consternation in the ranks of the Kuomintang leaders and, in the face of the problems mentioned and the armament embargo being enforced by the Western powers at the time, they turned with calculating eyes on the great arsenals of Hanyang, Nanking, and Shanghai—all of them larger than that at Canton.

With these rich prizes in mind, the National Government considered the several avenues open to it. It could surrender to the pressure of the Soviet and the Chinese communists and exchange its definite control for more and better equipment from the U.S.S.R. It could fall before the threat of the alliances of hostile warlords. Or, it could fight its way out. The National Government chose the latter course, a course coincident with a plan which Sun Yat-sen had often advocated —the launching of a northern expedition (*pei-fa*) for the unification of China.

II

In April-May 1926 the warlord T'ang Shen-chih, who had for some time been inclined to join his Hunanese forces with those of the National Government, was attacked and defeated by the powerful Marshal Wu Pei-fu, whose forces were among the best of the northern armies. This warfare in Hunan, the immediate neighborhood of the Kuomintang's base in Kwangtung, was regarded as a threat to the security of the National Government. A powerful unit of the National Revolutionary Army's Seventh (Kwangsite) Corps immediately rushed to T'ang's aid and scored a brilliant local victory against Wu's force. Led by the two aggressive Kwangsi generals, Li Tsung-jen and Li Chi-sen, the leaders of the Revolutionary Army advocated a policy of war in spite of the objections of the Soviet military advisers.

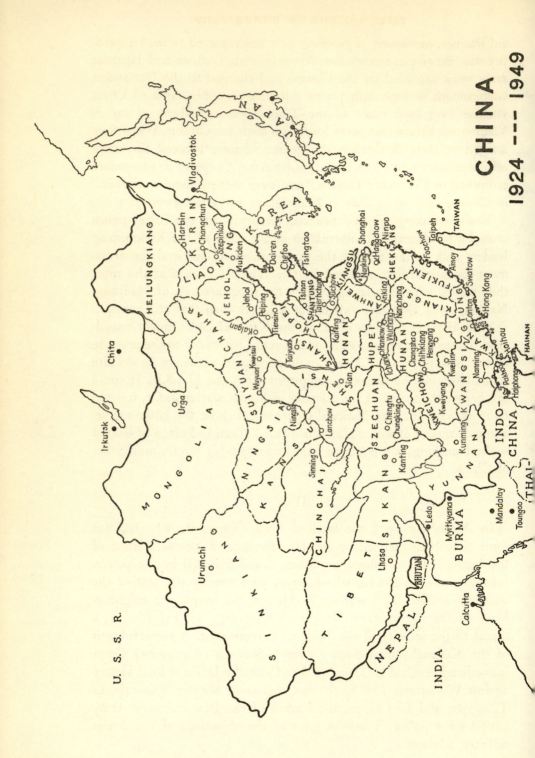

CHINA
1924 --- 1949

The spokesman of the Soviet objections was, however, Kisanka (Bubnov), then chief Soviet military adviser. As a newcomer he was not as yet entirely familiar with the Chinese situation, and he commanded so little respect from the veteran soldiers of the Kuomintang hierarchy that he was not destined to remain long enough to grasp the situation fully. He was recalled after only two months in China and replaced by a man of greater reputation and knowledge of strategy.

With such a man as Kisanka voicing the arguments against a northern expedition, Chiang Kai-shek had little difficulty in steering a resolution urging immediate action through an extraordinary meeting of the Kuomintang's central committee. Kisanka's counter-proposal was to ship troops by sea to North China to bolster the then leftish Kuominchun (People's Army) of Feng Yü-hsiang, a plan which was unrealistic in the face of the Kuomintang's lack of sufficient ships to convoy these forces through waters infested with enemy fleets. Feng could not even have supplied the port facilities for the debarkation of the army. Chiang argued that the whole plan suggested by Kisanka was suicidal, and though Kisanka was at that time even more powerful in the Soviet than Galen (according to General Chang Chih-chung, one of Chiang's closest friends) Chiang cabled Moscow for Kisanka's recall, using a tactic he was later to employ in the Stilwell case.[5] Moscow bowed to Chiang's request and the last obstacle in the path of the northern expedition was removed. The Communist Party continued, however, to attack the war policy in the publications they controlled—such as *Hsiang-tao* (*The Leader*)—contending that it was first necessary to consolidate the Kuomintang administration in Kwangtung. They questioned the unity of the Revolutionary Army, the loyalty of some of its generals, and the efficiency of its equipment.[6] Under cover of this attack, however, their chief concern was to gain time in which to repair the rifts in their own ranks, especially since the March coup had badly disorganized and disheartened

[5] Chang Chih-chung, "Address to the Central Military Academy, 1932," *Wei-tà-ti Chiang chu-hsi, op.cit.,* p. 31.

[6] For a more thorough study of the Kuomintang's decision to start the northern expedition, consult the following books: Chang Chi-yuen, *Tang-shih kai-yao, op.cit.,* II, pp. 515-516. Li Tsung-jen, *Li tsung-ssu-ling yen-lun-chih* (The Speeches and Writings of Commander-in-Chief Li) (Kweilin, 1934), p. 20. Yin Shi, *The Chiang-Lee Relationship and China,* in Chinese (Hongkong, 1954), pp. 12-19. *Soviet Plot in China, op.cit., passim.* Roy, M. N., *Revolution and Counter-Revolution in China* (Calcutta, 1946), *passim.* This is a revised version of *My Experience in China,* now out of print.

them. They were right that the technical equipment of Chiang's army could promise no more than an uncertain margin of victory over the northern forces at best, but (according to General Pai Chung-hsi) Chiang placed great confidence in the political principles of the party, regarding them as weapons fully as tangible and as effective as technical equipment.[7] He determined to use them to the greatest advantage by striking while, as far as morale was concerned, the iron was hot.

Surely a confident and dedicated force was necessary to face the formidable warlords arrayed against the National Government. The opposition was, practically speaking, under five or six banners in the field. Peking was in the hands of Chang Tso-lin, who ruled the provinces of Manchuria. From Honan, Wu Péi-fu extended his influence over a great part of central China. Sun Chuan-fang ruled seven provinces in southeast China, including the five maritime provinces, and strategic Shanghai. Shantung was controlled by the notorious Chang Tsung-ch'ang, whose power extended to the province of Chili (Hopeh). Yen Hsi-shan, the "model *tuchun*" (military governor) commanded the army of Shansi. Finally, Feng Yü-hsiang, though expelled from Peking, still retained control of the northwestern provinces of China. An idea of their comparative strength numerically may be seen in the chart on page 31.

Chiang's venture in the north was audacious. A number of northern armies—the Tung-pei-chun or Manchurian Army of Chang Tso-lin, for example—were better equipped than his. Chang Tso-lin, Sun Chuan-fang, and Chang Tsung-ch'ang all had the assistance of hireling Japanese officers in their armies. Chiang's confidence in eventual victory in the north—a confidence which proved to be well-founded—in the face of great opposing forces and stringent criticism in his own camp must be regarded as nothing less than visionary. No military virtue is comparable to boldness when boldness succeeds, and Chiang boldly hazarded everything in this northern expedition.

III

On June 9, 1926, the National Government at Canton appointed Chiang Kai-shek commander-in-chief of all the forces it had been

[7] Pai Chung-hsi, "President Chiang and China's Military Affairs during the Last Sixty Years," in Chinese, *Wei-ta-tī Chiang chu-hsi, op.cit.*, pp. 17-18; also, Yin Shi, *op.cit.*, pp. 12-19.

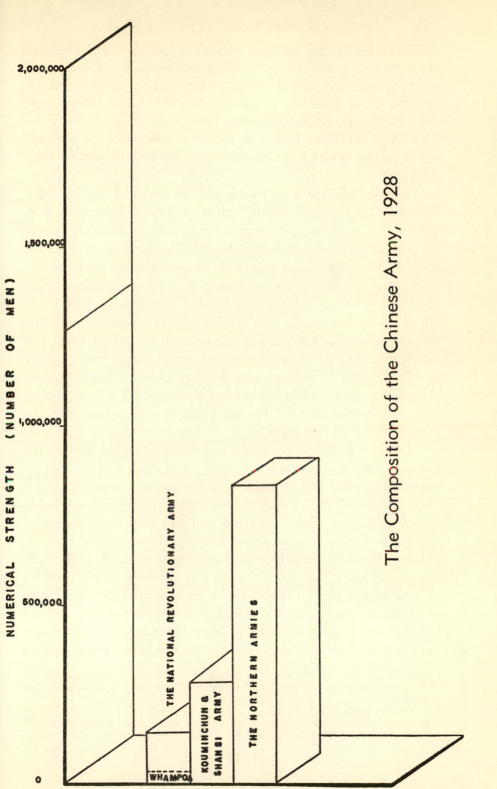

The Composition of the Chinese Army, 1928

NUMERICAL STRENGTH (NUMBER OF MEN)

2,000,000

1,500,000

1,000,000

500,000

0

THE NATIONAL REVOLUTIONARY ARMY

WHAMPOA

KOUMINCHUN & SHANSI ARMY

THE NORTHERN ARMIES

able to muster for the northern expedition, stating: "The object of the revolutionary war is to establish an independent and free nation and to promote the welfare of the country and people in accordance with the Three Principles of the People (Nationalism, Democracy, and Livelihood). All revolutionary forces must, therefore, be mobilized under the Three Principles for the overthrow of the warlords and of foreign imperialists upon whom the warlords depend for their existence."[8]

Commanding "the land, naval, and air forces on behalf of the National Government," Chiang set up a general headquarters on July 7 and began to operate in earnest, responsible solely to the National Government and to the Central Committee of the Kuomintang.[9] His power exceeded that of the chairman of the government's military council, and several sections of that organ (the department of political training and the general staff particularly) were transferred to his supervision, thus placing him in control of both the political commissars and the vital agencies of military planning and intelligence. The government complied with Chiang's request for a unified direction of military and political affairs (*t'ung-i-chün-ling cheng-ling*) and placed in his hands the reins of all military, party, civil, and financial control.[10] He was given supreme command of the conduct of the whole campaign.

Virtually a dictator empowered to act as he thought best on the grounds of military emergency, Chiang was the target of Communist Party charges that this assumption of the supreme command was a direct result of his March coup and the final step in a ruthless scramble to power. Chiang himself asserted that this step was a beneficial separation of military command (*chün-ling*) from military administration (*chün-cheng*), a long-needed wresting of power from the military council which had, under the guise of exercising political control over the armed forces, combined both the command and administrative functions. Perhaps some clarification of these two vaguely defined Chinese terms is called for at this juncture. *Chün-ling* deals with major military operations and the direction of the war in its various theatres

[8] National Government of China, "Manifesto of the National Revolutionary Army on the purpose of Northern Expedition," quoted in: Chiang Kai-shek, *China's Destiny*, authorized translation by Wang Chung-hui (N.Y.: Macmillan, 1947), p. 103.

[9] Chang Chi-yuen, *Tang-shih kai-yao*, *op.cit.*, II, pp. 518-520.

[10] National Government of China, "Organic Law of the General Headquarters of the Commander-in-Chief of the National Revolutionary Army, Canton, July 7, 1926."

on the highest and most comprehensive levels. *Chün-cheng* groups together those matters of personnel, equipment, and supplies; construction and operation of bases; transportation; hospitalization; management and training—the totality of what approaches the American phrase "the zone of the interior" or the Russian "the organization of the rear." Chiang's purpose was to confine the military council of the government to military administration and to vest military command in the single person of the commander-in-chief. His contention was simply that a committee cannot wage a war.

It was fortunate that Chiang had taken matters firmly in hand, for the Russians were of little help. It has often been stated that the participation of the Soviet advisers was responsible for many of the Kuomintang's military victories, but a close examination tends to minimize such claims. What actually happened was that the Chinese had begun to apply for themselves the political and military strategies they had assimilated from the Russians. The real military achievements must be credited to the Chinese commanders, notably to Chiang and Pei Chung-hsi in the development of the grand strategy; to Li Tsung-jen, Ho Ying-ch'in, Chang Fa-kuei, and Yeh T'ing in the tactical sphere; to Teng Yen-ta, Chou En-lai, and Lin Tsu-han in the realm of political warfare.

Borkenau, in his book *The Communist International*, stated that General Galen was strongly convinced of the possibility of the failure of the expedition and, that in order to dissociate himself from the defeat, he remained in Canton when the expedition set out.[11] The fact is that although Galen was concerned about maintaining his prestige intact he did, nevertheless, participate in the expedition, although every evidence indicates that the Russians were not overly enthusiastic. Despite the widening gulf between the Chinese and the Russians, many advisers (such as Cherapanoff, Sedich-Nossoff, and Rolland) were active in the field. A number of the Soviet advisers had been heroes in the civil wars of their own country and had meritorious records of service as political commissars in the Red Army. A few were the products of general staff training in the Tsarist Army, and a small number of General Galen's assistants were well versed in military science. Galen himself, according to the account of a high Chinese staff officer who served with him, confined himself largely to criticism of the operational plan originated by the Chinese staff, though con-

[11] Borkenau, F., *The Communist International* (London: Faber & Faber, 1938), p. 310.

tributing significantly to the logistics of the war where the Chinese were inexperienced and unlearned. Galen seldom, however, formulated or made any attempt to direct the expedition's course himself. Mobility, the element of surprise, speed of march, and enveloping tactics were the factors he constantly emphasized. Galen used German military phraseology freely, and his precision and thoroughness were reminiscent of the German Generalstab. Chiang admired Galen's efficiency and added personal friendship to professional respect, even offering to retain Galen's services after he parted ways with Soviet Russia. The Russians reciprocated in this admiration and extended it also to Chiang's acting chief of staff, General Pai Chung-hsi, the legendary "hsiao Chu-ko" (little Chu-ko)[12] of the northern expedition, one of the Revolutionary Army's most brilliant planners.

In two short months the Revolutionary Army swept over all of south China and entered the gates of Wuchan, in the Wu-ch'ang-Hankow-Hanyang area. The military victories were somewhat hampered by the design of the communist wing to turn the whole expedition into a revolution of the proletariat, and communist-instigated mobs rose in insurrections which often caused consternation to the leadership of the Kuomintang as the Reds availed themselves of the opportunities presented by military conquest to spread their organization and recruit new adherents while the armies marched northward. No quarter was given by the communists in the battle for men's minds, and their struggles were as earnest as those of the fighting armies on the bloody fields at Ting-sze-chiao and Ho-sheng-chiao.

The most notable of the military units engaged in this campaign was the "flying" Kwangsi Seventh Army Corps of Li Tsung-jen and the "ironside" Fourth Corps commanded by Chang Fa-kuei. The Fourth Corps, staffed by cadets from the Whampoa Academy, contained an appreciable number of the disbanded communist organization called The Workers' Guard. The Twenty-fourth Division of that corps was commanded by the communist General Yeh T'ing, and stood particularly high in Red favor. Yeh Chien-ying, another communist leader, was the chief of staff of this corps.

Despite the cooperation of certain communist strategists in the army and of the always interested if not always very valuable Soviet advisers, the campaign had been entered into by the Chinese against

[12] Chu-ko Liang (circa A.D. 206-260) was one of China's greatest statesman-strategists of the Han dynasty.

the advice of the Reds. Moreover, once the battle had begun, the Chinese communists involved in the fray did what they could to turn it to their advantage politically, without too much concern with the military hopes of the Kuomintang. During the early stage of the Sino-Russian alliance, the Kuomintang army received substantial assistance from the Soviets. When the Kuomintang was able to stand upon its own feet in Kwangtung, the purchase of military supplies from Russia had to be made on cash terms at the Soviet's quoted price. After the March coup, in an attempt to bring the greater majority of the Kuomintang force into line, the Soviets began to favor the more leftish elements of the Chinese army, but they were checked in their attempt to create another Red Army in China and gradually came to realize that Chiang and his associates would not be docile puppets. The China-for-the-Chinese and China-for-the-world-revolution movements clashed head-on. Chiang Kai-shek, M. N. Roy, Joseph Stalin, and Leon Trotsky all had their versions of the story,[13] but in the final analysis it comes down simply to the basic clash between the Reds, who wanted to enlist the Chinese in revolution and who were willing to expend money and men to accomplish this, and Chiang and the Kuomintang, who had different purposes and who were willing to accept all of the assistance but little of the domineering advice that the Soviets cared to give. The two bided their time as long as they conveniently could, each hoping for some favorable turn that would make possible closer cooperation without unacceptable demands. At last the split came, for the communists grew weary of laboring within the ranks of the Kuomintang army, and decided to create a new supreme military organization, a Red Army in China. When Chiang recognized this move for the serious threat it was to himself and to his whole party, at last no compromise was possible. The showdown was only a matter of time.

[13] Chang Chi-yuen, *op.cit.*, II, Ch. 21, pp. 615-657. Roy, M. N., *op.cit.*, Chs. XV, XVI, XVII. Stalin, J. V., *Marxism and the National and Colonial Question* (N.Y., n.d.), *passim*. Trotsky, L., *op.cit.*, *passim*.

4 · THE SOVIET MASTER PLAN FAILS. THE KUOMINTANG-COMMUNIST SPLIT

I. WUHAN: THE COMMUNIST MILITARY ATTEMPT. II. THE COMMUNIST POLITICAL ATTEMPT. III. CHIANG KAI-SHEK FIGHTS BACK. IV. THE COMMANDERS AND THE COMMISSARS—THE KUOMINGTANG-COMMUNIST SPLIT.

I

DISCOVERING that the northern expedition was to be forced upon them by the Chinese, the Soviet advisers under Michael Borodin set about devising a broad strategical plan which would turn the action as much as possible to their own interest. The immediate goal was the defeat of Marshal Wu Pei-fu's northern armies in central China.[1] The Soviets approved of the plan which sent the Revolutionary Army driving north through central China toward a juncture with the People's Army (Kuominchun) commanded by General Feng Yü-hsiang, then a military ally of Soviet Russia. Feng's forces were so situated in the northwest of China that a direct overland route of communication with Russia was open to the Soviets, in case they decided to bolster Feng's armies with material aid or to supply and equip a completely communist-controlled Red Army.[2] If such forces were raised to sufficient strength to sweep down the east coast of China by means of the Lunghai railway and the Yangtze River, arousing and organizing the masses on the way, they would hold the

---

[1] The mobilization order issued by Chiang to the troops participating in the northern expedition contained the following preamble:

". . . I thereby order the mobilization of our grand army—to secure san-Hsiang [literary description of the Hunan and Hupeh provinces], next, to liberate Wuhan [Wuchang-Hankow], and, then, to join force with our friendly Kuominchun. Our purpose is to unify China and to revive our nation. Our Fourth Army Corps (Commander, General Li Chi-sen) and Seventh Army Corps (Commander, General Li Tsung-jen) have already been dispatched to the front to coordinate with the Eighth Corps (Commander, General T'ang Shen-chih); they shall advance as situation permits. I hereby issue the enclosed operational orders, maps and charts for the guidance of the following operational units: First Corps (Commander, General Ho Ying-chin), Second Corps (T'ang Yen-k'ai), Third Corps (Chu Pei-teh), Fifth Corps (Li Fu-lin), and Sixth Corps (Cheng Chien). These units shall mobilize and concentrate in accordance to plan. . . ." *Mobilization Order*, July 1, 1926, at Canton.

[2] Roy, M. N., *op.cit.*, chs. XV, XVI, XVII.

key to victory—and the communists would have complete control of the progress of the revolution. Such a strong and dependable force would give the Reds the power to steer China's revolutionary course for her. This plan had been proposed to Chiang and the Kuomintang's central executive committee earlier, and Borodin had supported it vehemently.[3] Essentially it was the same suggestion that Kisanka had offered to the Kuomintang on June 4, 1926: to reach China's north-west and to effect a rendezvous with Feng's armies. The Chinese had turned down Kisanka's plan at that time.[4]

The Chinese accepted, it seems, the first move outlined by the Russians: advancing on Wuhan from Canton. At the same time, how-ever, Chiang entrusted his reliable First Army Corps at Kwantung with quite another mission. Commanded by Ho Ying-ch'in, Ch'en Ch'eng, and Ku Chu-t'ung, the First Army Corps struck through the rich coastal provinces of Fukien, Chekiang, and Kiangsu. Their aim was twofold: to seize China's financial and industrial center, Shanghai, and to capture her historic southern capital, Nanking. This invasion route would carry Chiang's army through some of China's richest cities and, through the capture of seaports, would provide the means of receiving whatever foreign arms might be available. The two great arsenals of Shanghai and Nanking were rich prizes, comparable to the strategic Hanyang Arsenal in the important city of Wuhan, the goal of the army despatched to the west.

Attacking northward from Canton were two of the Revolutionary Army's best fighting outfits: the Fourth Corps of General Li Chi-shen and the Seventh Corps commanded by General Li-Tsung-jen. Having rescued T'ang Shen-chih's force, now reorganized as the Eighth Corps, the three corps marched toward Changsha and Hankow as an united army, crushing the enemy forces all along the way. In August, the forces of Marshal Wu Pei-fu were destroyed by the veteran units under the command of Generals Li Tsung-jen and Chang Fa-kuei on the bloody battlefields around Ting-sze-chiao and Ho-shen-chiao. With the destruction of the most powerful northern force of that most feared warlord-marshal, the Revolutionary Army was assured of vic-tory in the first phase of the northern expedition. Amid these victories, Chiang Kai-shek assumed the over-all direction of the campaign against Wuhan, placing himself at the head of an army of varying

[3] Strong, A. L., *China's Million* (N.Y., 1935), p. 352.
[4] Chang Chi-chung, "Address to the Central Military Academy, 1952," *Wei-tà-ti Chiang chu-hsi, op.cit.*, p. 31.

political allegiance. Despite the fall of the Hankow-Wuchang area to Chiang's victorious army on October 10, 1926, it seemed for a time that the successes of this campaign were in reality losses for the Kuomintang, for the communists managed to deliver Hankow and the Hanyang Arsenal into the hands of the leftish elements. A spectacular increase in labor and peasant movements, largely directed by the communists, took place, erupting in a wave of strikes and uprisings in central China. The violence that ensued shocked Chiang and many of his military commanders. The political commissars, being in most cases behind the uprisings, became too dominant for the military commanders to bear. On the other hand, there were generals like T'ang Shen-chi, whose desire for power the communists thought they could neatly turn to their own advantage. Eventually, however, T'ang proved to be a less loyal comrade and less ready tool than the Reds thought.

The plot involving T'ang was only one of the multifarious activities that the Reds directed towards orienting the Kuomintang's force towards the left. Borodin strove vainly to persuade General Li Tsung-jen, a popular fighting general whom Galen held in great respect, to swing over to the communist side, for Li commanded the powerful Seventh Army Corps, the deciding factor in the whole situation. Li's unswerving loyalty to the Kuomintang and the continued efforts of his army of Kwangsi in behalf of the nationalist cause were deciding factors in preventing a military landslide in favor of the communists.[5]

The walled city of Wuchang, dominating both Hankow and Han-yang, was captured only after a prolonged siege during which the northern army of Sun Chuan-fang moved to cut off the revolutionary forces from their rear. Finding that the communists had controlled Wuhan, Chiang Kai-shek made the fateful decision to turn his general reserve force eastward into Kiangsi and, joining force with Li Tsung-jen, to move along the Yangtze toward Nanchang, Nanking, and Shanghai. The protests of the Soviet advisers were immediate, vociferous, and ineffective.[6] Only Galen saw the point that the threat from Sun Chuan-fang must be dealt with, knowing that Chiang's next move might well be the capture of the arsenals at Nanking and Shanghai upon which the latter's armies depended for continued existence. Chiang met with a serious military setback around Nanchang, the

[5] Li Tsung-jen, *Li tsung ssu-ling Yen-lun-chih* (Kweilin, 1934), p. 20.
[6] *Ibid.* See also Yin Shi, *The Chiang-Lee Relationship and China* (Hongkong, 1954), pp. 20-23.

capital of Kiangsi, during the early part of his eastward drive. But on his north, Li Tsung-jen's army fought its way through enemy encirclement and destroyed Sun Chuan-fang's forces at Yochi, Tehan, and Huang-chia-pu, earning the name "flying army" for its speedy and decisive *coup de grace*. Chiang's forces then captured Nanchang and from there he demanded that the seat of government be moved from Canton to Nanchang rather than to Hankow, where the communist influence was dominant. He even made a quick trip to Hankow to press his demand. The leftist elements there, momentarily exhilarated by the appearance of popular strength behind them, were bold enough to reject Chiang's demand. Back in Nanchang, Chiang boldly announced his anti-communist view: "Being known as a faithful believer in the doctrine of Dr. Sun Yat-sen, I have the right to say that every true member of the party must be just that and nothing else. Whoever goes against the aims and methods indicated by Dr. Sun Yat-sen will not be a comrade but an enemy who must not remain among us."[7]

The cleavage was widening.

II

The Reds, having failed on the military level (for Chiang obtained arsenals of his own and was no longer dependent upon Red-controlled Wuhan), opened another political attack. On March 30, 1927, the Wuhan group ordered a sudden reorganization of the military machinery under the slogan: "Return all power—political, military, financial, foreign affairs—to the Party."[8] Their hope was to place power in the weaker hands of the Kuomintang's committees, whence they could wrest it more easily than from Chiang's steel grip. A new "organic law" was passed at the left-dominated third plenary session of the Kuomintang, specifying the military council as the highest military organ of the government.[9] Previously Chiang's general headquarters and the military council of the government were legally equal in authority, with Chiang's headquarters, in actual fact, a superior body.

The military council's membership was limited to fifteen. Its stand-

[7] Chiang Kai-shek, "Speech, Feb. 19, 1927," *Chiang kai-Shek tī ke-ming kŭng-tso*, *op.cit.*, p. 2150. Wigner, *Chine Moderne*, VIII, pp. 23-24.
[8] Chow Mu-chia, *Hsin Chung-Kuo fa-chan shih* (The History of the Development of New China) (Shanghai, 1939), p. 114.
[9] National Government of China, *General Political Report*, May 1931, Section 1.

ing committee of three had to be composed entirely of party-elected civilians. At least four members of the council's presidium were required to subscribe to any decision that was put into effect. The resolution of the third plenary session also established the procedural limitation that mobilization orders for battle must be decided upon by the military council and approved by the central executive committee of the party. Only after such authorization could the order be executed by the general headquarters. This move was calculated to tie the hands of Chiang's general headquarters in all matters dealing with grand strategy.

Other steps were taken to strip Chiang of power. He was appointed a member of the presidium of the military council and of the Kuomintang's central executive committee, but his power as commander-in-chief to appoint personnel was taken from him and vested in the two committees, in each of which he had but a single vote. He was thus deprived of a potential weapon for building personal prestige and following. During the late campaign, enemy commanders had, one after another, joined the Revolutionary Army forces, bringing their troops with them into the Kuomintang's camp. Within the first six months of the campaign the army under Chiang's command had increased tenfold. Many of the defeated northern commanders had been Chiang's schoolmates at the Paoting Military Academy and this fact, coupled with his power of appointment as commander-in-chief, enabled him to enlist them in his ranks. The Reds viewed with alarm Chiang's power in counteracting the rise of the communist influence which, according to General Li Tsung-jen's firsthand account, had been so successful in the hands of the political agents assigned to the army that by the time the Revolutionary Army reached Wuhan the communist doctrine had spread almost everywhere and Chiang's own First Army Corps had not been immune to the infection.[10]

III

Chiang was obviously the greatest obstacle in the way of the communists. Just how important and zealous their master plan was may be inferred from a speech made by Stalin on November 30, 1926, before the Chinese Committee of the Communist International:

"The Chinese Communist Party workers should do their utmost to strengthen the political work among the troops, endeavoring to enable

[10] Li Tsung-jen, *op.cit.* Yin Shi, *op.cit.*, pp. 24-30.

the troops to shoulder the task of bringing to fulfillment the Chinese revolutionary ideology, and to become its model representatives. This is particularly important because the various militarists, who have no common ground with the Kuomintang, have now affiliated themselves with the Canton group. They allied themselves with the force designed to crush the Chinese people. When they joined the Canton group they (the militarists) brought corruptions to the troops. In order to neutralize such 'allies,' or to transform them into true members of the Kuomintang, the only method is to strengthen the political work and establish the methods of revolutionary supervision against them. Unless this is done, it is very likely that the troops will be placed in a most difficult position.

"Secondly, the Chinese revolutionaries, including the Communist Party men, should begin to make a thorough study of military affairs. They must not regard military affairs as of secondary importance because now they comprise a very important factor of the Chinese revolution. The Chinese revolutionaries, and that is to say including the Communist members, must study military affairs so as to advance themselves progressively and to occupy certain positions of leadership among the revolutionary troops. Herein lies the guarantee that the Chinese revolutionary military forces may march along a correct path until the objective is reached. Otherwise drifting and instability among the troops will be unavoidable. In the problems of the revolutionary army the responsibility of the Chinese Communist Party lies precisely here."[11]

If the communists had a master plan for China and were well aware of what they might accomplish there toward world revolution, Chiang Kai-shek and his party were also alert to their intentions. On April 7, 1927 a secret military conference was held at Shanghai, in which the powerful Kwangsi military leaders, Li Tsung-jen, Li Chi-shen, Pai Chung-hsi, and Huang Shao-hsiung pledged their support of Chiang's effort to cleanse the Kuomintang of communistic elements. Emboldened by their support, Chiang ordered a sweeping purge and on April 12 the military went into action against the communists in Shanghai, Canton, and Kwangsi. In a manifesto to the people, Chiang declared his understanding of communist intentions:

"In military affairs they saw the rapid advance made by our armies and feared an early success for the nationalist revolution which would

[11] Stalin, J. V., *op.cit.*, VIII, pp. 351-374.

allow no time for the communist propaganda work when the program of reconstruction commenced, so they alienated our comrades, interrupted our military movements, held up our provisions and ammunition, and did every other hindering thing in their power.

"The Communist Party has been spreading abroad all sorts of rumors concerning the 'oppression of the toiling masses by the Kuomintang' and 'Chiang Kai-shek, the new militarist.' These are due to my opposition to its repugnant policies. . . . The temporary surveillance of the Communists was ordered because they were hampering the military operations, a fact being exposed by the Kuomintang Central Censor Committee. For the safety of our soldiers and of the people it was imperative that their activities should be somewhat restricted in time of war. This is a military necessity. We shall retain them only until the military operations are completed, but we have no wish to endanger our lives. It was this which has given rise to the so-called 'Party Imprisonment.' . . ."[12]

Chiang had attempted to deal with the menace of the communist master plan to subvert the Chinese revolution to Soviet ends by imposing restrictive measures, calculated to limit the effectiveness of communist hindrance. The communists fully appreciated the danger Chiang represented, and even before the proclamation of the manifesto we have quoted in part the Wuhan group had acted to deprive Chiang of his full authority as commander-in-chief. Following that dismissal, the communists expelled Chiang from the Kuomintang accusing him on twelve counts of activities detrimental to the goals of the revolution, a response to his institution of the "temporary surveillance" he in turn had put upon them.

The measure of "temporary surveillance" had been adopted as a result of the interception of the following order, addressed by Stalin to the communist leadership in China. The copy intended for the Soviet military adviser to Chiang's own First Army Corps fell into Chiang's hands and he read this message:

"The work of the Kuomintang and communist cells in the army must be intensified; they must be organized wherever they do not exist and wherever their organization is possible. Where the organization of the communist cell is impossible, intensive work must be carried on with the help of concealed communists.

[12] Chiang Kai-shek, *Manifesto to the People, April 18, 1927* (Shanghai: Commercial Press, 1927), pp. 1-14.

"Our course must be steered towards the arming of the workers and peasants, the transformation of the peasants, the transformation of the peasants' committees in the various localities into actual organs of power accompanied by armed self-defense, etc."[13]

Chiang countered with his system of checks against the communists in April 1927. A month later, Stalin issued the following order:

"The most important thing in the internal policy of the Kuomintang now must be the development of the agrarian revolution systematically in all the provinces, and particularly in Kwangtung, under the slogan 'All Power to the Peasant Unions and the Committees in the Rural Districts.' This is fundamental to the success of the revolution and of the Kuomintang. It is fundamental to the creation in China of a large and powerful political and military army against imperialism and its agents. . . .

"The organization must immediately be undertaken of eight or ten divisions of revolutionary peasants and workers with an absolutely reliable command. This will serve as a guard for Wuhan both at the front and on the home-front for the disarming of unreliable divisions. This must not be delayed.

"Work must be intensified in the rear and within the divisions of Chiang Kai-shek, in order to disintegrate them, and assistance must be given to the peasant insurrectionists in Kwantung, where the rule of the landlords is particularly intolerable."[14]

IV

Some of the most important causes of the Kuomintang-Communist split had their roots in military affairs, chief among which was the role of the political commissars in the army. We have seen in an earlier chapter something of the activities of these commissars and political workers within the ranks of the Whampoa cadets. A brilliant and fiery young general of communist leanings, Teng Yen-ta, was entrusted with the leadership of the army's "political administration." Under his direction the party line dictated by Moscow filtered down to the troops and, through public meetings, demonstrations, and uprisings in various local areas, was put into operation among the masses. In the field the political commissars became independent of military direction and endangered the well-established Chinese tradition of

[13] Stalin, J. V., *Marxism and the National and Colonial Questions* (N.Y.: International Publications, no date).

[14] *Ibid.*

"unity of military command." Beloff and White in their studies have traced the chequered career of the political commissars in the army.[15] In Soviet Russia herself, after 1924, the desire of the Red Army's commanders in the field to take full control of their units was formally recognized in a declaration of the central committee of the Bolshevik Party, which stated the necessity of a single executive principle (*edinonachalie*) for the Red Army—the equivalent of the Chinese "unity of command." The great purge of the 1930's made political supervision once again a necessity, and political commissars were reinstated on an equal basis with the commanders. When there was more confidence in the loyalty of the armed forces to the party's cause during World War II and less suspicion of military unreliability, the political commissar system was once again suspended.

The incompatibility of the political police and the army command was well illustrated in China. Commissars and commanders were often in subtle and hidden conflict as the army's "political administration" fed more and more leftists and straight communists into the military machinery; the commander-in-chief, holding the power of "promotion or execution," silently fought these threats in the military personnel. When the Hankow regime stripped Chiang of his personnel appointive power, he countered by ordering the abolition of the "political administration" and the whole system of political commissars in his command. The confusion which resulted paralyzed the army's organization. The military commanders flocked around Chiang: most of the political commissars followed the lead of the left. The Kuomintang-Communist split tore the army apart.

The commander and the commissar had battled in nearly every division of the entire army. The troops, swayed by political idealism, revolutionary zeal, party loyalty, allegiance to their commander, obedience to military authority, and hope of advancement in something of a "career open to talent" system, were torn between army and party discipline. The coup of March 20 had some relation to the whole struggle for power between the army (Chiang, and his Whampoa force) and the political commissars (Wang Ching-wei, and his party representatives). In part, the coup was a reply to Wang Ching-wei's myriad pro-communist activities of 1926 and 1927, activities which Chiang well knew and described in *China's Destiny*.[16] The communists

[15] Beloff, M., *The Foreign Policy of Soviet Russia* (London: Oxford, 1943), p. 360. White, F. D., *The Growth of the Red Army* (Princeton, 1943), *passim*.
[16] Chiang Kai-shek, *China's Destiny*, trans. Wang Chung-huei (N.Y.: Macmillan,

were sowing the seeds of dissension in Chinese ranks for their own purposes, and such men as M. N. Roy, a Red agent at Hankow, were carrying out, step by step, a plan based on texts in the communist bible, Marx. Whenever Chiang saw evidences of this foreign plan, he sprang to crush it.

On March 24, 1927, nationalist troops entered Nanking. Reportedly goaded by the communist political commissars under Lin Tsu-han, the soldiers of the Fifth Army Corps unleashed an attack on all foreigners in the city, looting foreign consulates and dwellings. Foreign gunboats in the harbor began to shell the town. Some 30,000 foreign troops were despatched to Shanghai, and foreign warships converged on the trouble spot. It looked as if the communists had planned to widen the gulf between the government and foreign powers through a series of engineered incidents. Seeing the communists' deliberate lawlessness, Chiang and other conservative military leaders, Li Tsung-jen, Ho Ying-ch'in, and Pai Chung-hsi, feared that unless drastic steps were taken against the Reds further incidents might jeopardize the success of the entire revolution by inviting, at that inexpedient moment, large-scale foreign intervention. On April 12 they began to purge the communists from the party, beginning at Shanghai and later extending the purge to Canton.

Chiang was able to deal the communist element some serious blows. There were a number of reasons for this. For one, Borodin and Galen (and their whole section of the communist hierarchy which went under the name of the "common sense" school) were fully aware of Chiang's power and unwilling to launch an all-out political offensive against him until some circumstance arose to present them with a clear advantage. Moreover, just as Chiang Kai-shek and Wang Ching-wei, soldier and politician, battled for the mantle of Sun Yat-sen after the elder statesman's death, so, behind the scenes in the Kremlin, there was a contest of power between Stalin and Trotsky for the vacated throne of Lenin. Stalin and Chiang were, in a sense, allies in these intrigues. "The Man of Steel" met Chiang in Moscow in 1923, and was known to have directed the Soviet propaganda machine which built up Chiang's prestige as the leader of China's national renaissance. On many occasions after the March 20 coup, for instance, Stalin sided with Chiang. Trotsky, on the other hand, denounced

1945), pp. 105-106. See also Chiang Kai-shek, *Manifesto to the People, op.cit.*, pp. 1-14.

Stalin's alliance with Chiang and urged the Chinese communists to strive for a proletarian dictatorship on their own.[17]

Stalin had that disadvantage to which even the most powerful men are prey—incompetent assistants. His orders to the Wuhan group were often dictated by consideration of the reports he received from the Comintern's agents at Hankow, especially M. N. Roy. Roy was a Trotskyite, a Hindu with a certain degree of brilliance as a theorist but lacking the practical military sense and political acumen of such men as Borodin and Galen. His desire to impose Marxian theory rigidly was thwarted by his lack of real knowledge of Chinese affairs, and his book *Revolution and Counter-Revolution in China* reflects his misconceptions and failures and the concomitant over-simplifications and self-justifications.

On May 22, 1927, Stalin cabled a direct order to the Wuhan group: ". . . The dependence upon unreliable generals must be put to an end. Mobilize about 20,000 communists, add about 50,000 revolutionary workers from Hunan and Hupeh, forming several new army corps and utilizing the students of the school [Whampoa] as commanders. Organize your army before it is too late, otherwise there can be no guarantee against failure. It is a difficult matter, but there is no other course."[18]

The order was Roy's suggestion, a thoroughly impossible plan completely out of touch with the actual situation. The most likely nucleus for this army would have been the Fourth Army Corps—its numbers already decimated by heavy fighting and its morale and party loyalty at a new low. Surrounded by hostile forces and without any easy route by which communist supplies might reach them, they would clearly have been no match for Chiang Kai-shek's armies. On top of all this was Roy's greatest mistake: his failure in realizing that any palpable move on the part of the Reds to seize the Kuomintang leadership would be tantamount to precipitating an irreparable split between the communists and the Kuomintang. Against the advice of Borodin and Galen, Roy sent his plan of action to the Kremlin, a plan which Stalin, with misplaced trust in the efficiency of his remote-control system and his assistants, could not but accept.[19]

[17] Stalin, J. V., *Sochinenya*, VIII, pp. 358 and 373. Bukharin, S., "Speech," *Konferentsya Vsesoyuznoi Kom Partii*, pp. 27-29. Dallin, D. J., *op.cit.*, pp. 212-223. Deutscher, I., *Stalin, A Political Biography* (N.Y.: Oxford, 1946), p. 400.
[18] Stalin, J. V., *op. oppozitsii*, p. 661. Tewksbury, D. G., *Source Book On Far Eastern Political Ideologies*, p. 78.
[19] Roy, *op.cit.*, pp. 520-527.

Chiang Kai-shek's victory over Stalin in 1927 was a bold and precarious adventure—a testimony to his skill in military and political legerdemain. Stalin had many Chinese *t'ung-chih* (ideological comrades) deeply entrenched in Chiang's revolutionary army. Even in Chiang's own First Army Corps the communist influence was, at one time, sufficiently strong to force Ho Ying-ch'in, its commanding general, to attempt resignation when he learned that Chiang had decided to crack down on the communists. Li Tsung-jen, the successful Kwangsite general who commanded the famous Seventh Army Corps, reputedly an "army of steel," held the key to the situation. Li's army was the only outfit not seriously infected by the communist influence. He and his associate, Pai Chung-hsi, both nationalistic and conservative in their outlook, shared a soldier's suspicion of the motives of the Communist International in China. Having been assured of their support, Chiang had Li's corps redeployed in the Nanking area and, in a master stroke, purged the communists from the First Division of his own army *a la pointe des canons* of the Kwangsite troops.[20] He regained complete control of his own army and, as master of his own destiny, confidently challenged the Kremlin in the name of nationalism—the first principle of Dr. Sun Yat-sen's San-min-chu-i (The Three Principles of the People).

It was too late for Stalin to mobilize "new revolutionary regiments and divisions of revolutionary peasants"! The Stalin-Roy telegram of May 22, 1927, alienated even the generals previously sympathetic to the Wuhan's cause and turned them into "unreliable" generals ready to turn their guns against the communists. The time was ripe for Nanking to deliver the *coup de grace*.

Toward the end of June 1927, Chiang delivered his ultimatum to the Wuhan regime, for by then it was clear where the different loyalties lay. Chiang was joined by Li Tsung-jen and Feng Yü-hsiang, whom he had just created commanders-in-chief of two of the four group armies of the Revolutionary Army. They demanded that the Soviet advisers be relieved of their duties and the communists be expelled from the Kuomintang. With this done, the way was open to the reunion of the Kuomintang factions, and a conference was called which gave birth to the unrivaled authority of the National Government at Nanking.

[20] Yin Shi, *op.cit.*, pp. 24-30.

5 · THE CONSOLIDATION
OF CHIANG KAI-SHEK'S POWER

On April 18, 1927, Chiang Kai-shek, with the support of the moderate wing and the rightists of the Kuomintang, set up the new National Government in the ancient city of Nanking.

The rival Kuomintang elements who had established the Wuhan regime had yet to capitulate, and so China for a time had two governments and two main armies. However, the government at Nanking had the greater resources, both military and financial, and it prevailed. Thereafter Chiang set about setting his house in order in regard to both finances and military forces.

Chiang's solution to the March 24 uprising at Nanking assured all foreign powers that the nationalists deplored the use of mob violence or force to effect a change in the status of the foreign settlement in the new capital. The Washington Conference permitted China an increase in import duties and the English inspector of China's customs administration delivered $3 million to Chiang's government as the first installment of the amount due to China under the new regulations. The banking concerns of Shanghai promised their support to the Nanking regime, and a loan of $30 millions was floated in its behalf. The foreign powers quietly abandoned their agreements not to ship arms to China and, with the lifting of this embargo, the armed forces were in line for a lasting reorganization. Following the purge of the communists, from April 1927 until October 1928 the army underwent a series of reorganizations reflecting the successive administrative difficulties that beset the military organization.[1]

Nanking's policy hinged upon three basic concepts:

1. Party control over military command. This was the central feature of Nanking's military reorganization, designed to place the command of the armed forces firmly in the control of the Kuomintang's central executive committee.

2. Committee responsibility in military administration. This was an attempt to place matters of administration in the hands of a com-

[1] *The Official Bulletin of the National Government*, I, No. 2 (1927). Chien Tuan-shen and Sah Shih-chiung, *Min-Kuo cheng-chih shih* (History of Political Institutions under the Republic), (Chungking, 1945), I, p. 174.

mittee, and to prevent the chairman from assuming the privileges and responsibilities of his associates.

3. The separation of military command and military administration by vesting these powers respectively in the Kuomintang's central executive committee and the military committee mentioned under point 2.

The ingrained Chinese tradition of checks and balances emerged once again, for it is evident that an attempt was made, through the military council, to guard against and counteract the sweeping power of military command exercised by the central executive committee. At the same time the deficiencies inherent in a committee were compensated for by the existence of a single commander-in-chief.

While the Nanking government sought to stabilize itself, the Wuhan regime was in chaos. Soviet advisers, representatives of the Communist International of many nationalities, Chinese communists, and the leftist elements of the Kuomintang—all clustered around Hankow, all anxious to direct the great Chinese revolution. In the Kremlin itself, Stalin and Trotsky were engaged in a top-level struggle for power which confused the party line. Uncertain about what course of action to take regarding the Nanking forces, the forces of Wuhan largely avoided them, and instead undertook separate expeditions against the northern armies which the Nanking troops were then battling. Spearheaded by the veteran Fourth Army, the Wuhan forces defeated the Manchurian Army at Honan. This proved, however, to be a Pyrrhic victory, and it led in the long run to the collapse of Wuhan military power.

For a time the military politicians took over the show. General Feng Yü-hsiang, who had recently joined the revolutionary ranks after returning from Moscow, played sides with both Nanking and Wuhan. In the Chengchow conference of June 10, 1927, which he convened, it was resolved that the Wuhan force should leave the Honan area to him and that T'ang Shen-chih's troops should return to Hankow to suppress the radical movements of the left. The best of the Wuhan units, the "Ironside" Fourth Corps, was by now both frustrated and war-weary and decided to march homeward toward Canton. When they arrived at Nanchang on August 1, 1927, the communist revolt led by Ho Lung and Yeh T'ing split the army asunder and saw the better part of it lost to the Wuhan cause. All the principal military commanders had, since their discovery of the Stalin-

Roy order of May 22, deserted the communist cause. The Wuhan regime, having no military force to sustain it, could no longer survive. Borodin, Galen, and their communist entourage had to leave for Moscow.

But Chiang also had to step down temporarily to facilitate the re-union of the separate Kuomintang elements. Taking advantage of that party's difficulties, powerful northern forces, 70,000 strong, crossed the Yangtze River on August 25, 1927. Nanking was in imminent danger. Immediately Li Tsung-jen's Seventh Corps struck back against the northerners, supported by the forces of Ho Ying-chin and Pai Chung-hsi, and after five days of fierce battles annihilated the invaders at Lungtan. Thirty thousand of Sun Chuan-fang's northern troops surrendered to Nanking. It was said that in the battles at Lungtan and in Honan the generalship as well as the combat efficiency of the Revolutionary Army had reached its maturity. But much of the flower of revolutionary manhood was also being decimated there.

Now, with Chiang removed, the whole structure of command fell apart into a confusing handful of components—and opponents. At Nanking a triumvirate consisting of Li Tsung-jen, Ho Ying-ch'in, and Pai Chung-hsi shared the command of the troops in South China. But in North China, and in Canton, many powerful military leaders saw the opportunity of rising to power with the backing of loyal troops. No one of them was willing to accept an inferior status, and the weak-ened government at Nanking was compelled to devise a system to honor them all without exalting one above the other. On July 6, 1927, the Nanking government announced the names of forty-six members of a National Military Council, including even important militarists from Szechuan, Yunnan, and Kweichow. Many of the men thus honored had contributed little or nothing to the cause of the national revolution, and some were notoriously corrupt. The pre-sidium of the military council was reserved for a handful of the most powerful military leaders: it consisted of the most serious contenders for the supreme military power in China.

The Wuhan-Nanking bickering had impeded the progress of the Revolutionary Army in its drive northward, and now that the Wuhan faction had been silenced the supporters of the Nanking government looked for a renewed and united effort in the northern expedition. While the armies of the south had fought among themselves, the northern warlords had had time to band together, and they rallied under the banner of their chosen generalissimo, the Manchurian general, Chang Tso-lin. Under his strong hand, the 400,000 men who remained to support the northern cause gave some semblance of unity of command.[2] It was evident that the 700,000 troops of the south would have to meet them with something better in the way of command than a committee, a triumvirate, and a heterogeneous collection of petty independent commanders.

The answer was, of course, Chiang Kai-shek. At the request of the Kuomintang he emerged from his retirement and, in announcing his resumption of command on January 6, 1928, he pledged himself to complete the task of the northern campaign if he was granted unity of command. He was created commander-in-chief and chairman of the national military council. Taking command of the First Army, he immediately made General Li Chi-shen chief of the general staff. Li, a leader of the Kwangsi-Kwangtung military group (which consisted of some of the best fighting forces commanded by Li Tsung-jen, Pai Chung-hsi, and Chang Fa-kuei), was to be Chiang's righthand man. Together they planned a strategy which deployed the four formidable armies of the south on seven fronts. The battle line of almost 800 miles stretched from the eastern coast above the Yangtze to the Great Wall in the province of Shansi. Against such a terrible array of strength the northern warlords, whose power had always been more apparent than real, could not win. They suffered a series of disastrous reverses, and by the time the Revolutionary Army reached the Yellow River and was preparing to deliver the *coup de grâce* the routed northern forces were deserting their commanders in large numbers. Even Japanese intervention—such as that at Tsinan on May 3, 1928— could not save the northern cause.

The Second Army under General Feng Yü-hsiang and the Third Army under General Yen Hsi-shan displayed their sturdy fighting qualities on numerous occasions, and the soldiers of the Kuomintang remained popular with the people. Their relentless advance was one of the determining factors in the campaign.

When the four armies of the south converged upon their last defense perimeter, the morale of the northern army sank. The commander-in-chief, Chang Tso-lin, sensed imminent defeat and decided to withdraw his forces from the Great Wall, despite the strongest

[2] "The Orders of Battle of the Opposing Armies" listed in Chang Tze-sen "The War History of the Northern Expedition of the National Revolutionary Army," *The Eastern Miscellany*, in Chinese, xxv, 17 (Sept. 10, 1928), pp. 59-61.

kind of Japanese opposition to this move. On June 4, 1927, on the same day that Peking fell to the Revolutionary Army, Chang Tso-lin was assassinated by the Japanese while on his way to Mukden. He was succeeded by his son, Chang Hsueh-liang, who repulsed the Japanese and delivered Manchuria and his own allegiance into the hands of the nationalists in Nanking. By the fall of 1928 the Revolutionary Army had apparently achieved unification for the Kuomintang.

6 · A CRITICAL SUMMARY OF THE PERIOD 1924-1928

THE four years between 1924 and 1928 were a period of pace-setting in military affairs for the Kuomintang. Its first achievement was the creation of a nucleus around which could be built a strong, reliable military force designed specifically for the revolutionary cause. With the aid of Soviet Russia and the Chinese Communist Party members, the Kuomintang was able to build a centralized military machine capable of exploiting the revolutionary zeal of the small military cadre of Whampoa cadets. The new army formed around such a nucleus adapted the politico-military system of the Red Army to its own purposes and devised more effective techniques of organization. These were positive advances by which the Kuomintang paved the way in its initial military organization for its successes to come.

As the Kuomintang enlisted the support of the Reds in creating a new Chinese army, it also won over the educated class of its own nation. The Chinese people of the 1920's welcomed the promise of liberation from the rapacious warlordism under which they had suffered for so long. The government at Canton, with its revolutionary zeal, orderliness in structure, and relative democracy, won their sympathy and support. In addition, the iron discipline of the young army, its dedicated efforts in propaganda and public relations, and the selfless spirit exhibited by the revolutionary fighters, had enabled the new government to win over the great masses of China's *lao-pai-hsing*, the common people. To the strength resulting from popular support the Kuomintang forces added military growth as various military units of South China flocked to its banners and swelled its ranks. The new government seemed to be supported on all sides. All that remained, it appeared, was to crush the military forces of the hostile warlords.

Matters, however, were not so simple. For one thing, an analysis of the Kuomintang's early military nucleus reveals that it was constituted of two elements: the Whampoa military cadre led by Chiang Kai-shek, and the group of youthful political workers and commissars controlled, by and large, by Chinese communist organizations and Soviet advisers. As long as their aims were similar the two groups collaborated harmoniously: the Whampoa cadre shouldering much of the command responsibilities of the army, the political commissars managing a good deal of the army's organizational, administrative, and political functions. Then came the northern expedition, splitting the two forces and creating a dichotomy between the aims of Chiang and his group and the strict Communist Party line.

As the nucleus grew, the military leadership soon outgrew the civilian controls at Canton. The mere slogan of political control could not check the ascendancy of the military after the death of Dr. Sun Yat-sen and the assassination of Liao Chung-k'ai. Against the Chinese communists and their Soviet allies, military force became the sole effective instrument of self-preservation in the hands of the Kuomintang. The years 1924-1928, therefore, saw on the one hand the marked rise of communist influence and on the other the deliberate increase of Kuomintang military power. In the emergency the politicians of the Kuomintang placed themselves in the hands of the military leaders and made no attempt, instead, to subject those leaders to the dictates of the party's political control. The Chinese Communist Party was a politically disciplined force, but the Kuomintang's only real discipline was to be found in its military force. When the times called for discipline, the Kuomintang's hierarchy rallied around its military leadership.

As part of their master plan to seize control of the direction of the revolution, the communists infiltrated every section of the Kuomintang. Nationalism, ideological differences, military economics, and strategic disagreements compounded to precipitate the final showdown. The communist plan for China involved destructive and hampering activities which the Chinese could not but resent strongly, and this, combined with mismanagement at the Chinese end of the Kremlin's remote-control system, doomed it to failure, particularly when such a man as Chiang was poised to take advantage of Stalin's every mistake.

From the standpoint of history, the northern expedition was dictated by military economics as well as by the avowed aims of the Kuomintang. On this question, however, the Chinese and the Russian party lines parted company and the military commanders and political commissars split, after each side had tried to force capitulation by threats, deadlocks, and retaliations. Things were at a standstill during the brief period that Chiang resigned from the high command. The reassertion of his personal leadership enabled the northern expedition to roll on again toward its eventual success, but the same act divided Chiang's party and the communists into two irreconcilable camps. Chiang himself emerged as a factor in the success of the revolutionary campaign (both against the warlords in the north and the communists formerly in his own ranks), a factor at least as important as the highly-praised revolutionary spirit, organizing techniques, and teamwork.

Chiang, of course, had to have support behind him, and this support came in large part from the Whampoa group. While it is true that one cannot consider the Whampoa group the Chinese Army, it did form an essential and, especially to Chiang, important part of the whole. The army of a nation must be led by that nation's best qualified men, and Chiang's predisposition to grant the army's leadership to his Whampoa men was deleterious in its effect, a not surprising outcome when a highly political army, an army which had established the nation's political strength, regarded itself as heir to the nation's military power. If one compares the honor roll of Whampoa with the roster of the Nationalist Army's top echelons, one notices a remarkable similarity. As Chiang rose to power, his subordinates of the Whampoa days advanced in the military hierarchy. Those who had served as faculty members at Whampoa received the choicest plums that the nationalist administration could offer: posts as commanders-in-chief, provincial governors, ministerial appointments in government. The majority of Whampoa's early classmen, particularly the first and second classes graduated, moved into the key field command of the army, ranging from divisional commanders to commanders-in-chief. Even the top brackets of the navy and air force have, since 1945, been occupied by old Whampoa comrades, despite the fact that they have had no opportunity to gain any formal professional qualifications for their posts. The Russians were smarter than the Chinese in this respect, for Stalin, much as he treasured the memory of Tsaritsyn, did not entrust the entire World War II command to Tsaritsyn generals. Although Voroshilov and Budyenny remained in Stalin's entourage, the youthful and capable commanders (such as Zhukov, Vassilevsky, Rokossovsky, and Voronov) had been able to gain high commands and top administrative offices. In China, for a quarter of a century the same people ruled the armed forces.

The pattern of personnel administration in the nationalist military organization was fixed in the Whampoa period. Certain relevant social and political factors should be noted. First, the Chinese had long been dedicated to the proposition of mutual loyalty between a leader and his followers. It had been a tradition to entrust important assignments to one's personal confidants, not necessarily because of their competence (though they would have been chosen largely on this criterion in the first place) but chiefly because of their tested reliability. Nepotism, favoritism, and the need for trustworthy lieutenants had firmly established this procedure.

The second influence was largely ideological in nature. At Whampoa, for example, while an ardent communist minority constantly worked from within to subvert the whole to its own ends, the holder of power, in order to prevent these machinations, was increasingly inclined to confer appointments and vest authority only in those whom he considered indubitably loyal. Such discriminatory favoritism may be viewed as a by-product of "power preservation" in the *realpolitik* sense of the word.

Third, there is the undeniable contribution of the Whampoa group to the Kuomintang's success, a factor that Chiang Kai-shek would be the first to recognize. The term *Wham-poa-ching-shên* (Whampoa spirit) originated by Chiang, became almost synonymous with the spirit of gallant self-sacrifice. The Whampoa cadets became a living legend of heroism. Tales of their near contempt for life, their courage, their selflessness, were widely circulated in China. These accounts built up the *esprit de corps* of a new generation of Chinese military men who were the fighting cadres of both the nationalist and the Chinese communist army. Here is one of them, as an example:

"In the late Spring of 1927, during the Battle of Wuchang, it appeared that unless Kuei-shan (a mountain nearby) could be taken, the capture of the city by assault would be difficult. At the top of the mountain were strong defences—only a couple of narrow paths, commanded by several machine-guns, led to the top.

"Teng Yen-ta [one of Whampoa's early figures and then chief of the Revolutionary Army's political administration] decided that an assault on the hilltop should be made. He announced to the Whampoa cadets that five hundred men would be needed the next morning for the assault. Every one of the one-thousand-odd cadets there at the time volunteered for the mission. Then they had a dinner together which was in the nature of a common farewell party, for to join the assault was virtual suicide, and they all knew it. The dinner, nevertheless, was cheerful enough.

"Shortly before midnight Borodin heard of the order for the assault. He got in touch with Teng Yen-ta and suggested to him that the capture of the hill was not worth the sacrifice of so many of the very best men the Nationalists had. Borodin advised that Wuchang should be surrounded and besieged instead of being taken by assault.

"Early the next morning the cadets turned out every last man, ready for the assault. They were informed that the plan had been changed."[1]

Even the faculty of Whampoa and Chiang himself had on occasion joined the so-called *kan-ssu-tui* (do-or-die) detachments. During the attack on Waichow in October 1925 students and faculty members of Whampoa volunteered en masse for the suicidal mission of scaling the city wall of the fortressed stronghold. Chiang, unable to join such a mission, nevertheless swore before all the cadets to crush the forces of Ch'en Chiung-ming (the late Dr. Sun's most hated militarist traitor) and personally directed the assault immediately beneath the city wall. Refusing to take shelter, Chiang reiterated his pledge that unless the stronghold was taken within a certain time he would remain in that same spot. The embattled city, boasted by Ch'en as impregnable, fell before the appointed hour at the cost of the lives of many of Whampoa's veteran members, cut down by murderous enemy cross-fire.[2]

Many years of the agony of combat, of sweat and blood, of revolution and the struggle for power, had fostered the deepest kind of mutual loyalty between Chiang and his Whampoa comrades. Chiang's introductions to the Whampoa alumni books, with his own vivid revelation of the early death-defying struggles, reveal that Whampoa's success was neither accidental nor cheaply bought. In its founding days, Chiang had envisioned an academy built on heroism and sacrifice. He saw the school he founded live up to its fighting tradition and build up his personal power. With pride Chiang cited the martyrdom of old Whampoa comrades and extolled the spirit fostered by the academy, a spirit worthy of the other heroes of China's long military history. Chinese writers have recorded the deeds of Whampoa in their glowing annals. Among them is this one:

"At the Battle of Lungt'an in the Summer of 1927, Sun Chuan-fang [a northern warlord] had succeeded in transporting his troops

[1] *The Week in China*, XI, 170 (June 30, 1928), p. 23.
[2] Chang Chi-yuen, *Tang Shi Kai-yao*, II (Taipeh, 1951), pp. 488, 544.

across the Yangtze. Nanking was in a critical situation. Pai Chung-hsi had sent up reinforcements, due to arrive in half an hour or so, but the assault at one strategic point was extremely fierce. Resistance was practically gone.

"Two hundred Whampoa cadets, hearing of the state of things at the railway, asked permission to volunteer to hold the line. The permission was granted.

"They held the line. Not one of them lived to tell the tale. The Whampoa cadets had always shown a willingness to fight to the end."[3]

Whampoa's early training was not without some shortcomings. The few months' course given the cadets of the first three classes can hardly be regarded, by any modern standard, as adequate officers' training. The young army's logistics in those days were so rudimentary and simple that the entire system of supply, recruitment, and subsistence could be easily grasped. The same did not hold true, however, after the Nationalist Army had begun its modernization. By that time the early graduates and the old guard of Whampoa's faculty had climbed the ladder of rank. Confronted by the new and far more complicated problems of modern warfare, they were nonplused. It availed but little in such a dilemma to extol an *esprit de corps*. These were no "desk generals," for Whampoa had stressed experience in the field and baptism of its young graduates by fire, but these seasoned soldiers were too inadequate for anything more than the glory of field command. They sneered at administrative offices and looked with an air of ill-concealed contempt on the teaching staffs of the military schools, calling them *lo-wu fen-tzu* (the backward elements).[4] Such an attitude could not be without its dire effect on the soundness of the military organization. In the best military schools, the most important administrative and teaching duties are reserved for the best-qualified men. Today a sound system of rotation of duties is another almost indispensable factor in modern military administration. Generally speaking, the Nationalist Army's prevailing outlook on military affairs was fairly narrow and onesided. So anxious were the Whampoa men for field command that they forfeited their chances for higher education, fearing that once away from their post of command they would be unable to return. History records few great commanders who were not well versed in military administration. Napoleon was a

[3] *The Week in China, op.cit.,* p. 24.
[4] Wang Chun, *Chung-Kuo lu-chun chao-yu kai-kuan* (The General Condition of China's Military Education), (Chungking, 1943), pp. 10-11.

genius in this aspect, and Wellington and Marlborough were meticu-
lous about administrative arrangements.[5] Moltke of the German Generalstab stressed the value of *verwaltung*, and Foch displayed his
mastery of *la sagesse administrative*. In our own day, Generals Marshall and Eisenhower are perhaps best known as administrators. No
modern army can be efficient in which administrative posts become
havens of mediocrity, where, as was unfortunately the case in China,
the generals were simply sword-wavers.

Perhaps one of the greatest dangers of the "Whampoa mind" was
the excessive extolling of the interests of the Whampoa group. To
many this attitude has appeared chauvinistic and discriminative. The
desire to serve first the interests of the Whampoa group as such led
inevitably to schism and disharmony in the army. It threatened national solidarity and introduced petty politics in the military organization. But, for better or for worse, Chiang and the Whampoa group
emerged from the test of the northern campaign firmly entrenched.

[5] Wavell, A., *Generals and Generalship* (N.Y.: Macmillan, 1943), pp. 2, 19, 20.
White, L. D., et al., *Civil Service Abroad* (N.Y.: McGraw, 1935), Monograph 4.

7 · THE BEGINNINGS OF GERMAN INFLUENCE: REORGANIZATION

I. THE NEED FOR REORGANIZATION. II. THE SHORT AND IMPORTANT CAREER OF MAX BAUER. III. THE BACKGROUND OF THE REORGANIZATION: GERMAN MODELS. JAPANESE MODELS. CHINESE MODELS. IV. THE NATURE OF THE REORGANIZATION.

I

LATE in the summer of 1928 a victorious National Revolutionary Army entered the gates of the ancient capital of Peking. The northern expedition was officially concluded.

The victory, however, was not unmixed with difficulties. A warning of impending storm had been given the new Kuomintang regime on May 3, 1928, when Japan sent military forces to Tsinan in the province of Shantung in an effort to obstruct the advance of the Revolutionary Army in North China. Fearing that any resistance to the Japanese intervention might imperil the success of the northern expedition, Chiang Kai-shek restrained his angry troops from action against the Japanese. As a result, the new government and the Revolutionary Army lost face, and Chiang became the target of vituperative attacks from the people, who smarted from the humiliation of the unresisted Japanese attack. In an effort to pacify the army's antagonism to the act of Japanese imperialism, Chiang instructed his officers and men: "If we wish to redress the wrong done to our nation, to avenge our national humiliation, to free China from the oppression of imperialism, and to attain independence and freedom, we must for the present endure disgrace and shoulder our responsibility. We must remember what we have suffered and set apart ten years for developing our national strength and ten years for training our people. . . ."[1]

While the Chinese themselves, peeved at the Japanese insult, endangered the success of their own campaign by threats of diverting

[1] Chiang Kai-shek, "Manifesto to the Soldiers on May 3rd Incident," quoted in Chang Chi-yuen, *Tang Shi Kai-yao* (Taipeh, 1951), II, p. 577.

their forces against the Japanese, other matters complicated the successful completion of the task they had set for themselves. The forces massed to attain victory in the north were heterogeneous and scattered. During the late stages of the campaign, Chiang could barely coordinate the efforts of the three other army groups with those of the forces he personally commanded. Crowning all were the tremendous financial demands being made by these vast armies on the already depleted coffers of the government.

As soon as the northern campaign was concluded, the government hastened to put into action the plan which for some time it had seen to be a necessity—the blueprint for the demobilization of China's vast army and the creation of a smaller, more closely knit, less expensive defense force. This new army they elected to organize and train along the lines of Germany's Reichswehr, a suggestion advanced by the German military advisers under Dr. Max Bauer who replaced the Russian attachés after the Kuomintang-Soviet split. The new government settled in Nanking rather than in the precarious northern capital of Peking and determined, with the help of German advice, to consolidate its position, centralize authority, and strengthen the military defenses against the potential external threats from Soviet Russia and Japan.

II

Chiang Kai-shek, who in 1913 and again in 1918 had actually prepared to pursue military studies in Germany himself, had always shown a profound interest in German military methods.[2] He sent his favorite son, Chiang Wei-kuo, to receive military training in the German army in the mid-1930's. Chiang himself was always on the best of terms with his German advisers, and when the United States sent General Albert C. Wedemeyer to replace Stilwell in China it was Wedemeyer's brilliant record in the German Kriegsakademie which was chiefly responsible for his warm reception in China.

When, in the spring of 1927, Chiang decided to dispense with his Soviet military advisers, it was a former German colonel, Dr. Max Bauer, whom he appointed as his military aide. Bauer's acceptance of the position was said to be part of German industrial policy in China, and it has been suggested that his name was recommended to

[2] Tong, H. K., *op.cit.*, II, p. 622.

Chiang by a powerful German industrialist.[3] Bauer, onetime chief of operations under Field Marshal Erich Ludendorff, was regarded as an expert in artillery, engineering, and chemistry.[4] He had received his doctorate from the University of Berlin and was the author of several books, including the much-respected *Der Grosse Krieg in Feld und Heimat*. His experience included service with Ludendorff, the patronage of Kaiser Wilhelm II, and important staff posts. Politically he was an arch-royalist and he had been exiled for his part in the Kapp Putsch but later pardoned. In advisory capacities he had served the governments of Austria, Soviet Russia, Spain, and Argentina, on matters ranging from military aviation to the combatting of locust plagues.[5]

Arriving at Shanghai in November 1927, Bauer took over the post vacated by General Galen. He immediately won the favor of the Chinese military authorities. He had the advantage of experience in Soviet Russia, where he had served as a German adviser to the Red Army after the First World War. His familiarity with the strength and weaknesses of the Soviet military system stood him in good stead in his role in China. After he had established himself there he returned to Germany to recruit more military advisers and to arrange for procuring munitions and equipment. He brought back to China an unofficial Reichswehr group numbering some forty-six men—the beginning of a long line of German military advisers who were to dominate the reorganization of the Nationalist Army. Bauer played an important part in the initiation of a military intelligence system, a foreign publicity program, and a scheme of organized military training. Originally, in mid-1927, Chiang had planned to establish at Nanking a central military and political academy, patterned after Whampoa.[6] It was Bauer and his assistants who proposed the more thorough system of military education, based upon German instructional methods and entirely divorced from politics, which Chiang came to prefer. Bauer's services were granted a prominent role in many of Chiang's military successes in the next few years; Chiang's rapid victory over Li Tsung-jen's armies in Central China was one

[3] Bloch, K., *German Interests and Policy in the Far East* (N.Y.: I.P.R., 1939), pp. 12-13.
[4] Tschuppak, K., *Ludendorff* (Boston: Houghton Mifflin, 1933), p. 56f.
[5] *The Eastern Miscellany*, in Chinese, XXVI, p. 13, July 10, 1929.
[6] National Government "Official Decree, Nanking, June 17, 1927," *Kuo-fan Kung-pao* (Official Reports on National Defense), in Chinese (June, 1927).

example. During that campaign, Bauer followed Chiang's head-quarters to Hankow in April 1929, and it was there that he contracted small-pox. He died shortly after in a hospital in Shanghai.

III

The revamping of the army under German advice had its counter-part in administrative changes throughout the government. On October 10, 1928, the National Government was reorganized into a five-power system comprising five theoretically co-equal divisions called *yuans*: the Executive Yuan, the Legislative Yuan, the Judicial Yuan, the Administrative Yuan, and the Examining Yuan.[7] This new constitutional plan followed the broad outlines of the five-fold constitution conceived by the late Dr. Sun Yat-sen. The most striking feature of the reorganized government was the new military setup, which quickly established its dominance in practice despite the theoretical arrangements. In actual fact the country was ruled by a tripartite administration composed, in descending order of importance, of the military administration, the Kuomintang or party, and the Executive Yuan. In reality the new government in operation was not in any way related to Dr. Sun's original design. Chiang Kai-shek was elected president of the National Government by a caucus of the Kuomintang leaders, and in that capacity he became generalissimo of the Chinese army, navy, and air force.

In the accompanying military reorganization, which was of the most drastic order, the changes were principally based upon the principles of the Prussian and Japanese systems. So complete was the change that it may be said that the Chinese military organization had veered from one foreign system, the Russian, to an almost diametrically opposed pole. One outstanding feature of the new order was the parceling out of various military functions, in contradistinction to the previous attempts at integration. Formerly the military machinery had essayed to embody both the functions of command and administration. The military council which had normally been assigned these functions yielded the power of command in time of war, delegating this authority to the commander-in-chief. In the new setup, the subdivisions lined up as follows:

[7] For a detailed study of the Five-Yuan System see: Wang Shih-chieh, *Pi-chiao Hsien-fa* (Comparative Constitution Law) and Linebarger, P. M., *The China of Chiang Kai-Shek* (Boston, 1943), Ch. 11.

Major Division	Function
1. General staff	Defense planning
2. War ministry	Military administration
3. Military advisory council	Advisory
4. Directorate-General of military training	Military training
5. General headquarters of the commander-in-chief	Military command
6. National defense council	Defense policy-making
7. Metropolitan garrison headquarters	Security of the capital

All of these new military agencies, with the exception of the war ministry, which was subjected to the Executive Yuan, were made entirely independent of the five *yuans* and answerable directly to the National Government, specifically in the person of the president.[8] The military council expired (by an order dated November 7, 1927), and its powers were vested in the war ministry, the general staff, and the military advisory council. These moves put the direction of almost every phase of military operations in the hands of Chiang, as president.

To understand the nature of the new military organization, one has to examine its background in the military system of Imperial Germany. That system, as built up during the years 1870-1883, consisted of three principal organs: the Grossen Generalstab (the great general staff), which was responsible for war plans and, in time of war, had *ipso facto* all command of forces in the field; the Militär-Kabinett (the kaiser's cabinet for military affairs), in charge of all matters concerning the officer corps; and the Kriegsministerium (the ministry of war), which was in charge of all organization, supply, and other administrative functions. All three were directly answerable to the kaiser, with the exception of the minister of war, who answered to the Reichskanzler (the prime minister) and, in theory, the Reichstag (the German parliament). In addition to these three offices, there was the General Inspektion des Militär-Erziehungs und Bildungswesen—the office of the inspector-general of military training. The German plan was intended to enable the kaiser to exercise absolute control over the officer corps and the army as a whole, making him entirely free of interference from the Reichstag. As Bismarck, the Iron Chancellor, wrote to Kaiser Wilhelm I on February 24, 1883: "Any attempt to seek the favor of the parliament that does not maintain the independence of Royal Command above all possible doubt

---

[8] Ministry of War, *Chün-cheng Kung-pao* (Official Report of the War Ministry), No. 52, August, 1929.

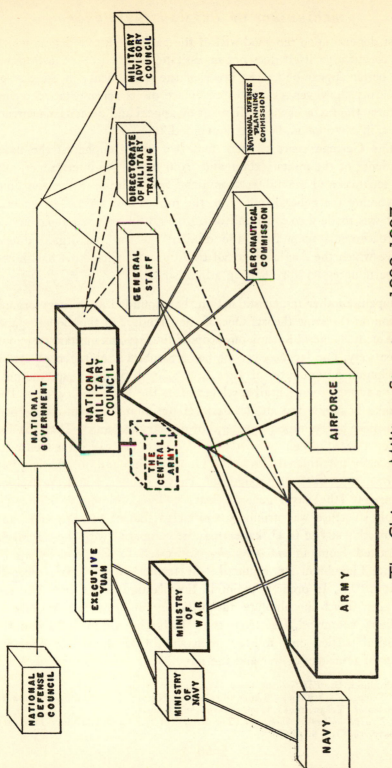

The Chinese Military Structure, 1932-1937

must depend upon the good will of the parliament to a degree which the constitution itself does not necessitate. . . . All other institutions can better appear under the favor of the parliament; in the case of the army, however, even the semblance of its representative trying to curry the favor of the parliament by appeal and devious maneuvers must, in my opinion, be strictly avoided."[9]

The German concept, then, had two main emphases: the independence of the military command from legislative interference, and the separation of the military command from administrative functions (divorcing the general staff from the ministry of war). The general staff was made a co-equal and distinct body in order to avoid undue encroachments upon it by the ministry of war, an organizational move which the Anglo-American tradition of civilian rule has shown to be unnecessary for effective administration.

Japan, another militaristic nation, had founded its military organization on the same theory. One of the founders of the modern Japanese army, General Katsura-taro, copied the German military system in its entirety. The Japanese version had a Sambo Hombu (general staff), a Rikugunshō (ministry of war), and a Gunji Sanjün (supreme military advisory council), all modeled after the Prussian originals. The Kyoiku Sokambo was an elevated version of its German counterpart (the office of the inspector-general of military training). The Japanese added a board of field marshals and fleet admirals called the Gensuifu. The navy participated also in the Gunji Sanjün and, in addition, had its own top offices: the Kaigunshō (navy ministry) and the Kaigun Gunreibu (the naval general staff).[10] The philosophy behind the whole structure was strikingly similar to that of the Prussians, and Bismarck's advice to his kaiser may be compared with these remarks extracted from an *aide-memoire* addressed to Emperor Meiji by Prince Hakubumi Ito, reputedly the framer of the Japanese constitution: ". . . In order to maintain the prestige of the armed forces, to keep intact the absolute authority of His Imperial Majesty in military command, free from the interference of the Diet and the political parties, only military men should be allowed to hold the posts of ministers of war and the navy."[11]

[9] Rosinski, H., *The German Army* (Washington, 1944), p. 146f.

[10] Yamagata, Aritomo, "Rikugunshi" (The History of the Army), *Kai-koku Eogunenshi* (Tokyo, 1908), I, pp. 267-292, in Japanese.

[11] *Kyokuto-saiban-kohan-kiroku* (The Record of Far Eastern Military Tribunal), (Tokyo, 1948), I, p. 203.

This attitude was reflected in Article VII of the Japanese constitution, where it was stated that the chiefs of the army and the navy general staffs had the right of direct access to the throne, similar to the German version of *Immediatvortrag*. So complete was the circumvention of civilian rule that even the ministers of war and of the navy, cabinet members theoretically subject to the prime minister, enjoyed the right of access to the emperor.

The Japanese system had three important features: the absolute power of the sovereign in military affairs; the unaccountability of the military to the Diet; and the rule that only professional military men could head the military administration.

In Japan this system resulted as early as 1931 in the adoption by the Minseito (the Japanese Democratic Party) of the issue of *gunbu bunkansei* (civilian rule of service ministries) as a plank in their election platform. They advocated that the following steps be taken: (1) the abolishment of the two independent army and navy general staffs, and the army's inspectorate-general of military training; (2) the creation of a single ministry of war and of the navy, the whole to be headed by a civilian; and (3) the abolishment of the military leaders' right of access to the throne.[12] These moves were hardly calculated to appeal to a militaristic people, and they fell on deaf ears. A Japanese political scientist, Professor Tomio Nankano, made an exhaustive study of his nation's military problems and concluded that the system of independent military command had an adverse effect upon the free and natural interaction between national policy and public opinion. It caused antagonism among the military leaders on the one hand and the legislature, civil government, and the people on the other.[13] The Germans found, in the acid test of World War I, that the system had many weaknesses in top-level military coordination and in the overall direction of the war. As a result of the lessons the war provided, Germany created the Oberkommando der Wehrmacht in 1938, designed to overcome those organizational weaknesses which contributed to the defeat of 1918.[14]

IV

How China happened to adopt the German system is a matter for

[12] Minseito-hombo, *Nippon-kaizo-hoan* (Tokyo, 1931).

[13] Nokano Tomio, *Tosuiken no dokuritsu* (The Independence of the Prerogative of Military Command), (Tokyo, 1934), pp. 728-729, in Japanese.

[14] Rosinski, *op.cit.*, p. 151.

conjecture. It is indeed difficult to explain how a professed revolutionary regime would select a system which was nothing but an organizational continuation of the pre-constitutional period. The presence of the arch-royalist Bauer cannot be discounted as a factor. The three principal architects of China's new governmental plan—Chiang Kai-shek, Tai Chi-t'ao, and Dr. Wang Chung-hui (who translated the German Weimar Constitution into English)—were by no means unfamiliar with the Kaiserliche military organization.

One of the possible explanations for China's adopting the new system has been that she was still in the military period of the three stages of her revolution: military unification, political tutelage, and the framing of a constitution. But this reasoning offers no satisfactory explanation for the adoption of an antiquated system known for its inadequacy. The most obvious explanation would seem to be that such a plan would enable Generalissimo Chiang, the newly elected president of the National Government, to secure, like the kaiser and the emperor, direct and undisputed control over the nation's armed forces. Another advantage of the system was that it opened up a number of equal high military offices for the most powerful military leaders of that time. The two northern leaders, Feng Yü-hsiang and Yen Hsi-shan, received their rewards as minister of war and minister of the interior, respectively, and were still subject to the president of the Executive Yuan. The leaders of the armies of the Kwangsi, Li Chi-shen and Li Tsung-jen, headed the general staff and the military advisory council. The second-ranking Whampoa leader, Ho Ying-ch'in, was to fill the office of the director-general of military training. A convenient method of dividing the spoils had been found, with Chiang remaining supreme. Again, by allowing personal considerations to prevail, the long-term soundness of the nation's defense organization was sadly hampered.

Germany had evolved the Prussian type of military organization to suit her own needs and, no matter how much in dispute its long-range merits might be, long experience had taught the Germans how to keep it operating smoothly. The Japanese had copied the German blueprint in minutest detail, but the Chinese were too proud to stoop to such slavish imitation and, while reacting violently to the Russian type of organization which they had previously favored, they took over the German system in large part—but added variations of their own. In this way they adopted the German plan without its spirit, and they suffered from both its inherent inadequacies and the problems created by the introduction of their own improvisations.

The new military advisory council was not unlike the defunct Ch'iang-chün-fu of the old Peking regime—the board of generals and admirals that Yuan Shi-k'ai had devised to accommodate the top-ranking military men both in and out of power. The council which replaced the Peking board was far from being the vigorous and experienced body that it ought to have been, capable of throwing the weight of the army's and navy's collective wisdom against ill-considered policies or personal dictation. Unlike the German Militär-Kabinett, it had no real control of higher policy, for it was actually no more than an unwieldy body of superannuated military leaders whose opinions no longer carried much force. It failed to serve the function of either the Militär-Kabinett or the Japanese Gunji Sanjiin.

As for the new military nerve center—the general staff—the situation was no less deplorable. First of all, in 1928 China had barely enough trained general staff officers to meet her immediate needs, and an examination of the records of the successive chiefs of staff of the Chinese army reveals that few of them had formal general staff training. Two of the basic principles of the German general staff system were these: the strict insistence upon a high level of competence among general staff officers, and an emphasis on the harmonious pairing of personalities and abilities in the case of the commander and his chief of staff, while at the same time ensuring that the chief of staff be, by character and training, capable of exercising competent and independent judgment—not just a "yes-man" to the commander.[15] The Germans always strove to place men of great professional ability and independent character in the vital post of Chef der Generalstab. In China, however, few of the incumbents of this office could be said to have conformed to those requirements. The chief of the general staff too often stood in danger of being intimidated by a strong-willed commander-in-chief.

In military affairs it is an undisputed tenet that authority must always be commensurate with responsibility. In the ministry of war, whether it was deliberately planned or not, an intricate system of checks and balances seems to have existed. A minister's power could be balanced by vice-ministers and strategically placed bureau chiefs who could be counted on to keep an eagle eye on the minister's loyalty

[15] von Seeckt, Hans, *Die Gedanken eines Soldaten* (Leipzig, 1935), *passim*.

to the ruling interest. True, a powerful warlord who became minister of war could offer a great potential danger to the administration, but annulments from above, circumvention from below, and an omnipresent spirit of distrust can hardly produce efficiency. The whole military organization suffered from the fear, weakness, and indecision of its central administration.

On the whole the reorganized military structure in the China of 1928 was cumbersome and unusually intricate. Too much complexity can always threaten to plunge a whole organization into anarchy, especially when there is a shortage of both competent administrators and working experience. Unstudied separation of functions in the 1928 organization had far-reaching and unfortunate ramifications. A number of equal and compartmentalized functions competed with another, while no machinery existed to integrate them and to direct the over-all effort into the proper channel. In the hands of the president alone rested the one opportunity of ultimate military coordination. If the same system had worked with tolerable efficiency in the German and Japanese forces, it was because they had highly trained personnel at ease in their jobs—men universally indoctrinated with a set of beliefs which made the coordination of their efforts feasible by clarifying the goals. In China, on the other hand, there was not yet an adequate general staff equipped either by formal schooling or by experience to run such a complicated military machine. The disjointed efforts of the multitudinous departments could hope for unification and direction from only one source: Generalissimo Chiang himself. Upon the powerful personality of Chiang, in the absence of other competent top-level administration, the whole burden rested.

8 · TOWARD MILITARIZATION WITH CHIANG KAI-SHEK

‖ᘓᘓᘓᘓᘓᘓᘓᘓᘓᘓᘓᘓᘓᘓᘓᘓᘓᘓᘓᘓᘓᘓᘓᘓᘓᘓᘓᘓᘓᘓᘓᘓᘓᘓᘓ‖

I. THE IMMEDIATE PROBLEM OF TROOP DISBANDMENT.
II. UNIFICATION OF THE NEW ARMY UNDER CHIANG.
III. GERMAN ADVISERS KRIEBEL AND WETZELL. IV. THE
CREATION OF A MILITARY COUNCIL. V. CHIANG CONTROLS
THE MILITARY COUNCIL: MILITARIZATION.

‖ᘓᘓᘓᘓᘓᘓᘓᘓᘓᘓᘓᘓᘓᘓᘓᘓᘓᘓᘓᘓᘓᘓᘓᘓᘓᘓᘓᘓᘓᘓᘓᘓᘓᘓᘓ‖

I

"There are two problems the solution of which is most essential to the successful administration of the National Government, namely, the disbandment of superfluous troops and the curtailment of military appropriation on the one hand and the reorganization of national finances on the other.

"Each problem stands in an independent category but, as they are fundamentally interrelated, the one and the other may be tackled simultaneously."[1]

This quotation, the theme of the manifesto issued in August 1928 by the National Government, states succinctly the chief concerns of the government at that time. Military operations had been brought to a successful conclusion, and the newly reorganized government was desirous, while consolidating its power on a firm basis, of introducing political and financial reforms which would demonstrate the wisdom of the reorganization.

Immediately after the Revolutionary Army entered Peking a conference of high military leaders was convened at Pei-t'ang-shan in July 1928. The central issue of debate, a problem of far-reaching importance and complexity, was troop disbandment. The government outlined the following policy:

"1. The National Government shall have supreme command of the armed forces.

"2. Unity of command shall be thus realized:

[1] "Official Proclamation of the National Government," *Chinese Affairs*, I, No. 27 (October 31, 1928); also *Kuowan Weekly*, July 22, 1928.

[71]

"a. the existing army units shall be reorganized by the central government into a truly national army;

"b. all right of command must be vested in the central government;

"c. the systems of organization, training, and supply shall be standardized; etc."[2]

By these and other like measures the government proposed:

"1. to better the quality of the nation's armed forces by reducing the huge, heterogeneous army to a manageable size;

"2. to centralize the military administration in the National Government (particularly the aspects of finance, supply, and personnel) and to curtail the illegal interception of revenues by the various warlords, then still a prevalent ill in the Chinese financial picture;

"3. to improve the standard of living of the common soldier; and

"4. to enforce a "soldier-labor" policy utilizing demobilized soldiers as a disciplined and trained labor force for reconstruction plans."[3]

This plan was ratified by the fifth plenary session of the Kuomintang, which went on record for unified command, nationally supervised military education, conscription, and decreased army strength, which would lead to greater unity and decreased military spending. It specified that the total number of the nation's military forces must be so reduced that the annual military budget would not exceed fifty per cent of the annual national revenue.

The government then convened a high-level conference to arrange partial demobilization of the armed forces. The four commanders-in-chief of the Revolutionary Army met with Finance Minister T. V. Soong, Chiang's lieutenant Ho Ying-ch'in, and the commander-in-chief of the naval forces. They decided that the army would be pared down to some fifty or sixty divisions, with the four army groups choosing the most meritorious and efficient units to remain intact, and directly subordinated to the unifying command of the National Government. From the current army of approximately 2,200,000 men, a standing army of 600,000 men, with a gendarmerie of an additional

---

[2] *Chinese Affairs*, I, No. 27 (Oct. 31, 1928).

[3] "Chiang Kai-shek's statement to the press at Peking on July 13, 1928," cited in *Kuowan Weekly* (July 22, 1928) and *Ta-kung-pao* (daily newspaper), July 14, 1928.

200,000, was to be preserved. The superfluous troops were to be separated as quickly as possible. The standing National Defense Army of 800,000 men could then be maintained at the cheapest cost by instituting a system of conscription, a plan which had the added advantage of reducing the opportunities for the militarists to raise their own private armies. By conscription, by unity of command, by governmental supervision of military education, the National Government hoped to achieve a tightly knit, centralized military authority.

But Feng Yü-hsiang, the strongest northern military leader south of the Great Wall, immediately reacted against the demobilization program, and, while upholding the general principle of disbandment, urged that measures be put into effect to prevent the program from being used by certain military leaders for personal power aggrandizement.[4] He, and many another power-conscious military man, feared that Chiang and his Whampoa group might turn the disbandment program to their own advantage, concentrating military power in a single, central authority and then seizing control of it. They regarded the move as dictated not so much by the financial necessity of cutting down the number of military mouths that had to be fed from over 2,000,000 to 800,000, but by the wish of Chiang and his party to place command in as few hands as possible at the top—their own.

The National Government in 1928 was still politically shaky and economically far from secure. It had not had sufficient time to build up the prestige necessary to buck the opposition of the warlords. From the vantage point of time, it would have seemed prudent of the government to make every effort to maintain its equilibrium, even at the cost of moving slowly toward its goals. When it had had sufficient time to establish itself by moderation and effectiveness and had attained a better comprehension of the domestic and external problems it had to face, it could then have opposed with vigor and confidence the warlords and all other factions which threatened the existence of a strictly impartial, broad-based administration, free from favoritism and factionalism. That would have been the ideal approach and, in a government under civilian rule, such a sober, conciliatory method might have been adopted. But, instead, the government was in the hands of a military authority which demanded the immediate obedience of a number of arrogant, powerful warlords. Personal pride and group loyalties played a strong part. By enforcing disbandment, the govern-

[4] Feng Yu-hsiang, "Circular Telegram to Military Commanders," July 5, 1928.

ment touched off a series of bloody civil wars. The plan to reduce the armed forces was scrapped. The civil wars swelled the strength of the army to over two hundred divisions of heterogeneous troops, and the only reductions were those effected by casualties as thousands of men perished in internecine war.

II

From 1929 to 1931 civil wars and communist uprisings mildewed the bright hopes of the National Government. Many powerful military leaders revoked their allegiance to Nanking. Chiang took upon himself the task of upholding the supremacy of that National Government of which he was the symbol and the head. In the name of national unification he clashed with Wang Ching-wei and all the others who plotted against the centralization of authority. He fought against his former ally, the Kwangsi group led by Li Tsung-jen, Pai Chung-hsi, and Li Chi-shen. He met a succession of rebellions led by T'ang Shen-chih, Chang Fa-kuei, Feng Yü-hsiang, and Yen Hsi-shan. In 1930 and 1931 Chiang's government forces were arrayed against the armies of Feng and Yen in North China, and against this coalition the National Government was obliged to throw its fiercest attacks. With the aid of the army of the northeast (Manchurian) under Chang Hsueh-liang, Chiang was able to secure a narrow margin of victory which made the region of North China a precarious unity from the Amur River to the Yangtze. The punitive campaigns of the National Government, to put down all rebellious opposition to the central authority, had succeeded in establishing its authority. The loyalty of the Whampoa group to Chiang; the authority of "government" he carried, and the epithet "traitors" given to all who opposed him; his superior generalship, equipment, and supplies; and, finally, his command of the seaports of the coastal provinces and of the finances of the nation—all these factors combined to give Chiang Kai-shek the victory. There was one more factor which contributed to the success of the National Government: the central authority could and did enlist the expert service of a number of German military advisers.

III

Following the death of Colonel Bauer, a German politician-soldier named Hermann Kriebel became Chiang's principal military adviser. Lieutenant Colonel Kriebel had been a member of Germany's armistice commission and, in making his farewells to the Allied commission at the conclusion of the negotiations, he had fired the last shot of World War I—or, perhaps, the first shot of World War II—for he said curtly, "See you again in twenty years." After that prophetic remark, he worked for its fulfillment and became a friend of Hitler and Ludendorff and one of the original participants in Hitler's Beer-Hall Putsch of 1923. Kriebel served in China initially for only a short time and, in August 1930, was replaced by Lieutenant General Georg Wetzell, a world-famed strategist even more useful to Chiang in those days of civil war, as chief operational adviser. Kriebel's part was not done, however, for upon his return to Germany he renewed his relationship with Hitler and in April 1934 he returned to China as German consul-general at Shanghai. He became the key representative in China of the Nazi Party's interests, and it was through him that much of China's munitions and industrial purchasing was arranged. As the confidant of both Chiang and the Fuehrer, Kriebel's influence in China was even greater than that of the German ambassador, Dr. Trautmann. He remained in that vital position until February 1941, when he was recalled to become chief of the personnel department of the German foreign office.

Georg Wetzell had had a distinguished career in the German army. As a noted member of the Grosse Generalstab, the supreme headquarters, he proved himself one of Germany's brilliant general staff officers in the First World War, having originated the plan under which the Italian army was defeated in 1917. He served as a principal operational officer under Hindenburg and Ludendorff, and after World War I occupied the key post of Chief of the Troops Office (Chef des Truppenamtes), which was actually the disguised general staff of the Reichswehr.[5] At that time his reputation outshone even such prominent German military men as von Blomberg and von Fritsch. His long-time superior, General von Seeckt, rated him as "very good in military operation," though questioning his organizing abilities.[6] As the author of *Der Bundniskrieg*, Wetzell was widely read by military experts. He had little interest in politics or, as von Seeckt pointed out, in administration, but was a man of action, in character rather

[5] Goerlitz, W., *Der Deutsche Generalstab* (Frankfurt am Main, 1950), pp. 217, 228.
[6] von Seeckt, H., "Ansprache an die Berater am 20 April, 1934," *Verzeichnis von Nachlass des Generalobersten Hans von Seeckt* (Heeresarchiv, Potsdam: Lager-No. 1864, now in the National Archives, Washington, D.C.), 5. Hereafter referred to as *Ansprache*.

like "Vinegar Joe" Stilwell of World War II. Behind his actions, however, was a rigid, pedantic set of military theories to which he clung with great obstinacy.

Upon his arrival in China, Wetzell advised Chiang on the strategy of the campaign against Feng Yü-hsiang and Yen Hsi-shan, but his advice was not always followed. At this stage the pronouncements of the German advisers were not carrying the weight that they later were to be given, for Chiang believed foreigners to be incapable of taking into account the habits and customs of the people and the psychology of the Chinese soldier. They were not, in addition, fully acquainted with the terrain, and Chiang was somewhat skeptical of their grasp of the particular Chinese situation. What contributions Kriebel and Wetzell did make, however, served to strengthen the position of the German advisers, and their successors were able to channel it into an increasingly strong influence.

<h1 style="text-align:center">IV</h1>

The political and military struggles of the period following the northern expedition were for Generalissimo Chiang the ordeals which tested his mettle. He emerged from those trying times with a better comprehension of the broad political and economic issues and a clearer picture of the opposition which confronted him. The costly civil wars taught him several lessons, one of which was that force could not magically change a recently crushed enemy into a cooperative ally. The memory of the Mukden incident—the Japanese attack of September 18, 1931, made possible by the necessity of Chiang's keeping Chang Hsueh-liang's Manchurian army within the Great Wall in order to assist in putting down rebellion—still smarted. Japanese aggression had served to pull together China's forces in a common cause and Chiang, having learned the value of compromise and the necessity of cooperation, found the nation uniting to turn on the outside intruder.

On October 26 a delegation from the dissident factions of the south presented the following demands to the Kuomintang:

"The presidency of the National Government should be filled in accordance with the presidential system of France and Germany—by a comrade [of the Kuomintang] both venerable in age and of established character and reputation. No military man in active service should be eligible for the post.

"The post of generalissimo of the national land, naval, and air forces should be abolished and a separate supreme military organ set in its place. The details should be determined separately."[7]

The demand represented a reaction against the recent seizure and centralization of the supreme military command. Chiang, who had grabbed all the reins of power lest the force of the party be dissipated by a number of factions all pulling in different directions, was ironically faced with a unification within the party which would make his continuation as coordinator less requisite, his total power less defensible. The party felt that it no longer needed a generalissimo-president, and Chiang, lest his future be entirely jeopardized and his past achievements set in a very unfavorable light, stepped down. The national military council was reestablished on March 11, 1931.

This move was, however, not without inharmonious ramifications. The new structure essayed to combine incompatibles. The underlying concept of the military council, whose function was to integrate all military functions in a common policy-making body, was Lenin's doctrine of "democratic centralism." One of its effects was to enlist civilian participation in the formulation of military decisions. On the other hand, there still existed the Prusso-Japanese type of military organization, which the nation had adopted in 1928; it fundamentally denied the principle of such a committee as the new military council and completely rejected the idea of civilian participation. The Prussian-sponsored plan was to allow the major military functions to operate independently, run by military men and not by civilians, and to coordinate the whole through the absolute control vested in the military head of the state. Here, clearly, was a case of trying to mix water and oil.

The South China group was able to press other measures, such as the reorganization of the office of the president. Once the focus of the whole military machine, the president was now reduced to a figurehead. His position of command dwindled into a nominal leadership, his power to coordinate and direct into the function of advice and assent. The Chinese had kept the German structure, but had scrapped their kaiser. The body remained, but it had been decapitated. The general staff, the military advisory council, and the other committees worked uncoordinated, subordinated to a fuzzy concept of the National Government. Whatever could be done to make things run smoothly

---

[7] "Official Text of Nanking-Canton Communication of 26 October, 1931," cited in *The China Nation* (Nov. 4, 1931), p. 732.

was in the hands of the national military council. Chiang Kai-shek, the chairman of this new committee, retained such control as there existed.

The establishment of the new military council profoundly affected the constitutional powers of the Executive Yuan. Its impact was readily appreciated. When the Executive Yuan was created in 1929, the war ministry (and, later, the navy ministry) was subordinated exclusively to it. These two ministries, under the new dispensation, were now also subjected to the military council, a fact which rendered incomplete the power of the Executive Yuan over the administrative functions. Chiang, the chairman of the military committee, had such personal prestige that the Executive Yuan's authority could hope to do no better than to run a poor second. If previously there had been a military dominance in the government, despite its structural unsoundness, it had been due to the fact that the presidential power was held by a man in whose mind the military aims were uppermost. In the new system, Chiang's dominant personality remained as powerful as ever but now with even less constitutional justification.

On close examination of the National Government of the years 1932-1946 it will appear that it actually consisted of a military and a civil administration, side by side. The war ministry linked the two. It was subordinate to both the military council and the Executive Yuan, and all orders to the army passed through its hands. Chiang kept General Ho Ying-ch'in, one of his closest friends and Whampoa's second-ranking figure, as minister of war from 1930-1944. In this manner he once again managed to control all that it was necessary to control, and Chiang and the Whampoa group remained at the helm of the state.

V

After the military reorganization of 1931, the military council became the supreme military authority of the nation. It began to extend its influence into the spheres of industrial development and economics and, by 1933, had created a subsidiary commission to investigate mineral reserves and sources of raw materials in the name of national defense planning. Under the guidance of the military council, this committee, headed by the internationally known Chinese geologist Dr. Weng Wen-hao, mapped out a three-year plan for the expansion of China's heavy industry and laid the foundations for the national resources commission which was to follow it.

Chiang branched out also into civil administration, even though this was nominally the province of the Executive Yuan, then headed by Wang Ching-wei. Wang was a capable and an ambitious man—he later served as the puppet head of the Japanese-controlled section of China during the Sino-Japanese war—and the tussle over civil administration was a personal tug-of-war between Chiang and himself. Wang's position would seem to have given him the edge in this battle, had it not been that Chiang managed to gain control of the Central Political Institute (Chung-yang cheng-chih hsueh-hsiao) and make it a sister institution of the new Central Military Academy. Chiang, as president of Whampoa, had previously directed both of these operations when they, under the Soviet system, were wedded in the Whampoa Academy. Now, although the Central Political Institute was training magistrates and other administrative personnel for the national government, and not the political commissars for the army that Whampoa used to produce, Chiang directed this operation and ensured himself of the allegiance of its graduates. He affiliated himself in this undertaking with a certain number of capable academic, financial, and business leaders—including the well-known political scientists' group (*cheng-hsueh-hsi*)—but at all times kept the final direction of the whole securely in his own hands. In him alone rested the only unifying power and, with Chiang's practical control of both the military and civil branches of the government, Wang Ching-wei was rendered virtually powerless. Chiang had once again contrived to bind various warring factions to himself in loyalty—factions among whom he alone could preserve any semblance of cooperation.

Chinese communist forces were rising to challenge the supremacy of the national government and Chiang, as military leader, was given the power to override the civil authority in troubled areas. As the communist threat spread, Chiang's authority extended to ever wider areas and the military domination over civil authority was given a *raison d'être*. He had not only unofficial control over the Central Political Institute but also legally delegated jurisdiction, under martial law, over all those areas where the communists were contending with the National Government.

The military council extended its influence over the country's affairs, created a number of dependent offices (a national aeronautical commission, a bureau of air defense, and other such organizations), and became in time, as H. H. Donald, an Australian adviser to the generalissimo, said, the "real core of the government." The whole structure rested on Chiang's personal ability to command the loyalty of the various organizations that composed this patchwork. China's National Government turned to militarism in the face of threats of extermination by both the communists and the Japanese and placed herself in the hands of her military leaders. In actual fact, she had entrusted her fate to Chiang Kai-shek alone.

9 · THE MOLDING OF "BASIC" MILITARY POWER

I. THE IMPORTANCE OF THE CENTRAL MILITARY ACADE-
MY. II. THE BASIC AND SPECIALIZED EDUCATIONAL PRO-
GRAMS. III. GENERAL STAFF TRAINING: THE SPIRIT OF THE
GENERAL STAFF COLLEGE. REGULAR AND SENIOR COM-
MAND COURSES. ADVANCED STUDY ABROAD. AN EVALUA-
TION OF THE CHINESE SYSTEM.

*"Toward a program for our country, today; basic army
units, basic geographic areas, basic organizations, and a nucleus of cadres, are the four vital items which must be
planned and established with speed and priority."—Chiang
Kai-shek, in a speech in April, 1932.*

I

EVER since the break with Soviet Russia, Chiang Kai-shek had gone
ahead with the task of building a powerful modern army of which
the nucleus was to be an efficient and dependable officer corps. He now
turned to the Germans for technical assistance and qualified instructors.

Chiang had always devoted a considerable part of his effort to the
perpetuation of the Whampoa educational system. By the time of the
northern expedition, the academy at Whampoa had graduated four
classes of cadets, approximately 5,000 officers. During the northern
expedition, 2,600 Whampoa graduates, according to Chiang, had
sacrificed themselves for the revolution. This comparatively small
group had in large measure contributed to the success of the revolution
and was a decisive factor in Chiang's own rise to power. When the
nation's capital was moved to Nanking, he immediately ordered that
the Whampoa Academy be transferred to the new site. His plan was
to reopen it there as the Central Military and Political Academy and
to continue to run it along its original—that is, Soviet—lines. In a
significant action the word "political" was dropped from the name

of the academy—a symbol of the nation's new attitude and the growing German influence. As a military college, the new Central Military Academy was to lay more stress on the second of its objectives: "To prepare junior officers adequately versed in political knowledge; and to provide advanced and specialized training to the officers of senior grades in the armed forces."[1]

In the northeast section of the walled city of Nanking, lying beneath a massive gate of the city wall called the Gate of Peace, many simple and neat buildings were erected, surrounded by various types of drill grounds and military installations. Chiang's personal residence was situated right in the center of the campus of the new Central Military Academy.

After the successful termination of the northern expedition, the ambition of the central government at Nanking, as we have stated in a previous chapter, was to transform the large and heterogeneous armies of the nation into a united national defense army, small enough to govern successfully and to support without undue financial strain. Military education was envisaged as the key to this program. The Kuomintang's Central Executive Committee affirmed this in August 1928, specifying, "That military education should be unified and all military schools in the country should be placed under the direct control of the government; and that the establishment of any military school or institution of like nature by individual commanders should be strictly prohibited."[2]

The new Central Military Academy—Whampoa moved to the seat of government for even closer surveillance—trained the backbone of the nation's army, the junior commanders, under the government's close supervision. Its work went on unimpeded, despite civil wars, and a program of modernization in facilities and curriculum was adopted. Many German instructors were hired and further training for selected Chinese faculty members was provided abroad. A training brigade, completely outfitted with the latest modern equipment, was set up as an integral part of the academy.

Candidates were selected on the basis of the results of a nation-wide competitive examination open to high-school graduates of acceptable physical condition and character. Prior to 1937, this system provided

[1] National Government, *Organic Law of the Central Military and Political Academy* (Nanking, June 17, 1927).
[2] International Relation Committee, *Chinese Affairs*, No. 12 (Shanghai, Aug. 25, 1928), p. 8.

the academy with an annual quota of about 3,000 entering cadets. They were given a rigorous military training, made to live a cadet life approximating as nearly as possible the austerities of wartime, and deliberately exposed to hardships which in severity surpassed even those of Japanese military education.

As the quality of the academy's education steadily improved, a gradual shift in its educational policy took place. The outlook of the early Whampoa days drifted toward a pattern more closely resembling the orthodox plan of Western military schools. This change may be traced in Chiang's numerous speeches at the academy. In 1942 he summarized its educational objective as one devoted to "teaching the cadets self-government, initiative, self-reliance, and self-respect. Its purpose is to give the cadets a sense of propriety, integrity, responsibility, and discipline. Its spirit is one of the sacrifice of individual comfort, life, and everything else for the success of the revolution. Lastly, its objective is to teach every cadet, as well as every soldier he may command after graduation, to be loyal to his nation, his people, party principle, and the Chinese revolution."[3]

These sentiments were also instilled in those officers of higher rank who availed themselves of the refresher courses offered at the academy —men who either had risen to command without any formal military schooling or who wished to take an up-to-date postgraduate course.

Hans von Seeckt has outlined the tremendous energy which Chiang Kai-shek devoted to the academy after 1932.[4] When he could manage it, Chiang personally conducted the weekly memorial services. He treasured his title as president first at Whampoa and later of the Central Military Academy. The importance of the academy was reflected in the fact that its leaders were always of high rank; its president a generalissimo, its vice-president a full general, and its superintendent a general or a lieutenant-general.

II

Much of the development of China's military training in the days before World War II was influenced by German concepts and owed much to General Hans von Seeckt, the builder of the German Reichswehr, a force of 100,000 men created by the Weimar government

[3] Chiang Kai-shek, "Speech on the 18th Anniversary of the Central Military Academy, June 16, 1942."
[4] Chinese Ministry of National Defense, *Wei-tà-ti Chiang chu-hsi, op.cit.*

after World War I. Two of von Seeckt's principal assistants in this program of training were Wetzell and von Falkenhausen. Wetzell's Truppenamt amounted to a secret general staff, and it trained officers for general staff and other duties. Von Falkenhausen, as commandant of the famous infantry school, developed an efficient system of specialization which was instrumental in producing the high quality of the Reichswehr. These three men brought their valuable experience to the solution of China's military problems. On their advice, Generalissimo Chiang created a small but effective Kerntruppe, or nucleus, as the core around which China's defense army could be built. Essential to that plan was, of course, an efficient officer-training scheme, and the German plan in this regard may be succinctly stated under three headings:

1. *On the basic level.* The Central Military Academy was to be responsible for the unified training of cadets. This training had two stages. First came the *ju-wu*, the Chinese equivalent of boot training, where the cadets were all educated together, whether they were army, air force, or police trainees. Later special training was given to each of the different groups, but only after they had been indoctrinated with a common outlook and given the basic military doctrine.

2. *On the intermediate level.* The courses of specialization begun in the second phase of basic training were continued on a postgraduate level for one or more years in one of the army's special service schools.

3. *On the higher level.* In addition to offering advanced education abroad to selected candidates, the Chinese army staff college offered general staff training at home to selected officers of the armed forces. The aim was to reintegrate their specialization, broaden their outlook, and develop promising officers for command and staff duties.

A number of special service schools, most of them located at or near the capital (Nanking), were established with German instructional aid and made available to officers who, after a compulsory two-year service in the field following graduation and commissioning, were selected for advanced specialization. In 1937 the following special service schools existed: Army Staff College (Nanking), Infantry School, Cavalry School, Artillery School, Engineering School, Gendarmerie Training School, Chemical Warfare School, Anti-Aircraft Defense School, Armor and Mechanized School, Communications School, Transport and Supply School, Fortress Artillery School, Quartermaster School, Naval Academy at Mamoi (Fukien), Air Academy at Hangchow (Chekiang).

In addition to the above schools for line officers, the following specialized schools offered longer courses for staff officers of the army: Army Finance School, Army Surveying School, Army Medical School, Army Veterinary School, Ordnance Technical School, Foreign Language School.

These schools gave modern instruction to both commissioned and selected non-commissioned officers. Their objective was to train competent combat leaders for all arms or services, and to keep the army alert to modern military thought and techniques. One of their functions was to develop, test, and train men in new military tactics and procedures. An effort was made to standardize the official training manuals and regulations which hitherto had admitted of a wide diversity in practice. These schools quickly developed into highly efficient specialized organizations and, once a year, there was a joint maneuver in which all the special service schools, the Central Military Academy, the training brigade, and other military units participated. Japanese aggression came soon after the schools had been established, but they had been in operation long enough to afford modern military training to cadres from both the central and non-central armies and to provide a degree of common background and experience which was keenly appreciated when all the Chinese armies fought side-by-side against the Japanese foe.

III

"The education of the Army Staff College has its objective in the training of selected officers for command and staff duties, aiming to instill in them advanced military principles, military rules, and the necessary knowledge of military science.

"Special emphasis must be given to ethical training, for leadership through moral inspiration is indispensable to high commanders and important staff officers. Great attention, therefore, must be directed to inculcating, besides the necessary military knowledge and techniques, military morality and martial spirit."[5]

In such words was the educational policy of the Chinese Army Staff College set forth by its ex officio president, Generalissimo Chiang. Moral qualities and military ethics have always received important emphasis in the Chinese tradition and Chiang, the traditionalist, was

[5] Army Staff College, *Lu-chün-ta-hsueh chiao-yu-k'an-ling* (The Educational Policy of the Army Staff College), (Nanking, 1930).

anxious to stress the classical Chinese virtues in all Chinese military educational institutions. He wrote in 1930:

"The educational concept of the college is centered in the shaping of fine and persevering qualities in the students' personalities; to develop in them the attributes of virtuous citizenship and soldierly spirit and to harmonize these with scientific knowledge of military principles, of the skill of command, and the procedures of war. It aims to bring forth the students' instinctive ability to face exigency, the power of comprehending military principles, the art of applying these principles in practice, and the ability to handle administrative affairs.

"The fundamental approach lies in the students' correct understanding of the meaning of *responsibility*; their appreciation of initiative, flexibility, and speedy decisiveness; their obstinate spiritual courage; their broad comprehension of the situation confronting them, and their constructiveness in applying their knowledge."[6]

The Army Staff College of China (Lu-chün ta-hsüeh-hsiao, abbreviated to Lu-ta) was a reorganization of the old staff college at Peking under German supervision. The influence of the German Kriegsakademie was marked, brought into the picture by the German advisers invited to lecture in military science at the new school. Some Japanese influences went into its curriculum also, for a number of the Chinese members of the faculty had received their training in the Rikugun Taigakko (the Japanese staff college) and were, in those days when China was preparing to fight the Japanese, listened to with more than usual interest. French tactics of the Ecole Superieure de Guerre and the history of the Napoleonic wars were introduced into the curriculum by a French general and his staff of French military experts who taught for a time at Lu-ta. Of all the foreign instructional groups, however, the Germans enjoyed the highest professional prestige among the Chinese.

The Lu-ta offered two courses: a regular staff course and a special command course. The regular students were selected from the younger army officers, above the rank of captain, who had at least three years of service experience. Upon recommendation through the proper channels, candidates had to pass a special board appointed by the chief of the general staff before they could take the competitive examinations. This, by Chinese standards, was a stringent process of selection. The regular three-year course concentrated largely on the

[6] *Ibid.*

study of staff techniques, military strategy, history, logistics, and ended with planning large-scale military operations. Courses in social science, mathematics, and foreign languages were also taught, providing a kind of university curriculum meant to further the future general staff officers' general education. The course was regarded as a difficult one, and competition was keen among the students. One special feature of Lu-ta, not unlike that which prevailed in the German Kriegsakademie, was the rather thorough observation of the students' character, ability, and talent. The students were constantly under a microscope. Such a system, well developed at Lu-ta, later found its way into almost all the higher political and military training courses in Nationalist China, particularly in the Central Training Institute. There was, however, a slight modification in the Chinese concept. Whereas in the Western and the earlier Prussian general staff system the aim was to evaluate the originality, strength of character, and attainment of an incumbent, the trend in China, revealing the influence of the Soviet political commissar system, put great stress on conformity and political loyalty.

The special command course offered by the college lasted only a year. It was offered to senior military officers in the hope that it would broaden their outlook, unify their strategic concept, and prepare them for important commands. Although the younger senior officers took the course in earnest, the older officers were both arrogant and afraid to leave their command lest they lose it.

The Nationalist Army, in addition to setting up the general staff program we have outlined, also sent a great many students abroad to foreign military schools. During the early days a good percentage of Whampoa's graduates did postgraduate work in Soviet Russia in the Red Army's military, political, or aeronautical schools or at Moscow's Sun Yat-sen or Eastern Universities. In 1925, for instance, the Whampoa Academy sent 150 men to Russia. The number was increasing steadily until 1927, when China broke off relations with the Kremlin.

Up until 1928 an appreciable number of Chinese military students were sent to Europe by provincial military authorities or, in the expectation of short-cuts to high position in China, at private expense. China, thinking that such action might tend to jeopardize her interests abroad, acted through the National Military Council to stop the unauthorized sending of military students to foreign countries. She vested in the central military authorities all power to determine the country's foreign military training program.[7] After 1930 a system of competitive selection was put into force and the army alone received a quota of 176 foreign studentships abroad annually, with the navy and air force quota in proportion.[8] These figures had to be raised as China's military program expanded and, by the 1930's, Chinese military students could be found in numerous outstanding foreign schools at West Point, V.M.I., and Fort Leavenworth in the United States; at France's St. Cyr, Ecole Polytechnique, and Ecole Superieure de Guerre; at England's Sandhurst; and in Japan's Shikan Gakko, Rikugun Taigakko, and other schools. The greatest number went to Germany, where they studied everything from artillery and ordnance to military hygiene, taking courses in various staff and war colleges.

Here, as elsewhere throughout Generalissimo Chiang's program, was his abiding interest in developing a "modern" army for China: an army which would preserve the military tradition of classic China and, in an age of progressing technology, be soundly conceived and built upon the best of foreign ideas.

Before 1933 the regular army staff course was given to about 100 officers a year. By 1937, on the eve of the war against Japan, Lu-ta by virtue of an accelerated course and a broader admissions program, had trained as many as 2,000 general staff officers. They had all been given the valuable experience of conducting maneuvers on the divisional scale with modernized outfits of the Central Army, and, in the third year, field trips to designated areas in the manner of the Generalstabsreisen to familiarize them with larger operations on the national defense scale. One month out of each year of the three-year course was spent in field duty with the troops, where officers were encouraged to familiarize themselves with services other than their own. Tours of duty with naval and air force units or in key defense industries were likewise arranged.

The army staff college, as a training ground for an elite corps of well-prepared officers, was a success, but it was never permitted to spread its healthy influence throughout the length and breadth of the armed forces and to become more than a mere technical school. A

[7] National Government, *Rules Governing the Military Students Abroad* (Nanking, July 20, 1929).

[8] Ministry of War, *Rules Governing the Selection of Military Students for Advanced Studies Abroad* (Nanking, Dec. 16, 1929).

wider influence had been achieved by the German general staff college ever since its inception in 1868 and by many other military academies of like nature throughout the world, but in China the stress on technical information which the school had to impart and the lack of co-operation on the highest command levels made this impossible.

The British military authority General Ian Hamilton has said that the so-called "staff-mind" must be the planning and organizing mind.[9] Lu-ta sacrificed some of this necessarily broad and balanced education to mere technical proficiency and, in many cases, produced officers who, to speak metaphorically, knew a great deal about the trees but could not plan a way out of the forest.

Critics have also cited the lack of a realistic approach in Lu-ta's education. The students at the college spoke of Moltke and Schlieffen so frequently that they knew all about Sedan and Cannae, but they spent much less time on the basic problems of mobilizing the Chinese peasants against Japan. The rigidity of the curriculum, plus the absence of a rotation system for the teaching personnel, so that many lost touch with the actual conditions of the battlefield, contributed to this unfortunate situation. Lastly, those in Lu-ta tended to regard all those outside the military profession as amateurs, and they failed to enlist the invaluable assistance of outstanding civilian scholars and scientists. Experience taught the policy-makers of Lu-ta something of the error of their ways. By 1935, for instance, they began to lay much more stress on research projects at the college, as the articles in the college's quarterly journals and the establishment of a postgraduate military research institute testify.

But the greatest improvement the general staff school might have made in the army's personnel system it was unable to accomplish. It failed, in the face of deep-rooted Chinese tradition and short-sighted modern generals, to consider, in choosing candidates for positions of responsibility, merit, record, proven ability, and qualities of leadership, instead of patronage.

[9] Hamilton, Ian, *The Soul and Body of an Army* (N.Y.: Doran, 1921), pp. 27-28.

10 · GERMAN MILITARY AND INDUSTRIAL INFLUENCE: VON SEECKT AND VON FALKENHAUSEN

I. MUTUAL COOPERATION: THE SINO-GERMAN RELATIONSHIP DEFINED. II. VON SEECKT'S FIRST CHINESE MISSION: THE *DENKSCHRIFT FUER MARSCHALL CHIANG KAI-SHEK*. III. VON SEECKT'S SECOND CHINESE MISSION: HIS AIMS AND HIS SUCCESS. IV. COOPERATION IN HIGH GEAR: VON FALKENHAUSEN.

I

Prior to Hitler's regime, the Weimar government's attitude toward sending German military advisers to China was not openly favorable. Outwardly and officially theirs was a position of a strict adherence to the Treaty of Versailles. In 1929 the German government, in answer to the protest of Wang Ching-wei that German advisers were assisting Chiang in the civil wars, made the following declaration:

"1. It is untrue that the German government has sent military officers to China. The German government did not even recommend any. They have been selected in Germany by Chiang Kai-shek or by his deputies in Germany.

"2. The German government, as a matter of principle, does not favor Germans participating in military actions abroad.

"3. Germans going abroad to face the hazard of warfare, are doing so at their own risk. . . ."[1]

In another official statement in 1930, the German government attempted to clarify its position regarding the export of German arms to China and the involvement of German military personnel in China's civil war: "The export of arms for the purpose of warfare, ammunition and poison gas from Germany has been prohibited by statute, and such prohibition is strictly enforced. The German mili-

[1] Bloch, K., *German Interests and Policies in the Far East* (N.Y.: I.P.R., 1939), p. 14.

tary advisers to the Chinese Army are employed against the wishes of the German government. . . ."[2]

This was Germany's declared position, but German military aid to China was being sustained unofficially by the cooperation of the Reichswehr and a powerful group of German industrialists. Max Bauer had openly stated in Germany that he was working for China in the interests of German business and German science. Bauer had been recommended to Chiang by the famous General Erich Ludendorff and by certain prominent industrialists in Germany.[3]

The Reichswehr had long pursued a policy of sending its military personnel to advise foreign forces. The disarmament clauses of the Treaty of Versailles were then restricting Germany's military preparations, and in an effort to circumvent these restrictions the Reichswehr had trained some men at the expense of foreign governments by entering into certain advisory schemes with Russia and, more especially, with China. We now know that in the years after World War I the Reichswehr maintained close contacts with munition industrialists at home and abroad. For example, it had an active interest in the development of the Swedish Bofors (Krupp), the Swiss Oerlikon (Rheinmetall-Borsig), the munitions plants of the Netherlands, and other foreign firms. The development of a munitions market in China was obviously, for the Reichswehr and the Reichsverband der Deutschen Industrie, a profitable enterprise.

The difference between the German and the several other advisory missions in China was, perhaps, simply this: the German military advisers were there to contribute to their own country's interests, business and military. They were profiting by their relationship with China, and they were cooperative and friendly to their Chinese "customers." Their service in China was designed not only to put their well-earned salaries in their pockets but also to stimulate Germany's export trade. With the sale of products from Krupp-Bofors, Rheinmetall-Borsig, M.A.N., I. G. Farben, and other such firms, the Reichswehr was receiving many indirect benefits along its road to rearmament.

II

In May 1933, General Wetzell wrote from China to his former superior General Hans von Seeckt, then living in retirement after

[2] *Ibid.*   [3] *Ibid.*, p. 13.

resigning as commander-in-chief of the Reichswehr, which he had commanded from 1919 to 1926. Wetzell said in part: "The Chinese government has previously extended its invitation to prominent personages, evidently with the intention of promoting understanding and seeking world interest in China through such persons. Concerning the invitation extended to Your Excellency, there was also the expectation of learning about the valuable German systems of organization and, above all, military know-how and imaginativeness. . . . The Marshal [Generalissimo Chiang Kai-shek] has often asked me about Your Excellency's work in the building of the Reichswehr. . . ."[4]

At Chiang's invitation, von Seeckt came to China. The value of German military assistance had been amply demonstrated in the successes of German-trained units of the Central Army (notably the Fifth Army) against the invading Japanese forces in the Shanghai campaign of 1932, and von Seeckt was met with high hopes. Generalissimo Chiang had great plans for a modernized army trained and built with German assistance, and he had every confidence in von Seeckt, of whom Herbert Rosinski has written that his "superiority, as a political leader, as a military organizer, as an educator, above all as a brilliant strategist, was incontestible."[5] In Liddell Hart's opinion, von Seeckt's influence and his contribution to the German army between the two World Wars was at least comparable to, if it did not surpass, that of Schlieffen in the period prior to World War I.[6]

Von Seeckt made the first of his two trips to China in the spring of 1933. He was treated royally and paid sumptuously by the Chinese government. Asked by Chiang to build a Chinese army patterned after the Reichswehr, he demurred, saying that the different circumstances in China did not make such a plan feasible. Von Seeckt expressed his willingness, however, to give advice on specific problems, and Chiang consulted him on political matters, probably in an attempt to recognize and benefit from von Seeckt's prestige in his homeland, in the hope that China might thus obtain more active military assistance from Germany, who was then rearming.[7] Von Seeckt, on the other hand, assumed that Chiang planned to use his fame as a means of uniting the Chinese army, a misconception which quite likely arose because

[4] Rabenau, Friedrich. *Seeckt, aus seinem Leben 1918-1936* (Leipzig, 1940), p. 678.
[5] Rosinski, *The German Army*, p. 104.
[6] Liddell Hart, *The German Generals Talk* (N.Y.: 1948), Ch. 1.
[7] von Seeckt, *Ansprache*, p. 5.

Chiang had asked von Seeckt to lecture to China's top military leaders in Chiang's own study at Peking.[8]

Soon after his arrival von Seeckt embarked on a three-month fact-finding tour of North China. He was greatly impressed with the ancient Chinese culture and lingered admiringly over the birthplace of Confucius, the palace and the Kuo-tze-chien (Imperial University and Hall of Classics) at Peiping, and the Great Wall of China. The trip was not just tourist sightseeing, however, for out of it came the celebrated memorandum *Denkschrift fuer Marschall Chiang Kai-shek*, von Seeckt's observations on China's military situation which were to have a signal influence on subsequent military development there. Von Seeckt presented this memorandum to Chiang at Peiping on June 30, 1933, and soon after returned to Germany to assume the high honor of *Generalberater*, resident general adviser to the National Government of China.

General von Seeckt's memorandum was immediately seized upon as a blueprint for China's military organization. It began: "The hypothesis of every reorganization of an army is, first of all, peace on the outer borders. That means several years of external peace and a state of political calm. . . . Before these conditions are achieved a successful military reorganization cannot be accomplished. Success cannot be attained while you are in a continual state of war."[9]

Foremost among von Seeckt's many suggestions was the caveat that it would be unwise to attempt to build a large army all at once. He stressed quality as the most essential ingredient and suggested that the creation of a "nucleus" was the first step to be taken. Von Seeckt's central concepts were three, and they may be summarized as follows:

1. The army is the foundation of the ruling power [*Regierungsgewalt*] and a shield of national security against aggression from without.

2. The effectiveness of an army lies in its qualitative superiority.

3. The value of an army depends upon the worth of its officer corps.[10]

Upon these assumptions von Seeckt based his suggestions. He recommended the immediate establishment of a training brigade (*Lehrbrigade*), a device whereby officers of all grades up to divisional generals might familiarize themselves with the most modern military

---

[8] *Ibid.*

[9] von Seeckt, H., *Denkschrift für Marschall Chiang Kai-shek* (hereafter to be referred as *Denkschrift*), (German Heeresarchiv, Potsdam, Sg. 60, Lager-No. 1864, Karten 15, Stüeck 205), p. 1.

[10] *Ibid.*

techniques. Through this brigade, he affirmed, the general staff officers and the students of the general staff college would be enabled to increase their abilities for the direction of war (*Kriegsfuehrung*). The objective was also to train a cadre "well versed in the principles of modern warfare as well as their application; the trainees thus could be imbued with the kind of feeling proper to a modern field commander." Von Seeckt emphasized that the older Chinese officers, especially those at the level of divisional command, should be extended every possible opportunity for such experience. Evidently he recognized that these older officers were the weakest links in the Chinese army. As the Central Military Academy trained the younger officers, so the training brigade, armed with the most modern equipment and led by energetic German advisers and battle-experienced Chinese soldiers, would educate the higher echelons of the army in infantry, artillery, engineering, communications, armor, and air operations.

Von Seeckt's next major proposal was related to the personnel system. On this he had the following remarks: "The employment, promotion, and dismissal of the officers must be managed from a single officer in accordance with a uniform principle and standard. The decision over the employment and the destinies of the officers can rest only in the hands of the commander-in-chief of the army. In this a personnel officer [*Personalamtes*] is especially needed, established under him and dealing with the lists [personnel documentary matters]. Based upon these, judgment can be passed on the achievements of any officer in military school as to whether or not he has the capacity to rise to a higher position. On the basis of capacity, officers will be prepared for a command or sent to the War College [*Kriegsakademie*] or assigned to the general staff."[11]

Financial reform in the army was called for by von Seeckt with unusual candor: "Side by side, and independent of the War Ministry is to be established a special control authority after the model of the German General Accounting Office [*Oberrechnungshofes*]. To put the financial administration in order, no office may be allowed to spend money on its own authority. There must be precise budgets established for the individual formations, divisions, military schools, training brigades, etc., and the newly-established [auditing] authority is to check the expenditure with the budget. The form and procedure of

[11] *Ibid.*, p. 9.

the accounting and auditing must be prescribed beforehand and made into a uniform practice everywhere. Such an authority may be put into operation by a suitable German official [*Beamten*] but it must be put under Chinese leadership thereafter. Through such an organization the essential economy of the military budget [*militär-Etat*] can be achieved, and judicial spending for essential purposes can thus be safeguarded."[12]

The reorganization suggested by von Seeckt had, it will be noted, its administrative as well as its military side. Along with the reconstruction of the army in accordance with the demands of modern warfare went a suggestion for the establishment of the ministry of war on an up-to-date basis. As for the overall military organization, von Seeckt's views may be summarized in three points:

1. Clarity in organization throughout the entire military system is a prerequisite to administrative success. In the military chain of command authority and responsibility must be clearly regulated.

2. The entire military machine—the elements of training, administration, and command—must be integrated and subordinated to the commander-in-chief. He is a member of the government, and he alone is responsible to the government. Directly subordinated to him are the war minister, the army commanders, the chief of the general staff, the training brigade, etc. There must be unity of command.

3. It is essential to delegate authority and responsibility in a proper manner.

Von Seeckt had found that lack of centralized authority, ill-defined powers and responsibilities, and the absence of unity of command were weaknesses prevalent in the Chinese army:

"A side-by-side arrangement of higher positions as was the case in North China during the late war and which still seems to be in existence, can never lead to victory.

"When the commander-in-chief does not personally take charge of the command at the front, he must appoint a special person to serve in his place with unrestricted authority. Here at Peiping it is not clear whether the war minister, the minister of the interior, or the representative of the chief of the general staff is in command of troops. In any case, there is no unity of command."[13]

The Chinese traditions of balances of power and the characteristic reluctance to delegate authority were seen by von Seeckt as weaknesses

[12] *Ibid.*   [13] *Ibid.*

which the army could no longer afford to permit. The first desideratum was a clearly organized, unified command; then, quality:

"It appears to me that it is better to have ten good divisions than to establish twenty mediocre divisions within the same period.

"The coordination between infantry and artillery is the necessary condition of all modern warfare. If one cannot at least approximate the strength of the Japanese artillery and air force, then the prospect of conducting a skillful resistance against Japan cannot be counted on."[14]

Finally, von Seeckt took up the question of the German advisers in China, stating:

"An excellent choice for the chief of troop training may not necessarily rest in one's capacity as a lecturer in the War College. One who is experienced in the techniques of weapons is not, perhaps, always suitable for training the troops. The right person for the right position is the criterion of success. It is quite natural that the German advisers summoned to China would meet with adverse resistance in this country which would prevent the broadening of their influence. Only Your Excellency's influence [Chiang's] is capable of breaking up this resistance.

"In this respect it seems possible for the Chinese as well as the Germans to work together under these difficulties and to determine where the difficulties lie, whether with the Chinese or with the Germans, and how cooperation might be effected. Your Excellency's German advisers are also in a position to make recommendations regarding the problems of organization and armament, but you must consider the external and internal factors and bring their recommendations into line with the prevailing state of affairs. In this, Your Excellency, sound counseling demands the cooperation of a competent German and Chinese staff in order to enable their various tasks to be fulfilled."[15]

III

During von Seeckt's first mission to China, General Wetzell (a long-time subordinate of von Seeckt) was serving as chief German military adviser to Chiang. Wetzell and von Seeckt often took drastically different views of the Chinese situation, and von Seeckt noted in his diary under July 28, 1933: "It is regrettable that Wetzell is

14 *Ibid.*   15 *Ibid.*

seldom satisfied with me. I feel sorry, because he had a great attachment for me and has his very good qualities: above all, his energy to work and his devotion to his task. . . . It is understandable that with his long years of experience he would know things better than I could during a single week. On the other hand, my view is freer and less skeptical. Perhaps he is right in every respect, but that should not alter my right to express my own opinion. . . ."[16]

Shortly after von Seeckt returned to Germany, Wetzell resigned and Dr. Chu Chia-hua, then a cabinet member, dispatched a telegram on October 2, 1933 to von Seeckt: "General Wetzell has contemplated resignation. He feels that he is no longer able to work for Marshal Chiang. Would prefer a man of your background. You are requested to come."[17]

At the same time Colonel Heins, a trusted German adviser to Chiang, was sent to Berlin, bearing a personal letter from the generalissimo to von Seeckt. As a result, in the spring of 1934, von Seeckt left Germany for China. His departure was the occasion of receiving the blessings of President Hindenburg and Field Marshal von Mackensen.[18] Von Seeckt departed, as he said, to take up the "full responsibility" himself.[19]

Part of von Seeckt's function in China was to be to build up Sino-German trade and to put China on her feet in a program of prewar industrialization. As he told Chiang, von Seeckt regarded the building of a modern army as impossible unless accompanied by industrial reconstruction. The entire nation had to reorganize its economy and set up an armament industry (*Rustungindustrie*) with German technical and material assistance. The Chinese, in this establishment of a *kuo-fang kung-yeh* (national defense industry) dealt largely with the German industrial organization Hapro and, under the military council, set up a national resources planning commission. The Chinese finance minister, H. H. Kung, went to Germany in 1935. A barter-agreement and a revolving credit was given by the German national bank, the president of which was Schacht, who was considered a friend of China. Trade with Germany, involving many hundreds of millions of marks, had its inception here. German assistance, and

[16] Rabenau, *Seeckt, op.cit.*, p. 690.
[17] von Seeckt, *Ansprache*, p. 3.
[18] See letters from Hindenburg and von Mackensen in von Seeckt's file, *Verzeichnis vom Nachlass des Generalobersten Hans von Seeckt.*
[19] von Seeckt, *Ansprache*, pp. 5-6.

the threat of Japanese expansion, spurred Chinese industrialization to great achievements. Highways and railways, with war as well as peace in mind, were speedily built.[20] Factories sprang up. Arsenals were expanded and modernized. The new industrial tempo was geared to the feverish military preparations. Turning more to this industrial development and giving his military chief of staff General von Falkenhausen a free hand in military matters, the ailing von Seeckt masterminded China's industrial expansion. Many foreign observers have credited von Seeckt with the encircling plan which drove the Chinese communists from their base at Kiangsi, but von Seeckt's precise involvement in these plans cannot be accurately determined. His overall plans for reconstructing the army and certain broad general strategies were of great value, but his most far-reaching work was that concerned with the establishment of Chinese war industries and the encouragement of Sino-German trade. In general, it may be said that his proposals were earnestly followed by the Chinese and that von Seeckt's mission to China must be regarded as highly successful. In the sphere of international politics, however, von Seeckt's effort was not nearly so successful. Upon his return to Germany, he recommended to Hitler, in the presence of Blomberg, Neurath, and Schacht, that there was a need of pursuing a clear-cut German policy with respect to China.[21] For some time von Seeckt was under the illusion that Hitler had followed his advice. Then suddenly something happened: Ribbentrop signed the anti-Comintern pact with Japan on November 25, 1936.

Why had von Seeckt been able to do so much in his two brief missions to China? His military prestige earned him the respect of Chiang and the cooperation of his associates, and, moreover, he took advantage of his ability to get things done by effecting immediately some of the most needed defense preparations against Japan. His personality—his inspiring bearing, his correctness, his attention to details—pleased Chiang. His military sagacity and his doctrine of the *Eliteheeres* (elite army) won over many of the Chinese leaders, while his concept of the centralization of military control coincided exactly

[20] The material for the strategic Hangchow-Nanchang Railway was supplied by the German concern of Otto Wolff-Cologne. Wolff was twice in China, during 1934 and 1935.

[21] Goerlitz, Walter, *Der Deutsche Generalstab: Geschichte und Gestalt 1657-1945* (Frankfurt am Main, 1951), p. 428.

with what Chiang was advocating.[22] His experience enabled him to step into a strange situation and in a very short time not only detect what was wrong but offer constructive and concrete suggestions. He did not attempt the Stilwellian method of overwhelming Chinese opposition by sarcasm, logic, and evidence. Instead, he inspired confidence by his reputation and his assurance and, by cordiality and respect, won over the Chinese. He had a real admiration for the Chinese and especially for Chiang, whom he once described to the noted Swedish explorer Sven Hedin as a judicious, wise, and prudent statesman, a skillful but careful strategist, and a splendid and noble personality.[23]

So great was von Seeckt's influence in Chinese military circles that his writings, especially his *Gedanken eines Soldaten* (*The Thought of a Soldier*), were widely quoted in China. When he died in December 1946 a solemn memorial service held in China's capital was attended by almost the entire military hierarchy of Nanking. The Chinese minister of war, General Ho Ying-ch'in, who spoke for Generalissimo Chiang on this occasion, said: "The entire Chinese officer corps can find in the personality of General von Seeckt a wonderful example for themselves."[24]

IV

On June 30, 1933, General Hans von Seeckt presented his first memorandum *Denkschrift fuer Marschall Chiang Kai-shek,* in the same year that an important conference was held at Nanchang under the guise of a military disbandment conference. This, and another conference held in 1934, established the policy that the National Government of China would build up a powerful and modern army in several stages. The second conference with General von Seeckt was held in May 1934 at Kuling. There were not enough funds for the complete plan laid down by von Seeckt, but it was being pushed as far as possible. From 1934 to 1936 the government was to reorganize and reequip 20 divisions. In 1936 another top-level military conference was convened out of which came China's Three-year Plan of rearmament. The National Government at Nanking was to reorganize 60 modern army divisions and to readjust another 60 existing

[22] von Seeckt, "Moderne Heere," *Gedanken eines Soldaten, op.cit.,* pp. 51-61.
[23] Hedin, Sven, *Chiang Kai-shek* (N.Y.: John Day, 1940), pp. 59, 68f.
[24] Rabenau, *Seeckt, op.cit.,* p. 735.

divisions, putting these on a more or less modern basis. These divisions were to be supported by an appropriate number of special fighting units, such as armored, artillery and chemical warfare.[25]

At Kuling General von Seeckt fell ill, from an illness from which he could not completely recover. When, in March 1935, he left for home because of rapidly failing health, he recommended that his chief of staff, General Alexander von Falkenhausen, succeed him as head of the German military mission in China.

Famous as a brilliant strategist of Germany's pre-World War I great general staff and honored with the order Pour le Mérite for his achievements, von Falkenhausen had combined diplomatic service with a brilliant military career. He was in Turkey during 1916-1919 as chief of an army; in 1918 he became military plenipotentiary there. From 1910 to 1914 he served as German military attaché in Tokyo. Having prepared himself at the School for Oriental Studies in Berlin, he understood China's problems and had the advantage of being able to converse directly with Chiang in Japanese. Von Falkenhausen had been one of Germany's outstanding general staff officers during World War I and in the postwar years had commanded the German infantry school and contributed much to the building of the Reichswehr. With this useful background, and with the respect of the Chinese and the recommendation of von Seeckt ("I can praise him with my whole heart"), von Falkenhausen came into his position of high responsibility at a crucial time in China's modern history.

Cognizant of China's industrial limitations and the pressing need for an armed force, von Falkenhausen adopted the scheme on which the 100,000-man Reichswehr had been constructed: great reliance was placed on a high proportion of light automatic weapons, and mortars were largely for heavier artillery. The military training plan went forward in high gear. An 80,000-man force was soon under arms.[26] A number of modern artillery regiments were built around well-trained nuclei. An anti-aircraft and air defense system had to be constructed from scratch, a move which the coming war was soon to justify. An armored brigade, equipped with two kinds of old British tanks and artillery, trained near Nanking. Although mobility was the keynote of the Chinese preparations, it was nevertheless thought advisable to build certain defense lines between Nanking and the sea-

[25] Chang Chi-yüen, *Tang-shih kai-yao* (Taipeh, 1951), Vol. II, Ch. 27.
[26] Chennault, C. L., *Way of a Fighter* (N.Y.: Putnam, 1949), p. 38. Carlson, E. F., *The Chinese Army* (N.Y.: I.P.R., 1940), p. 46.

port of Shanghai, where the Japanese had gained a foothold and had established a military base. To General Chang Chih-chung, then superintendent of the Central Military Academy, was assigned this task. He worked in secret headquarters at Soochow, with the assistance of German fortifications experts. A plan to reorganize the coastal defense, especially the Yangtze River (originally largely defended by very old guns) at Kiangyin, Chinkiang, and Nanking, was being actively pursued. Unfortunately, the new German guns came too late—barely a few weeks before the Japanese attack. Equally fruitless was the effort on the Chinese counterpart of the "Hindenburg" line, which consisted of a network of pillboxes and fortresses between the capital and Shanghai. This line did not live up to expectations when the test came, and it went the way of the Maginot, the Siegfried, and all such "impregnable" lines of defense.

The Germans, well aware of China's industrial backwardness, made every effort to advise the Chinese on the expansion and acceleration of the munitions industries. Under the direction of General Yü Ta-wei, the arsenals at Nanking, Kung-hsien, and Hanyang produced weapons of original German design, such as the Maxim machine gun, the 82 mm. trench mortar, and the Mauser rifles and pistols. The standard Chinese rifle, the Chung-cheng or "Generalissimo Chiang model," was actually a Mauser design. For the first time, due chiefly to machinery and tools imported from Germany, Chinese-made weapons embodied quality and precision. Chemical plants for the munitions program were constructed with technical advice from I. G. Farben. With German financing, the Chinese projected a modern steel mill to be erected at Chuchow, in the province of Hunan. These are only a few indications of the vast Chinese defense preparations. Behind the scenes a certain Captain Klein, who was instrumental in bringing to China the original Bauer group, reaped the rewards of the huge Sino-German trade which he, and other German industrial diplomats like him, had fostered.[27]

A barter agreement involving 100 million marks in trade was signed by China and Germany on July 25, 1936. Tungsten headed the list of Chinese raw materials exchanged for German-made munitions and other industrial products. Hitler's defense minister, Field Marshal Werner Fritz von Blomberg, conducted the negotiations, and von Seeckt, the resident adviser to China, played an important role in

[27] von Dircksen, H., *Moscow, Tokyo, London, Twenty Years of German Foreign Policy* (Norman, Oklahoma: 1952), p. 171.

the deal, as did General von Reichenau, who made a special trip to China as Hitler's representative, and Major General Thomas, chief of economic warfare in Germany.

The Germans had put their stamp on China's war preparations. In 1933 there were 61 German advisers and officers with the Chinese armed forces, 22 of them in key positions.[28] In 1935 this number had increased to 70, and in 1938 the remaining military advisers numbered only 30. German 88 mm. flak manned by Chinese soldiers in German-style helmets were seen around Nanking. German 75 mm. guns, Bofors (Krupp) guns, Daimler-Benz Henschel, and M.A.N. tractors, and other powerful German weapons paraded in the streets of the capital. The Chinese navy (formerly based on British models) and the air force (formerly taking its cue from American and Italian systems) were remodeled along German lines. Hermann Goering delegated General Milch to see to it that the Chinese air force received assistance from the Luftwaffe, and a submarine expert of World War I became resident chief German naval adviser of China. There were great plans for the navy. The Hapro organization contracted to build a dozen submarines for China in an initial order, and a number of German warships, from cruisers to motor torpedo boats, were earmarked for the Chinese. The war, however, broke out before the deliveries of naval equipment could be made.

Had the war been delayed for two more years, China might have had 60 German-trained army divisions to throw against the Japanese invaders. In the air Messerschmitt and Stuka planes would have carried her markings and, under the sea, Chinese-manned U-boats would have harassed Japanese shipping in submarine wolf-packs. As it turned out, much of her equipment was German-made, many of her officers German-trained, and her whole military organization and industrial development German-inspired. Had German influence been given more time to work and spread in China, the Japanese might have met a far different foe. Continued German influence might well have drastically changed the world picture by eventually enlisting China as a partner of Germany and turning China's formidable manpower in an entirely different direction.

[28] These figures were obtained from Chinese war ministry sources and from the lists of names included in General von Seeckt's file. According to the figures given by the *New York Herald Tribune's* file on General von Falkenhausen, a total of 137 Germans served as advisers in China in the 10-year period inaugurated by Bauer's arrival there. The largest at any one time (in 1934) was 64. Nine died in China of disease and two were killed in accidents while demonstrating the techniques of handling hand grenades.

11 · 1937, THE TIME FOR WAR

I. *K'ANG CHANG TAO-TI* : A FIGHT TO THE LAST. II. CHINA'S STRATEGY. III. PREPARATION AND THE LACK OF IT. IV. THE NATIONALIST ARMY: FORTH TO BATTLE.

> *"Wars spring from unseen and generally insignificant causes, the first outbreak being often but an explosion of anger."*—Thucydides II.11.4.

I

THE war between China and Japan broke out on July 7, 1937. Generalissimo Chiang declared to the nation that the Chinese had reached the "limit of endurance":

"From the military point of view we may say that Japan's preparations are complete in all respects. . . . Now let us look at our own situation. How do we stand? Have we fulfilled the conditions necessary for resisting the enemy? We ourselves can answer that question simply and sadly in one brief sentence: we have made no preparations whatsoever. Not only have we not organized our resources, but we are not even unified in thought and spirit."[1]

"Since we are a weak nation there is only one thing to do now that we have reached the limit of endurance: we must throw every ounce of energy into the struggle for national survival and independence. That done, neither time nor circumstance will permit our stopping midway to seek peace. . . . Let our people realize the meaning of 'the limit of endurance' and the extent of the sacrifice implied, for once that stage is reached we can only sacrifice and fight to the bitter end. Only a determination to sacrifice ourselves to the utmost can bring us ultimate victory."[2]

Up to this point the National Government's policy had been

[1] Chiang Kai-shek, "Resistance to Aggression and Renaissance of the Nation," *The Collected Wartime Messages of Generalissimo Chiang Kai-shek* (N.Y.: John Day, 1946), I, pp. 1-2.
[2] Chiang Kai-shek, "Limit of China's Endurance," *op.cit.*, I, p. 22.

summed up in these words: "The National Government of China will not abandon peace until all hope of peace is gone; it will not lightly talk of sacrifice until the last stage is reached when sacrifice becomes necessary." But on July 7, 1937, the Japanese occupied the Lukouchiao area in North China, cutting communication between North and South China and bringing the old capital of Peiping completely under their control. The Chinese realized that the danger was insupportable. The time for full-scale war had arrived.

On August 13, the Chinese defenders of Shanghai resolutely confronted the Japanese invaders in the bloodiest battle that the world had seen since Verdun. The opposition was as unexpected as it was brave. The Japanese, having taken Peiping and Tientsin, were hoping for what they regarded as quick war and a quick settlement (*sokk-sen sokk-katsu*) before China could increase her military power, strengthen and stabilize her economy, and further expand her industry. Though they saw signs of Chinese unification, they were of the opinion that they still had the opportunity to strike before it could be effectively accomplished. They little realized that the military leaders from all parts of China who met in the auditorium of the Central Military Academy on July 21 to pledge their loyalty to the nation and to unite under the supreme command of Generalissimo Chiang were determined to offer a united front against the invader or that the forces of China were at last prepared to pool their efforts in a policy of *k'ang-chang tao-ti* (a fight to the last).

II

In developing her grand strategy against Japan, China had applied the lessons learned in the northern campaigns, and particularly the expeditions to quell communist uprisings. The strategy took into consideration all the essentials: China's huge manpower, her far-flung territory, the nature of the terrain, and the character of the enemy. Several strategies may be perceived. Generalissimo Chiang Kai-shek advocated the concept of sacrifice and of achieving international support for China's political aims through tenacious and prolonged military struggle.[3] General Pai Chung-hsi, the Chinese strategist noted for his slogans "trading space for time" and "accumulating minor successes into major victory," contributed the idea of a powerful army

[3] Chang Chi-yuen, *Tang-shih kai-yao, op.cit.*, II, Chs. 26, 27, 28.

held in constant readiness to strike decisive blows whenever and wherever the Japanese-held lines were weakened by dispersion. He reinforced Chiang's call for sacrifice by suggesting that his countrymen fight their enemy with a determination sufficient even to carry out a policy of "scorched earth" resistance—a phrase coined by his close partner General Li Tsung-jen. From Mao Tse-tung and the communists—the old masters of guerrilla warfare—came the policy of a protracted war. The German influence on China's war strategy should not be discounted. General von Falkenhausen, Chiang's military adviser, founded his argument for China's "final victory" on demographic and geographic grounds, paralleling his theory with the concept of *Die Abwehr* propounded by another German strategist, von Leeb; both were influential in the Chinese general staff college.[4] Above all, Chiang, though not discounting the importance of the fact that the Japanese were better trained and better equipped, chose to place great confidence in the spirit of his soldiers and the patriotism of his people. General Pai Chung-hsi wrote of Chiang: "The President conceives his strategical basis in the development of revolutionary morale to the highest degree. . . . He chooses to de-emphasize the more tangible factors, thinking that there is little hope of success in waiting for the realization of all the tangible, material considerations. He depends rather upon the revolutionary spirit, the party's organization, and faith in the party's doctrines. These are the highest sort of weapons. This theory was a new discovery at that time (of the northern expedition)—a bold and justifiable innovation which had its continuing influence during the war of resistance."[5]

China settled down to a long war, resigned to the cost and relying upon the willing sacrifice of her people. Her only hope, in the face of Japan's superior preparation, was in a prolonged war of attrition. Recognizing the Japanese habit of clinging to the Cannae[6] style of war, Pai's strategy called for harrying the Japanese with guerrilla tactics in the rear, waging mobile warfare on the enemy's front and flank, yielding cities and drawing the Japanese into the vast interior of the country, and preserving the main Chinese fighting force intact

[4] von Leeb, Ritter Wilhelm, *Die Abwehr* (Berlin, 1933), *passim*.
[5] Pai Chung-hsi, "President Chiang and China's Military Development during the Last Sixty Years," *Wei-tà-ti Chiang chu-hsi, op.cit.*, pp. 17f. Chiang Kai-shek, *China's Destiny, op.cit.*, pp. 130-131, 134.
[6] The battle of Cannae, in which Hannibal's Carthaginian army won a decisive victory over the Romans, is considered a classic example of the battle of annihilation.

by avoiding direct and expensive clashes with the Japanese. All-out contests for fixed points were to be avoided wherever possible, for there were no "strategic points"—only the strategy of compelling the enemy to be drawn deeper and deeper into the quagmire. After the significant Chinese victory at Tai-erh-chuang and the subsequent retreat from Hsuchow, the Chinese began to adopt this strategy of offensive defense more often. The strategy of sacrifice, which had produced the gallant and costly defense of Shanghai, was gradually abandoned. Although the defense of Shanghai and Nanking did gain time, time in which a substantial amount of industrial potential was evacuated to the interior of China, that campaign cost the Chinese valuable striking power—striking power which Pai felt would better have been conserved for a strategical counteroffensive when the Japanese penetrated into the interior. A number of German military analysts saw in Pai's doctrine a strong emphasis of *verteidigung durch Angriff* (defense through attack).[7] The early sacrifice proved to the world that China was determined to resist Japanese aggression, regardless of the cost; then China settled down to a calculated and less spectacular strategy of dissipating Japanese might and forcing Japan to overextend herself.

One important factor in any war strategy which no one can afford to neglect but which is sometimes overshadowed by the display of verbiage on grand strategy is the group of men—the general staff officers—who execute the strategic plan and transform orders into actions. Up to 1937 the Chinese Army Staff College had graduated 2,000 general staff officers; by 1945, a total of 3,000 had completed their training. These were the men who actually influenced China's war strategy. The general staff officers trained during the prewar days were of good caliber, having received careful instruction from competent German military experts. However, their studies and discussions were largely confined to the lessons of the First World War, with heavy emphasis on trench warfare and positional war. The French instructional team led by General Balny had further infused the concept of defense in the Chinese war college; the French looked with scornful eyes upon the German-designed curriculum based on a war of movement. It was because of their influence that many of the

[7] Schenke, Wolf, *Reise an der Gelbenfront* (Berlin, 1941), p. 249. Yin Shi, *The Chiang-Lee Relationship and China*, op.cit., p. 75. *Far Eastern Mirror Fortnightly*, I, 5 (May 5, 1938), pp. 35-38.

Chinese general staff officers had become unduly Maginot-conscious, and overmagnified the role of Hindenburg-type trench lines in their own war. These men had performed invaluable service in the war by virtue of the fact that they were the only group capable of conducting large-scale operations. Near the end of the war, however, the system of general staff training in China had been changed from one of the Kriegsakademie-style to one following the pattern of the U.S. Fort Leavenworth school.

Experience, the fountainhead of strategy, cannot always be acquired in classrooms, nor is imaginativeness the monoply of Occidental strategical thinkers. The Chinese communist Mao Tse-tung is a man whose genius in strategy is not the product of any military school. His plan for a protracted war depended upon the organization of the peasantry into guerrilla groups which would harass Japanese patrols and disrupt their economy and communication in the rear. In his *Strategic Problems in the Anti-Japanese Guerrilla War*, Mao raised guerrilla warfare from the level of tactics to that of strategy:

"The strategic problem in guerrilla warfare arises out of the fact that China is not a small but a big country; yet unlike the Soviet Union, she is weak. While in a period of progress, this big but weak country is attacked by a small but strong country. When that happens, a whole set of problem arises.

"It was under such circumstances that the territory seized by our enemy became rather extensive and the war took on a protracted character.

"When our enemy, a small country with insufficient armed forces, seizes an extensive area in this big country of ours, he cannot but leave many sections of that area ungarrisoned. The anti-Japanese guerrilla war is conducted, therefore, primarily not on interior lines to coordinate with the regulars in their campaigns, but independently on exterior lines. . . ."

Then Mao reiterated: "Initiative, flexibility, and planning in the offensive in a defensive war, of battles of quick decision in a protracted war, and of exterior line operative within interior line operation constitute the central problem regarding the strategic principles of guerrilla warfare."[8]

[8] Nieh Jung-chen, Chief of the General Staff of the Chinese (Communist) People's Liberation Army, "How the Chinese People Defeated the Japanese Fascist Aggressor," *China's Revolutionary Wars* (Peking, 1951), p. 24. Mao Tse-tung, *On Protracted War* (Chungking, 1941), *passim*. Mao Tse-tung, *Chung-kuo ke-ming-chang-tseng tī*

The communists under Mao Tse-tung had suggested this strategy, and they undertook to organize it. They set up local organizations to develop guerrilla tactics, indoctrinating them with the regular communist party line. On the pretext of winning people for guerrilla tactics to advance the immediate cause of the war, they distributed the property of landowners to the peasant and laboring classes. They won to their side a loyal pro-communist segment of the population. The communists were making plans for the days after the conclusion of the Sino-Japanese war.

It is clear enough to all now and it was evident to the shrewd observer even then that Mao Tse-tung had plans which, in their long-range purpose, were broader than the strategies for the day, though most of his associates were military men with their eyes on immediate goals. The nationalists had a basically workable over-all plan, but they were not organized well enough on all levels to provide that general mobilization of all resources which *total* war, by the very nature of its name, demands. Founded upon a primarily agricultural economy, China was deficient in centralized industry, although perhaps her leaders could feel a compensating advantage in the fact that there were therefore fewer crucial targets vulnerable to air blows.

China's sprawling industrial resources were one problem. Another was the lamentable fact that the Chinese military strategists had not planned in advance any effective system of civilian cooperation with the military—a necessity of modern warfare. She had difficulty in mobilizing the best brains from all walks of civilian life when the military called for their assistance. Economic problems were another consideration and China's uncontrollable inflationary spiral was as big a headache in her own morale and security as was the nation's difficult terrain to the mechanized armies of Japan.

The Chinese were indeed fortunate that the Japanese militarists were no more imaginative in their tactics than they were. With all of Nippon's technological superiority, the armies of Japan not only bogged down drastically in China's vast land, but also failed to exploit many of the military and economic mistakes and weaknesses of the Chinese. The Chinese were fighting with considerable success, considering the strength of their opponent, and were sustained perhaps more by morale and dogged determination than by solid economic backing and an air-tight, fool-proof grand strategy.

---

chang-lo wen-t'i (The Strategic Problems of China's Revolutionary Wars), (Harbin, 1948) *passim.*

III

In *The Comments of Moung Ka* "Saki" wrote that "a little inaccuracy sometimes saves tons of explanation," but we must resist all the pat and facile answers to the important question of the prelude to the Sino-Japanese war of 1937-1945. It might be said that China prepared for war as long as she was given time to do so, and, time having run out, then fought. That would be inaccurate. Nor is it sufficiently true to state unqualifiedly that Japanese aggression was borne with patience until this or that incident eventually precipitated China into war. The truth lies somewhere between the statement that China went to war when sufficiently ready to do so and the assertion that she, all unprepared, was at last forced unwillingly to check Japanese imperialism and turn her soil into a war-torn battlefield.

It is undeniable that for five years, from 1932 to 1937, the Japanese —sometimes with comparative freedom and sometimes bitterly opposed—harried the Chinese with aggressive advances. During these five years militarists on both sides were most outspoken in urging their people into war. Why, then, did not war break out before 1937?

The declaration of war, it may be said, rested with the Chinese. The Japanese had taken the first action toward war and their aggression at almost any time was sufficient cause for China to declare war. On the other hand, it seemed that large-scale Japanese offensives against China might not be undertaken as long as the Chinese were willing to tolerate these infringements upon their sovereignty. The conditions under which China would declare war seemed to be simply these: (1) Japan's aggression would have to be sufficient to arouse the Chinese people to all-out war despite the terrible toll they knew would be exacted; (2) the Chinese armies had to be sufficiently prepared. The menace of Japan became sufficient cause to the Chinese after a few Chinese victories in minor skirmishes had raised morale, after the armed forces had felt the humiliation of defeat and tasted something of the blood of victory, and after the student group (in their idealism) and the communist group (for political reasons) had made the cry for war against Japan articulate.[9] At the same time, the government's plans to unify China's heterogeneous armies and to centralize command had met with reasonable success, and the new

[9] Consult MacNair, H. F., and Lach, H. F., *Modern Far Eastern International Relations* (N.Y.: Van Nostrand, 1950), pp. 491-495. Elmquist, P. O., "The Sino-Japanese Undeclared War of 1932," *Harvard Regional Study Monogram, Papers on China*, v (May 1951) pp. 39-74.

Central Army showed sufficient promise of effectiveness in war. Militarily, China was not, of course, really ready for war against Japan, any more than she was fully prepared, economically or industrially, but the government had enough confidence in the newly unified and centralized army, the idealists and the militarists were demanding retribution, and, finally the communists found it politically advantageous to throw in their lot with Chiang Kai-shek and to call on him to lead all the Chinese forces against Imperial Japan. The Chinese Red Army joined with the Central Army, forming what Westerners usually call the nationalists, and the Nationalist Army was put into the field against the superior forces of Japan.

IV

The growth of the Nationalist Army from the cadre of Whampoa into a great fighting force capable of defending the nation against a first-class military power can be sketched only in outline here. The new army grew by accretion; Whampoa furnished its nucleus. The famous National Revolutionary Army which swept across China during the northern campaign was an amalgam of several forces of different geographical origins. The Kuomintang army, led by Whampoa cadets and composed of Chiang's loyal Chekiang and Kwangtung troops, formed the First Army Corps, and the armies of the province of Hunan the Second. From Yunnan came the troops of the Third Army Corps, and the Cantonese forces in the West River area (who fought at Wuhan and sustained the greatest losses) comprised the Fourth Army Corps. From the Kwangsi province came the Seventh Army Corps, a hard-fighting and fast-moving battalion led by Li Tsung-jen and Pai Chung-hsi. With these army corps for its backbone, the Revolutionary Army began the northern expedition some 100,000 strong. Fighting their way from Canton to the banks of the Yangtze, they crushed the best that the northern warlords had to oppose them (the crack units commanded by Wu Pei-fu, Sun Chuen-fang, and Chang Tso-lin) and won over many of their opponents to their side, so that when Chiang established the new capital at Nanking he was able to speak of his army as half a million strong.

The successes of the Revolutionary Army encouraged Feng Yu-hsiang's army of the northwest, the Kuominchun, and Yen Hsi-shan's army of Shansi to throw in their lot with Chiang.[10] Chiang then com-

[10] For the background of the Kuominchun consult: *Kuominchun ke-ming shih* (The

manded a total strength of 179 divisions and some 30 independent brigades; he reorganized the Revolutionary Army into four group armies. The First Group Army was comprised chiefly of the Kuomintang army corps, the Second of the Kuominchun, the Third of the army of Shansi, and the Fourth built around the Kwangsi troops.[11]

The Revolutionary Army was either actively or potentially opposed, after the northern campaign, by two forces: the communists and the Northeastern or Manchurian Army. The communist forces who openly rebelled against the Central Government were built around a 30,000-man force which broke away from the newly reorganized Revolutionary Army on August 1, 1927. The Manchurian Army of Marshal Chang Hsueh-liang was largely intact after the conclusion of the northern expedition. Supported by the rich resources beyond the Great Wall, it possessed powerful artillery and cavalry forces.

The program of troop disbandment of the central government added to the opposition, and the army of Kwangsi (Fourth Group Army) and the Second Group Army (Kuominchun) joined the army of Shansi (Third Group Army) in defying Nanking. These rebels were defeated in bloody civil war, and their troops were then reincorporated into the government forces. In 1931, when Japan seized China's four northeastern provinces, the Manchurian army was compelled to place itself more and more under the control of the government. The armies of China—except, of course, for the communists— were at last united.

The most powerful military force then in China was the Central Army, or Chung-yang chün, the successor of the earlier First Group Army. Next came the Kwangsi Army, which had a bold fighting tradition and excellent leadership in the persons of Li Tsung-jen and Pai Chung-hsi. Only about 12 divisions in all, the Kwangsi Army consisted of a small but highly trained regular army nucleus (about 10 regiments) and a large body of well-trained militia. By 1935 95 per cent of this army's officers had received thorough officers' training and its percentage of Army Staff College graduates was the highest in China.[12] Due to the efficient system of popular education in the province of Kwangsi, the literacy rate among its soldiers was higher

History of Kuominchun in Revolution), 1928, and Weisshart, Herbert, "Feng Yü-hsiang: His Rise as a Militarist and His Training Program," *Harvard Regional Study Monogram, Papers on China,* VI (March 1952), p. 75.

[11] Li Tsung-jen, *Li-tsung-ssu-ling yen-lun-chi, op.cit., passim.*

[12] *Ibid.,* especially p. 219.

than that of any other Chinese unit. According to the German advisers, the Kwangsi Army expanded its original regiments so that it was able to supply a vital fighting force of 143,000 well-trained men against the Japanese invaders and bore the brunt of numerous Japanese offensives on many major fronts.[13]

The Central Army's growth was a military achievement of great significance in the history of contemporary China. It grew out of the Whampoa force and was formed around the First Army Corps after the program of troop disbandment was put into effect in an attempt to consolidate China's forces. Its German-trained divisions were, with the navy and the air force, Generalissimo Chiang's most dependable and efficient units. At the outbreak of hostilities with Japan, the Central Army was largely equipped with German weapons and stood about 300,000 strong. The hard core was a force of 80,000 men equipped and organized according to the pre-World War II German standard for an infantry division and called "The Generalissimo's Own." It had most of China's artillery, armor, and other specialized units and was under the direct command of either the generalissimo or the minister of war. Eventually another 350,000 men were added to the Central Army's original 300,000 and the total force was classified by the Japanese general staff—perhaps the closest observers of Chinese military affairs—as "direct units of the Central Army" (Chung-yang-chih-hsi-chün). In addition, there were "subsidiary units of the Central Army" (Chung-yang-p'ang-hsi-chün) to the number of 550,000 men.[14]

The entire Central Army thus varied in fighting efficiency and, on the grounds of training and equipment differences, may be considered as composed of several strata. The highest efficiency was found in the generalissimo's own force, which had received his personal attention, as well as the best-trained officers (mostly graduates of the Central Military Academy) and the lion's share of the best equipment. This resulted, consequently, in a reliable force, strictly loyal to Chiang and to the Kuomintang, of a somewhat arrogant and overbearing nature.

[13] Abegg, Lily, *China's Erneurung* (Frankfurt, 1940), p. 149.
[14] To-a ken-kiu-kai, *Saishin Shina Yoran* (The Latest Issue of the Pocket Manual on China), in Japanese (Tokyo, 1943), p. 380. Such Japanese estimates on Chinese military forces fluctuated from year to year; for instance, in 1939, the strength of the Central Army was estimated to be 390,000 and the rest of the Chinese army, 540,000 men. For the official estimates given by the Japanese War Ministry, see Japanese War Ministry, *Taikoku oyobi Retsukoku no Rikugun* (The Armies of the Japanese Empire and Other Powers), (Tokyo, 1940), pp. 105-113.

This elite force was unswervingly loyal to Chiang and proud of itself, but it was by no means the only force determined to defend the nation against the inroads of the Japanese.

The youth of China who rose in the May Fourth Literary Renaissance and the May Thirtieth labor movement were galled by Chinese defeats in Japanese-engineered incidents at Tsinan, Wan-pao-shan, and in the other preludes to the Mukden incident. During 1929, China's Manchurian Army and Soviet Russia's Far-Eastern Army, commanded by General Bluecher (Galen), locked in a brief struggle from which the Chinese emerged in humiliating defeat. The National Government suffered this and other setbacks and humiliations but endeavored to avoid premature conflict with foreign powers. This policy caused the hotter bloods of the country to ridicule the government for cowardice and to brand many governmental and military leaders with the sneering appellation of "non-resistant persons." The one bright show of courage came late in 1931, when the Manchurian general, Ma Chan-shan, led his cavalry regiments in defiance of the Japanese for the defense of his home province, Heilungkiang. Overnight he and his men were acclaimed as national heroes, and the pride of their admiring countrymen rose.

The morale of the armed forces was visibly heightened, and it increased even more after the stand of the Chinese Nineteenth Route Army at Shanghai on January 28, 1932. They were later reinforced by the Fifth Army Corps, but at the time of the initial Japanese attack on Shanghai, the Nineteenth Route Army poorly equipped as they were (composed chiefly of Cantonese troops, derived from the Fourth Army Corps of northern expedition fame, and commanded by General Tsai T'ing-K'ai) repulsed the Japanese and gained a victory which electrified the Chinese army.[15] With only rifles and machine guns, they withstood the Japanese assaults from land, sea, and air, receiving the wholehearted cooperation of the population of Shanghai —a kind of public support rarely given in China, where common soldiers were generally depreciated. This first battle at Shanghai marked a definite turning point in Chinese morale.

After the battle of Shanghai, the Japanese advance in China took the form of creating Japanese-sponsored local governments in the Hopei-Chahar region and in Inner Mongolia and of wholesale smug-

[15] Compare Elmquist, P. O., *op.cit.*, pp. 39-74.

gling to rob China of much of her important custom revenue.[16] There were incidents at Yukwan, Jehol, and the Great Wall which proved that Chinese troops would fight back when attacked. The skirmishes along the Great Wall, where units of the Chinese Army commanded by Generals Sung Che-yuan and Fu Tso-yi clashed with the Japanese, were examples of successful campaigns waged against a better-equipped foe. Those who charged with Chinese broadswords in do-or-die attacks inspired a wave of illusive "broadsword psychology" throughout the nation. Patriotic organizations presented the front-line troops with thousands of broadswords, encouraging them to defend their country with deeds of valor.

By now the National Government had determined to repel the invader, and Generalissimo Chiang's presence in the front-line area was evidence that the matter was going to be taken seriously. In the fall of 1936, the Manchurian and Mongol troops of the Japanese Kwantung Army, supported by Japanese airplanes, tanks, and artillery, was routed by General Fu Tso-yi's Chinese forces and failed in the attempt to invade the province of Suiyuan. A government spokesman at Nanking gave the official position of the Chinese on the Japanese attempt to absorb Suiyuan: "The Japanese Kwantung Army underestimates the determination of the Chinese people and their government. The time has ended when foreign nations could safely nibble away at Chinese territorial fringes. If the Kwantung Army think they can do this, they will come into contact with the forces of the Central Government, and, if they hope to localize the incident, they will be sadly mistaken. This would mean war."[17]

This defiant declaration was backed up with reinforcements sent to the armies in the north. All China was thrilled when Fu Tso-yi and Wang Ching-kuo captured Pailingmiao on November 24, 1936, defeating a superior number of Japanese-directed forces. Generalissimo Chiang himself said that "the fall of Pailingmiao must be regarded as a turning point in the history of the national renaissance and independence of China."[18] The Nationalist Army was in the field.

[16] MacNair and Lach, *op.cit.*, Chs. IV, XVII.
[17] *Chung-yang Jih-pao* (The Central Daily News), Nov. 28, 1936.
[18] *Ibid.*, Nov. 30, 1936. Chang Chi-yuen, *Tang-shih kai-yao, op.cit.*, II, p. 1100.

12 · THE STATE IN ARMS: WARTIME ORGANIZATION

I. THE THEORY: CONCENTRATION OF POWER FOR TOTAL WAR. II. THE GROWTH AND PROBLEMS OF THE MILITARY COUNCIL. III. THE SUPREME NATIONAL DEFENSE CONFERENCE AND THE SUPREME DEFENSE COUNCIL. IV. THE GOVERNMENT WITHIN THE GOVERNMENT: THE GENERALISSIMO'S PERSONAL STAFF. V. THE CHINESE FIELD ORGANIZATION.

I

LUDENDORFF's concept of *totale Krieg* (total war) stresses the all-powerful role of the military commander. It specifies that in times of crisis the supreme military commander and the military staff should take over the direct control of all the significant elements of the nation's economy.[1] In the constitution of China before the war the National Government held "the supreme command of the land, naval, and air forces."[2] Upon the outbreak of war this power was delegated and vested in the person of the chairman of the military council when, in September 1937, the government declared: "The chairman of the national military council, in shouldering the full responsibility of national defense, shall have supreme command of the land, naval, and air forces and shall direct the people of the nation."[3]

The same proclamation empowered the chairman of the military council (Chiang Kai-shek) to exert a unifying direction over the party (Kuomintang) and the government. The generalissimo had been given all authority to lead the forces of the nation in the prosecution of total war.

This arrangement had replaced the abortive original plans of the central political conference—the nation's highest policymaking body—which met in August 1937 to transform the military council into a

[1] Ludendorff, Erich, *Der totale Krieg* (München, 1935), pp. 111-112.
[2] *China Handbook, 1938-1939*, pp. 88-91.
[3] National Government of China, *The Organic Law of the National Military Council*, Sept. 1, 1939.

ta-pen-ying (supreme headquarters) roughly analogous to the *daihonei* (the wartime imperial headquarters) of Japan. The conference had advocated the centralization of all the nation's effort under this proposed organization. But, stating that the national government would thereby become a Japanese-styled military dictatorship, Chiang objected to the resolution which was passed and it was never put into effect.

II

Soon after the commencement of hostilities, a wholesale reorganization took place in the Chinese government. The chief change in the military sphere was the subordination of all military organs to the supreme military council. The Prussian military structure, which was characterized by a number of independent high military organs, gave place to the return of the Soviet organizational influence, which demanded the assertion of the military council's superiority over the general staff, the military advisory council, and the directorate-general of military training. The military council expanded to embrace the control of military operation (reorganized from the general staff), political policies, heavy industries, national economy (light industries and commerce), international relations, and civilian defense. For almost a year the military council was in a state of continual expansion and was obliged to establish committees on agricultural production, mining and manufacturing, trade and commerce, and land and water transportation.[4]

The rapid growth of the military council created problems in management and coordination. The government's mandate to the military council to take over so many functions of administration did not at the same time eliminate many overlapping functions of the Executive Yuan. In many cases these two top-level organs were maintaining agencies which were practically identical in nature and in function. The military council, to cite an example, had a department of industries which practically duplicated the function of the ministry of commerce and industries operating under the Executive Yuan. Costly delays and confusions resulted from inaction, dislocation, and duplication of effort, and these were especially hazardous in the face of the

[4] Chien Tuan-sheng and Sah Shi-chiung, *Min-kuo cheng-chih shih* (The Political Institutions of the Republic), (Chungking, 1943) I, p. 291.

military reversals which compelled the government's retreat to the interior.[5]

Successive reorganizations brought one change upon the heels of another under the so-called "program for readjusting the organizations and for the disposal of party personnel, administrative officers, and the military establishment during the period of emergency."[6] The military council assumed unwieldy proportions and bewildering complexity until the situation became so chaotic that the council was forced to request the supreme national defense conference to order another sweeping reorganization—this time to effect simplicity. The hope was to restore to the military, administrative, and party affairs their respective identities. Even with this accomplished, the military council, despite attempts to streamline the structure, governed the following imposing list of military departments:[7]

Military operations (reorganized from the general staff)
Military affairs (reorganized from the war ministry)
Military training (reorganized from the directorate-general of military training)
Political affairs
Navy general headquarters (reorganized from the naval ministry)
Aeronautical affairs commission
Rear area services
Military advisory council
Directorate-general of courts martial

The military council could now devote its full time to military affairs, though these alone were such a tangled skein that administration was exceptionally difficult. The lack of coordination between the various departments of the military, and between the administration and the fighting forces in the field, remained a serious problem. There was virtually no integration within the military council, for, though its general office had certain coordinative functions, these were largely limited to matters of routine and it had neither the initiative nor the authority to take an active role in over-all coordination.

[5] *Ibid*. See also Chen Chi-mai, *Chung-kuo cheng-fu* (China's Government), (Shanghai, 1946).
[6] National Government of China, *The Decree for the Re-adjustment of the Party, Government, and Military Organizations and for the Dispersal of the Personnel under the Emergency Act*, Jan. 1, 1948.
[7] National Government of China, *Executive Order Number 55*, Chungking, Feb. 12, 1938.

By July 1940 the situation had become critical and could no longer be ignored. The office of the chief of the supreme staff (*ts'an-mou tsung-chang*) was created within the military council, its head becoming the chief of staff to the chairman of the council. The head of this new department was empowered to direct all the military departments, commissions, and bureaus of the council and to assist the chairman in the broad administration of military affairs. The new office provided an assistant for Chiang where one was certainly most needed.

The Americans, one of the most industrially experienced and technologically efficient people of the world, required the trials and errors of two world wars to comprehend the problems involved in total war.[8] In grappling with the single aspect of organizing for industrial mobilization, the United States marshalled the ideas and abilities of numerous scholars, industrialists, scientists, and engineers, as well as leaders of civil and military administration. The Germans, who originated the term *der totale Krieg* and who had experimented over a decade of war-geared economy, were hardly successful in all respects in their military-economic effort, despite the efficiency of their general staff, their characteristic thoroughness, and the backing of their best military minds.[9] The Chinese, without all of these assets, embarked upon a military bureaucracy designed to conduct a total war unaided. Experience taught them that this ambitious plan was unrealistic, and they were forced to surrender many of the political and economic functions of government which they had assumed and to call upon a large number of civilian experts for assistance.

III

To understand the nature of China's reorganization for war, a study of the nation's supreme governing body becomes necessary. In August 1937, when the war was already a reality, the ruling body of the Kuomintang created a supreme national defense conference. The chairman of this board was Generalissimo Chiang, then also the leader of the Kuomintang party and the chairman of the military council; its

[8] Baruch, Bernard M., *American Industry in the War* (N.Y.: Prentice Hall, 1941), pp. v-vi. Bureau of the Budget, War Record Section, *The United States at War* (Washington: G.P.O., 1946), particularly, Chs. 3, 4, 12, 16. Bush, Vannevar, *Modern Arms and Free Men* (N.Y.: Simon and Schuster, 1949), Ch. 1.
[9] Graham, F. D., and Scanlon, J. J., *Economic Preparation and Conduct of War under the Nazi Regime* (Historical Division, War Department Special Staff, 1946), pp. 42-49.

members were drawn from the incumbents of China's highest and most responsible political and military posts.[10]

The wisdom of permitting a committee to conduct a war has always been a debatable issue, especially when the committee lacks a sufficient administrative set-up to execute its orders. China's supreme defense conference, which ought to have confined itself to policy decisions, was rapidly inundated by the routine matters which it had taken over from the party's central political council. A prominent Chinese political scientist has listed some of the problems arising from this state of affairs:

"1. With the transfer of the nation's political center from Nanking to Hankow and thence to Chungking, Generalissimo Chiang could not always attend the conference in person. The vice-chairman, who acted for the generalissimo in his absence, was not always able to exercise his power.

"2. Owing to the number, the diversity, and the different viewpoints of the political, party, and military leaders, unity of outlook could not easily be reached, especially when the generalissimo was not there for the final decision. As a result the conference was rendered somewhat impotent.

"3. The conference agenda was swamped with routine matters which left less time for the deliberation of the major political and military issues."[11]

The result was that the overburdened conference unloaded more and more of its obligations on the military council, of which Chiang was likewise chairman. The military council was composed of men who were more than willing to buy power by accepting responsibility, but their appetites proved to be larger than their capacities and their actions resulted in the eventual breakdown of the military council's sprawling network of departments which we have described above.

On January 29, 1939, the supreme national defense council was created, designed to administer all the non-military aspects which the military council had been compelled to relinquish and replacing the national defense conference, although Chiang was once again chairman —this time as *tsung-ts'ai* or director-general of the party and not in his capacity as chairman of the military council, the basis for his chairmanship of the now-defunct conference.[12] If this account sounds con-

[10] Chen Chi-mai, *Chung-kuo cheng-fu, op.cit.,* pp. 117f.
[11] *Ibid.,* p. 119.
[12] Tsiang Ting-fu, "Reorganization of the National Government," *The Chinese Year Book, 1938-1939.*

fused, one may plead that Pooh-Bah and his many powers is called to mind by the list of the generalissimo's positions.

With the confining of the military council to strictly military affairs, a number of influential civilians entered into the civil administration and the party leadership in consultative and managerial positions. A number of leading political scientists (Drs. Tsiang Ting-fu, Ch'en Chi-mai, and Wang Shih-chieh) left their university posts to accept assignments in government. Dr. Hu Shih, acknowledged as one of China's foremost scholars, accepted the key diplomatic post as ambassador to the United States. Dr. Wang Ch'ung-hui, a prominent jurist, became secretary-general of the new supreme national defense council. Civilian officials like Drs. Wong Wen-hao, Chu Chia-hua, and Chang Chia-ngau rose to important offices. Despite the omnipresent and powerful influence of the generalissimo and the membership on the defense council of the chief of the supreme staff, the deputy chiefs, the heads of various military departments, and the chairman of the military advisory council, nevertheless the council served to lessen the military's domination of national affairs, and the party and administration representatives on the council were outspoken and influential.

It must be remembered, however, despite the increasing influence of civilian administrators and advisers, that the whole military structure pivoted on the generalissimo himself. Chiang, as chairman, held emergency power and still exercised the unified direction of all military, party, and governmental affairs. He was the supreme military commander, the director of the party, and (in effect) the head of the government. He was not called upon to adhere to any iron-bound procedures and he had the authority to issue any decree demanded by the situation and, to the detriment of the defense council (the highest governing body), he most often chose to act through the military council.

In certain aspects the supreme national defense council was not unlike the British war cabinet but even more closely resembled the Reichsverteidigungsrat, the Reich defense council of Nazi Germany, which was likewise the highest body of the state and designed to coordinate the three elements of the government: party, military, and administration.[13] Such structural features of the Chinese defense coun-

[13] Roger, Lindsay, "National Defense, Plan or Patchwork," *Foreign Affairs*, Oct. 1940.

cil as the central planning board bespoke the debt to Soviet organizational methods.

The military council, the chairmanship of which was Chiang's favorite post, was composed of a number of high military officials whose function was specified as assisting the chairman "in the planning of broad policies pertaining to national defense."[14] These full members of the military council must not be confused with the military counselors of the military advisory council or the civilian counselors of the military council, who were empowered only "to furnish advice in case it is needed by the chairman"; Chiang could call them into consultation or not, as he chose. The full members of the military council, however, had the power to force their advice upon the chairman, who had only "the authority to command" and who was reminded by the law that in matters of military policy and administration "the deciding power can be derived only through conference and may in no wise by subserved to dictatorial power."[15]

It might be imagined that in practice Chiang's forceful personality informally modified this regulation. Perhaps few persons could give a more qualified opinion regarding the inner operation of the military organization than General Ho Ying-ch'in, a member of the military council and chief of the supreme staff. In a lecture delivered at the Central Training Institute, Ho asserted that the members of the military council served in no more than an advisory capacity, that almost all major decisions rested with the generalissimo. In praising Chiang's interest in every detail and his tireless energy, Ho clearly implied that the generalissimo was responsible for most of the policy-making. An examination of the membership of the military council tends to confirm this judgment. Take, for an example, the composition of that body in the 1944-1945 period. There were at that time ten regular and six ex officio members (military officials holding key posts in the national military establishment).[16] Of the ten regular members, not one was a civilian and only one—an admiral, the commander-in-chief of the navy—was not an army man. More than half of the regular councilmen held commands in the field and were not normally in the wartime capital. The council included seven leaders of major politico-military groups, almost all of whom had, at one time or

[14] National Government of China, *The Organic Law of the National Government* revised, 1938.

[15] Wang Shi-chieh, *Pi-chiao hsien-fa* (Comparative Constitutional Laws), (Chungking ed., 1942), II, p. 224.

[16] The roster of the National Military Council.

another in the past, been on the opposite side of the fence from Chiang, but the councilmen whose duties normally required their residence in the capital were all ardent followers of Chiang. The few exceptions were the former leaders of military factions who had been pacified with the honor of membership on the council but, having relinquished their field commands, were now potential rather than actual threats. Of the ex-officio members of the council, practically all were trusted lieutenants of the generalissimo.

Membership in the military council was thus an honor roll of important military men—Chiang's friends and the opponents he had to pacify—created in the interests of national unity on the domestic scene. Something of a symbol of compromise, such a body might be deemed incapable of concerted action, but it has been said that the best system of governing is by means of a committee all of whose members, save one, are temporarily incapacitated, and the military council approached this ideal. Though Chiang headed a committee of both supporters and opponents, his supporters were generally on hand in the capital and his opponents were generally detained in the field. Under these circumstances, positive action could come only from the generalissimo. Chiang thereby enjoyed the most favored of all governing positions: that of the strong man who can arrive at policies on his own and then give them the blessing of collective responsibility.

Thus the self-reliant generalissimo stood at the top, and below him three broad command levels of the hierarchy were to be observed. The first of these was the military council which Chiang ran, whose policies he put into force or vetoed out of existence. Next, as an assistant to the generalissimo, was the chief of the supreme staff, Chiang's principal military aide. With the generalissimo, he represented the supreme command element and, in theory, was responsible for the coordination and direction of the over-all grand strategy recommended by the policy-making council. Beneath the supreme command level were the various echelons of central administrative departments, commanders-in-chief, and major fields commands. Responsible directly to the supreme command was a general strategic reserve force which consisted usually of ten full-strength army corps and certain special auxiliary units.

IV

Generalissimo Chiang once acknowledged that "the key to my

THE STATE IN ARMS

success lies in my employment of the chief-of-staff system."[17] It is true that as Chiang's power became greater and his duties became more pressing he shared his growing responsibilities with his lieutenants. The creation of the post of chief of the supreme staff was prompted by such motives. Let us consider precisely how much authority Chiang delegated, to whom it was entrusted, and how it was handled.

Although the German influence was considerable in Chinese military thinking, the Chinese conception of the chief-of-staff system differed radically from the German, the Chinese regarding the chief-of-staff not as an alter ego of the supreme commander but as his second in command.[18] When the first chief of the supreme command, Ho Ying-ch'in, was appointed, he was a man who for some time had been universally recognized as second in rank in Chiang's Whampoa hierarchy. Ho, a close friend of Chiang since the early days of Whampoa, had risen through numerous important positions to serve for a long time as minister of war, the post from which (though it had equipped him to deal with politico-administrative concerns more than with military strategy) he was elevated to the office of chief of the supreme staff. For assistants he was given two vice-chiefs, Generals Pai Chung-hsi and Cheng Ch'ien, who had commanded large and important forces in the field.

Pai was regarded both at home and abroad as a brilliant strategist and a highly skillful field commander. With Li Tsung-jen he had led the hard-fighting army of the Kwangsi in the northern expedition and in the resistance against Japan. Foreign military experts like Galen, von Falkenhausen, and even some top Japanese leaders had praised him for his contributions to China's major military victories. General Stilwell had strongly recommended that Pai be made chief of the supreme staff in 1944, but Pai was not one of the inner circle and he had also dared to countermand orders from above when he considered that the situation warranted it. Thus this distinguished soldier, whom Edgar Snow rated "one of the most intelligent and efficient commanders boasted by any army in the world,"[19] had to be content with a secondary role. Pai's colleague as vice-chief was General Cheng Ch'ien, appointed on the basis of the numerically impressive

[17] Chiang Kai-shek, *Hsin-cheng san-nien-chih* (Chungking, 1943), *passim*.
[18] von Seeckt, Hans, *Thoughts of a Soldier*, English trans. (London 1935), Introduction by Ian Hamilton.
[19] Snow, Edgar, *The Battle for Asia* (N.Y., 1940), p. 184.

Hunanese troops which he commanded. He did nothing of significance until he went over to the communist camp when the Red tide swept over China in 1949. He was regarded by Chiang's close friends even before that as a *fan-t'ung*, which literally means a "rice bucket," but which actually signifies something more like a ne'er-do-well.

Next to the chief of the supreme staff and his two deputies came the chief of the department of military operations, actually the general staff of the Chinese army. During the war the position was filled by General Hsu Yung-ch'ang, a principal figure in Yen Hsi-shan's Shansi army. A graduate of the army's staff college, Hsu had neither conspicuous talent nor personality, although he occupied a highly important office directly connected with the execution of war plans. He was but another example of China's wartime military rule, where group interests and the balance of internal military politics were chief concerns in the structure which the generalissimo created and supervised. Such an organization surely could not assert the kind of leadership requisite for the most effective prosecution of the war and, dominated by the generalissimo, both because of his power and personality and because of its own inherent weaknesses, it had to shoulder the responsibility for all mistakes even when these stemmed from the supreme commander's own judgment and decisions.

Closest to the generalissimo and potentially as powerful as any of the formal military offices was Chiang's own personal staff (*shih ts'ung shih*). It had a large though carefully selected personnel and an unusually fat budget, the full extent of which was never disclosed. It was literally the last court of military and governmental decisions and its staff of relatively young and well-trained officers, chosen by Chiang himself and not invariably based upon the official recommendations of the service chiefs, was unswervingly loyal to all the principles the generalissimo represented. Many of them had had the advantage of foreign study and most had received general staff training in their respective services, for the usual channels for reaching this inner circle were the Central Training Institute and post-graduate instruction in the National Defense College, similar in nature to the United States National War College or Britain's Imperial Defense College.

The functions of the generalissimo's personal military staff were varied. Its members did research on problems of current interest to Chiang and were available for consultation on a wide variety of military matters. Unlike aides de camp or the service aides to the American president, the generalissimo's personal staff was strictly a confidential and largely anonymous body which made few if any personal appearances. The chief of the office, usually a high-ranking general officer, carried out for the generalissimo a certain amount of confidential protocol functions, particularly in dealing with foreigners. General Lin Wei, in that office, for instance, was often delegated to deal with General Stilwell when he was serving as chief of staff to the supreme commander in the China theater.

The personal military staff was, of course, only part of the establishment. The entire organization had three departments and many bureaus.[20] In addition there was a crack regiment of personal guards, highly trained and afforded the best equipment available in China. Hitler was said to have presented Chiang with the weapons sufficient to arm an entire battalion of guards, and a German officer, Captain Stennes, served for a time as adviser to this group. The guards were entitled to receive military decorations, not for meritorious service in combat action, but on the basis of long-time loyalty and devoted service. As a sub-department there was a security division which took charge of intelligence, counter-espionage, and screening of all persons who had appointments with the generalissimo and of all materials intended to reach him.

A powerful department conducted all the government's top-level personnel management and, under the scrutiny of Ch'en Kuo-fu, one of Chiang's closest confidants, wielded great power. It was empowered to review all personnel appointments, promotions, rewards, and punishments in all governmental agencies, and for this purpose compiled and maintained an extensive and highly confidential file containing dossiers on the more important persons in all walks of life. It was a clearinghouse for information on all potential sources of danger and assistance.

A secretariat managed the regular duties of such an office and drafted speeches, public announcements, and directives for the generalissimo. The key figure here was Ch'en Pu-lei, a brilliant Kuomintang writer who was regarded by some as a member of the brain trust as well as Chiang's ghost-writer.

Very close to the personal staff, though created as an organ of the military council, was the office of the counselors, composed chiefly of political scientists and other scholars. This office conducted research,

[20] Chang Chi-yuen, *Tang-shih kai-yao*, op.cit., II, p. 913.

offered analyses, and gave advice on broad problems of constitutional, administrative, economic, and international significance. By virtue of its close affiliation with the generalissimo, it was exceedingly influential. Many of its activities overlapped those of formal government agencies, yet it was maintained despite a certain duplication of effort. On matters of foreign policy it at times outweighed the ministry of foreign affairs, yet it shouldered no responsibility.[21] This was but another example of the many cases where authority did not necessarily involve responsibility. The overlapping of functions was characteristic. Not only had the generalissimo provided himself with a government in microcosm in his personal staff, but the military council of which he was chairman also attempted to branch out from purely military matters to embrace many other concerns of the government. General Albert C. Wedemeyer, a man with a close working knowledge of the complex Chinese governmental machinery, once wrote: "There must be a streamlined organization and clear-cut enunciation of the duties of all the ministries and bureaus of the government. In April a year ago [1946] I discovered that there were well over sixty sections in the National Military Council with duplicating functions and conflicting authorities. There was little coordination between the various groups or sections. Actually there were some groups within the National Military Council that were handling matters which had nothing whatsoever to do with national defense matters. Today in the Ministry of Defense we have grouped sixty sections under six general heads and reduced the personnel about fifty per cent. Actually over 75,000 individuals were eliminated."[22]

V

In wartime China the basic field organization was this: the tactical unit was the division, the strategical unit the army corps. A wartime infantry division had a full strength of 10,000 men; two or three divisions together formed an army corps. The chain of command, however, was not so simple. It was complex and cumbersome in the early part of the war, as the diagram on page 127 indicates. Once again Chiang was at the top as commander-in-chief. He was assisted by the chief and vice-chiefs of the supreme staff and the department

[21] Chien Tuan-sheng, "The Role of the Military in Chinese Government," *Pacific Affairs*, XXI, 3 (Sept. 1948), pp. 239-251.
[22] U.S. Department of State, *United States Relations with China* (Washington: G.P.O., 1949), p. 760.

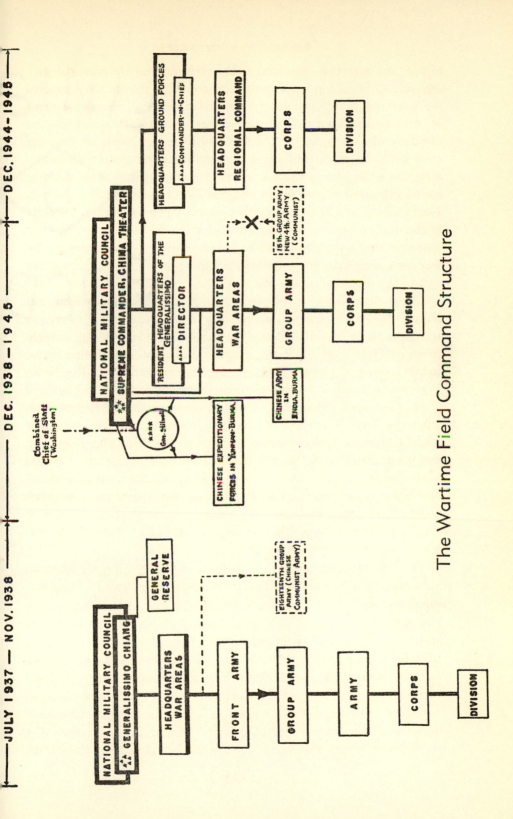

The Wartime Field Command Structure

of military operations (or, during the early days of the war, the general staff). The supreme command rested with the military council, the development of general operational plans with the department of military operations. When these were realized, the control and direction of the armies in the field were in the hands of regional commands or "war areas," major theaters of operations. In the beginning, the setting up of these war areas stemmed partly from political considerations; for instance, by the creation of the First War Area in North China and the transfer of General Cheng Ch'ien from chief of the general staff to the command of that area, the government at once removed a week strategist from the general staff and cleared the way for Cheng's deputy, General Pai Chung-hsi, to take a more active part in the direction of the war.

The commander of a war area theoretically exercised operational control over all troops in that locality. Thus General Li Tsung-jen was supreme in the Fifth War Area in which the victories of Tai-erh-chuang, Tsao-yang, northern Hopeh, and southern Honan were fought; General Hsueh Yueh directed the operations in the Ninth War Area, where the three victorious campaigns of Changsha took place; General Ch'en Ch'eng directed the defense of Hankow and, later, the Sixth War Area. From these names it will be noted that while Chiang may have rewarded a few deserving devotees with minor commands, these were in the less important areas; in the crucial places he posted men like the commanders we have mentioned, invariably battle-experienced soldiers of proven ability and integrity. Some of the most important war areas were assigned to leaders of the "non-Central" group (not direct followers of Chiang): Li Tsung-jen, Hsueh Yueh, Sun Lien-chung, and Fu Tso-yi.

The field organization of the early part of the war, largely German-influenced, displays certain Russian features. The Soviet Union was supplying military aid to China during the first three years of the war and it was not entirely coincidence that such terms as "front army," "route army," "rear area service" (familiar in the Red Army) were being employed by the Chinese forces. One thing the Chinese had been unable to copy successfully was the clear-cut chain of command and the mobility of the Soviet system. The Chinese chain of command (like the military council and supreme command we have discussed earlier) was elaborate, over-manned, and cumbersome. War soon demonstrated that some action must be taken to eliminate the unnecessary steps between the supreme command and the basic operational units. Responsibility was ill-defined, communication slow, and coordination tedious. An order had to pass through six separate offices between the general staff and the operational division which was to execute it.

When the first phase of the war came to an end, the military administration made an earnest effort to iron out the difficulties in the field organization. Conferences held at Changsha and Nanyo in November 1938 and the autumn of 1941 decided to reduce the number of steps in the chain of command to a minimum. Two intermediate units of the period of German-influence—the army group and the front army—were eliminated. The brigade was no longer the tactical unit; the division assumed this place. The corps became the strategical unit. China would no longer have continuous defense lines and would no longer risk the larger units which, being large, inflexible, and often poorly equipped, might be destroyed in a Japanese Cannae-type battle of annihilation. The new order stressed defense in depth and attack from all directions with small, mobile forces. The employment of concentrated masses in a power-drive frontal attack gave way to less orthodox strategies of speed and to guerrilla warfare. So long as the Japanese could not destroy the Chinese force en masse, the small and mobile Chinese units could continue a widespread and punishing war.

By 1944 the nine war areas of 1939 had increased to twelve. Indicative of the spread of the war and the Chinese plan to disperse and harass the Japanese force, the increased number of war areas produced an even greater need for coordination. For this purpose three field headquarters were created by the generalissimo at Kweiling, Han-chung, and T'ien-shui. These three new commands were awarded on the basis of seniority to high-ranking generals, though their power was not so great as might be imagined, for Chiang's conception of a field commander differed from the Western conception. Chiefly for reasons of expediency the generalissimo often chose to by-pass the normal chain of command by issuing orders directly to the lower echelons, ignoring or contradicting the field commanders.[23] The field commanders had the whole responsibility, but the generalissimo had the last word in authority. Although some of the most successful field commanders—Li Tsung-jen, Pai Chung-hsi, and Hsueh Yueh—had de-

[23] Stilwell, J. W., *The Stilwell Papers* (N.Y.: W. M. Sloane, 1948), p. 331.

vious ways of countering Chiang's interference, thus preserving the integrity of their own command, even so responsible a person as the chief of the supreme staff did not dare to displease the generalissimo. However, the areas which did the best fighting were those of the Fifth under Li Tsung-jen and the Ninth under Hsueh Yueh; both were commanders of outstanding coordinating ability and independent character. Chiang's arbitrary disregard for the chain of command and the rights of commanders grew until it reached the stage where the system of responsibility in the Chinese army was submerged under Chiang's personal authority. Councils at the highest echelons achieved coordination but usually met with the generalissimo to receive his decisions ready-made.

As American aid became an increasingly important factor in the military picture, Chinese field organization underwent a tightening process. In December 1944 a general headquarters of the Chinese ground forces was established at Kunming. Its purpose was to coordinate the equipping and training of ground troops, particularly the thirty-six divisions under the Alpha program, for the forthcoming Allied counteroffensive against the Japanese on the Chinese mainland. Four initial regional commands were set up under the general headquarters to prepare for the first offensive, code-named "Operation Rashness," and the whole organization of the American-trained and equipped forces was streamlined under General Wedemeyer's direction. Before more could be done, atom bombs fell on Japan and the imperial government announced to its people and to the world that it could no longer sustain the war. Aboard the battleship *Missouri* in Tokyo Bay, the representatives of the emperor signed the articles of surrender. It was V-J in Asia.

13 · THE PEOPLE IN ARMS: MANPOWER MOBILIZATION

⎯⎯⎯⎯⎯⎯⎯⎯⎯⎯⎯⎯⎯⎯⎯⎯⎯⎯⎯⎯⎯⎯⎯⎯⎯⎯⎯⎯⎯⎯⎯

THE PROBLEMS: I. CONSCRIPTION. II. MALNUTRITION
AND DISEASE. III. ILLITERACY. IV. *SSU SHOU*: DO OR DIE!
V. LEADERSHIP. VI. COMMANDERS.

⎯⎯⎯⎯⎯⎯⎯⎯⎯⎯⎯⎯⎯⎯⎯⎯⎯⎯⎯⎯⎯⎯⎯⎯⎯⎯⎯⎯⎯⎯⎯

I

FEW Western observers or even the Japanese enemy could understand how the motley crew of ragged, poorly equipped, largely illiterate, and underfed Chinese soldiers held at bay for such a long period
the heavily armed might of Imperial Japan. We have seen that the
answer did not lie in a smooth-working and clear-cut command system. Let us examine the important facts about the mobilization and
utilization of China's manpower.

The notion about China's inexhaustible manpower and the un-
limited hordes that she can put into the field is an inaccuracy dear to
the heart of every schoolboy. To begin with, there is a vast difference
between the size of a nation's population and her potential military
manpower. Although Voltaire observed that God is always on the side
of the largest battalions, he failed to note that superiority in numbers
is not an automatic guarantee of victory in modern technological warfare, and even Clausewitz qualified his reliance upon superior masses
by insisting on the proper time and place.[1] Geography, topography,
climatical conditions, mobility, and communications also enter the picture, of course.

About 1930, Dr. Chao Chi-ming conducted an investigation of
China's demographical problems.[2] Subsequently in 1946, Professor
Chen Ta published his *Population in Modern China*.[3] Chao's statistics
were:

[1] Clausewitz, Karl, *Vom Kriege*, trans. by J. J. Graham (London: Kegan Paul,
1918), p. 91.
[2] Chao Chi-ming, "A Study of the Chinese Population," *Milbank Memorial Fund
Quarterly Bulletin*, XI, 4 (Oct. 1933), Tables 6 and 10.
[3] Chen Ta, *Population in Modern China* (Chicago, 1946), Tables 5, 8 and 9.

PERCENTAGE OF AGE DISTRIBUTION

AGE BRACKET	*Male and Chao's*	*Female Chen's*	*Male*	*Female*
15-19	9.2		9.6	8.9
20-24	8.8	16.92	8.7	8.8
25-29	8.4		8.3	8.5
30-34	6.9	16.37	7.0	6.7
35-39	6.9		7.0	6.7
40-44	5.6	13.62	5.5	5.5
45-59	5.6		4.0	4.1

Ta Chen's figures are based on the Kunming Lake region

Male to Female Ratio

Chao's   109: 100
Chen's   106.77: 100   Highest
         95.67: 100   Lowest

If the male population of military age is computed from Chao's figures (that is, in the 18-45 bracket), it would be close to 90 million under China's wartime population of 450 million[4] or, one out of every five persons was of military age. This ratio agreed fairly well with another computation wherein Chen's figures were used.

A wartime survey of thirteen army conscription districts, containing about 340,430,000 persons in all, was used as the basis of General Ho Ying-ch'in's estimate, as wartime chief of the supreme staff, that around 1940 Free China had 50 million men of military age.[5] Another source for an estimate are the vital statistics of the province of Szechuan, whose population was 49,948,943 in 1939.[6] This single province had 8 million men of military age or, as in the previous case, roughly one out of every six persons. This would mean that China had a war potential of 75 million. The great discrepancy between these figures and the results of the survey summarized above in the table is indicative of the lack of dependable population statistics for China.

[4] *China Handbook, 1937-1945*, p. 2. This figure is a compromise of a number of estimates on China's population. Chen Ta's estimate is 400 million; George B. Cressey in his *Asia's Lands and People* (N.Y.: McGraw-Hill, 1944), p. 44, gives the best available figure as 472,580,216. In 1954, the Chinese communist government stated that China had a population of 600 million.

[5] National Military Council, *K'an-ch'ang-ssu-nien* (Four Years of Resistance), (Chungking, 1941), p. 146.

[6] Chen Yu-pei, *Chün-shih tsa-chih* (Chinese Journal of Military Affairs), No. 116 (Aug. 1939), pp. 120-130.

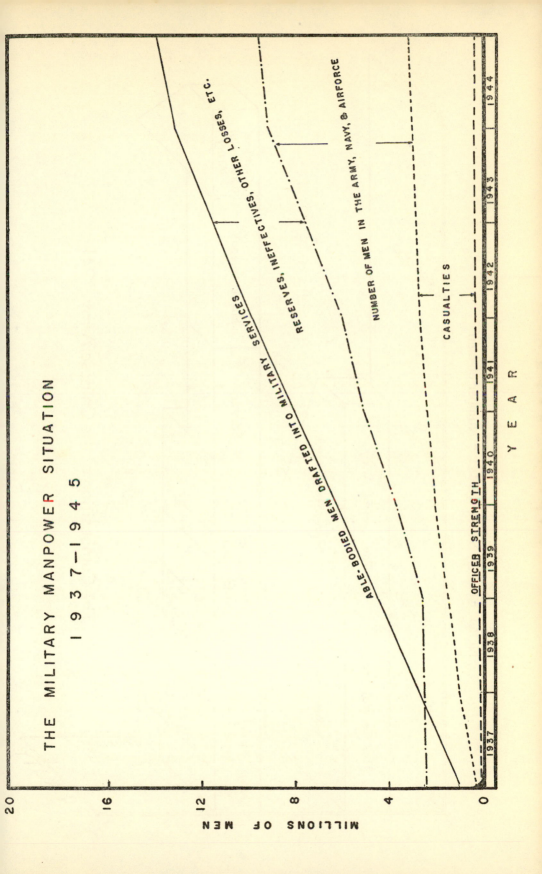

THE MILITARY MANPOWER SITUATION
1937—1945

ABLE-BODIED MEN DRAFTED INTO MILITARY SERVICES

RESERVES, INEFFECTIVES, OTHER LOSSES, ETC.

NUMBER OF MEN IN THE ARMY, NAVY, & AIRFORCE

OFFICER STRENGTH

CASUALTIES

YEAR

1937 1938 1939 1940 1941 1942 1943 1944

MILLIONS OF MEN

0   4   8   12   16   20

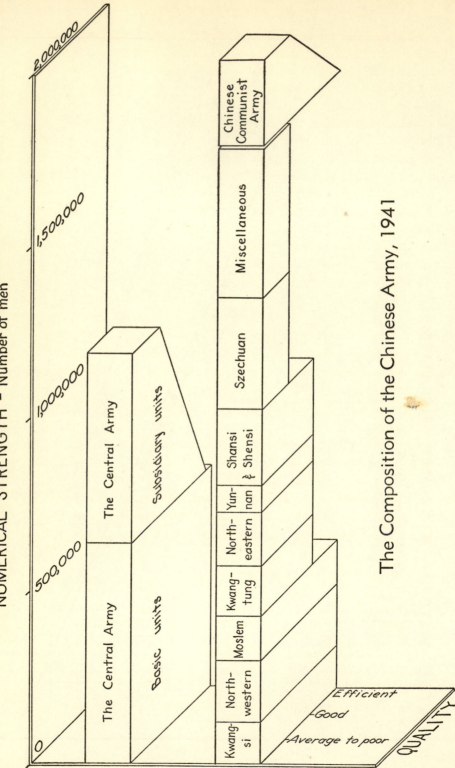

NUMERICAL STRENGTH – Number of men

2,000,000

1,500,000

1,000,000

500,000

0

The Central Army
Subsidiary units

The Central Army
Basic units

Chinese Communist Army

Miscellaneous

Szechuan

Shansi & Shensi

Yun-nan

North-eastern

Kwang-tung

Moslem

North-western

Kwang-si

Efficient
Good
Average to poor

QUALITY

The Composition of the Chinese Army, 1941

Whatever the number China had to draw upon, the strength of the actual army is known. After the outbreak of the war in 1937 the government built up its forces from a standing army of 1,700,000 regulars and 518,400 reservists.[7] The Japanese, taking into account the conscripts trained in 1936-1937, estimated that China's forces at this period numbered 2.27 million.[8] The initial stage of the war meant heavy casualties for the Chinese, and her forces sank to a low of one million before the upswing was felt. By 1941 the Chinese claimed to have 5.7 million under arms, with approximately 3 million effective front-line strength. The military reorganization of 1945, near the end of the war, set up the objective of maintaining an active force of 3.5 million. However, if needed, as General Pai Chung-hsi once stated, wartime China could put 15 million soldiers into the field to defend the nation.[9]

To maintain her wartime force, the Chinese government drafted a total of 14,053,988 men between 1937 and 1945.[10] The conscription policy called for one soldier from each *chia*, a group of from six to fifteen families. During the later stage of the war, drafting was based on a conscription ratio of one-half to one per cent of the population. The government planned to induct from 2.25 to 4.5 million each year into military service. The table on page 136 will indicate how China fell behind the other leading powers of World War II in mobilization of manpower.[11]

Two of the reasons for China's failure to reach her full mobilization were the inefficiency of her war machinery and the restrictions imposed by the limitations of her industrial capacity.

China's casualties were enormous, yet when it came to providing the necessary replacements she astonished the Japanese general staff. Such a responsible high commander as Field Marshal Count Hisachi

---

[7] National Military Council, *The National Troop Return of War Years*.

[8] *Japan Year Book, 1940-1941*, p. 1001.

[9] Pai Chung-hsi, "Statement to Foreign Correspondents at Hsuchow," quoted in *Far Eastern Mirror Fortnightly*, I, 6 (May 25, 1938), p. 8.

[10] Ministry of Defense source, quoted in *China Handbook*, 1950.

[11] A number of statistical sources have been consulted in the compilation of this table: U.S. War Department, *Biennial Report of the Chief of Staff July 1943 to June 1945* (Washington, 1945), p. 101. (a) Chen Ta, *Population in Modern China, op.cit., passim.* (b) The United States Strategic Bombing Survey, *The Effect of Strategic Bombing on Japan's War Economy* (Washington, 1946), Appendices A, B, C, on "Overall Economic Effect Division." (c) Minobe, Ryokichi, *Nippon keizai zusetsu, 1949* (Tokyo, 1950), p. 54. (d) 550 divisions computed on a basis of 11,000 men per division. (e) Figure was given at the end of 1944, *Encyclopedia Britannica*, Supplement 1946.

Country	Population	Manpower Mobilized for Military Service		Mobili-zation Index (%)**	Strength of Armed Forces (million men)***
China	450,000,000(a)*	14,054,000	July '37–Sept. '45	0.4	5.7
Japan	77,045,000(b)	8,040,000(c)		1.3	3.98(b)
U.K.	141,700,000	12,000,000	Sept. '39–Sept. '45	1.4	
U.S.	156,687,000	14,000,000	Dec. '41–Sept. '45	2.4	8.3
U.S.S.R.	170,467,000	22,000,000	July '41–Sept. '45	3.0	6.0(d)
Germany	79,530,000	17,000,000	Sept. '39–May '45	3.8	6.0(e)

* The Communist Peking Government's claim for China's population is 650,000,000. This figure is used in the above table.

** The "Mobilization Index" shown above is the average number of men mobilized per year expressed as a percentage of the total population.

*** The "Strength of Armed Forces" shown above indicates the maximum reported, or estimated strength of the nation's armed forces at any time. In a few cases, such maximum strength figures were unobtainable at the time of compiling the above table, and the figures given (particularly in the case of the U.S.S.R.) may not be the maximum strength of those nations throughout their war period.

Terauchi thought that severe losses would knock China out of the war. Despite her tremendous losses, China continued to fill the gaps in her lines, though the front-line replacement rate sometimes soared to 120 per cent annually and never fell below 60 per cent.[12] It became obvious that, if her armies could avoid "total destruction" in the Clausewitz usage of the term, China was prepared to absorb shocking losses and to continue the war as long as the material situation was tolerable, providing that the administration could retain the support of the people.

The official returns of the Chinese army from 1937 to 1945 record a total of 3,211,419 casualties in the armed forces.[13] Since a total of 14 million were drafted during this period, these figures mean that roughly 1 out of every 4 men became a casualty. At the peak of her strength, according to the 1941 claim of an army of 5.7 million, China had to draft between 2.5 and 4 men for every soldier who was to be kept at the front. These figures reflect the high percentage of wounded, sick, and replaced men, and the mismanagement of manpower by the military administration. Had China mobilized the 50 million suggested by the general staff, the efficiency of her front-line troops (in that case some 20 million) would have been much lower.

One significant limiting factor was the problem of training. When

[12] Japanese War Ministry figure quoted in *Saishin Toa Yoran, 1943*.
[13] *China Handbook, 1950*, p. 182.

the war broke out in 1937 China's experience with training conscripts was a short one. The experiment had begun in 1936 and, by the end of that year, about half a million men had been processed. During the eight war years China trained some 12 million, or about an average of 1.5 million annually. This training rate, however, was barely sufficient to enable her troops to meet the demands of modern war, and the management of her conscription system was shockingly inadequate. It is more than reasonable to assume that greater numbers would have been afforded even less efficient training, that an increase quantitatively would have meant a disastrous drop in quality.

In addition, the Chinese system of conscription was not entirely fair and impartial. In innumerable cases the well-to-do classes were afforded opportunities to circumvent the conscription law, and the burden of military service was shouldered almost exclusively by the underprivileged peasants. China could not catch the rich or afford to spare the industrially trained for military service. Her draftees were chiefly from the lowest classes, and they were often treated as military coolies. Many conscripts had to walk hundreds of miles to join their units—the replacements for the Szechuanese army, stationed in the coastal area, had to march for months from their conscription districts —and suffered from lack of food, shelter, warm clothing, and medical attention. It is not surprising that thousands upon thousands were lost, through desertion or death, before they could reach their units. General Stilwell found that in 1943 only 56 per cent of all recruits reached their assigned units. The rest died or "went over the hill" on the way.[14] That year the conscription board reported having drafted 1.67 million.[15] If these estimates are correct, almost three quarters of a million recruits were lost in this way—a factor which could not but affect the military situation adversely in 1944 and 1945. The Japanese general staff had its own estimate of the loss of Chinese manpower, stating that in 1940 and 1941 desertions from the Chinese forces amounted to 10 per cent of her total strength.[16]

Those who did not desert were treated poorly. The following incident occurred around 1944. Generalissimo Chiang learned from his elder son, Chiang Ching-kuo, that at a certain place a number of recruits had committed suicide while locked in their barracks. The generalissimo summoned the chief of the conscription board and went

[14] Stilwell, J. W., *The Stilwell Papers, op.cit.*
[15] *China Handbook, 1950*, Section on Military Affairs, p. 185.
[16] *Saishin Toa Yoran, 1943, op.cit.*, p. 182.

to inspect the situation himself. Upon discovering the unbearable conditions under which the conscripts lived without attention and died without care, the generalissimo broke down and wept. In great fury he attacked the chief of the conscription board, beating him with his cane and shouting, "You are murdering my soldiers!" He ordered the death penalty on the spot for the recruiting officer responsible for the mistreatment.

Chiang was convinced that a reform of the conscription system was imperative. Upon American advice he ordered the establishment of the ministry of conscription in November 1944, a body which was to assume responsibility for the recruit in both training and transfer. A number of hospitals and clinics were set up to care for the health and medical needs of conscripts. Finally, barracks and rest stations were built along the highways and routes along which replacements moved to the front lines. The Americans made arrangements for the air transport of those American-trained troops and replacements destined for such areas as the Burma theater of operations. The lot of the common soldier was vastly improved.

II

Malnutrition, disease, and epidemic are factors as important in war as enemy guns. No modern soldier suffered more from these enemies than the Chinese soldier.

The diet of the average Chinese home is adequate in calories but deficient in animal protein, vitamins, and certain essential salts. During wartime the soldiery could not dream of reaching even the usual standard. All they had was rice, a few vegetables, and more rice. Between 1939 and 1941 the average college student in Kunming, Chengtu, and Chungking consumed individually no more than 50 to 60 grams of protein per day, of which from 5 to 10 grams were of animal origin.[17] These college students were of a socially privileged class; the soldiers undoubtedly fared much worse. The average Chinese soldier ate meat only once or twice a month.

Prolonged malnutrition rendered the soldiers acutely susceptible to xerophthalmia, trachoma, skin infections of all sorts, parasitic infections, and anemia. Experiments proved that these debilitated men, after three months of adequate food, visibly improved in mental per-

[17] Tsia Chiao, "Problems of Nutrition in Present Day China," *Voices from Unoccupied China* (Chicago, 1943), p. 17.

formance and physical strength and endurance.[18] The Chinese health and medical officers repeatedly urged the military authorities to take action to improve the diet of the common soldier, but little amelioration was felt until the Americans entered the picture.

Meanwhile the men fell easy prey to epidemic and disease, and there were few regularly trained medical men and few drugs and facilities available to care for them. By minimum modern standards an army the size of the Chinese wartime forces needed 30,000 doctors.[19] Dr. Chang Chien, China's wartime superintendent of the Army Medical College, once estimated that even prior to the war the army required 8,000 medical officers, 30 per cent of whom should be well-trained doctors over the rank of major. In 1936 the army had only half that number, and the top 30 per cent were chiefly graduates of the Army Medical College—a school none too respected by the Chinese medical profession.[20] In 1937 the war found China with only 7 per cent of her medical corps—about 2,000 officers—qualified medical men, the rest having only scant training in orderly work or practical nursing.[21] It was not until 1940 that the nation began to draft medical personnel. Between 1940 and 1944 she drafted only 791 doctors.[22] By the postwar year 1948-1949, China had still not reached her modest goal for the medical corps, for only 2,700 doctors were in her ranks.[23]

According to one of the leaders of China's medical profession, Dr. Lim Ko-sheng, of the 10,000 registered doctors in wartime China no more than 2,000 could meet Western standards of competence.[24] Postwar statistics of the Chinese medical association at its second national congress reported a membership of less than 22,500 doctors—only a tenth of the minimum requirement set by the government's five-year medical plan. The rate of training in the profession in the postwar year of 1947 may be seen in the following table:[25]

[18] Liu, J. Heng, "The Origin and Development of Public Service in China," *Voices from Unoccupied China, op.cit.,* pp. 40-45.

[19] *China Handbook, 1950,* "Section on Military Affairs," p. 199.

[20] Chang Chien, "On the Army's Medical Services," *Chün-shih tsa chih,* No. 120 (Dec. 31, 1939), p. 55.

[21] *Ibid.*

[22] *China Handbook, 1937-1945,* p. 499.

[23] *Ibid.*

[24] Interview with Dr. Lim Ko-sheng on medical conditions in wartime China. Dr. Lim was a prominent wartime medical figure of the Chinese Red Cross. He also served as surgeon general of the army during the postwar period.

[25] Chinese Ministry of Education source. *National Reconstruction Journal,* VI, 3 (Jan. 1946), p. 6.

MEDICAL SCHOOLS	NUMBER OF GRADUATES			YEARLY AVERAGE
	1936-1945	*1945*	*Total*	
42 medical colleges	5,119	976	6,095	555 doctors
6 dental colleges	167	17	194	17 dentists
11 pharmacist schools			713	65 pharmacists
1 army medical center	(established 1947)			500 medical officers (projected)
1 army medical college				50-60 medical officers

That rate of output meant that, by Western standards, China would have to wait until 1970 before there could be a doctor for every 2,000 persons.[26] During World War II the United States Army alone had 45,000 doctors in its service, assisted by an equal number of nurses and by half a million trained first-aid men and medical orderlies.[27] Little wonder that the Americans were taken aback by the deplorable health conditions of the Chinese forces! American aid raised the health standards of Chinese soldiers fighting in India and Burma with, to the Chinese, an astonishing abundance of medical supplies. In the Salween campaigns American-manned hospitals took in more than 15,000 casualties from the 100,000-man Chinese expeditionary force involved. Thanks largely to American aid, only 5 per cent of these cases died, and only 2,000 died from other than battle wounds, despite the malaria-ridden battle area.[28] The Americans were instrumental in creating the program of medical aid under which Dr. Robert K. S. Lim organized emergency training schools to train thousands of medical assistants in elementary nursing, surgery, and dietetics.

During the war all kinds of medical men were in great demand. Many of the 600,000 Chinese "herb doctors" put themselves and their ancient recipes at the service of the troops and, despite the scoffing of Western medical men at their traditional remedies, proved psychologically helpful and valuable in treating many sorts of internal diseases.[29] In surgery, of course, they could be of little assistance.

Along with the acute shortage of trained medical men went a critical

[26] Under the Chinese communist regime, Li Teh-chuan, minister of health of the Peking government, stated that since the communists came to power, 11,000 doctors had been graduated in China (presumably from 1949 to August 1954) and that by 1957 there will be at least 40,000 highly trained medical men. Ridley, John, "China Revisited: Changes of Eight Years," *The New York Times Magazine*, Aug. 29, 1954, p. 5.

[27] U.S. War Department, *Biennial Report of the Chief of Staff, July 1943 to June 30, 1945* (Washington, U.S. News publication), p. 108.

[28] Chow, F., "The Salween Campaign," *China at War*, xv, 1 (July 1945), p. 58f.

[29] Chu, C. K., "The Modern Public Health Movement in China," *Voices from Unoccupied China, op.cit.*, p. 32.

shortage of all types of pharmaceutical and surgical supplies. Plasma, whole blood, penicillin, and sulfa drugs were largely unobtainable. Even quinine and aspirin were luxuries. Seldom did supplies permit every wounded soldier to receive a dose of antitoxin. When the Chinese troops retreated inland, drugs became even scarcer, and were precious items in the trading market. A single sulfa pill would cost a soldier his entire salary for several months. All the Chinese army pharmaceutical plants, plus all the private factories under government contract, together produced a mere 10,580 tons of medical supplies during the whole period of the war.[30] A small American chemical manufacturer could easily have surpassed that total many times.

The impact of these shortages of men and materials was stupendous, and the deplorable health conditions were reflected in the broad manpower picture. For example, when replacements were sent for the American training program at Ramgarh in 1943, out of 1,800 Chinese recruits as many as 68 per cent were rejected on physical grounds.[31] In 1945, medical examination eliminated some 23,000 men, or 37.3 per cent of the 60,000 hand-picked force which the generalissimo had placed at the disposal of General Wedemeyer.[32] In another case, out of 200 men earmarked for the Ramgarh program, 65 were rejected by Chinese doctors, and 30 more by the American doctors, who could pass only 105 or a bare 52.5 per cent of the whole.[33] The data compiled after the war revealed that by American standards only about 30 per cent of the Chinese wartime conscripts would be regarded as fit to fight.

III

In the present technological age, military efficiency depends in large part on the general educational level and degree of literacy of the people. The era of brute force is gone, and the age of refined, expensive, and extensive killing has arrived. Alexander the Great conquered at the rate of a very few cents a life, but modern nations require a great many dollars for each enemy casualty. The difference lies in the complex machinery of modern war, which requires a number of special technical skills. Despite the resourcefulness and native intelligence of the Chinese people, great technical proficiency in her forces was checked by illiteracy.

[30] *China Handbook, 1938-1945*, p. 290.
[31] *The Stilwell Papers, op.cit.*, p. 209.
[32] *Collier's*, July 7, 1945.   [33] *The Stilwell Papers, op.cit.*, p. 213.

Modern China has made many efforts to combat illiteracy among her people. Progress has by no means been slight: during two decades of its regime the Nationalist Government claimed to have decreased illiteracy by almost 20 per cent.[34] Although we must view this estimate with some suspicion, here are the official figures on Chinese literacy:[35]

Year	Percentage of Literates in the Population
1925	20.0
1937	23.42
1943	30.34
1944	44.90
1945	48.94

As for the literacy rate among the troops, we have the results of several surveys. In the early 1920's Dr. James Yen conducted an investigation among the soldiers of the notoriously illiterate Manchurian armies. Yen found that on the average about 25 out of every 150 soldiers could read and write—16.7 per cent.[36] Then around 1930 Professor Tao Meng-ho of the Academia Sinica conducted a survey that revealed that only 13 per cent of the soldiers polled could write letters: 87 per cent could neither read nor write.[37] Compare these figures with those of the American forces during World War II. The United States Army inducted 400,000 illiterates, a figure which will surprise a great many Americans.[38] Although this figure represented only about 2.9 per cent of the drafted manpower, it caused considerable alarm among some American authorities. The Chinese army, by dint of great effort, had reduced its illiteracy from 70 to 30 per cent. Some units, such as the Training Brigade, took pride in having only 10 per cent illiterate. All units of the Nationalist Army held training classes to teach reading, writing, arithmetic, and political indoctrination, though the system was rather like the Soviet scheme of political education and involved no professional educational method comparable, say, to the British army educational corps.

Illiteracy meant fewer men to handle highly technical weapons of

[34] "Chinese Government Memorandum to Lt. General A. C. Wedemeyer, Sept. 1947," Annex 137, *U.S. Relations with China, op.cit.*, p. 821.

[35] Han Li-wu, *The China Magazine* (Dec. 1948), p. 14.

[36] Yen, James Y. C., *The Mass Education Movement in China* (Shanghai: Commercial Press, 1925), p. 15.

[37] Tao Meng-ho, *Quarterly Review of the Institute of Social Science, Academia Sinica* (July 1930), pp. 92-115.

[38] *New York Times* (Dec. 13, 1950), p. 21.

war and more dependence upon oral instructions—a greater officer-to-enlisted-man ratio. In addition to raising the literacy rate of her armies, China also had to call upon the educated youth of the country to shoulder arms. In 1944 a great many educated young men, including students and faculty members from institutions of higher learning, volunteered for military service and bettered the government's goal of 100,000 by 50 per cent.[39] By early 1945, there were 43,000 of these men training, with many thousands more waiting their turn. Girl students also volunteered and were organized into a women's army corps (starting with an initial force of 2,811) to assume medical, political, and clerical duties in the armed forces.[40] China had for the first time summoned her social elite—the educated class—to bear arms in the nation's service.

IV

Statistics quoted previously indicate that during China's bitter eight-year struggle approximately one out of every four conscripts was a casualty. China's huge losses were not entirely unrelated to her basic strategical concepts. From the beginning the keynote of the war was one of sacrifice. "Only a determination to sacrifice ourselves to the utmost can bring us ultimate victory,"[41] the generalissimo had declared. Catchwords of the army express the philosophy that produced those fanatical mass charges: *Ssu-shou* (Defend to the death), *Yü-chen-ti-kung ts'un-wang* (Live or die with the defense position), *Hsi-sheng tao-ti* (Sacrifice to the last).

From von Falkenhausen to Stilwell, not one Western military adviser had failed to criticize China's overindulgence in the "do-or-die" concept. Numerous Chinese commanders also argued against this creed, but it had its supporters, as it always has had in every country. The United States saw manifestations of the same sort of reckless courage, especially in the Marine Corps, and applauded it as heroism. In China, during the Shanghai and Nanking campaigns of 1937, this do-or-die attitude in the face of overwhelmingly superior forces cost the Chinese some of their most valuable and best-trained troops, troops who could have been withdrawn in the face of hopeless odds and saved for some later defense of the defensible. Hundreds of thousands died to make the point that China was ready to sacrifice.

[39] *China Handbook, 1937-1945*, pp. 287-288.   [40] *Ibid.*
[41] Chiang Kai-shek, "Limit of China's Endurance," *op.cit.*, I, p. 22.

Generalissimo Chiang once related to General Stilwell his idea behind the strategy of the battle of Chengchow. One division was deployed near Chengchow with orders to stand to the last man. Two other divisions were then withdrawn some fifty miles to the rear. The Japanese attacked in force and annihilated the single division which stood its ground—but then they advanced no farther. This, said Chiang, was a matter of psychology: the Japanese were so impressed by the determined defense of the one division they wiped out that they did not advance upon the other two. Chiang considered that he had stopped the Japanese advance at the cost of only one-third of his force.[42] In another situation, namely the forty-seven-day Chinese defense of Henyang in August 1944, more than 15,000 of the 16,275 defenders perished, exacting some 20,000 Japanese casualties.[43] To Occidentals this type of warfare generally seems incomprehensible when it involves their own troops, though it is admired from a distance: the charge of the Light Brigade at Balaclava, the heroic American stand at the Alamo against the Mexicans, the equally heroic stand at Chapultapeque by the Mexicans during the American invasion of Mexico, and so on. The battleflags of British regiments bear many honors recording courageous and costly stands. Yet the Japanese, committing hara-kiri after losing some engagement, or the Chinese and even the Russians, charging wildly into the cannon's mouth and over the mine fields to their utter destruction, sometimes seem less comprehensible to Westerners, who generally prefer George Bernard Shaw's more thoughtful strategy: "Soldiering, my dear madam, is the coward's art of attacking mercilessly when you are strong, and keeping out of harm's way when you are weak."

Orientals are prone to regard human losses as renewable, materials as harder to come by. They will trade not only space but human lives for time and enemy weariness. Western military thinkers do not generally undertake to gamble human lives against enemy superiority in manpower or material. They wait until they have the upper hand. They do not take chances if they can help it. Listen to Montgomery of Alamein: "I am not a bit anxious about my battles. If I am anxious I don't fight them. I wait until I am ready."[44]

[42] *The Stilwell Papers, op.cit.*, p. 66.
[43] Chao, S. M., "The Eighth War Year in Review," *China at War*, xv, 1 (July 1945), p. 2.
[44] Montgomery, Bernard Law, quoted in British Information Bulletin, *British Commanders*, 1945.

The Chinese strategy was of necessity different. It cost them an average of 23 per cent of all the able-bodied men drafted in the eight years of war:[45]

CHINESE BATTLE CASUALTIES

Year	Japanese Estimates	Chinese Estimates
1937		367,362 (July-Dec.)
1938	823,296 (July 1937 to Nov.1938)	735,017
1939	395,166	346,543
1940	847,000	
1941	708,000	299,483
1942		247,167
1943		162,895
1944		210,734
1945		168,850

Few other nations could have withstood losses of such magnitude year after year. The battles of 1940 alone cost the Chinese 28 per cent of their forces. In the Shanghai campaign the Chinese paid with ten of her own for every Japanese casualty. (This ratio was reduced to three to one in the later part of the war.) Chinese losses in equipment caused their losses in men to mount even higher. When well-equipped and adequately trained, as in the Northern Burma campaign of 1944, they were able to make the Japanese pay ten to one.[46] The death-stand attitude had far-reaching and unfortunate ramifications: it tended to de-emphasize training, and it exacted material losses that made further stands more and more expensive. It terrified troops and led to more desertions. To some extent great sacrifices were demanded of the Chinese—sacrifices they could not escape with honor, and they met them with courage—but the unwarranted sacrifices resulting from overemphasis on the do-or-die philosophy proved to be unintelligent and inadvisable. The attitude of "Liberty's in every blow! Let us do or die,"[47] must be tempered by some consideration of the necessity of discretion in valor and the efficacy of living to fight another day.

V

A nation's military manpower may be large, but it cannot be strong if its leadership is weak. There is a direct correlation between the

[45] Table compiled from data contained in: "Statement of the Japanese War Ministry," quoted from *Tokyo Gazette*, III, 1 (March 1940), pp. 391-393. *Saishin Shina Yoran, op.cit.*, p. 383. *China Handbook, 1950*
[46] *Stilwell Papers, op.cit.*, p. 304.   [47] *Scots, Wha Hae*, Robert Burns.

caliber of an armed force's commissioned and non-commissioned officers and its effectiveness.

In 1930, not long after the culmination of the northern expedition, a highly illuminating statistical study of the personnel in the new Nationalist Government central military establishment revealed these facts:[48]

THE EDUCATIONAL BACKGROUND OF CHINESE ARMY OFFICERS
(1930)

Education Received	General	Lt. Gen. to Maj. Gen.	Colonel to Major	Captain to 2nd Lt.
		Percentage (%)		
Regular military academies	—	16.02	24.41	11.50
Auxiliary military academies	—	11.17	12.93	17.06
Other military schools	16.67	8.25	14.21	13.75
Returned students from foreign countries	66.67	39.32	14.02	1.81
From the ranks	—	—	.18	2.12
Staff college	—	14.56	3.10	.31
Non-military schools	—	6.32	29.51	47.06
Unknown	16.66	4.37	1.64	6.38
Percentage of total	100.00	100.00	100.00	100.00
Number of persons in the sample	6	206	549	1600

One immediately notices the heterogeneity of qualifications at all levels and the scarcity of well-trained officers in positions of high responsibility. At the general officer level 70 per cent had not been graduated from the regular military academies.

At the time of the 1937-1945 war approximately the same group occupied the top positions in the military or had been entrusted with high offices in the civil administration—the governorships of provinces, for example. In the interim very few had received any further formal education; most had left such schooling twenty or thirty years behind. In a period of rapid progress in military science, men on the top level were compelled to cope with the complexities of modern war equipped with whatever learning they had acquired a score of years back, plus whatever experience might have taught them. China's case had been, at the beginning of her revolution, closely akin to that in

[48] Lin, Peter Wei, "A Statistical Study of Personnel of Chinese National Government," *XIX.e Session de Institute International de Statistique* (Shanghai, 1930), Table VIII.

which Russia, on a similar occasion, had found herself. In contra-distinction to China, however, Russia's educational standards for of-ficers soared after the revolutionary days, as White tells us, and Guil-laume recorded that Red Army officers spent half of their military careers in schools of various sorts.[49]

In the middle and lower ranks of China's officers corps matters were not bad. She had trained about 2,000 general staff officers between 1929 and 1937, the Central Military Academy turning out well-trained junior officers at the rate of about 3,000 a year. Generalissimo Chiang's initial goal was to build up an officer corps of somewhere near 170,000 men, the bulk of them being provided by the military academy and other military schools.[50] The Japanese saw clearly the threat that this plan offered and took whatever steps they could (in-cluding posting Japanese intelligence agents, who posed as Chinese cadets, within the academy) to learn the details of the plan and dis-rupt it. The Japanese feared the qualitative improvement of the Chinese forces, which this officer-training program would ensure, more than they did the quantitative development of China's consolidating armies. When the Japanese commenced the full-scale war in 1937, China had 90,000 soundly trained officers.

The outbreak of war caught China with only 40 newly adjusted divisions—300,000 men. About 80,000 of these were first-rate fight-ing troops equipped with German-made weapons.[51] Most of these (about three-fifths) were deployed around Shanghai and Nanking, the backbone of the 450,000-man force ordered to make a death stand in defense of that area. In this untenable position, 60 per cent of the total strength was lost and the casualties among the junior officers were particularly high.[52] In a single blow China lost 10,000 junior officers and many hundreds of thousands of her best troops, potential junior officers. For many months thereafter the Central Army felt the lack of leadership and the weakness of her green replacements, as well as the virtually irreparable loss of much valuable foreign-made equip-ment. Of all the losses which this ill-calculated stand had effected, the

[49] Guillaume, A., *Soviet Arms and Soviet Power*, op.cit., p. 106; also compare White, D. Fedotoff, *The Growth of the Red Army* (Princeton, 1943), pp. 367-374.
[50] Central Military Academy, *Document 34 June 1936*, Nanking, 1936.
[51] Chennault, *Ways of a Fighter*, op.cit., p. 40.
[52] Tsao Chü-jen and Shu Tsung-chiao, *K'an-chang hua-shih* (Pictorial History of China's War of Resistance), (Shanghai, 1946), pp. 107, 120.

loss in one battle of 10 per cent of the officer corps which China had taken nearly ten years to train was the greatest.

This setback forced China to replace her losses as soon as possible, and an accelerated program to train officers on a large scale was immediately put into effect. Under the veteran general, Pai Chung-hsi, chief of military training, 190,000 officers were trained during the war years.[53] China's wartime officer strength was estimated by the Japanese at roughly 180,000 men.[54] To maintain this strength in the face of heavy casualties (perhaps overestimated by the Japanese at 54,000 officers annually) the training schools of wartime China graduated between 42,000 and 43,000 officer cadets each year, while 12,000 junior officers were commissioned each year from the ranks.[55]

Between 1929 and 1944 the Whampoa and Central Military Academies graduated a total of 146,449 cadets in 19 classes, an average of about 7,700 a class. The refresher and advanced courses offered by the Central Military Academy and its branches trained a total of 86,236 student officers in the same period. When these statistics were officially released in the early months of 1945, the regular academy courses and the advanced courses had enrollments of 18,715 and 1,246 respectively.[56] In 1945 these cadets were organized into 15 cadet brigades, and in previous years into 32 cadet brigades.[57] In that peak war year the schools mentioned, plus the special service schools, training classes, and training centers, turned out 47,289 graduates, well above the average annual wartime output of 25,000 junior officers. In the twenty years between 1924 and 1944 the Nationalist Army trained, in academies and elsewhere, a total of 280,000 officers.

During the years immediately preceding the war, the students in higher educational institutions received compulsory military training and engaged in summer maneuvers in conjunction with regular army units. On the eve of war, 18,000 students had received this training, but less than 1,000 college students were fully qualified to receive reserve commissions.[58] The Chinese army was essentially a career army, and not much thought had been given to reservists—until war

[53] *Chung-kuo tăng-tăi ming-jen-chuan* (Biographies of Famous Persons of China), (Shanghai, 1947), Biography of General Pai Chung-hsi.
[54] *Saishin Shina Yoran*, *1943*, *op.cit.*, p. 382.
[55] *Ibid.*
[56] *China Handbook, 1937-1945*, section on military education, p. 288.
[57] Pai Chung-hsi, "Lecture Delivered at the Army Staff College on Modern Military Education" (Shanghai: International Publisher, 1946), p. 10.
[58] Tsao and Shu, *op.cit.*, p. 85.

broke out. By 1944, in 1,132 institutions of learning, 175,028 students were receiving military training.[59] Compare these figures with those of the United States R.O.T.C. program in 1939, when American schools turned out 162,000 reserve officers for the armed services.[60] Of course the number of Chinese youths receiving higher education has always been small—the total enrollment in her higher educational institutions was only 41,922 in 1937, with about 390,000 in secondary schools. In 1943 these figures had risen to 73,669 and 1,100,000 respectively, or about one-quarter of one per cent of the population.[61] These figures include female students, so the potential officer reserve was even smaller.

With a small potential officer reserve, and with comparatively small classes being graduated at the academies, the leadership situation was difficult. The Chinese forces had no sound rotation scheme and the constant strain of being exposed to battle conditions took its toll in valuable veteran officers at the front. The inexperience of the green replacements caused even more casualties. By the late years of the war, an average Chinese battalion of infantry had only about 20 per cent of its officer complement properly filled with academy graduates. Sometimes there were as few as 4 or 5 in a battalion. It was the ill-considered sacrifice of the Shanghai and other such campaigns that had chiefly caused the figure to drop from the 80 per cent of 1937.

In China, as in every other nation at war, the exigencies of the emergency caused the marked acceleration of the training courses offered and the necessary lowering of standards. At the academies the three-year curriculum was cut to one year. Many received their training in hastily established and poorly equipped substitute training schools where the instructors had neither the time nor the means to ready the cadets properly for battle. Officers promoted from the ranks, with no special officer training, were often regarded by commanders and the rank and file alike as more reliable in action than the graduates of officer programs, especially since the latter had often received training more properly described as shortened than as intensified. Even the Central Military Academy's entrance requirements suffered markedly. Before the war, candidates had to be high-school graduates; in wartime the academy was open to applicants with

[59] *China Handbook, 1937-1945,* p. 289.
[60] U.S. Senate, *The Army of the United States, op.cit.,* p. 141.
[61] *China Handbook, 1937-1945,* pp. 321-336.

only junior-high-school training. Since much of the most valuable
pre-college scientific training was concentrated in the senior years of
high school, these candidates were vastly inferior to the pre-war
applicants and consequently less able to grasp technical subjects
in the training curriculum.

VI

> "*The military commander is the fate of the nation. Only
> the seasoned soldier, the general staff officer, who has re-
> ceived a thorough training in war or devoted himself to
> serious study and has been tested in a great variety of peace-
> time assignments, will qualify as a military commander.*"
> —*von Moltke.*[62]

As late as the nationalist period, a Chinese commander was partly
a combat leader and partly a medieval lord who commanded the
allegiance of his followers as a sort of district governor and family
head. Most had had some variety of narrow military training at such
schools as Paoting, Whampoa, or Peiyang, but few indeed had enjoyed the benefit of training at Chinese or foreign staff colleges.
Hardly a handful had had the combination of administrative, teaching,
and command assignments which go into the making of the average
Occidental commander.[63] The Chinese commander's school had been
the battlefield and there he had learned his tactics. His chief qualifications were some talent for personal leadership, courage, and resourcefulness.

Behind the field commander the organization was weak. No adequate general staff—that group which Liddell Hart defined as "a collective substitute for genius which no army could count on producing
at need"—existed to plan the broad strategical patterns within which
the tactics of the commanders in the field operated.[64] The Nationalist
Government, in power for less than ten years when the Japanese
attacked, had not had time to build one: Colonel J. M. Palmer records
that it took fourteen years to establish the United States general staff
corps, a statement which General Otto Nelson's study also seems to

[62] von Moltke, Helmuth, *Gesammelte Schriften und Denkwürdigkeiten* (Berlin, 1891), VI, p. 193.
[63] Chen Yi-fu, "Prize Essay, 1943," *Chün-shih tsa-chih*, No. 165 (May 1945), p. 45.
[64] Liddell Hart, B. H., *The German Generals Talk* (N.Y.: W. Morrow, 1948), p. 18.

have corroborated.[65] China, with her huge army, would have needed an even longer period to do so, especially since the times were troublesome and unstable.

Up to 1937 China's staff college had trained less than 2,000 general staff officers, and many of the highest-placed field commanders had not taken this training, considering that their experience and wisdom could not be so enhanced. The field commander tended also to draw his staff from his relatives and his schoolmates, distributing offices among his friends in what Westerners would regard as nepotism but what he regarded as justifiable *jen-ch'ing shih-ku* (human relations and social conventions). Favoritism and personal loyalty appeared to him to be virtues. He thought of good administration in terms of precedents and bureaucratic procedures. In problems of personnel he strove for a marriage of convenience between the official regulations and his principles of social convention.

The commander had control over the purse-strings of his unit. He determined how much and when his men should be paid. Some seized the opportunity to enrich themselves through padding, grafting, and other manipulations, though most tried to find a decent solution to the problems presented by the army's financial red tape on the one hand and the empty stomachs of their troops on the other. Struggling with domestic politics and foreign enemies, lacking adequate supervision and often adequate financing from the government, the commander was largely on his own in the management of his band of mostly illiterate peasants. There were some good leaders and some bad ones. They received little effective commendation or condemnation.

One of the best examples of the old-fashioned field commanders was the heroic General Chang Tzu-chung, whose portrait hung in a conspicuous place in Generalissimo Chiang's private study. He had come in for a good deal of adverse criticism when, as mayor of Tientsin, he was forced to do some diplomatic bargaining with the Japanese, but he had redeemed himself with his part in the brilliant victory at Tai-erh-chuang and finally fell in battle in defense of his country. Other heroes, perhaps more enlightened, were General Fang Hsien-chueh, who conducted the gallant defense of Hengyang for forty-seven days against overwhelming odds; General Hsueh Yueh, thrice

<hr>

[65] Hamilton, *The Soul and Body of an Army, op.cit.*, p. 245; Nelson, O., *National Security and the General Staff* (Washington, 1946), *passim*; Palmer, J. M., *America in Arms: The Experience of the U.S. with Military Organization* (New Haven, 1941), *passim*.

the victor at Changsha; General Li Tsung-jen, who distinguished him-
self as the victorious high commander capable of successfully coordi-
nating a large heterogeneous field army on the bloody field of
Tai-erh-chuang; and General Sun Li-jen, the hero of northern Burma.
Few if any of their deeds received the praise they deserved from
Western admirers of valor.

The outside world has shown more interest of late in the Chinese
communist generals. Imbued with the dogmas of Marx and Lenin,
from which no deviation was permitted, they had one advantage
over the non-communist Chinese commanders: a doctrinal unity, a
collective strength. This, of course, was partly canceled out by those
concomitant defects of following a strict party-line: stilting rigidity,
blinding bias, and a lack of initiative. The communist leaders, most
of whom had received thorough training abroad (particularly in
Russia), were, on the whole, more competent than the representatives of the "feudalistic" codes they decried. As combat leaders they
gave more attention to the unity of their troops, and specialized in
ruthless and fanatical guerrilla tactics, but their determination and
courage were matched by their anti-communist cousins.

14 · THE MOBILIZATION OF INDUSTRY

I. NATIVE POTENTIALITIES. II. FOREIGN IMPORTS. III.
MANAGEMENT AND MISMANAGEMENT.

I

THE chief limitations of China's military potential were the nation's industrial backwardness and maladministration. It is not improbable, as some critics have hastened to point out, that military control of the nation's industrial development did more harm than good. The military men, who were anxious to have guns in a hurry, neglected to build Chinese factories, preferring to import what they needed. They discovered too late that the finest foreign-made weapons were useless to them if they could not be shipped in, and that the newest German-made 88mms, when out of ammunition, were even less effective than the old Chinese muzzle-loader firing black powder and assorted metal scraps.

Reliance upon foreign supplies relegated Chinese industrialization to a position of minor importance in the military program. It was not that China was altogether without considerable industry. The Kiangnan dockyard, China's first and largest industrial undertaking, was established for building warships and as an arsenal. In its early days it produced the first machine gun in China, shortly after Maxim had perfected the first working model, with Chinese skill and initiative. The Hanyang steel works—at the time of its erection in 1891 one of the larger steel mills in the world—was another example of great Chinese industry. But these were merely erected as arsenals for the production of weapons. Dominated by military men without technical knowledge and given neither opportunity nor incentive to expand and improve, these and other industries in China rapidly declined.[1]

On the eve of war, China's total blast furnace capacity in 1936 was a pathetic 870,000 tons of pig iron a year, all from small furnaces which were often idle. The government was planning to erect four new steel mills, but only one small private plant, the Hoshing Steel

[1] Ch'uan Han-sheng, "The Kiangnan Arsenal of the Ch'ing Dynasty," *Bulletin of the Institute of History and Philology, Academia Sinica,* XXIII (Dec. 1951).

Works of Shanghai, was in full-shift continuous production. It had a 10-ton baby furnace. The only mill capable of producing quality alloy steel was not a steel works at all but the metallurgical laboratory of the Academia Sinica, which maintained several small electric furnaces for research purposes. In electrical manufacturing, up to the eve of war in 1937, there were approximately 200 factories, medium or small, 159 of which (three-fourths of the total) were concentrated around the vulnerable Shanghai area. Petroleum, another vital war need, was previously produced in China in mere hundreds of *catties*[2] a day. Only when the war showed signs of being long-drawn-out, and when China had to fall back on her own resources, did the quest for oil start. Notwithstanding great difficulties in the importation of equipment from abroad, China's Kansu Petroleum Administration managed to maintain an annual production of more than 400,000 barrels of crude oil, and more than 100,000 barrels of gasoline.[3] As long as China thought in terms of importing high-grade steel, petroleum, and finished arms, her native industry was bound to remain undeveloped.

The prewar administration actually put a "five-year military production plan" into effect, but it was concerned chiefly with the standardization of the army's multifarious types of small arms. In those days a single Chinese division might have five kinds of light machine guns: the French Hotchkiss, the American Browning, the German Solothorn MG-34, and both Czech- and Chinese-made Brnos. The situation was similar for other weapons. Supply problems were increased by the many varieties of ammunition and the fact that some were not interchangeable. Even the drill manual had to provide instructions for many kinds of weapons. The plan was finally adopted to standardize equipment and, by the outbreak of the war, China had readjusted the light arms of nearly all the Central Army units.[4]

Light arms, because of China's weakness in heavy industry, were to be the basis of the army's firepower. Automatic weapons were

[2] A *catty* is equivalent to 1.10231 pounds.
[3] *The Chinese Year Book, 1937* (Shanghai: Commercial Press, 1937), pp. 748-750. "China Starts to Tap Her Oil Deposits," *China Economist*, II, 8 (Aug. 23, 1948), p. 179. Central Electrical Manufacturing Works, *List of Electrical Manufacturing Enterprises in China* (Nanking: National Resource Commission, 1937).
[4] The 1936 part of the Five Year Ordnance Reconstruction and Munition Reserve Plan had as its annual goal the reequipment of 30 readjusted divisions, 1 training brigade, 1 heavy artillery regiment. All the light arms were to be supplied by domestic arsenals.

heavily relied on, and mortars remedied the shortage of heavier artillery. The Chinese arsenals manufactured some light arms of good quality and by 1937 the supply of light weapons was said to be sufficient to equip practically all of the Chinese infantry divisions. About 1941 there were only 800-odd pieces of artillery, a motley assortment from the arsenals of Europe and Japan. The small arms picture was brighter. In 1942 the Chinese had 1,000,000 rifles, 6,600 light machine guns, 17,000 heavy machine guns, 1,000 anti-tank guns, 8,200 trench mortars, and about 250 million rounds of small arms ammunition.[5]

Foreign sources provided by far the largest share of the heavier weapons. Between 1932 and 1937 the published figures on German exports to China totaled 610 millions in registered marks.[6] Since a substantial part of the military equipment exported to Germany may reasonably be assumed to have been kept secret, this figure can only permit us to guess at the total. In the same period, German imports from China amounted to 365.2 millions of registered marks. But China's total wartime industrial capital equipment was valued at less than $1,395 billions (Chinese). Obviously she had determined to import rather than produce wherever she could.[7]

When full-scale hostilities began, the Chinese government, realizing the great value of her industrial equipment, made a supreme effort to move inland whatever industrial facilities she could. The defense of Shanghai was one of the calculated moves in this effort, and the machinery saved in the evacuation was dearly bought. The effectiveness of this plan may be questioned when one balances, in addition to the human lives expended to buy time, the loss of equipment on the Shanghai front with what could be produced by the machinery saved.

By January 1939 the ministry of economic affairs announced that 300 factories had been transplanted from the coastal area to the interior. At the end of the first phase of the war, 41 per cent of the 516 factories of the Wuhan area (which included the cities of Wu-

[5] "Statement of Gen. Yu Ta-wei, Chinese Chief of Ordnance, to Dr. L. Currie U.S. Presidential Representative, on 31 July, 1942," quoted in Romanus, C. F., and Sunderland, R., *U.S. Army in World War II, China-Burma-India Theater, Stilwell Mission to China* (Washington, 1953), p. 234.
[6] Bloch, K., *German Interest and Policies, op.cit.*, p. 27.
[7] Chinese Ministry of Economic Affairs, "Registration of Chinese Industries 1941," *China Handbook, 1937-1945*, pp. 363-364.

chang, Hankow, and Hanyang) had been moved to safer locations deep within China, and another 12 per cent which could not be moved had been deliberately destroyed by the Chinese.[8] Perhaps the Soviets learned something from the Chinese, for about a year later Russia moved her industrial equipment behind the Urals to defend it from German attack.[9]

II

China's munitions production depended largely on imported materials. During the first sixteen months of the war, an estimated 60,000 tons of such materials were brought in each month through Hong Kong. A total of over 700,000 tons reached Hankow before that city fell into Japanese hands. Another 2,000 tons a month came in through French Indochina, and limited quantities of vital supplies came from the Russians via the long overland route from the north. Between 1937 and 1939 some 60,000 tons of ammunition reached China by ships from the Soviet Black Sea port of Odessa.[10] Later, the Burma Road was to supply about 7,500 tons of American lend-lease goods per month, but before this Germany provided about 60 per cent of the Chinese imports and Denmark, Sweden, the Soviet Union, and the United States most of the rest.[11] Between May 1941 and April 1942, some 110,864 tons of American lend-lease supplies were earmarked for China, and most of it reached its destination. During the next three years, the United States delivered 736,374 tons of material "over the Hump" into China, much of it for the support of Chinese-based American forces.[12]

China's dependence upon foreign imports may be gauged from the following estimates of tonnage reaching unoccupied wartime China each month:[13]

[8] "Statement of Japanese Cabinet Information Bureau," *Tokyo Gazette*, IV, 5 (Nov. 1940), pp. 92-96.

[9] Consult Lesueur, L., *Twelve Months that Changed the World* (N.Y.: A. Knopf, 1943), *passim*.

[10] Wu, Aitchin K., *China and the Soviet Union* (N.Y.: John Day, 1950), p. 269.

[11] U.S. Office of Coordination of Information, *Memorandum No. B.R.T.; American Aid to China*, pp. 37-42.

[12] Romanus and Sunderland, *op.cit.*, p. 47.

[13] Table compiled from information and data given in: U.S. Office of Coordination of Information, *op.cit.*, pp. 37-42. Feis, H., *The China Tangle* (Princeton, 1953), p. 275. Romanus and Sunderland, *op.cit.*, p. 47.

Period	Estimated Monthly Tonnage
July 1937 to Nov. 1938	62,000
Nov. 1938 to Nov. 1939	6,800
1937 to 1939	60,000†
Nov. 1939 to July 1940	7,800
July 1940 to Oct. 1940	3,800
Oct. 1940 to Dec. 1940	5,000
Early 1941 to Jan. 1942	7,500-10,000
May 1945 to June 1945*	28,000
July 1945 to Sept. 1945*	15,900-23,000

* Over the Stilwell Road, including weight of trucks.
† From Soviet Russia by way of Odessa.

After the United States entered the war against Japan, of course, the supply situation brightened, though for three years following the spring of 1942 China's main land routes to the outside were cut off and supplies reached her almost exclusively by the perilous airlift over the Himalayan range. Although the airlift over the Hump operated with amazing efficiency, its effectiveness was limited: over a three-year period it brought into China about the same total tonnage as had been transported over the difficult land routes in the previous sixteen months of the war. The Stilwell Road was finally opened in 1945; its completion was too late for the purpose initially envisioned by General Stilwell. Tonnage actually brought into China during the rest of 1945 over this road and the parallel pipeline was much smaller than that carried by air over the Hump. The following breakdown gives a closer picture of the airlift's achievement:[14]

Period	Monthly Tonnage
Sept. 1942	1,986
June 1943	3,000
July 1943	5,000
Jan. 1944	13,500
Jan. 1945	46,000
June 1945	58,300
July 1945	73,700
Aug. 1945	63,100
Sept. 1945	49,200

The airlift was a highly laudable achievement, but it was by no means the perfect answer to China's problems. To begin with, with an army of 1½ million fighting on a modest infantry scale, China

[14] Chennault, *op.cit.*, pp. 225, 235, 247, 273. Feis, *op.cit.*, p. 275.

needed a continuous flow of at least 100,000 tons per month to sustain optimum efficiency. Reliance upon imports caused scientific research at home to go stale and transportation costs to cut deeply into funds allocated to buy commodities; it also presented constant threats to uninterrupted supply because of political issues, allocation problems, and matters of priority. Finally, foreign-made equipment created serious maintenance problems. China's wartime airplane purchases were a typical example; unprepared to produce the necessary spare parts at home, the Chinese had a difficult time keeping the planes in flying condition.

The suppliers had their problems too. German military aid was on a strict business basis—strictly a *quid pro quo* deal. Soviet Russia's investment in China was a calculated move for political and strategic profit. The United States, while a generous donor, gave grudgingly, fearing incompetence in Chinese purchasing agencies, waste, or hoarding of supplies for anti-communist purposes. The Chinese actually received less than 10 per cent of what they had been promised by the United States authorities. America had other allies to support, and she naturally felt closer ties to her British comrades in arms. The *Tulsa* incident was touched off by Chungking's resentment of the reallocation, to the British in Burma, of supplies destined for China. Chinese tempers ran high, and the American reassignment of munitions vital to the Chinese caused a serious break in Sino-British relations. Sometime later, Chiang Kai-shek issued his famous Three Demands on the subject of lend-lease aid which further strained relations.[15]

In his Three Demands Generalissimo Chiang requested that three United States divisions be dispatched forthwith to the Burma front; that 500 planes with concomitant replacements be assured him; that the United States guarantee him 5,000 tons a month of airborne supplies over the Hump by August 1942.

In presenting this ultimatum-like request to Washington, Chiang had made a serious misjudgment of the material situation of his allies. In the Middle East, where Rommel's powerful forces were knocking at the door of Alexandria, the situation was perilous. All the resources the United States could spare from her own campaigns were going to the embattled British at Cairo and to the Russians at Stalingrad. The three U.S. divisions which Chiang requested were

[15] Romanus and Sunderland, *op.cit.*, pp. 169-187.

simply not available. Aircraft production in the United States had, in the summer of 1942, not yet reached its peak. Transport carriers designed to fly the height of the Hump had not yet been developed, and the few C-47's were bringing into China only about 100 tons a month. Not realizing these difficulties, China was becoming increasingly dissatisfied with the decisions of the Anglo-American-controlled munitions assignment board, which—especially since China had no voice in the council of the combined chiefs of staff—was consistently repossessing China's lend-lease stockpiles in the United States and India for reallocation to other theaters.

III

China's own wartime munitions effort was oriented around three important arsenals. In the days before the war, the arsenals at Nanking, Hanyang, Kung-hsien, and Taiyuan shouldered the greater part of the production burden, working largely with imported raw materials. The migration of industries to the interior for defense against the Japanese caused these four units to be consolidated into three arsenals well behind the battlelines. Some production went on in bomb-proof tunnels miles long and hewn out of solid rock.

Due to the losses of heavy machinery early in the war, even China's largest unit, the Twenty-First Arsenal, suffered a severe cut in efficiency. At the nadir of its production level, its monthly output was a mere 200 machine guns, 120,000 trench mortar shells, and a comparative trickle of small arms.[16] In the vital sphere of military communication, throughout the war years there were only about 20,000 sets of field telephones for the 5-million-man army.[17] Gradually almost all of the machine shops in the interior were enlisted for direct or indirect war production and by 1944, despite crucial material shortages, China's arsenals had stepped up five times the prewar production of mortars and were turning out 10,000 light machine guns a year.[18] The Japanese offensive in the latter part of 1944 brought about considerable destruction in the sprouting Chinese industries located in the Hengyang-Kweilin area. In a three months' period interior China had lost a substantial part of her war-supporting

[16] Snow, Edgar, *The Battle for Asia, op.cit.,* p. 180.
[17] Yun, C., "Electrical Manufacturing in China," *China Economist*, II, 12 (Sept. 20, 1948), p. 267.
[18] *China Handbook, 1937-1945,* p. 289f.

industries which she had painfully established during the previous seven years. The blow to the war production program, therefore, can be well imagined.

The Japanese general staff's estimate of China's munitions situation was this:[19]

Light machine guns: Half produced in China, half foreign-made.
Heavy machine guns: All heavy machine guns used produced in China.
Machine cannons: All machine cannons, whether for anti-aircraft or anti-tank operations, foreign-made.
Artillery: All heavy caliber guns foreign-made.

The Japanese gave the Chinese-manufactured weapons, with the exception of a few prewar models, the rating of "medium" quality.

Because of the partial destruction of her arsenal capacity, China even as late as the postwar year of 1947 could scarcely meet 70 to 90 per cent of the needs of the peak National Army of 2.5 million.[20] She manufactured no heavy artillery and, after the Russians had seized Manchuria's production centers and stripped the Mukden arsenal, even her production of light arms was cut appreciably.

All through the war the supply of ammunition had never been plentiful, a fact which was felt acutely on the front and in training in the rear. In July 1942 China had a stockpile of about 250 million rounds of small arms ammunition, but, by the middle of 1943, the backlog of rifle bullets in the depots dwindled to 40 million rounds.[21] This, assuming a similar amount was in the hands of the troops, amounted to approximately 20 bullets per man. Yet in a single major operation—say the conflict in the Inchang area during May 1943— 10 million rounds of rifle ammunition might be used.[22] When American aid entered the picture, the situation was somewhat relieved, although ammunition never became plentiful. In the postwar year 1947 the governmental arsenals even then could supply only 20 per cent of the army's need for small arms ammunition and a mere 3 per cent of the normal demand for artillery shells.[23]

Clearly China was irrevocably committed to the necessity of foreign aid. Her reliance upon outside help, originally dictated by the in-

---

[19] Captured Japanese document, *Tekigawa guntai o tzu giti mitaru; Keizei kosen ryoku kansatsu shiryo*, Japanese Army *Riku-shi*-secret transmit No. 2570 (Nov. 3, 1942).
[20] Chinese Ministry of Defense source, quoted in *China Handbook, 1950*, p. 201.
[21] Romanus and Sunderland, *op.cit.*, p. 234. *The Stilwell Papers, op.cit.*, p. 208.
[22] *The Stilwell Papers, op.cit.*, p. 208.
[23] Chinese Ministry of Defense figure quoted in *China Handbook, 1950*, p. 208.

sufficiency of her own industries, gradually rendered those industries even less capable. Money needed for vital industrial developments at home was sent abroad for more arms. Von Seeckt's *Rüstungs-industrie* plan for China, instituted with German technical assistance, received insufficient backing. Civilian industries which might be turned to war production were generally ignored, and defense contracts went to foreign bidders. In prewar days, little thought had been given to any plan to mobilize and utilize the public and private production facilities of the nation in time of emergency. Almost no research projects had been supported in Chinese universities. When war came, the military, demanding complete control over industry in the name of total war, did not know how to harness China's industrial power to the tasks of war. The military council was finally forced to acknowledge its incapacity to deal with industrial mobilization and to place the task in the hands of a civilian-controlled national resources commission which, after an understandably slow start, became one of China's most efficient wartime organizations, managing both government arsenals, the private industries and the amazing and ingenious industrial cooperatives operating in the villages with makeshift equipment. Many of these small industries, of course, went into bankruptcy when American aid at last offered an easy and reliable source of materials.

China not only neglected her home industries but also her trained personnel and her scientific research program. In World War II the United States had approximately 30,000 scientists and engineers conducting research on new weapons and medicine for war.[24] Science played a vital part in the war effort and made some truly astounding contributions. In China there were not even 300 scientists and engineers engaged in this kind of work, engaged, as President Eisenhower has said, in effecting "the constant change that modern science, working under the compelling urge of national self-preservation, brings to the battlefield."[25] China's military men, insufficiently aware of the realities of modern technological warfare, have too often merely applied foreign methods and have always slighted the nation's needs in education, science, and industrial development.

[24] Bush, Vannevar, *Modern Arms and Free Men* (N.Y.: Simon and Schuster, 1949), p. 6.
[25] Eisenhower, Dwight, quoted in Bush, *op.cit.*, p. 249.

15 · GERMAN AND SOVIET FACTORS

I. THE DEPENDABILITY OF THE GERMAN ADVISERS. II. THE CRAFTINESS OF THE KREMLIN: THE SINO-SOVIET NON-AGGRESSION PACT. SINO-SOVIET TRADE. THE SOVIET MILITARY MEN IN CHINA. III. THE DETERIORATION OF SINO-SOVIET RELATIONS.

I

WHEN the Sino-Japanese war broke out in July 1937, General von Falkenhausen and his German advisory group were rated highly by the rank and file of the government for their valuable work in building China's fighting strength. They had also won the confidence of the generalissimo himself. Germany's relations with Imperial Japan were at that time growing increasingly close, but von Falkenhausen and his associates continued to work faithfully to assist China. With the generalissimo's full confidence, von Falkenhausen was immediately dispatched to the North China theater headquarters at Paoting soon after the war broke out. Then he was ordered to the Shanghai front with a number of his staff officers and remained there during the battle of Shanghai until November. After the fall of Nanking, by special order of the generalissimo, von Falkenhausen assisted every day in the supreme headquarters at Wuchang. Several high-ranking German advisers, among them General Streccius, served in confidential capacity in Shangtung and Shansi, albeit their contributions have been exaggerated and their functions misunderstood. The German advisers themselves admitted that many successful strategies attributed to them by rumor (such as the Tai-erh-chuang campaign) were entirely Chinese in origin and execution, although von Falkenhausen had a hand in the Tai-erh-chuang strategy.[1]

Von Falkenhausen had had differences of opinion with the generalissimo on a number of occasions, but he usually bowed to Chiang's final decision on the Chinese situation, with a loyalty and tact commensurate with his abilities as a soldier. One source of disagree-

[1] United Press dispatch, June 13, 1938.

ment between the Chinese and their advisers arose out of the Oriental philosophy regarding the value of human life. The Germans were continually objecting to the commitment of troops to futile defenses. The chief German adviser, for instance, in one of his confidential memoranda to the generalissimo, while praising the stand of the Chinese forces at Shanghai—and indeed many of the crack outfits of the Central Army fighting there owed their efficiency to German-supervised training—could nevertheless not refrain from implying that, in the face of undeniable superiority in enemy firepower, the tenacious defense of the fixed positions at Shanghai had been courageous but ill-advised.[2] He hinted that excessive sacrifice would eventually cost China her main striking power and be detrimental to her long-term military interests. The German advisers were at complete variance with the Chinese concept of "live and die in defense." Stanch death-stand strategies for the defense of walled cities, particularly Nanking and Taiyuan, drew sharp German criticism and advice to rely instead on highly trained, mobile striking forces and swift, calculated attacks.[3]

Military supplies continued to pour in from Germany, expedited by such "pro-Chinese" among the high German leaders as the war minister, Field Marshal von Blomberg. According to Herbert von Dircksen, Germany's ambassador to Tokyo, the German general staff became increasingly favorable to the Chinese and viewed Hitler's impending Berlin-Tokyo collaboration with great reservations.[4] The German chief of the general staff, General Beck, a good friend of von Falkenhausen, maintained that China's friendship must be preserved. Beck was anti-Nazi in his belief; he later shot himself on July 20, 1944, after having been involved with a number of generals, including Erwin Rommel, in the plot to assassinate Hitler. However, in 1938, after Ribbentrop became foreign minister, Hitler overruled the opposition of his general staff and decided to go along with the Japanese.

Japan, of course, was exerting pressure upon Germany to withdraw her military advisers from China, and Hitler at the beginning of

[2] Quoted from a declassified secret Chinese army document circulated for the study of selected senior officers during the latter stage of the Shanghai campaign and dated September 1937. The document was in the form of a report from von Falkenhausen.
[3] Author's conversation in 1937 with Colonel F. Hummel, a German general staff officer assigned as adviser to China's training brigade at the Central Military Academy.
[4] von Dircksen, H., *op.cit.*, p. 171.

1938 offered German assistance in mediating a peace between China and Japan. Chiang Kai-shek rejected this proposal summarily but tactfully.[5] The Nazis retaliated by recalling her German advisers from China. Just previous to this in February 1938, however, Hitler had forced out von Blomberg and von Fritsch, seizing control of the German army. Both were anti-Japanese and, like von Seeckt, friendly to the Chinese. This abrupt action had alienated many of the German advisory personnel, and about a dozen of them resigned from German military service and elected to stay on in China. In this way, even after some of China's friends in Germany had dropped out of power and many of the advisers were compelled to return to Germany, some military men remained to work for Chiang; von Falkenhausen tried to avoid Hitler's strict order as long as he could. Hitler, however, compelled the reluctant von Falkenhausen to return to Germany —under the threat of reprisal against his family.[6] Many German advisers were non-military men and remained unaffected by the recall of the professional soldiers. Among them was Dr. Horst Baerensprung, once police chief of Saxony, who had been with Chiang's headquarters for seven years, reportedly advising on matters of intelligence and counterespionage.

A certain feeling of loyalty had grown up between the German advisers and the Chinese, an attitude quite different from that revealed in the notorious conduct of a number of Mussolini's air officers who had been loaned to China. The Italians built up elaborate aerial survey mosaics of the strategic Nanking-Hangchow-Shanghai triangle —surveys which found their way, at a handsome profit, into the hands of the Japanese.[7] In contrast, von Falkenhausen, even when the official Nazi policy was becoming pronouncedly pro-Japanese and the German mission in China was being broken up, took precautions to see that no German advisers returned home via Japan or in any other way communicated their intimate knowledge of Chinese affairs to China's enemy. Von Falkenhausen and his associates left China retaining the confidence, high respect, and regard of the Chinese.

The German advisers had contributed markedly to the efficiency of the Chinese forces. The pick of the Reichswehr, they had upon

[5] Consult Liu, T. C., "German Mediation in the Sino-Japanese War," *Far Eastern Quarterly*, VIII (1949).

[6] Goerlitz, Walter, *Der Deutsche Generalstab; Geschichte und Gestalt 1657-1945* (Frankfurt am Main, 1951), p. 428.

[7] Chennault, *Ways of a Fighter, op.cit.*, p. 38.

arrival the respect of Chinese military leaders, and they went on to enlist their cooperation and to further win their regard. Generalissimo Chiang, especially captivated by German efficiency, placed considerable trust in these advisers and sought to employ them in several respects: to advise in the training of a nucleus force to resist the Japanese invasion; to advance the modernization of the provincial armies and, through increased strength in the outlying areas, to enhance the unifying effect of the central government; and, lastly, to build up an entente which would promote better military, political, and industrial relations.

The German advisers met with knotty problems. Not all the Chinese military men had as much respect for and awe of the Germans as Chiang had of von Seeckt; not all the Germans were so well wined and dined as von Falkenhausen, who was led to inquire: "What am I supposed to do here, give military advice or eat these huge dinners?"[8] Some Chinese were more amenable to advice than others. Some, like the graduates of the Central Military Academy who had been trained to be receptive to new ideas, led German advisers to dub the Chinese "the cleverest students in the world."[9] Considering the lack of cooperation the Germans had to encounter in some areas and the staggering difficulties engendered by such obstacles as widespread illiteracy and largely undeveloped industry, it must be granted that the German mission in China was valuable beyond any expectation that could reasonably have been held. Great credit must be given to General von Falkenhausen, that tall, erect, tight-lipped soldier of Junker tradition, who since 1933 had been peering firsthand at China's problems through his thick pince-nez. With him went more than twenty high-ranking officers who saw in China the opportunity denied them at home because of treaty restrictions on the size of the German forces or by their own lack of sympathy with the growing Nazi party. They had been highly successful in assisting Chiang to create the powerful Central Army and the small nucleus of officers which formed China's general staff. Had these well-trained troops not been squandered during the campaigns at Shanghai and Nanking, and had Chiang and many of his officers given greater considerations to their German advisers, the course of war might have been quite different. As von Falkenhausen left he told his friends that he would someday

[8] Chinese War Ministry Source.
[9] Abegg, Lily, *Chinas Erneurung, op.cit.*, p. 145.

return "by way of Chinese Turkistan." He was convinced that the "barbarian" Japanese could never wholly control the Chinese even in their occupied areas and aware that Japan's manpower was limited. He said that China could wage war for fifty years, if necessary, and that she was ultimately invincible. After only a few months of war service with the Chinese troops, whom he considered "magnificent," von Falkenhausen left China assured that Japan would eventually lose on the vast mainland of China and equally convinced that Soviet Russia was a great threat to China's future.

II

In *China's Destiny*, Generalissimo Chiang Kai-shek asserted that after 1931 Japan had attempted to force upon the Chinese acceptance of Hirota's Three Principles, among which was a clause entitled "Joint Defense against Communism." Chiang presented the Japanese motives as follows: " 'Joint Defense against Communism' meant that with the four northeastern provinces (Manchuria) as a base, Japan would annex the rest of China's territory piecemeal, dominate the Chinese government, and, in conspiracy with the Axis Powers in Europe, concentrate forces from the east and the west in a joint attack on the Soviet Union. Knowing these to be the premeditated steps in Japan's continental policy, the Chinese government resolutely rejected the demands, and as a countermove concluded a treaty of non-aggression with the Soviet Union in August 1937."[10]

Initially, in April 1937, the Soviet ambassador Dimitri Bogomoloff had proposed to Nanking that China and the Soviet Union sign a mutual assistance pact, promising that the Soviet government would be willing to float a loan of $50 million (Chinese)—about $12.5 million in U.S. currency—to supply the Chinese with ammunition and the machinery to manufacture it.[11] At that stage the responsible Chinese government officials inclined toward the West and, because of their trade relationship with Germany, hesitated to enter into such an understanding with the Soviets. By July the Lukouchiao incident had radically altered China's outlook and she regarded the proposed mutual assistance pact with favor. Then, however, Bogomoloff betrayed his country's own changed attitude and demonstrated that the

[10] Chiang Kai-shek, *China's Destiny*, *op.cit.*, p. 130.
[11] Consult Wu, Aitchin K., *China and the Soviet Union, A Study of Sino-Soviet Relations* (N.Y.: John Day, 1950), p. 264.

Soviets were no longer anxious to conclude such a pact. Chinese official circles, the Russian complained, were not in full accord, an anti-Soviet attitude still prevailed in some quarters, and China was too weak militarily and economically to be able to resist on all fronts. He counseled the Chinese that the whole incident would blow over in a week or two. Even when large-scale operations began in the Shanghai area, Bogomoloff still did not believe that the Chinese were determined to fight on all fronts.[12] The best that China could now extract from the Soviet Union was a non-aggression pact. It was signed on August 21, 1937.[13]

China, assured in the secret clauses of the pact of material aid from the Soviet Union in fighting Japan, was more confident in her resistance to the aggressor. The Soviet manipulation of the whole situation, the substitution of a non-aggression pact for a mutual assistance agreement, and the secret terms of the treaty eventually signed, were extremely clever.

Following the signing of the pact, an agreement was reached, but never signed, with the Kremlin which promised China a loan of $100 million (Chinese)—about $20 million U.S.—intended to supply 24 Chinese divisions with Soviet arms.[14] Arrangements were also made for Soviet military and air advisers to go to China. For the first time since 1924, Russian "comrades," guns, tanks, and planes made their appearance in the Chinese armed forces. No less a personage than Marshal Klimenti Voroshilov handled the details.

Late in 1937 Bogomoloff was recalled and a former Soviet adviser to Canton, M. Smirnov, deputy commissar of war under Voroshilov, replaced him as ambassador to China. Smirnov used the assumed name of Lugants-Orelsky. This was the beginning of a formidable array of Soviet talent in China. One of Smirnov's successors as ambassador was Alexander S. Panyushkin, also a professional army man, a graduate of Frunze Academy. Soviet Russia's most brilliant military commander, Georgi Zhukov, came to China as Soviet military attaché and made a tremendous impression on Chinese military men well before his climb to wider fame in World War II and thereafter. Chief of the Soviet military mission was the former adviser to the

[12] *Ibid.*, pp. 264f.

[13] Consult text in Moore, H. L., *Soviet Far Eastern Policy 1931-45* (Princeton, 1945), pp. 224-225.

[14] Wu, *op.cit.*, p. 268.

Whampoa Academy, who called himself Comrade Cherapanoff. One of Chiang's new advisers was General Vassily I. Chuikov, later the heroic defender of Stalingrad, at that time fresh from successes in the Russo-Finnish war and highly regarded by the Chinese high command at Chungking. The Chinese, on their part, gave ample evidence (if more were needed) of the military nature of the short-lived Sino-Soviet alliance. Their ambassador to the Kremlin was the former deputy chief of the general staff and commandant of the army staff college, General Yang Chieh.

The problem of supply routes into China for the materials from Russia was partly solved by the construction of a 1,700-mile north-western highway from Lanchow to the Soviet border. Soviet equipment poured into China. From 1938 to 1940, it was estimated, Soviet Russia's first loan to China actually supplied part of the promised equipment, probably sufficient for the reorganization of about ten Chinese divisions. However, the monetary value of this first loan was now fixed by Stalin, in a meeting with Dr. Sun Fo in March 1938, as equivalent to $50 million (U.S.) instead of the originally agreed $20 million (U.S.).[15] Between 1937 and 1939, according to several reports, some 60,000 tons of ammunition reached China through Odessa.[16] Soviet air aid was more impressive. Altogether, 885 aircraft of all types were sent to China, though not transferred outright to the Chinese air force.[17] Five flights of Soviet aircraft were maintained in China, largely manned by Russian airmen. At one time a General Asanov commanded the Soviet squadrons, which were assigned to protect the main Chinese bases at Nanking, Hankow, Chungking, and, especially, Lanchow, a position in China's north-west which Russia considered of vital strategic importance to her own security. These air groups were supplied with fuel and ammunition transported by trucks, camels, and pack animals from the Soviet Union across Chinese Turkistan by way of the famous Silk Road.

Even before the first Soviet loan was exhausted, Dr. Sun Fo, at Chiang Kai-shek's request, returned to Moscow in March 1938 in an attempt to negotiate a second loan. After having fixed the first unsigned loan as $50 million (U.S.), Premier Stalin suggested that

[15] *Ibid.*   [16] *Ibid.*, p. 269.
[17] Chow Chi-jou, "The Chinese Air Force," *China Year Book 1944-1945*, p. 315.

the amount was sufficient and promised, if the need arose, that a third loan of another $50 million would be forthcoming. The second loan was practically exhausted by November 1938, and after that no ammunition was received in China.

In April 1939, the Chinese became alarmed at both their dwindling supplies and the rapidly cooling Soviet friendship, and Dr. Sun Fo was once again sent to Moscow. For some weeks the Chinese envoy waited without avail to see Stalin and then, on May 13, he was finally received at the Kremlin. After two hours of discussion, Stalin gave his verdict tersely: "You may have a loan of any amount you require without putting forward any reasons." Sun proposed an amount equal to $150 million in U.S. currency. He signed the loan agreement with Mikoyan and straightened out ammunition supply matters with Voroshilov. The total value of the loan was officially reported as equivalent to $250 million (U.S.), with interest at 3 per cent. Ammunition was arranged for and, to expedite matters, General Yang Chieh, stationed in Moscow as Chinese ambassador, was either forced by the Kremlin or empowered by Chungking to fix prices on all ammunition intended for China without having to await instructions from Chungking. China undertook to barter tea, wool, tungsten, lead, and other strategic materials to the Soviet Union. All these terms were laid down by Moscow in negotiations reminding one of the characteristic pattern of Soviet techniques which today have become well-known to the diplomats of the Orient and the West alike.[18]

The Soviets were once again investing in China for their own benefit. By maintaining China in the war against Japan, Russia assured herself that her own eastern borders were relatively secure, and she concentrated her attention on the West. Soviet military men, furthermore, were afforded the opportunity of studying the capabilities of the Chinese and Japanese forces and of testing German concepts, training systems, and equipment on the Chinese battlefront. About 500 Soviet military advisers were attached to the Chinese army, serving not with the front-line forces but rather at the higher field headquarters (where they were available for consultation on technical matters but did no actual routine staff work), the tank and artillery training centers, and the flying school at Inning on

[18] Consult Bennett, R., and Johnson, J. E. (ed.), *Negotiating with the Russians* (World Peace Foundation, 1951), particularly articles by Maj. Gen. J. R. Deane and J. N. Hazard.

the Sino-Soviet border. Certain higher-ranking Soviet military experts occasionally lectured at the staff college. Their chief military and air advisers held advisory positions on the national military council. All of them, from the lowest to the highest, were instructed to keep their eyes open at all times and to learn as much as they taught. China was a laboratory into which Russia had sent scientifically trained personnel to make tests and observations.

On the whole, the influence of the Soviet military advisers in this period never approached the importance of the years between 1924 and 1927. Their role in the Sino-Japanese war was limited, their commanding general of far less influence than von Falkenhausen. Generalissimo Chiang made it clear that he retained them for technical consultation only, and the Russians had little opportunity to formulate war strategy.[19] Many of them, indeed, were too specialized in their knowledge and experience to be of any use in that respect anyway—experts on a single Soviet weapon, for instance. Even the famous artillery men of the Red Army failed to give a good account of themselves when faced with the problems of China's forces: the Russian concept was one of mass, concentrated firepower, but in China ammunition was scarce.

The Soviet advisers, however, lived well and watched closely. They may have been spending lavishly on fine clothing, watches, jewelry, etc., but they were making other uses of their time in China. As they looked for German pistols and binoculars to buy, they also kept an eye open to learn what they could of German equipment and German training methods, both of which they admired and studied. They were much taken by German efficiency and thoroughness, the opposite of the Russian philosophy of *nichevo* (it can't be helped) and the Chinese *mei-yu fa-tzu* (nothing to be done about it).

III

While receiving military aid from the Soviet Union, the Chinese government could not permit itself to rest secure in the belief that Russia would provide continuous and dependable assistance in the prosecution of the war. The Soviet Union's *volte face* regarding Germany and Japan and her subsequent non-aggression pacts with these nations kept the Chinese wary of Stalin's next move. Russia was play-

---

[19] Information given by an undisclosed high Chinese source.

ing both sides. In April 1941 she signed her non-aggression pact with Japan, tacitly recognized Manchukuo, and won from the Japanese a recognition of the Mongolian People's Republic. It looked as if Soviet Russia and Japan were willing to unite in order to cut themselves large slices of the Chinese pie. The Soviet Union, of course, gained another advantage: she secured her eastern borders in anticipation of the incipient German attack on her western front which came two months later, on June 22, 1941. The Soviet-Japanese neutrality pact permitted Japan to withdraw 100,000 men of her crack Kwantung army from Manchuria, a force which she was to use to great advantage in the coming Pacific war.[20] The Soviet-Japanese pact drew vigorous protests from Chungking; it seemed to China that she had not only lost the support of Soviet Russia but that Japan had succeeded in enlisting her as an ally. Two months later, however, a Sino-Soviet military conference was held secretly at Chita in Siberia. The object under discussion: mutual aid against Japan.

Ever since it had become apparent that China was determined to battle Japan to the finish, Soviet Russia had cut down on the supplies she had so willingly furnished from the summer of 1937 through the summer of 1939. At the same time, the Soviet Union gradually tightened her hold on China's province of Sinkiang, which was rich in natural resources such as tungsten and oil. Sinkiang was governed by Sheng Shih-tsai, a member of the Russian (but not the Chinese) Communist Party. With him Moscow had signed the secret Sheng-Bakulin and Karpov Agreement of November 26, 1940 in which the Russians demanded greater political control of Sinkiang and the exclusive right to exploit the mineral resources of that province. The Soviet pressure brought upon Governor Sheng Shih-tsai had driven him closer and closer to Generalissimo Chiang Kai-shek, with whom he maintained secret communication. When the German *blitzkrieg* sent Russia reeling back on the western front, Russia put increasing pressure on Sheng and attempted to control more Chinese resources. Chiang Kai-shek blocked this move with a political counterstroke which snatched Sinkiang out of Soviet hands. This was Chiang's second contest with Stalin after 1927, and Chiang won it with the assistance of Sheng Shih-tsai, who shifted his allegiance from Moscow to Chungking.[21]

There had never been much love lost between Chiang and Stalin.

[20] Estimate of the Chinese Board of Military Operation.
[21] Li, Chang, "The Soviet Grip on Sinkiang," *Foreign Affairs*, XXXII, 2 (1954), pp. 491-503.

Chiang always had a deep-rooted suspicion that the ultimate Soviet goal was to communize China and to establish the nation as an indomitable base for world communist operations. Stalin, for his part, placed little trust in Chiang as a friend of Soviet Russia, even though he praised him to American ambassador Patrick J. Hurley in April 1945 as "selfless," "a patriot," and a man who was aware of the contribution which Soviet assistance in the past had made to his rise.[22]

Sino-Soviet relations were further strained when, after the outbreak of the Pacific war, American supplies destined for China and routed through Soviet-controlled areas were intercepted by the Russians and seized for their own use. The nationalists were battling the pro-communist forces in Sinkiang and, by May of 1943, forced out all Soviet personnel except a tiny consular staff, an act which contributed to the deterioration of Sino-Soviet friendship. In April 1944 pro-communist troops in Outer Mongolia clashed with Chinese forces. After the victory at Stalingrad, the Soviet Union took a strong position. Chungking's policy, the Soviet military attaché at Chungking stated, was to worsen Sino-Soviet relations, and Russia recalled all of her military advisers to the Chungking government.[23] Simultaneously she recalled her ambassador, A. S. Panyushkin, and it was not until April 1945 that A. A. Petrov arrived in China to fill the vacancy.

The evidence of a Sino-Soviet falling out alarmed Washington and, in September 1944, Vice-President Henry Wallace went to Chungking to encourage Chiang to repair the rift between China and the Soviet Union. He received the reply from Chiang that "anything not detrimental to Chinese sovereignty would be done to avoid such a conflict" and that China had already gone far out of her way to avoid a break with the U.S.S.R.[24] Stalin was equally diplomatic and even more vehement in his denials that the fault lay with the Soviet Union.

Underneath it all, however, the two-parties had fundamentally contradictory purposes. In spite of all the scrupulous care which the Soviet personnel in Chungking had been instructed to exercise lest it appear that Stalin was backing the Chinese communists rather than supporting President Chiang's government, it can be clearly seen, at least from the vantage point of time, just where Soviet sympathies lay

[22] "Ambassador Patrick J. Hurley's interview with Stalin, April 15, 1945," quoted in *U.S. Relations with China, op.cit.*, pp. 94f.

[23] U.S. General Staff, *The Chinese Communist Movement, 5 July 1945*, published as U.S. Senate Document (Washington: G.P.O., 1952), pp. 2386ff.

[24] *U.S. Relations with China*, p. 57, Annexes 43, 44.

and, when the time came to operate openly, where Soviet energies would be expended. But Stalin had the Yalta agreement on his side. On August 8, 1945, two days after the atom bomb was dropped on Hiroshima and eight years after the Chinese first took up arms against the Japanese invaders, the Soviet Union entered the war against the already defeated nation of Japan. Soviet armies crossed the Manchurian borders for the kill—but not until Stalin had exacted ample reward from his war-depleted Chinese neighbor.[25] Meanwhile Chiang, quite aware of the real situation, was content to enlist the support of the devil himself if, with supreme caution and skill, he could turn it to his own ends.

[25] Consult Feis, *The China Tangle, op.cit.,* Chs. 28, 29, 30.

16 · VINEGAR AND HONEY:
THE STILWELL AND WEDEMEYER MISSIONS
IN CHINA

᠎

PART ONE: STILWELL'S FAILURE. I. EARLY MISSIONS TO
CHINA. II. "A SMALL-FRY COLONEL" RETURNS AS A GEN-
ERAL. III. PROBLEMS FOR "VINEGAR JOE." IV. STILWELL
IS RECALLED.

PART TWO: STILWELL'S SUCCESS. I. THE PLAN FOR
BURMA: CHINESE TROOPS, AMERICAN-TRAINED. II. RAM-
GARH: THE PROGRAM IN INDIA. III. AN EVALUATION OF
RAMGARH'S SUCCESS. IV. KUNMING AND KWEILIN: THE
PROGRAM IN CHINA. V. THE PINCER MOVEMENT: THE
RECOVERY OF BURMA.

PART THREE: WEDEMEYER'S SUCCESS.

"More flies are caught with a drop of honey than with a
cask of vinegar"—Dutch Proverb.

᠎

PART ONE: STILWELL'S FAILURE

I

THE United States, although a traditional friend of China, did not
enter the Chinese military picture until 1941, when her involvement
in a general war in the Pacific appeared imminent. Before this, however, her interest in the maintenance of Chinese administrative and
territorial integrity, her political and moral support of China's cause,
and her material assistance had long been recognized as significant
factors contributing to China's war strength.

Prior to the war, the Chinese air force was the only branch of the
armed services in which the Americans could claim any influence. In
1931 Colonel Jack Jouett came to the Chinese Air Force Academy
with a small instructional team and laid a sound foundation for the
Chinese through his introduction of the highly efficient American air-

training system. As the air force became American-oriented, many more Americans came to China's service. Prominent among them was Claire L. Chennault, later the commanding general of the Flying Tigers.

The first military assistance to China sponsored by the United States government came as part of the American air program for China.[1] At the request of Chiang Kai-shek, the United States sent an air mission to China in May 1941 for the purpose of making a report on the Chinese air forces, with particular reference to the American volunteer program, which would serve as a basis for the allocation of United States aid. General H. B. Clagett USAAF, arrived in Chungking and remained for about a month. The Chinese proposals at that time were formulated around three basic points: (1) creating a modern Chinese air force, (2) instituting and maintaining an efficient line of communication into China, and (3) arming 30 Chinese divisions.[2] By this time, President Roosevelt, Harry Hopkins, and Secretary Cordell Hull were looking seriously into the problem of providing material aid to China in the form of ordnance, motor transport, and military supplies.

Washington, feeling that China did not have sufficiently qualified military personnel in the capital to plan lend-lease aid effectively and economically, established the American Military Mission to China (AMMISCA) in July 1941.[3] Its function was to find out precisely how much the Chinese really needed, how the foundations laid by the German mission could be built upon, and to offer certain organizational and instructional assistance. The well-balanced team of American military experts was led by capable and experienced Brigadier General John Magruder. The group was composed of six men who had had some experience in China, three of whom had studied the language for four years or more; they were prepared to offer expert advice on economic warfare, medicine, railroad management, artillery, and pursuit aircraft.[4]

By mid-November 1941 twenty officers (two-thirds of the mission) reached China.[5] By the time the Japanese attack on Pearl Harbor catapulted the United States into the war, American military special-

---

[1] U.S. Coordinator of Information, Far Eastern Section, *American Aid to China*, *op.cit.*, p. 32.
[2] Romanus and Sunderland, *op.cit.*, pp. 48-49.
[3] U.S. Coordinator of Information, *op.cit.*, pp. 32-35.
[4] *Ibid.*   [5] *Ibid.*

ists were already established in China. The outbreak of war called
for an even closer cooperation between the Americans and the Chinese,
and General Magruder was directed to supply his superiors with a
plan under which 30 Chinese army divisions were to be armed and
trained by the Americans. On March 15, 1941, President Roosevelt
pledged assistance to China: "China likewise expresses the magnificent
will of millions of plain people to resist the dismemberment of their
nation. China, through the generalissimo, Chiang Kai-shek, asks our
help. America has said that she shall have our help."[6] On May 16,
1941, the president again declared that the defense of China was
vital to the United States.

Until Pearl Harbor was attacked, the United States remained, in
the Chinese war, merely a sympathetic bystander. She was on the
whole in favor of retaining China's friendship, maintaining her territorial integrity, and preserving her independence, but American policy
in detail, both political and military, was neither clear-cut nor firmly
established. The United States was determined to help China to help
herself, and she was ready in some manner to execute the policy tersely
stated by General Marshall: to "arm, equip, and train Chinese forces
in China."[7] The most effective result of this policy in the early stages,
however, concerned Americans more than American-trained Chinese:
air aid to China provided by the American volunteer group, the
Flying Tigers, under Chennault. They provided effective air defense
for southwest China. Subsequently, the U.S. Navy also dispatched
a highly effective naval mission to China under the leadership of
Rear Admiral Milton E. Miles, the activities of which were believed
to have far-reaching consequences in later American naval operations.
The success of this mission was an anonymous one, although it was
not unrelated to the great American naval victory at Midway in June
1942, where the Japanese Combined Fleet suffered its most devastating defeat in the entire Pacific war.

II

In January 1942, soon after the United States found herself directly concerned with the turmoil in the Far East, Generalissimo
Chiang accepted the nomination as supreme commander of an allied

[6] "Address of President Franklin D. Roosevelt on March 15, 1941," quoted in
United States Relations with China, p. 26.
[7] Romanus and Sunderland, *op.cit.,* p. 49.

China theater. In appreciation of this nomination, Chiang requested the United States government to send a high-ranking officer to be the chief of the allied staff. Chiang's letter noted: ". . . this officer need not be an expert on the Far East; on the contrary, he (the generalissimo) thinks that military men who have a knowledge of Chinese armies when China was under the warlords operate at a disadvantage when they think of the present Chinese national armies in terms of the armies of the warlords."[8]

Originally, the United States war department had planned to send one of its senior generals, Hugh A. Drum, to China. Facing administrative confusion and divided counsel in Washington, General Drum determined to obtain a clear-cut, workable directive from the war department in regard to his mission to China. Secretary Stimson was unable to reach full agreement with General Marshall, then chief of staff, and Major General Joseph W. Stilwell was eventually granted the China appointment. He was to be chief of staff of the allied officers from China, the United States, the United Kingdom, and the Netherlands, and was to serve, with General Ho Ying-ch'in, chief of the supreme Chinese staff, as one of Chiang's two top assistants. He was, in addition, commanding general of the American forces in the China-Burma-India theater and of such other troops as the generalissimo might assign to him. Such a multiplicity of duties doomed Stilwell from the beginning. In summary his functions were described as "to increase the effectiveness of the United States assistance to the Chinese government for the prosecution of the war and to assist in improving the combat efficiency of the Chinese army."[9]

Not only was Stilwell harnessed with a number of duties which may indeed have been too much for any one man to discharge successfully, but he was not by nature the sort of man which the Chinese situation demanded. On the other hand, the Chinese leadership at Chungking was far from being faultless, nor was it open-minded enough to be receptive to sincere advice. In his *Great Mistakes of the War*, the brilliant military analyst Hanson W. Baldwin summarized the objections to Stilwell: "But we made other grievous errors in China which compounded the basic one. . . . One was a mistake in personnel. General Joseph W. Stilwell was a lovable character and a

[8] "Letter from Soong to Under Secretary of War J. J. McCloy, 6 Jan. 1942," quoted in Romanus and Sunderland, *op.cit.*, p. 66.
[9] Romanus and Sunderland, *op.cit.*, p. 74.

fine soldier, but his nickname 'Vinegar Joe,' the difficulty he had in working with the British, and his natural tendency to give primacy to military, rather than political considerations did not make him the ideal theater commander in the most difficult theater of war: one where toughness needed to be combined with urbanity and with greater political *savoir faire*."[10]

III

The command was indeed a most difficult one, and the diplomacy that Stilwell lacked was not the only problem. General Marshall described Stilwell's position thus: "He was out at the end of the *thinnest* supply line of all. . . . He had a most difficult physical problem of great distances, almost impossible terrain, widespread disease and unfavorable climate; he faced an extremely complex political problem and his purely military problem of opposing large numbers of enemy with few resources was unmatched in any theater."[11]

To a job of unmatched difficulty Stilwell brought the courage and know-how of a veteran fighting general, the knowledge of an old hand in China, and a monumental absence of tact. He detested inefficiency and corruption. He did not attempt to disguise his contempt of Chinese officialdom, the head of the state not excepted. Chiang remarked on Stilwell's blatant "superiority complex."[12] Stilwell spoke of Roosevelt as "Old Softie"; of Chiang as "Peanut," a "tribal chieftain"; of Field Marshal Wavell as "Bumble," whose favorite words were "can't," "goddam difficult," and "impracticable." Admiral Mountbatten was a "glamor boy," and General Wedemeyer came in for his share of insults.[13]

Stilwell had other talents in addition to his undoubted gifts of infuriating his allies, discouraging cooperation, and maintaining incompetent or prejudicial staff assistants rather than suffering criticism or suggestions from his deputies.[14] He had amazing vigor and a capacity for any kind of hard work—except paper work, which he hated. His passion for justice endeared him to the common soldiers,

[10] Baldwin, Hanson W., *Great Mistakes of the War* (N.Y.: Harper, 1950), p. 60.
[11] U.S. War Department, "Biennial Report of the Chief of Staff of the U.S. Army, July 1, 1943 to June 30, 1945 to the Secretary of the War," *The U.S. News* (Washington, Oct. 10, 1945), p. 59.
[12] *The Stilwell Papers*, *op.cit.*, pp. 232f.   [13] *Ibid., passim.*
[14] Ho Yung-chi, *The Big Circle* (N.Y., 1948), p. 47.

to whom he was devoted. He was brilliant in thought and fearless in battle. He could train soldiers and he could lead them.

Almost immediately he was precipitated into the Burma campaign without an adequate staff, a thorough acquaintance with the local situation, or a clarification of his ambiguous command over the Chinese forces in Burma, where the Chinese commanders were willing to accept his suggestions in strategic direction and tactical planning but hardly ready to acknowledge his supreme command. The British expected Stilwell to take orders from General R. L. G. Alexander, who in turn expected to command the Chinese.

Misjudging the enemy, Stilwell advocated the ill-fated strategy of *attack*, the attempt to recapture Rangoon, in the face of Chiang's pleas that defense was all the allies could achieve at the time. The error was never wholly forgotten during the entire time that Stilwell remained in the East, despite the Second Burma Campaign, one of the outstanding military feats of World War II, which might be said to have atoned for it. In the latter campaign, Stilwell, commanding a well-knit Chinese and American force, fought terrain, monsoons, and crack Japanese divisions. He endeared himself to the Chinese soldiers, who saw a foreign commander marching with them fearlessly in the thick of the fight and the worst of the jungles. He proved himself considerably better than the "World War I foot soldier, Walking Joe" or "the best goddam four-star battalion commander" his detractors talked about. In fact, General Marshall and Secretary of War Stimson both concurred that "No American officer had demonstrated more clearly his knowledge of the strength and weakness of the Japanese force as General Stilwell."[15] He performed his duty with single-minded determination, never retreating an inch from his conviction that "the Chinese troops if well trained, equipped and led can match the valor of soldiers everywhere."[16]

One of Stilwell's problems was the self-defensive arrogance that the China appointment brought out in him. Only a few years earlier he had been in China as a military attaché, in a greatly inferior position. When the appointment as chief of staff in China was being discussed, he wrote: "George [the chief of staff] looking for a high-ranking man to go. Drum? Pompous, stubborn, new to them, high

[15] U.S. War Department, *Biennial Report, op.cit.*, p. 60.
[16] Stimson, H. L., and Bundy, M., *On Active Service in Peace and War* (1st ed., N.Y.: Harper, 1948), p. 540.

rank. Me? No, thank you. They remember me as a small-fry colonel that they kicked around."[17] The former colonel had to return to China (where both he and Brigadier General Evan F. Carlson, USMC, were regarded as inclined to be too friendly to the Chinese communists) in the wake of such distinguished foreign generals as Galen, Wetzell, von Seeckt, von Falkenhausen, and Zhukov—and the Chinese always tended to judge foreigners by their rank and prestige at home.

It was arrogance on Stilwell's part that led to the break with Chiang. The general not only asserted his power in military affairs but also began to dabble in Chinese politics. As Major General Robert B. McClure, the United States deputy chief of staff in China, reported of Stilwell:

"His long experience in China convinced him that the only way to achieve the objective was through extensive reorganization not only of the *Chinese Army*, but of the *National Government* as well. The deadwood, the incompetent, and the corrupt must be forcibly removed. The Communists and the Nationalists must be forced to join forces and fight the Japanese! Thus, as the military situation in China became steadily worse, Stilwell insisted that the price of increased U.S. help must be the appointment of himself as the Commander-in-Chief of all Chinese Armies. The appointment was made in 1944 by the GMO [Generalissimo Chiang].

"At that time the Chinese Communist forces were not strong or well equipped, and were fighting only sporadic actions against both the Japanese and the Nationalists. . . . During these months the Communist forces gave neither Nationalists nor Americans real help or assistance when it was so sorely needed."[18]

Stilwell demanded and received the ostensible power to unify these forces against the Japanese, and called for a governmental shake-up to produce more efficiency. His weapon in these battles was the promise of continued or increased American aid. The British influence was strong in the ranks of the combined chiefs of staff, however, and Chinese stockpiles rapidly diminished while material was reallocated to other recipients. When aircraft originally intended for

---

[17] *The Stilwell Papers, op.cit.,* p. 19.
[18] "Major General R. B. McClure's Address at the University of Colorado, August 8, 1949," quoted in Chen Chi-mai, *Kuomintang and Communist Relationship, A Historical Study,* a mimeographed pamphlet prepared by the chancellor of the Chinese Embassy at Washington, p. 11.

the Chinese theater was reallocated by Washington, Stilwell complained: "Now what can I say to the G-mo? We fail in all our commitments and blithely tell him to just carry on, old top."[19]

General Stilwell addressed Generalissimo Chiang thus in regard to the Chinese army: "The Chinese Army is weak partly because of lack of equipment, but mostly for other reasons. It is too large to equip properly with the material now available, but a reduced number of divisions could be furnished with suitable weapons, including artillery, if a determined effort were made to get it together. . . . The lack of artillery, A.A. guns, tanks, and planes has been evident for a long time. There is no use in continuing this complaint. . . ."

Then Stilwell made three demands: (1) that the Chinese divisions be merged to bring all units up to full strength; (2) a "rigid purge" of inefficient Chinese high commanders; (3) that in further operation "one man be chosen with complete authority to direct the action with complete control over the services, and with no staff other than his own present . . . this absolute control over the troops must not be infringed upon."[20] Twenty days later Madame Chiang Kai-shek told Stilwell that his demands were "unrealistic."

Throughout his stay in China, Stilwell, giving primacy to military matters, consistently ignored the worsening economic situation in nationalist China. On several occasions he urged his own government to refuse loans to Chungking. The Chinese government, on the other hand, was being asked to provide great sums of Chinese paper money to pay for the construction of air fields and the building of roads— all connected with the expansion of American military activities in China. To meet this deficit, the Chinese government, apathetic in its economic efforts, resorted to issuing unbacked notes. Although Stilwell was in no way to be blamed for the deteriorating war economy, inflation was cutting deeply into the livelihood of the millions of Chinese soldiers and their families, causing serious effects on their fighting morale and, in many ways, indirectly nullifying the American effort to improve the Chinese military efficiency.

IV

In the United States, where policy at that time was to keep China in the war and to retain her friendship, the Chinese anger at Stilwell's

[19] *The Stilwell Papers, op.cit.,* p. 119.
[20] Romanus and Sunderland, *op.cit.,* pp. 372-373.

arrogant demands and his inability to fulfill his commitments about aid became a matter of some concern. The president indicated his strong dissatisfaction with the turn matters had taken in China. Stilwell's sarcastic cablegrams about the Chinese reflected, the president felt, his hatred of the Chinese. It was common knowledge that there was no love lost between the generalissimo and Stilwell. There was some discussion about replacing Stilwell. When Vice-President Henry A. Wallace returned from his fact-finding trip to China, one of his proposals was that General Albert C. Wedemeyer replace Stilwell in the China command.[21] General Marshall and Admiral King, however, were vehement in their support of Stilwell, and General Marshall argued that Stilwell was the only high-ranking officer who could speak Chinese and that, though his dislike of Chinese officialdom could not be denied, he had a high regard for the Chinese people.[22]

Stilwell's recall was a result, not of Washington deliberations, but of his own actions. Despite the strong opposition of many ranking Americans in Chungking, Stilwell contemptuously delivered a strongly worded message from President Roosevelt to Chiang Kai-shek. The Chinese reacted violently, replying that this was but another in the long succession of attempts to use American aid as a club with which to beat the Chinese into submission. The government's highest body in Chungking unanimously backed Chiang in this ultimatum: if Stilwell's dictation was to be the American price for aid to China, then China would rather fight the Japanese alone. That was the end of Stilwell in China.[23]

Stilwell's recall by no means ended the friction between China and the United States. The strain he had put on their friendship had far-reaching repercussions. Insofar as he had been instructed to improve Sino-American relations, Stilwell had failed dismally. The fault could not be his alone; the Chinese leadership at Chungking was not blameless. Perhaps his assignment had been an impossible one. General Marshall wrote of his recall: "Nevertheless, General Stilwell sought with amazing vigor to carry out his mission exactly as it had been stated. His great effort brought a natural conflict of personalities. He stood, as it were, the middle man between two great governments

[21] "Letter, Vice President H. A. Wallace to President Roosevelt, July 10, 1944," *New York Times* (Sept. 24, 1951), p. 20.

[22] Sherwood, Robert E., *Roosevelt and Hopkins* (Bantam Revised Ed., 1950), p. 352.

[23] Consult Feis, *op.cit.*, Ch. 19.

other than his own, with slender resources and problems somewhat overwhelming in their complexity. As a consequence it was deemed necessary in the fall of 1944 to relieve General Stilwell of the burden of his heavy responsibilities in Asia and give him respite from attempting the impossible."[24]

But China did stay in the war, and Stilwell had proved his hypothesis that Chinese troops when well trained could match the valor of soldiers anywhere. The next section will record the outstanding success of Stilwell's training programs and his confidence in Chinese troops. Some of Japan's best army divisions from northern and central Burma had been wiped out—even the so-called invincible Eighteenth Division. The blockade of China had been broken and an overland route from Ledo to China was being opened according to Stilwell's original plan. The overland route was Stilwell's "baby." In General Wedemeyer's words: "The strongest proponent of a land route to China has been General Stilwell. He conceived the plan and fought it through the council rooms."[25]

Even the generalissimo acknowledged Stilwell's achievement in that regard. Chiang Kai-shek commented: ". . . Let us name this road after General Joseph Stilwell in memory of his distinctive contribution, of the signal part which the Allied and Chinese forces under his direction played in the Burma campaign and in the building of this road."[26]

PART TWO: STILWELL'S SUCCESS

I

Stilwell was determined to "fight back to Burma." After the failure of the first Burmese expedition in 1942, he offered the Chinese high command a training program at Ramgarh in northeast India, pursuing a plan approved by the joint chiefs of staff in Washington. Its purpose was to provide the Chinese forces in India with the techniques and tactics that would make the fullest possible use of the new weapons

[24] U.S. War Department, *Biennial Report of the Chief of Staff, op.cit.,* p. 59.
[25] Wedemeyer, A. C., "Broadcast on Jan. 28, 1945 on the Opening of the Stilwell Road," *China Handbook, 1937-1945,* pp. 224f.
[26] Chiang Kai-shek, "Broadcast to the American, British, and Allied Peoples, Jan. 28, 1945," *China Handbook, 1937-1945,* p. 224.

with which they were to be equipped. Around the Ramgarh-trained forces Stilwell planned to build his 30 Chinese divisions.[27]

The nucleus for the training program was a part of the Chinese expeditionary force (the Twenty-Second and the Thirty-Sixth divisions) which had retreated into India during the reverses of the first Burma campaign in the spring of 1942. Not only were there men in India, but the cutting off of the land route to China had stockpiled a considerable amount of equipment there. The decision was made to reverse the usual procedure: the troops would be brought to the equipment. In India, free from Chinese political interference, Chinese troops would be trained along American lines.

With the exception of Bren guns and some Bren gun carriers, where the British lent a hand, all arms and ammunition were to come from the rich, avuncular Americans. The British provided rations, gas, and oil—and turned over to the plan such field installations as infantry, artillery, and tank training grounds. The Americans set up medical facilities and staffed them with their own personnel. The Chinese were to be responsible for unit administration and discipline, and would also supply the trainees.

The Americans made a great initial stride toward cooperation and success by their choice of commanding and instructional personnel. Colonels G. W. Sliney (highly respected by the Chinese for his earlier performance in the Burmese campaign), J. H. Hinwood, C. C. Benson, E. F. Easterbrook, C. H. Brown, and W. H. Holcomb were placed in charge of the training centers for artillery, infantry, armor, tactics, and the services of supply. The forceful but diplomatic Brigadier General Frederick McCabe was appointed commanding general for the Ramgarh scheme, and Brigadier General W. E. Bergin, the chief-of-staff. General McCabe was later succeeded by Colonel D. A. Young.

The Chinese commanders, too, were of the highest caliber. Lieutenant Generals Sun Li-jen and Liao Yao-hsiang were two of the best-educated and most battle-experienced younger Chinese generals. Sun, who had studied at Purdue University, was a graduate of the Virginia Military Institute, and Liao was a product of France's military academy, St. Cyr. Their Chinese assistants were predominantly officers from the Central Army units, and thus regular graduates of

[27] U.S. War Department, *Biennial Report of the Chief of Staff*, op.cit., p. 22.

the Chinese military academy and training schools. They handled staff work for the Chinese forces at Ramgarh and, later, in the fighting in northern Burma.

The efficiency, sincerity, and smooth cooperation of the instructional and administrative teams were matched by the eagerness of the Chinese troops to learn. They arrived ragged, hungry, and ridden with disease. They were fed and clothed, given proper medical care, and transformed into efficient, self-confident, proud new units. For once Americans and Chinese showed what their wholehearted team-work could produce.

This efficiency, and mutual understanding and admiration, came only after some hurdles had been cleared. There was inevitable friction at the beginning. The American and Chinese officers had different concepts of the nature of military command, the traditional Chinese attitude of an officer toward his men being summed up in the phrase *tzu-ti-ping* (translated roughly as "children and companions in arms"). The Chinese objected to the Americans being put in direct command of Chinese troops, by-passing Chinese authority, and conceived of a plan where Chinese officers would first receive training from Americans and then hand it on to their own men. The Chinese officer wanted to preserve in training that same relationship with his men that he would have when the training came at last to be tested in battle.[28] The Americans feared that the Chinese officers were largely under the influence of preconceived notions resulting from seven years of defensive action, notions which would hamper the inculcation of aggressive training for attack.[29] The Chinese countered that their seven years in combat had taught them valuable lessons for any war situation, and they did not take kindly to criticism from American instructors who had never been under fire. Even in supply there were problems. When American personnel failed to consult the Chinese, they often forgot to supply, for example, water bottles, trenching tools, or pack animals. With understanding and patience on both sides, however, everything came out right eventually.

American training methods, based on their own mobilization training programs, utilized every aid from films to Donald Duck comic books.

[28] Ho Yung-chi, *The Big Circle*, *op.cit.*, p. 45.
[29] Consult a series of articles (in Chinese) in *Shih-ssu-sing-pao*, Chungking, written by that newspaper's correspondent in India entitled "Chung-kuo yuan-ch'eng-chün chu-In-chün-chü," which appeared between Nov. 1944 and Jan. 1945.

Because of the ever-present language barrier and the shortage of inter-preters, however, the Americans chiefly taught by example: "Thank God we don't speak Chinese, and we don't have interpreters, *remarked Colonel Sliney, the director of Ramgarh's artillery training*. We dem-onstrate and they copy. They are the greatest mimics in the world and are learning very fast."[30]

Colonel Sliney thought highly of the Chinese artillerymen he trained, and his opinion was shared by Brigadier General McCabe. The Chinese mastered the use of mortars in almost miraculous time. Instructed by Colonel R. M. Cannon's men, former infantrymen learned to fire the vicious 75 mm. pack howitzer in a week. The more complex Browning machine gun and the Bren gun took a little longer, but progress was rapid.[31] These trainees, coming from homes where technological standards are many decades behind the American stand-ards, caught on amazingly. Without any previous knowledge of Eng-lish, more than 90 per cent of the Chinese radio operators were able to receive 15 words a minute in English after 7 weeks of training. Ordinarily, in the United States, about 60 per cent of the men made the grade after 13 weeks of training.[32] The main Chinese weakness was poor rifle marksmanship. Fortunately there was usually enough ammunition so that the soldiers could practice until the instructors were satisfied with the results. The Chinese had cause for pride and the Americans at Ramgarh (particularly, their successive chiefs of operations, Colonels J. A. Andrews and R. R. Tourtillott) had a pleasant sense of achievement. Morale was high and various difficulties, such as an occasional lack of supplies and equipment, served only to knit the Americans and the Chinese more closely together.

II

The training received at Ramgarh may be classified under three headings. The officers were to receive instructions in combat techniques, tactics, and teamwork coordination; the soldiers were trained to master their weapons and taught how to use their equipment to perform specialized combat duties. The idea was to develop task forces capable of an efficient, sustained, and coordinated effort on the battlefield. On

[30] Eldridge, F., *Wrath in Burma* (N.Y., 1946), p. 142.
[31] *Ibid.*
[32] "Statement of Brig. Gen. T. S. Arms to the correspondents," quoted in *China, After Seven Years of War* (N.Y.: Macmillan, 1945), p. 208.

a higher level there was a special training program for the staff officers and field commanders, from colonels to generals, who were flown over the Hump from various war areas in China, were given a course of training, and then flown back to put their new knowledge into immediate practice. They received a six-week version of the wartime course administered at the United States command and general staff school at Leavenworth, Kansas, in American staff procedures, strategy and tactics, and logistics. This program formed part of a long-range scheme which transcended the Burma front and aimed at an eventual counteroffensive on the mainland of China.

One of the best-handled aspects in the administration of the plan was the medical service. Outstanding American doctors and specialists (Drs. I. V. Ravdin, C. TenBroeck, G. S. Seagrave) performed yeoman service in supplying much-needed medical care in well-equipped hospitals in India and Burma and in front-line surgical units.

General Pai Chung-hsi, vice-chief of the supreme staff and Chinese minister in charge of military training, lauded what he had seen at the Kunming training center: "According to our observation, we found the good traits in the American system of military education to consist of the ability for self-consciousness, initiative, autonomy, perseverance and industry. Whatever the weather conditions there was no relaxation of technical training and practical maneuvers. The methods used consisted of preparation, instruction, demonstration, practice, tests, and evaluation. There was an ample supply of arms and ammunition. By the methods used and a system of rotation, it is possible to train a large number of officers and men within the short period dictated by wartime demands. We must indeed adopt such methods of education ourselves. We must never lose sight of [the importance of] educational facilities and the condition of arms, equipment, and ammunition."[33]

Pai's tour of inspection gave him an opportunity to observe at first hand the smoothly efficient scheme and, when asked by General Stilwell for his comments, he tendered the suggestion that Sino-American cooperation might well be extended with joint exercises designed to promote inter-service harmony and teamwork between the army and the air forces based at Kunming. This, and a plan to have such joint exercises also at Ramgarh, was subsequently adopted.

[33] Pai Chung-hsi, "Lecture to the Chinese Army Staff College," *Military Education and Training in China* (Shanghai: International Publisher, 1946), pp. 7f.

The Americans were happy to extend their operations, and the success of the Ramgarh training program up to the time had disposed Chiang to look favorably on proposals to continue it on an enlarged basis. At the time Stilwell and the whole corps of American instructors were firmly set in the generalissimo's favor. American prestige reached a new high, and by the end of 1943 Stilwell assumed full command of the Chinese army in India whose successes the training programs had done so much to ensure.

III

The proof of Ramgarh's achievement was the northern Burma campaign. General Tojo, the Japanese premier, had openly admitted to the puppet Burmese government: "On the defense of Burma, the Imperial Japanese army itself can shoulder the full responsibility; but the Chinese army in India, now concentrating in East India's Assam province, is a highly trained crack army to which we should give our close attention."[34] The importance of the training was stressed in all of Stilwell's reports to the generalissimo. The following is an extract from one such report, dealing with a Chinese-manned tank battalion commanded by Colonel Rothwell H. Brown:

"The Chinese tank corps in particular covered itself with glory in operation. Not too much was expected of them, as they are not seasoned troops, veterans of many battles and possessors of a mechanical heritage. They are green men in the military sense, and many of them have come from China's paddy fields to drive a motor-driven vehicle for the first time in their lives. . . . The tanks and supporting infantry killed about five hundred Japanese in addition to spreading consternation throughout enemy positions wherever they operated. (These were about the Maingkwan-Walawbum area tank action in the Hukwang Valley in March, 1942.) It represented a series of actions that would have done credit to a seasoned unit and was especially meritorious considering the amount of training (only three months) and other preparation that had gone into this group. . . ."[35]

For seventeen months the Chinese forces fought in northern Burma, advancing more than 600 miles from their operational base in India without sustaining a single defeat. Often they were numerically in-

[34] Tojo, Hideji, "Statement on the Anniversary of Burmese Independence Day 1944," *Domei*, 1944.
[35] Eldridge, *op.cit.*, p. 142.

ferior to the enemy, but sheer tenacity and fighting won through for them. Stilwell exulted: "The Chinese troops have been grand—and they will do what I say now. Their tails are up and they tear into the Japs with full confidence that they can beat the hell out of them. It is what you may call very satisfying to say the least. Also our score of dead Japs counted is now over 20,000."[36]

Colonel Rothwell H. Brown, whom Stilwell praised in the report to Chiang quoted above and who was in direct command of Chinese troops, remarked: "The Chinese are the bravest soldiers I have ever seen. With the little training they have had, I must take off my hat to them for what they have accomplished. They've got guts. I'm willing to go anywhere with them."[37]

For a Chinese evaluation of the success of the Ramgarh plan, let a Chinese commander, Lieutenant General Sun Li-jen, speak: "The victory of the Chinese Expeditionary Forces in northern Burma is the happiest result of the Chinese fighting spirit combined with American equipment and training. Through these long years of war the Chinese soldier has a tried and true record. Now he has been given a chance to prove what he can do when placed shoulder to shoulder with his ally and on equal terms with the enemy."[38]

IV

Other American-manned training centers were established as a result of the Ramgarh experiment. In China they were set up principally in the provinces of Kwangsi and Yunnan. At Kunming an infantry training center was established under Brigadier General Thomas S. Arms, with Chiang Kai-shek as its nominal commandant. Later another was situated at Kweilin. An artillery school was established under Brigadier General J. J. Waters. The trainees were withdrawn from the front, given six weeks of accelerated indoctrination in American methods, and put back in the front lines to put their newly acquired skills to practical use. They learned the handling of weapons and something of tactics from American instructors and Chinese assistants and also a little about medical aid, veterinary

[36] *The Stilwell Papers, op.cit.*, p. 308.
[37] Cheng, H., "Chinese Courage in the Burma Jungle," *China, After Seven Years of War*, p. 213.
[38] Sun Li-jen, "Opening Words to Burma-Yunnan Victory," *China at War*, XV, 1 (July, 1945), p. 26.

science, signaling, and engineering. Some of the fighting methods were especially modified to fit local conditions.

Equipment in the Chinese centers posed problems unheard of in the Ramgarh operation. Once again the Americans provided instructional personnel, but this time the rifles and heavy machine guns were made in China, not U.S.-supplied. The Bren guns were a Czech model made in Canada, and Canadian and British arsenals supplied some automatic rifles. The Tommy guns, carbines, and mortars were of American make and, although the ammunition for small arms was mostly Chinese, substantial quantities were shipped from the United States and flown into China.

The trainees were selected at the division level, and divisional and army commanders were ordered to training centers by the generalissimo to attend command and general staff courses or to serve as administrative officers. They attended courses and shared barracks with junior student officers. Some of the commanders were at first skeptical of the scheme, and refused to send their best men for training, but after taking the course themselves (and observing the improved tactical ability and marksmanship of the graduates) they recognized its benefits. Results were good because the majority of the trainees had had considerable battle experience prior to their training and knew the value, and the specific uses, of the new information they received. They had long sustained a defensive action, and one of the objectives of the training program was to inculcate offensive concepts in preparation for the counteroffensive in the offing. Assured of American support and a continued source of material aid, and confident in their new skills, the trainees were zealous in their preparation to fight back against the Japanese.

The generalissimo himself inspected the infantry installation at Kweilin and expressed his complete satisfaction in its methods, morale, and results. He was impressed, as many of his battle-hardened subordinate officers had been, with the surprising success the Americans were having with the brief six-week course. The mutual satisfaction engendered by the success of the program greatly improved Sino-American relations and produced admiration on both sides. Those Americans who participated in the plan in China gained a new understanding and appreciation of the Chinese soldier's potential and fighting spirit. They were especially taken by his aggressiveness. General Arms remarked: "This is perhaps the greatest difference between a

Chinese and an American soldier. The American soldier asks when he is going out to the front. But the Chinese asks when he is going back to the front." He continued: "When a man has gone through the kind of hell a Chinese soldier has gone through in the last seven years and is still anxious to go back and get even with the enemy, you can't beat him if he has the necessary training and equipment—which we are trying to give him in the center."[39]

V

The training program in China was primarily designed to build up another Chinese expeditionary force which would, in conjunction with the Stilwell force in India, join in a pincer movement for the attack on Burma. Stilwell and his deputies (especially Brigadier General Frank "Pinky" Dorn) pinned their hopes on getting the Chinese to mobilize all the available manpower and materials for a concerted effort at the conquest of Burma. Part of the material, they assumed, the United States lend-lease program could provide. Chiang stated, on November 3, 1942, that he could contribute 20 picked divisions, with appropriate artillery.[40] Stilwell hoped to exact more strength from the generalissimo and reorganize it into 24 new-type assault divisions, 2 old-style divisions, and 6 replacements. All were expected to operate as self-contained combat teams.[41]

Although the American demands on Chinese troop supplies were unrealistic in view of the situation on the Chinese front, a force of 100,000 men was mobilized. Under General Wei Li-huang they crossed the Salween River on May 11, 1944 and captured the Japanese strongholds in the steep fastnesses of the Kaolikung mountain ranges, despite raging monsoons and stiff Japanese defense of strong positions. On January 27, 1945, the two pincer forces met at Mu-se. Stilwell's dream of recapturing Burma with American-trained Chinese forces was at last a reality.

PART THREE: WEDEMEYER'S SUCCESS

Lieutenant General Albert C. Wedemeyer came to Chungking at an awkward time. The Chinese had grown increasingly touchy,

[39] Chao, S. M., "American Know-How for Chinese Soldiers," *China, After Seven Years of War, op.cit.*, p. 212.
[40] Romanus and Sunderland, *op.cit.*, p. 182.   [41] *Ibid.*, p. 234.

and the slightest misstep might have provided sufficient to cause a serious and permanent break in Sino-American relations.

Wedemeyer's first press conference at Chungking made it clear that his job was to serve the Chinese in the war against Japan and to stay out of Chinese politics. He gave frank notice to the American military personnel in China of what his policy would be. He was determined, first, to formulate a plan to hold American supply bases at all costs; second, to improve the fighting effectiveness of the Chinese army; third, to see that all Americans in China "act like Americans."

These instructions followed the spirit of a new directive which the Joint Chiefs of Staff issued to Wedemeyer on October 24, 1944, and which was to remain the governing order for American military activity in China until the end of war. It specified:

"1. That in regard to the United States combat forces under his command his primary mission was to carry out air operations from China.

"2. He was also to continue to assist the Chinese air and ground forces in operation, training, and logistical support.

"3. He was to control the allocation of Lend-Lease supplies delivered into China, within priorities set by the Joint Chiefs of Staff.

"4. In regard to the Chinese forces he was authorized to advise and to assist the Generalissimo in the conduct of military operations against Japan.

"5. He was not to use United States resources to suppress civil strife except insofar as necessary to protect United States lives and property."[42]

It was clear that Wedemeyer's tact and diplomacy would appeal to the Chinese. His ability as a strategist was no less. He earned the admiration of the Chinese by his unreserved cooperation with their government in repelling the Japanese offensive against Kweiyang, by quickly ordering an airlift to transport Chinese troops from the northwest to the critical spot. With Chennault's U.S. Fourteenth Air Force under his command, Wedemeyer directed against the Japanese forces powerful air assaults which succeeded in slowing their advance. Fresh reinforcements and air support enabled the Chinese to send the enemy reeling back from Kweichow, and the tide of war took a definite turn

[42] Feis, *op.cit.*, p. 202.

in favor of the allies. Wedemeyer had succeeded in the fulfillment of his first objective: to hold American supply bases in China.

Within a month, Wedemeyer was able to report gratifying successes on the battlefield. Toward the end of November 1944, the long-demanded changes in the Chinese government—the overhaul of the military administration and the reorganization of the army—were announced as adopted. The Chinese military administration consented to put into force Wedemeyer's proposals to reorganize the army by reducing its size from 327 divisions to 84 effective combat divisions; and of these, Wedemeyer suggested that the United States train and equip 39 divisions and China the rest.[43] The Chinese even agreed to Wedemeyer's insistence that Americans supervise the purchase of food locally when paid for with lend-lease funds. One of the general's reforms in the Chinese army concerned the amelioration of the Chinese soldier's diet, a necessary and popular move. Wedemeyer also urged that the officer corps be thoroughly culled, that the command be drawn together, and that armies be relocated.

As a soldier Wedemeyer was aptly described in an official citation as a man of "outstanding ability, resourcefulness, tact, initiative and profound strategical judgment."[44] He came to China comparatively young and with less seniority than some of the men with whom that nation had dealt, but he had behind him an impressive record as one of the few American officers ever graduated from the German war college, the Kriegsakademie, and as a leading light of the United States war department planning staff. His record, his abilities, and his pleasant personality won him favor with Chiang and his associates, both American and Chinese. Though an infantry general, he made great use of the air force, and he was especially known for his bold, effective strategies—indeed Generals Stratemeyer and Marshall regarded him as a "strategist of the whole war."[45]

In his plan to improve the effectiveness of the Chinese army, Wedemeyer instituted joint U.S.-Chinese staffs at all the major echelons. American officers were placed in all branches of services and in combat commands. Policies were arrived at and executed by the Chinese and the Americans as allies and equals, and so completely had Wedemeyer

[43] *Ibid.*, p. 296.
[44] "United States War Department on Awarding Lt. Gen. Albert C. Wedemeyer the Distinguished Service Medal," quoted in *Current Biography*, *1945*, p. 664.
[45] Utley, Freda, *Last Chance in China* (Indianapolis, 1947), p. 278.

been able to win back Chiang's confidence that the generalissimo himself directed that, in the event of disagreement at the highest level, the American view should prevail. By the summer of 1945, about 500 American officers and 500 enlisted men were serving in the Chinese armed forces.

Wedemeyer not only repaired the breach in the Sino-American entente that Stilwell's actions had created, but he conserved and strengthened the good work that Stilwell had been able to do in the training programs. The training of the Chinese staff nucleus was accelerated. Wedemeyer even took an interest in the operation of the Chinese Army Staff College and the National Defense Institute.

Flying across China, and always on the alert for necessary reforms —a merit system, improved rations, etc.—Wedemeyer gained an intimate knowledge of the performance of Chinese units on the several war fronts. Everywhere he went he stressed the importance of establishing a good relationship between the officers and the enlisted men, while maintaining strict discipline and fighting efficiency.[46] His reports on the recruits prompted the government to improve the conscription system, and he also got action on the voluntary tightening up of the army's size while improving its fighting power, a program which Stilwell had often urged before but which his lack of diplomacy had previously made unacceptable to the government. The all-out Chinese military organization of 1945 was testimony to Wedemeyer's ability not only to perceive where changes had to be made but to enlist the wholehearted support of the Chinese officials in making them.

Under Wedemeyer's direction an expanded military program was set in operation. The command and general staff courses turned out officers qualified to assume duties as chiefs of staff or operational officers in various military commands. Instruction was now offered in infantry, heavy mortars, engineering, signals, motor corps, ordnance, medical and veterinary sciences, and the service of supply. In due course the China combat command was created, headed by Major General Robert B. McClure, the American equivalent of the commander-in-chief of the Chinese ground forces. Roughly paralleling the Chinese army organization, the group supplied liaison teams of Americans to be attached to Chinese units for training troops in the field and advising Chinese commanders in operations, medical services, and other respects.

[46] *U.S. Relations with China, op.cit.*, p. 759.

American methods were adopted to remedy the well-known Chinese defects in administration and supply. A vigorous program was inaugurated to train the Chinese in military finance and in procedures for handling men and materials. For the first time in Chinese military annals a foreigner—the American Major General Gilbert X. Cheves —was appointed by the generalissimo as commanding general of the entire Chinese service of supply.

The delivery of American lend-lease material to China was expedited. Wedemeyer secured the approval of Washington's combined chiefs of staff for sending more planes to the China theater. More resources to back the training programs initiated by Magruder and Stilwell were obtained, and an improved supervisory system over American supplies was instituted.

Plans were ambitious. A total of 39 Chinese divisions were to be trained and equipped. The Alpha program then instituted envisaged the training of half a million Chinese troops, of which 300,000 were to be armed soldiers. If completed, this plan would have affected approximately one-sixth of the entire Chinese regular army as reorganized. Of the 39 divisions, however, the plan was fully realized for only 12, as far as equipment was concerned, but under Wedemeyer 36 divisions had retrained within half a year. Even greater plans were afoot: a secret provision of the Cairo Conference talked of arming 90 Chinese divisions. Wedemeyer's headquarters, nevertheless, never visualized organizing more than 60 divisions along American lines. At one time it was thought that the surrendered equipment of the defeated German Wehrmacht might be made available for the Chinese offensive against Japan.[47]

. By mid-1945 General Wedemeyer had built the Chinese fighting effectiveness to a new high, and the American war department assigned to him two of the top commanders who had helped to crush the German army: General Truscott of the Fifth Army and General Simpson of the Ninth. By August of that year Chinese forces, concentrated in the south, were set for a major offensive against the Japanese forces along the South China coast.[48] For this purpose, General Wedemeyer restrained the Chinese commanders from premature and piecemeal local offensives which used up their limited resources. The intention was

[47] *China Monthly*, XI, 3 (March 1950), pp. 44-47.
[48] *General Offensive Plan, Operation Rashness*, General Headquarters, Chinese Ground Forces, 1945.

to conserve a maximum of striking strength for a vital blow under the code name of Operation Rashness. But other things happened during that fateful month. Hiroshima was blasted by an atomic bomb on August 6. Two days later, Russia declared war on Japan. The next day Nagasaki suffered a crushing atomic attack. On August 10 Japan began to inquire whether the emperor could retain his sovereignty under terms of surrender. The war with Japan was over.

Appraising Wedemeyer's achievement in China, one may say that he "cracked down" on the American forces there while treating the Chinese with tact and diplomacy. He recognized the innumerable weaknesses of the Chinese government and its army, but his respect for and understanding of the Chinese was great. He was able to gain the confidence and cooperation of officials from Chiang on down. He wrote: "We Americans hail the courage of China and the vision of her great leader, Generalissimo Chiang Kai-shek. We confidently face the problems that must yet be solved, knowing that the mutual trust and respect between our two countries remains the basis for lasting peace between China and the United States."[49]

Stilwell had tried vinegar and achieved, he said, these effects: "Holding in general to a purely advisory role, the Americans were often regarded with a jaundiced look of suspicion. In some instances our honest efforts and our impartial action demonstrated an altruistic motive which won the respect and trust of certain field commanders. This favorable action did not always hold true in the Chungking Government. In high places we were generally regarded as interlopers of cunning demeanor distributing largesse, most of which failed to materialize."[50]

Wedemeyer had tried a little bit of honied diplomacy along with the decisiveness and strength that were needed. His mission was successful; Stilwell's was not.

[49] Wedemeyer, A. C., "Broadcast on Jan. 28, 1945 on the Opening of Stilwell Road," *China Handbook, 1937-1945*, p. 225.
[50] *U.S. Relations with China, op.cit.*, p. 69.

17 · THE SINO-JAPANESE WAR, 1937-1945

FIRST PHASE: FROM WANPING TO THE FALL OF HANKOW.
SECOND PHASE: THE CHINESE REDS PLAY THEIR OWN
GAME. *THIRD PHASE*: I. ENTER THE AMERICAN ALLY.
II. THE FIRST BURMA CAMPAIGN. III. VICTORY IN BURMA
AND ITS AFTERMATH. IV. OPERATION *ICHI-GŌ*: THE JAPA-
NESE OFFENSIVE. V. THE CONCLUSION OF THE WAR. *SUM-
MARY*.

FIRST PHASE

THE great conflict between China and Imperial Japan is generally
regarded as having begun on the night of July 7, 1937, with an
exchange of shots between a Japanese force conducting maneuvers and
the Chinese garrison of Wanping. Wanping, standing at the eastern
end of the Lukouchiao or Marco Polo Bridge, was a small city, but
it strategically linked the important Peiping-Tientsin line with the
vital Peiping-Hankow railroad. The Chinese sued for a local settlement and were prepared to make concessions, but the Japanese took
advantage of the occasion as an excuse for sending heavy reinforcements to northern China. Within twenty days Peiping had been encircled and fell to the Japanese. Her historic northern capital in enemy
hands, China could not but enter the war.[1] In Tokyo, the Japanese
war minister General Sugiyama reported confidently to Emperor
Hirohito that the war would end within one month and that Japan
would *win*!

Chinese public opinion was stronger than the doubts of her leaders
regarding the advisability of fighting. Upon learning that the Chinese
were determined to blockade and defend the lower approaches to the

[1] According to a noted Japanese journalist, Tamura Masasaku, the touching-off of
the Lukouchiao incident was due to a premeditated plot on the part of a small group
of Japanese militarists, the so-called "China section" in the general staff and war
ministry. They wanted to extend the incident as a means of broadening their military
influence in China. Opposing such a militaristic policy was a small minority led by
the noted Japanese military expert, Colonel Kanji Ishiwara, who pleaded futilely for
a policy of non-extension. See Masasaku, Tamura, *Miao-ping jin-ken* (Tokyo, 1953),
pp. 23-25, 33-41, 48-49.

Yangtze, the Japanese government ordered the instant evacuation of her nationals from the Chinese cities along that river. An incident in Shanghai ignited that tinderbox when the Japanese attempted to pour heavy land and naval reinforcement into the area in order to augment the already large Japanese fleet lying in the Whampoo River. The Chinese and Japanese clashed there on August 13, and the war began in eastern China.

The defense of the Nanking-Shanghai area was vital to the security of China's capital and, partly for that reason and partly to relieve Japanese pressure on northern China, the National Government threw units of the Central Army into the Shanghai battle. This move was an attempt to force a stand in the south, for China realized that the Japanese strategy called for not only the conquest of northern China (concentrating chiefly on the occupation of Hopei, Shantung, Chahar, Suiyuan, and probably Shansi and Shensi as well) but also an invasion in force of the vital Nanking-Shanghai area. The Chinese decision to pour troops into Shanghai forced the Japanese to commit their major strength in eastern China to counter the numerically superior Chinese, leaving the northern provinces largely unassailed.

The three major battles of this early stage of the conflict were those of Shanghai-Nanking (August-December 1937), Tai-erh-chuang-Hsuchow (March-June 1938), and the siege of Hankow (June-October 1938). The bloodiest of these campaigns was unquestionably fought in the Shanghai-Nanking area. There the Japanese offered a powerful 200,000-man striking force drawn from a large number of divisions, heavily supported by sea and air. Against them the Chinese high command deployed the main strength of the Central Army's crack divisions. Due to tremendous naval and air bombardment, which was made possible by the short sea route between Japan and Shanghai, 60 per cent of the 450,000 defenders fell in the do-or-die battle.[2] The Japanese losses, by no means inconsiderable, have been estimated at over 40,000 men. At such a price did China buy time for continued resistance in the interior and accomplish certain political ends at home and abroad to strengthen that resistance. The battle raged for three costly months and was won by a successful Japanese turning movement on the right flank, a move made possible

[2] Tsao Chu-jen and Shu Tsung-chiao, *Pictorial History of China's War of Resistance* (Shanghai, 1946), p. 120.

by the failure of less stanch defenders at Hangchow Bay. The Chinese forces began to retire from Shanghai on November 9.

The retreat was to Nanking, where the Chinese, insisting on making another death stand in that walled city, incurred further heavy losses. Originally the Chinese plan had called for a redeployment of the Shanghai defending force along a strongly fortified line between Sungshan and Wushih, a strategy calculated to bring the Japanese to a halt through carefully prepared positions. Inexperienced commanders failed to organize an orderly withdrawal from Shanghai, and the disorganized torrent of retreating soldiers destroyed any hope of defending that "Maginot" line. At Nanking the Chinese high command made a gallant gesture only to squander a number of its best fighting units to hold a walled city which could not offer much of a defense.[3] Nanking fell to the Japanese on December 12-13, 1937. The National Government, however, had transferred the capital to Hankow the previous month and thence to the mountain city of Chungking.

Two of the greatest strategical mistakes of the Sino-Japanese war, according to some military critics, were, first, the Chinese insistence on holding Nanking by attempting a heroic sacrifice of their best fighting men, and, second, the Japanese failure to press the advantage and continue to drive to almost undefended Hankow. The chance Japan had to disrupt China's war effort by disorganization slipped by. Actually, however, as a matter of historic fact, there was a reason for the Japanese hesitancy, other than their hope that Hitler's efforts at a Sino-Japanese truce would prove effective. From a military viewpoint, the Japanese were stunned and badly set back by the heroic Chinese stand at Shanghai, and they feared that further overextension of their already fully committed forces might invite tragic defeat at the hands of the Chinese. From a purely strategic point of view, the Japanese could not drive farther westward. The powerful Chinese armies under General Li Tsung-jen, a soldier whom the Japanese commanders held in great respect, controlled the

---

[3] "Generalissimo Chiang's Operational Instruction to the Senior Commanders, Nov. 28, 1937," as quoted in Tsao and Shu, *op.cit.*, pp. 125-126. In this instruction the generalissimo cautioned the commanders concerned not to wage a rigid defensive battle at Nanking, and warned them that only a short-period defense should be the goal. He instructed these commanders not to commit all their basic forces to a death stand and to quickly replenish their losses during the previous campaigns in order to strike back at the enemy from a more advantageous terrain.

throat of the Yangtze River north of the strategic Huei region, ready to cut off from the rear any overextended Japanese force venturing westward. Moreover, Li's armies blocked the line of communication between the Japanese forces in their northern and southern theaters.

The early months of 1938 were a critical period for China. The Chinese sustained widespread defeats, but at the depth of their depression Hankow suddenly announced China's first victory at Tai-erh-chuang. That "tiger" general, Li Tsung-jen, directing his men on the front line as the commander-in-chief of China's strategic Fifth War Area, soundly trounced the Japanese forces commanded by the two best-known young generals of the Japanese army, Generals Itagaki and Isogai. Li's 133,000-man Chinese force poured into attack against the two advancing Japanese columns and, as postwar Japanese sources have admitted, "dealt fatal blows at the Japanese forces, writing an immortal page in Chinese military history."[4] A humiliating blow to the hitherto "invincible" Japanese armies, the savage fighting at Tai-erh-chuang campaign cost the Japanese 30,000 men. Their attempt to avenge this defeat, in which they assembled ten divisions of from 20,000 to 25,000 men each with a view toward trapping and annihilating the Chinese, was checked by Li's masterfully executed retreat to new lines of defense. Encirclement was avoided, and all the Chinese heavy equipment successfully withdrawn. The Chinese defense of the strategic Hsuchow area lasted six months after the Chinese retreat from Shanghai and Nanking. Six months of vitally needed time was gained by the courageous fighting of a relatively small and poorly equipped force (largely made up of provincial armies); China was allowed a breathing spell to redeploy her forces for the defense of Hankow, and for waging a protracted war that eventually lasted eight years. Li's generalship, both in his victory and his strategic withdrawal, was of inestimable value to China's continued resistance.

Meanwhile, in September 1937, the Chinese Red Army—now

[4] For a more detailed study of the Tai-erh-chuang campaign, consult: Li Tsung-jen, *Tai-erh-chuang K'ang chang hui-i-lu* (Hongkong, 1954), *passim*. Asahi Shimbun, *Sekai no kujuku meijin* (World's Ninety-nine Famous Men), (Tokyo, 1953) p. 93. Fan Chang-chiang, "The Battle of Tai-erh-chuang," *Ta-kung-pao War Zone Correspondence*, April-May, 1938. Levitsky, K., "Japan's Sedan Tactics in the China War," originally an article in Moscow's *Izvestia*, in Russian trans., *Pacific Digest*, II, 4 (April 1938), pp. 29-33.

renamed the Eighth Route Army—sent the Japanese reeling back
from the P'ing-hsing Pass and under General Lin Piao ambushed a
large Japanese column in the eastern Shansi mountain valley, a
victory described by the German military journals as a "classic of
mobile warfare."

Elsewhere, however, the Chinese met with reverses. In September
1937, the Japanese launched campaigns against the Peiping-Hankow
and Tientsin-Pukow railways, the two main rail lines from north
China to the valley of the Yangtze. In the campaign along the latter
rail line the Japanese paid with their defeats at Tai-erh-chuang and
the Hsuchow area. But along the Peiping-Hankow route the ill-
trained and poorly-equipped provincial armies could offer but weak
resistance to the Japanese thrusts and were mown down on the flat
north China plain by tanks, heavy guns, and devastating air attack.
The coordinating command which had proved so successful at Tai-
erh-chuang was non-existent in other war areas, and the lack of
unified effort took its toll.

May and June saw the loss of some of the best-trained units of
the Central Army near the key rail city of Lan-feng, in the province
of Honan. Initially the much-hated Japanese Doihara division was
on the verge of total defeat in this action, being surrounded by a
crack Chinese force, but faulty coordination between the Chinese
field commands permitted the Japanese to escape the trap. Strongly
reinforced, the Japanese struck back against the forces commanded
by General Kwei Yung-chin and for some reason Kwei's heroic resistance had to be effected without the support of nearby Chinese
forces under Hu Tsung-nan. This disunity cost the Chinese almost
irreparable damage in trained soldiers and materiel.

The stubborn defense put up by the Chinese at Shanghai, Tai-erh-
chuang, and Chengchow had made the enemy hesitant about pursuing
the long and hazardous advance upon Hankow without further
reinforcements. Not until they had assembled a force of twelve
divisions were they content to face the stubborn resistance of the
Central Army, a foe they had learned to respect through bitter
experience. Previously the Japanese had underestimated the Chinese,
but now the reverse was the case. Their strongly reinforced armies
advanced on Hankow cautiously from the north, supported by naval
forces brought up the Yangtze and an attack on Kwangtung (to the
south) which cut off an important Chinese pipeline. In October 1938,

they entered another abandoned wartime capital—a city of rubble. Japanese precautions against underestimating the Chinese had worked against them this time and, as Generalissimo Chiang put it, the battle of Wuchang-Hankow was the point at which "the victor lost the war."[5]

With the fall of Hankow, the first phase of the war came to a close. Throughout this phase, although there were many instances of stubborn resistance on the part of the Chinese, the policy of Chiang's government had been to trade land for time—time for the mobilization of the nation's resources for a protracted war. The Chinese lost most of the battles and paid dearly in trained men in the last-ditch stands and ill-organized retreat operations.

During this first phase, however, despite costly defeats, the various provincial armies of China were united under the National Government. Temporarily the aims of Chiang and of the communists coincided, a factor which contributed to a united defense. But although China's armies were enjoying a somewhat unaccustomed unity, and the wholehearted support of the people, all was not well. War destruction was mounting, and the nation's production picture was bleak. Inflation sapped the country's economy, and corruption and bureaucracy undermined the government to such an extent that the Nanyo military conference was called in November 1938 to reexamine the national situation.

SECOND PHASE

By the time the second phase of the war opened, the Japanese had overrun a large section of Chinese territory. In November 1938 they occupied the Peiping-Tientsin area in the north, the Canton sector to the south, Hankow and part of central China, and the Shanghai-Nanking area to the east. The three great rivers—the Yellow, the West, and the Yangtze—the major cities, the coast, were all in Japanese hands.

With such an area under their control the Japanese adopted a new

[5] For an appraisal of the strategy of this period, consult Levitsky, *op.cit.* Liu, Fei, Vice-Chief of the Board of Military Operation, "A Study of Our Strategy and the Japanese Strategy," *War Pamphlet* (Chungking: Military Press, 1940). Anon (A Japanese military writer), "The Military Significance of the Battle for Hankow," *Tokyo Gazette*, No. 17, Nov. 1938, p. 2.

policy of *gen-chi Ho-kyn* (roughly translated as "supplying the war with local [Chinese] resources"). In other words, they proposed to live off their occupied territories while consolidating their gains, extending their control, and waiting for what seemed to them to be the inevitable collapse of Chiang's regime. To facilitate this policy, the Japanese attempted to capture the railroad networks—the Peiping-Hankow, Hangchow-Nanchang, and Canton-Hankow lines—but this was not to be accomplished easily. Because of her spirit, her refusal to accept defeat, China was not easily subdued; another weapon in her favor was her land—its size and difficult terrain. If one draws a straight line on the map of China between Aigun in Heilungkiang and Tengchung in Yunnan one notices two strikingly contrasting regions. Northwest of this line, the region is characterized by plateaus and mountain ranges with altitudes from more than 3,000 feet to more than 13,000 feet above sea level, with comparatively few basins and valleys. Southwest of the line, however, the main features become wide plains and low hills, few of which are more than 3,000 feet in height. Even before the Japanese could reach that line, the river gorges and mountain passes defended by the Chinese became formidable obstacles. In the battle of Tsaoyang (in the province of Hupeh, in May 1939) the Chinese, under General Li Tsung-jen, turned back the invading force with heavy Japanese losses. Since that battle the gateway to Chungking was always under Chinese control. Thrice at Changsha the Chinese, under General Hsueh Yueh, routed the Japanese, who were unable to occupy the vital Canton-Hankow railway before 1945.

Nevertheless the Japanese triumphed on most occasions. Heavy losses earlier in the war and the fairly effective Japanese blockade had combined to deprive the Chinese of supplies. Moreover, Chinese forces deteriorated while Japanese troops became more seasoned and experienced. Taking the equipment of a typical Chinese division, one would find the following picture:

Year	Rifles	Light Machine Guns	Heavy Machine Guns
1937	7,000	200	60
1939	2,500	100	33

Thus, in the second phase of the war the Chinese strategy, except in important engagements where a pitched battle and frontal attack of the better-equipped enemy appeared mandatory, was to yield in front, close in on the flanks and the rear, and attack thinly manned defense points and lines of communication. This policy has come in for a considerable amount of adverse criticism by Western military observers, although no one has yet advanced a better solution to the Chinese problem. The criticism was chiefly that the Chinese were not fighting aggressively enough, that the Japanese moved about pretty much as they pleased. It was even suggested by some misinformed individuals that the Japanese never lost a battle, never suffered a single reversal. Many of these criticisms, of course, were prompted by ulterior political motives, but some were based upon the firm and unshakable basis of ignorance. The Japanese were undoubtedly successful most of the time, but not without reversal. In November 1939, a strong Japanese force, drawn from the crack army units of the Japanese Kwangtung Army in Manchuria and from other units in Formosa, landed in the Chingchow Bay area north of the Gulf of Tonkin. The surprise move routed a number of Chinese defense units and enabled the Japanese to capture Nanning, the capital of Kwangsi. The Japanese plan was to seize the railway center at Liuchow and, from there, to control the entire south and southwest of China. But at the strategic gateway of Kunlungkwan they met a serious reversal; an entire brigade was destroyed there by the Chinese under the over-all command of General Pai Chung-hsi. The Japanese force was, despite further reinforcement, virtually immobilized by the 150,000 Chinese troops and the day-and-night harassment of Kwangsi guerrilla fighters. The Japanese retreated after ten months of futile occupation. Japanese war records reveal that in 1937 the war in China engaged 16 of Japan's 24 divisions and, after four years of war, still with no end in sight, 27 Japanese divisions (out of a total of 51) were immobilized by the poorly equipped Chinese troops which often met defeat on the battlefield.[6]

Many of China's severest critics abroad were ignorant of China's true plight. They knew nothing of her industrial and economic difficulties. Having lost the north and her coastal areas, China had no large factories capable of producing heavy weapons. There were a number of small arsenals left to her—whose combined annual output of small arms and ammunition could supply perhaps a month's

[6] Hattori, Takushiro, *Daitoa Senso Zenshi* (The Complete History of the Greater East Asia War) in Japanese (Tokyo, 1953), Vol. 1, pp. 314, 319, Tables 1 and 8.

The Disposition of Japanese Army Forces in Various
War Theatres between 1937 and 1941
(in number of divisions)

YEAR	WAR THEATRES				TOTAL STRENGTH OF THE JAPANESE ARMY
	China	Japan and Korea	Manchuria	Total	
1937	16	3	5	24	950,000
1938	24	2	8	34	1,130,000
1939	25	7	9	41	1,240,000
1940	27	11	12	50	1,350,000
1941	27	11	13	51	2,110,500

Source: Hattori, Daitōa Senso Zenshi (Tokyo, 1953) Vol. 1, Tables 6 and 8, pp. 314, 319.

intensive fighting. There was in all of China not one factory that could produce a truck, or a tank, or an airplane. And so the Chinese, with less than 800 artillery pieces of all kinds, planned a war of attrition against the mechanized might of Japan.

Another reason for Chiang's defensive policy was that his government had learned from a secret communist directive that Mao Tse-tung and the communists at Yenan were deliberately conserving their strength, holding back a good part of the force they might have directed against the Japanese in preparation for the eventual clash with Chiang's government. The signing of the Soviet-Japanese neutrality pact in April 1941 marked the beginning of an even greater period of calculated inactivity on the part of the Chinese communists. In order to counter this communist policy (stated in the words of Mao Tse-tung, as "to cooperate with the Kuomintang and struggle against it at the same time") Chiang blockaded the communists in the north with a force which eventually totaled sixteen corps.[7] Some 150,000 to 200,000 of the government's best troops were diverted to his *other* war—the communists.

After the fall of Hankow the communists had extended their political influence, especially behind Japanese lines. From the town of Yenan on the Yen River, the communists conducted their dual campaign: the new war against Japan and the old war against the Kuomintang. According to a secret communist document brought over

[7] Nieh Jung-chen, one-time chief of staff of the Chinese Red Army, "How the Chinese People Defeated the Japanese Fascist Aggressor," *China's Revolutionary Wars* (Peking, 1951), p. 28, a communist account of the war.

by a dissident communist leader, Chang Kuo-t'ao, communist policy was to be "70 per cent expansion, 20 per cent dealing with the Kuomintang and 10 per cent resisting Japan."[8] Mao, the military and spiritual leader of the tight-knit community of communist leaders, was primarily a long-range planner, a man with a genius for seeing clearly the distant goal. But the keynote of the whole Yenan group was not the planning that went on interminably in the two gray brick buildings at Yenan; it was positive, decisive action. The communists organized the peasants against the Japanese and, at the same time, were preparing them for rebellion against the whole system that Chiang and the nationalists stood for. Indeed, the communist and nationalist "allies" even clashed openly. In January 1941 occurred the so-called Huang-chiao incident. The government's forces battled with the communist New Fourth Army in the region of the Lower Yangtze, and captured its famous commanding general, Yeh Ting. Later, in April 1941, large-scale operations were conducted by the pro-Chiang Moslem armies against the Chinese communists active in the Kansu and Ninghsia areas. While the communists aided Chiang with brilliantly executed organization of guerrillas, they also hampered the nationalist effort against Japan.

Through the first and second phases of the war, the Japanese held sway over the sea and air. The small Chinese air force, even when reinforced by Russian-manned squadrons, was totally unable to wrest control from the Japanese until, eventually, United States forces came to the Pacific. Throughout 1939, 1940, and 1941 the Japanese undertook the destruction of the principal cities of China by air bombardment. The caves nearby Chungking, the wartime capital, became of increasing importance to its beleaguered inhabitants as the city achieved the dubious distinction of being at the time the most-bombed place on earth. The Japanese thought they could destroy Chinese resistance by bombing their cities and their homes, but they had miscalculated the tenacity of the Chinese people.

Failing to win a decision on the battlefield, or by air bombardment, the Japanese made the economic blockade of Free China an important policy in her strategy. This plan was put into effect shortly before Japan's entry into the Pacific war. Subsequently, in his presentation before the historic conference on December 21, 1942, with the Japa-

[8] U.S. General Staff, *The Chinese Communist Movement* (Washington, 1952), p. 2307.

nese emperor presiding, General Sugiyama, the Japanese chief of general staff, gave particular emphasis to the importance of cutting off China's supply line from the outside world. During this second phase of the war, China was practically isolated from the rest of the world except in the south through Hanoi, in French Indochina, and in the northwest, where the line of communication with Soviet Russia stretched across 2,000 miles of sandy waste. Fearful that the line through Hanoi might be severed at any moment, the Chinese constructed an all-weather highway from Kunming, in the province of Yunnan, to Lashio, in Burma. China had a well-established concept of the geographic needs of a protracted war against Japan, which was outlined even as early as July 1935 in these words of Generalissimo Chiang Kai-shek: "To fight the Japanese, the main (battle) front should be located in the area south of the Yangtze River and west of the Peiping-Hankow railway; Loyang, Siangyang-Fancheng, Kingmen-Ichang, and Changteh should constitute the last line (of defense). The three provinces of Szechuan, Kweichow and Shensi would form the nucleus and the provinces of Kansu and Yunnan, the rear areas."[9]

One of the basic policies of wartime China was, therefore, to secure the lines of communication with the outside world. For two years hundreds of thousands of Chinese laborers toiled to build by hand this highway right through the southern spur of the Himalayas. The construction of the highway regardless of cost indicated two important things: (1) that the maintenance of China's war effort depended to a substantial degree on material supply from the outside world; (2) that—and this is a point Chiang had been stressing repeatedly ever since he threw the doomed troops into the battle of Shanghai to make it clear—China was determined to wage a prolonged war against Japan, irrespective of changes in the international situation.

Fears about Hanoi soon proved justified. War broke out in Europe in September 1939 and, the following February, Japan took advantage of the French crisis and seized Hainan Island. Subsequently the French forces in Indochina were defeated and China's supply route through Hanoi was severed. A further Japanese attempt to isolate China, in preparation for her long-contemplated southward push, led to pressure upon Britain's Prime Minister Churchill which forced him to declare the Burma Road closed for three months.

During the first years of the war, Soviet loans to China, in the form

[9] Chang chi-yuen, *Tang-shih kai-yao*, *op.cit.*, Vol. II, p. 1014.

of barter agreements, had been the chief source of foreign aid. Up to the fateful day of Pearl Harbor, Soviet Russia is reported to have concluded barter agreements totaling the equivalent of $300,000,000 (U.S.), compared with the American total of $170,000,000 and the British total of £18,000,000. The American volunteer air group was actively fighting the Japanese in China, but so were private Soviet citizens in appreciable numbers.

After 1939, when the Chinese government and the Chinese communists came to a parting of the ways, Soviet aid was gradually withdrawn from Chiang and his followers. It was clear that the Soviet concern, official and popular, was with the Chinese communists. The signing of a Japanese-Soviet neutrality pact on April 13, 1941 eliminated the danger of any immediate Japanese attack on the Soviet Union and caused Soviet assistance to Chiang's forces to cease, although support of the Chinese communists (by now more the enemies of Chungking than of Japan) continued, and Kremlin sources strove to belittle the nationalists' usefulness before their Western allies and the rest of the world.

Meanwhile Chiang persisted in his long-cherished belief that, if a quick Japanese victory could be prevented, changes in the international situation would eventually create a climate favorable to China. Since communist support was being withdrawn, China no longer imagined that her hope lay in close collaboration with Soviet Russia, and Chungking began to turn her eyes more and more to the West, where the United States, long a determined and outspoken foe of Japanese aggression, was emerging ever more clearly as a strong and sympathetic ally.

THIRD PHASE

I

On December 7, 1941, the Japanese unmasked their next objective: the conquest of the Pacific and the establishment of what their propagandists termed a "greater East Asia sphere of co-prosperity." China immediately declared war on Germany and Italy, and the generalissimo presented proposals for allied unity and a four-power pact (to include China, the United States, Britain, and the Soviet Union) against the Axis powers.

While Japanese arms were being almost universally successful in the Pacific campaigns against the unprepared American forces and the once proud British and Dutch forces in their colonial areas, the defeat of the Japanese at Changsha by forces commanded by the renowned Chinese general Hsueh Yueh caught the attention and aroused the sympathies of the West. The Chinese were then engaging 22 Japanese divisions and 20 brigades on the battlefields, as compared with the 10 divisions and 3 brigades which the Japanese had employed in their successful southward offensives in the Pacific and Indian oceans.[10]

The Disposition of the Japanese Army Forces in December 1941

	China	Pacific and Southeast Asia	Manchuria	Japan	Korea and Formosa
Army division	21*	10**	13	4	2
Mixed brigade or equivalent	20*	3	24	11	
Army air squadron	16	70	56	9	

* plus one cavalry group army and one army division at Shanghai under the direct command of the Imperial General Headquarters.
** plus one special column. Of these ten divisions two were shipped from China theater.

Source: Japanese General Staff Statistics quoted in:
    Hattori, *Daitoa Senso Zenshi*, I, p. 330.

On January 3, 1942 President Franklin D. Roosevelt announced: "General Chiang Kai-shek has accepted the supreme command over all land and air forces of the nations which are now, or may in the future, be operating in the Chinese theater, including such portion of Indo-China and Thailand as may become available to troops of the United Nations. United States and British representatives will serve on his joint headquarters planning staff."[11]

This announcement was in accord with Roosevelt's decision to "treat China as a great power." Great authority and trust were vested in the generalissimo by the West, although China, despite repeated bids for admission was excluded from membership among the combined chiefs of staff. Chiang, therefore, was supreme in the China theater and not responsible to that body but answerable only to his own party and

[10] Hattori, *op.cit.*, II, p. 330.
[11] Sherwood, *Roosevelt and Hopkins, op.cit.*, II, p. 24.

government—a unique situation among allied commanders. Coincident with Chiang's appointment was that of Field Marshal Sir Archibald P. Wavell as supreme commander of the A.B.D.A. (the American, British, Dutch, and Australian) area.

II

One of Chiang's first moves was toward assuring the protection of China's main line of communication through Burma. He was prepared to send a Chinese expeditionary force, including the Fifth, Sixth, and Sixty-Sixth Armies, to face the impending Japanese invasion. When Washington sent General Stilwell to China, as his chief of Staff, Chiang placed him in charge of this expeditionary force, even before the American had sufficient time to acquaint himself with the current war situation in the Far East.

The war that Stilwell fought in Burma has made highly controversial history. The American side of the picture has been reported with admirable objectivity and impressive scholarship by C. F. Romanus and Riley Sutherland. Tokushiro Hattori, in his *Daitoa Senso Zenshi*, presented a well-written account of that campaign from the Japanese point of view. The British have published a little to justify their retreat from the First Burma Campaign. The Chinese view, except for a few unofficial works, none of them pretending to be exhaustive, has, however, yet to be presented.

The situation in Stilwell's new command was a strange one. The Americans were anxious to keep China in the war, and so were prepared to assist in Burma. The Chinese were anxious to hold Burma open, and willing to employ, if necessary, every ounce of American strength; of their own forces they were more chary and, since Pearl Harbor had precipitated the United States into the war, they were inclined to rely heavily on Uncle Sam. The British were anxious to recover Burma, but they wanted to do so themselves, if possible, in order to retain it as a colony. They were not entirely unafraid of American and Chinese help. Even among the Americans, who seemed to be stuck with the job, there was no agreement. General Claire Chennault, who had been in China since 1936 (when his beliefs had forced him to submit his resignation to the United States army), thought that the solution in the Chinese theater was air power, and particularly his own China Air Task Force, later to become the Fourteenth Air Force. Chennault, now back in uniform as a brigadier general, was not the least of Stilwell's problems in that vast theater which extended from Karachi to Sian, a distance of 3,000 miles.

Despite the various motives of the Americans, the British, and the Chinese, it was clear enough that the objectives had to be three: to protect China's land route to the outside world through Burma, to secure the defense of southwest China, and to meet the Japanese threat to Burma. Chiang's goals were modest; knowing the limitations of his troops and the difficulties of unfamiliar terrain in unfriendly Burma, he aimed at the prevention of total loss instead of the accomplishment of total victory. The Americans stressed *attack*, intending to employ the Chinese troops in a major offensive directed toward the recapture of Rangoon, thus opening the Burma Road. The British in India, the striking point from which such an expedition would set out, were anxious to recapture Burma, but, in their imperial defense plan, desirous above all to safeguard India. Churchill declared in the Commons that Wavell "is not therefore at present in a position to denude himself to any large extent and he must not cast away his resources."[12]

The command was complex in the extreme. The British commander in Burma, General Sir Harold R. L. G. Alexander, wanted to command the Chinese troops; Stilwell's presence, as a commander in Burma without an adequate staff, was not to the British liking. But Stilwell was under the ultimate control of three headquarters: the U.S. War Department at Washington; Generalissimo Chiang, whose chiefs of staff were General Ho Ying-ch'in in Chungking and General Stilwell in Burma; the British supreme commander of India and Malaya, Field Marshal Sir Archibald Wavell, with his field army in Burma commanded by General Harold Alexander. Stilwell, answerable to both Chiang and Wavell, would appear to be the uniting factor, but, under Stilwell, the Americans were in no position to unite anything. The two American air commanders, General L. H. Brereton, in command of American air forces in India, and General C. L. Chennault, were again subjected to the divided control by the British and Chinese high commands. To add to the difficulties, the Chinese objected to Stilwell's attempts to command, asserting that he was charged only with the strategic direction of the war and the duty of giving advice to Chinese commanders—the Chinese concept of a chief of staff. The British were no better organized, for although at the top they had

[12] Churchill, Winston, "Secret Session Speeches," pp. 57-60.

such names as Wavell, Alexander, and Slim, the lower echelons, according to F. Eldridge, were officered by men "taken from law offices and plantations" and given "ranks commensurate with their financial and social standing in the Colony."[13] Stilwell had trouble with the British on the spot and with the effect their influence on the combined chiefs of staff and the United States war department produced. At a time when the Japanese virtually commanded the air, he had to bicker with Major General Chennault (influenced by the Chinese) and Lieutenant General Brereton (influenced by the British), as well as with Washington and New Delhi.

The first engagements in the Burma campaign were not entirely encouraging to the allies, although the Chinese 200th Division, commanded by General Tai An-lan, who was recognized by the Americans as a man of "ability and force and considerable courage," put up a stiff, twelve-day defense of Toungoo against a superior Japanese force and chalked up a record for the most tenacious fighting in the First Burma Campaign.[14] The only allied victory of the whole campaign must be credited to General Sun Li-jen, whose 38th Division drove back the Japanese and rescued the hard-pressed British forces who were making a stand at Yenangyaung. The subsequent retreat of that force to India as an intact fighting unit was described by the Americans as an "epic" achievement.[15]

Exploiting allied disunity and weakness, the seasoned Japanese units under General Shojiro Iido outmaneuvered the allied forces, which consisted of 9 Chinese divisions under Lieutenant Generals Tu Yü-ming and Kan Li-ch'u, 5 Indian infantry brigades, 1 British armored brigade and 6 infantry battalions under the command of Lieutenant General T. J. Hutton. This made up a total of perhaps 81,000 men, supported by a modest complement of artillery, a Chinese-American fighter group, and several squadrons of the R.A.F. The Japanese victory resulted in the loss of Burma and the complete isolation of China except for the incredible airline over the Hump, a 500-mile route of uncharted and jagged terrain.

The loss of the Burma Road began to reduce Chinese fighting efficiency sharply, despite the gradual increase in tonnage flown over the Hump—an increase which became appreciable only in late 1943.

[13] Elderidge, *Wrath in Burma*, *op.cit.*, p. 40.
[14] U.S. Army, Japanese Study 88, "Interrogation Col. Kouchi, Staff Officer, 15th. Japanese Army, Jan. 8, 1948," quoted in Romanus and Sunderland, *op.cit.*, p. 109.
[15] Ho, *The Big Circle*, *op.cit.*, p. 18. Romanus and Sunderland, *op.cit.*, p. 140-141.

In the spring of 1942 the transports of the airlift moved only 80 tons a month, though this figure had increased a thousandfold by the end of the war. At no time, however, did the airlift furnish more than a tantalizing trickle of supplies. The temporary isolation of China, however, gave hope to Japan that the war in China might be brought to an end by negotiating directly with Chungking for a separate peace when the government was in distress. The Japanese knew that in 1942 a minimum of 600,000 of their fighting men were tied down by the China war. To enable the employment of this powerful force in other theaters, the Japanese high command was anxious to find a political settlement with Chungking. But in Chiang Kai-shek the Japanese found a stone wall blocking all their peace efforts.

However, China was beginning to get into growing military difficulties. A factor which contributed to the decline of Chinese effectiveness was the loss of her two key armies in the First Burma Campaign. Up to this time her policy had called for the maintenance of about 10 army corps, to be placed directly under the command of the national military council and to be employed as general strategic reserves in vital campaigns. The backbone of this force was composed of the Fifth and Sixth Armies, partly German-trained and German-equipped. Together with the 300,000 men (16 armies) under Hu Tsung-nan and T'ang En-po in the northwest, these were probably the best-equipped forces Chiang had at his disposal. The Japanese general headquarters had estimated the strength of this mobilizable force as 250,000 men. Before their loss in Burma, the Fifth and Sixth Armies served widely as roving troubleshooters plugging the most critical breaches in Chinese defenses as they occurred under the brunt of major enemy offensives. The loss of these forces and of their heavy equipment deprived China of more than a third of her strategic reserve, a fact that has never before received proper attention, even in the famous Stilwell papers.

Partly to consolidate after this loss, Stilwell suggested a radical reform of the Chinese army in order to whip it into shape for the forthcoming campaign to retake Burma. His plan advocated the reduction of Chinese army units to half the existing number, the elimination of incompetent commanders, and the reconstruction of China's forces around 2 field armies, each to consist of 30 divisions. Chiang did not consider the plan feasible at the time, although it was carried out in a modified form later under General Wedemeyer.[16] When Stilwell deplored Chiang's failure to cooperate in this plan, the generalissimo reminded him that the promise of American aid was far from being fulfilled, due largely to the limitations of the Hump and of India's transportation system and to the priority assigned to other war theaters.[17] Air support supplied by the U.S. Fourteenth Air Force was about the only truly efficient aid being extended at the time. Even of it, however, the Japanese had estimated that in 1943 the United States Air Force had only 130 planes in China; the Chinese, 200 planes. However, the estimate for 1944 raised the figure to a total of 500 allied planes in China—still woefully small by the standards of the European theaters.[18]

Meanwhile, Japanese strength increased in China, especially after the Stalin-Matsuoka agreement of 1941 had freed Japan's crack Kwantung Army from the necessity of defending the borders of Manchuria, and after the Chinese communists became increasingly hostile to the National Government, so that less and less support could be hoped from that quarter.

III

Up to this time no concrete over-all war plan concerning the China theater had been evolved by the allies, although it was clear that the American members of the combined chiefs of staff were agreed that China was needed for its manpower and its geographic position and that the allies must ultimately meet the Japanese on the mainland of Asia.[19] All parties concerned concurred in this reasoning, but Churchill and the British members repeatedly forced the abandonment of certain strategies that had been planned by the Chinese and Americans, who were acting on these assumptions.[20] The Cairo conference came up with one general agreement stated in broad terms: the Chinese should put into action 30 divisions initially, 30 more as soon as practicable, and still another 30 eventually. The allies agreed

[16] "Program for China; Note from Gen. Stilwell to Generalissimo Chiang," quoted in Romanus and Sunderland, op.cit., pp. 372-373.
[17] "Ltr. President Roosevelt to Gen. G. C. Marshall, Oct. 15, 1943," quoted in Romanus and Sunderland, op.cit., p. 382.
[18] Hattori, op.cit., III, p. 246.
[19] King, E. J., and Whitehill, W. M., Fleet Admiral King, A Naval Record (N.Y.: Norton, 1952), p. 436.
[20] Ibid., p. 525.

that this could not be accomplished without the opening of a land route to China over which supplies could flow. To provide such a route they jointly planned a land offensive from northern Burma to southwest China, to be accompanied by an amphibious American and British attack launched simultaneously against the Andaman Islands. Although this projected supporting campaign was soon abandoned, Stilwell was still anxious to push ahead with his campaign in northern Burma.

At Ramgarh in the Indian province of Behar, Stilwell had trained and reequipped those Chinese troops which had been successfully withdrawn from Burma earlier, building around the 22nd and 38th Divisions which had escaped to Assam. To this force in India he added troops flown over the Hump from China, working up a new First Army (commanded by General Sun Li-jen) and a new Sixth Army (under General Liao Yao-hsiang). This was the "X-Force" which, with Stilwell himself as over-all commander, was to attack Burma from India. The "Y-Force" was being trained at Kunming, in the Chinese province of Yunnan. The one operating from Ledo in northern Assam and the other from Salween in western China would smash the Burma blockade from both sides.

In March 1944 Stilwell set the X-Force in motion. Fighting a slow and difficult war in the wilds of Burma against such trained jungle fighters as the Japanese 18th Division, the Chinese captured the strongholds of central and northern Burma one after another, often against heavy odds.[21] Together with General Frank Merrill's famous Marauders, the Allies killed or wounded over 75,000 Japanese troops and took 3,023 prisoners. By August of the same year, the strongest Japanese base, at Myitkyina, fell and all the Japanese defenders there were annihilated. Despite the difficulties of jungle warfare, despite such differences in viewpoint as that evidenced by Brigadier General Haydon Boatner's handling of the Hukawng Valley operation, the X-Force forged ahead and achieved a victory in what General George Marshall described as the "most difficult campaign of World War II." Victory was the result of close Chinese-American cooperation, brilliant leadership, efficient training, supply, air and logistic support, flexibility of strategy, and plain hard fighting and indomitable will.[22]

[21] Cheng Tung-kuo, "Success of a Mission," *China at War*, xv, 1 (July 1945), pp. 27-32.
[22] Ho, *op.cit.*, pp. 60-80.

While the X-Force was besieging Myitkyina, General Wei Li-huang's 100,000 Chinese crossed the Salween River in strength and began to use the Y-Force side of the pincers. They fought on, up the steep Kaolikung Mountains, which rise to 9,000 feet, in terrible monsoon weather. An American army officer wrote: "The ruggedness of these mountains is incredible, and it is doubtful if any people other than the Chinese could have successfully traversed them, particularly, with the stubborn Japs defending fanatically at every possible strategical point. . . . To cross [them] on a ration of rice is a feat worthy of admiration."[23]

On September 7 the Chinese occupied Sungshan, the Gibraltar of the Burma Road. It stood on a high peak, crisscrossed by trenches, dotted with pillboxes and blockhouses, and undermined with a network of tunnels linking all the principal defense points. Chinese courage, American technical know-how, and fierce air support made the conquest possible.

After this Chinese victory, the Japanese were fighting a losing battle.[24] Tangchung, Lungling, Chefang and Wanting all fell to the Chinese. On January 21, 1945, the advance elements of the X-Force joined hands at Mu-se with the Y-Force from western Yunnan. Stilwell's dream was realized. The first convoy to China in almost three years soon rolled into Wanting over the road from Ledo which Brigadier General Lewis Ayen Pick and his engineers had built. Generalissimo Chiang subsequently named it the Stilwell Road.

General Henri-Eugène Navarre, commander of the French campaign in Indochina in 1953, once remarked that "victory is a woman. She does not give herself except to those who know how to take her." Part of this know-how and much of the equipment which made the Chinese victory possible came from the Americans, whose 300-man operations staff in the Salween campaign was roundly praised by General Wei Li-huang, commander-in-chief of the Chinese expeditionary force. American assistance proved useful in all spheres of activity, but perhaps it was nowhere more appreciated than in the medical services rendered. Never before in all the military history of China had Chinese troops been so well taken care of in heavy cam-

[23] Chow, F., "The Salween Campaign," *China at War*, xv, 1 (July 1945), pp. 54-70. National Military Council, *Kuo-chün Tien-hsi tsien-ti chi* (The Campaign of the National Army in Western Yunnan), (Nanking, 1946) *passim*.

[24] Liu Wei-chang, Vice-Chief of the Board of Military Operation, "Japan's Plight in 1945," *Ta-kung-pao*, June 1945.

paigns. Also, American air support, furnished by the U.S. Tenth and Fourteenth Air Forces, took part in bombing and strafing Japanese positions and created a line of supply by air without which, a high Chinese commander asserted, fighting in that area would have been totally impossible.[25]

The reopening of the Burma Road made it possible once again, in compliance with the policy that President Roosevelt had laid down, to "regard China as a vital part of our common war effort and depend upon the maintenance of the China theater as an urgent necessity for the defeat of our enemies." At Washington, New Delhi, and Cairo the British were reluctant to cooperate with the Chinese-American plan to retake Burma, but Stilwell, its chief defender, won out. The opening of the Burma Road made it possible not only to pour supplies into China for the support of the air war,[26] but also to redeploy trained Chinese forces for the final continental assaults. The Y-Force, having completed its part in the pincer movement in Burma, was to move east to Kweichow and Hunan and prepare to besiege Hankow. Encircled from the vicinity of Kiukiang, Hankow was certain to fall, and the subsequent occupation of Hsuchow would provide the base from which to direct bombers against Japan.[27]

Major General Claire L. Chennault, commanding the U.S. Fourteenth Air Force, was the leading proponent of the plan to bomb Japan from bases in China, a plan which greatly appealed to the generalissimo. In Washington, General H. H. Arnold was advocating the need "to strengthen Chennault's air force and get at the bombing of Japan as soon as possible."[28]

Chennault was anxious to bring up his air strength to a total of 105 fighters plus 30 medium and 12 heavy bombers—a drop in the bucket compared to the air strength of the European theater. The maximum monthly supply load that he requested to come over the Hump was only 7,000 tons. With this force he proposed to defeat the enemy air forces utterly in China and to cripple all Japanese rail and river communications in China, to sweep Japanese shipping off the

[25] Chow, F., *op.cit.*

[26] The strategic plan as set forth in a letter of rebuttal from General Marshall to a study by Field Marshal Sir John Dill contains the following paragraph: "Our great objective in the China theater is the build-up of air operation in China with a view to carrying out destructive attacks against Japanese shipping and supply."

[27] Memo from Gen. Stilwell to Soong, Stilwell Document, Hoover Library.

[28] "Harry Hopkins' Note to Chief Ship's Clerk Terry, Jan. 19, 1943," quoted in Sherwood, *op.cit.*, II, p. 284.

China seas between French Indochina and Korea, and—having accomplished all this—to commence bombing the Japanese islands themselves. Although he did not even receive the minimum supplies for which he asked, he nevertheless succeeded in realizing the better part of these plans, with the exception of the bombing of Japan. That attack was entrusted to General Curtis Lemay's superfortresses.

Stilwell was cool about these air plans, fearing that American use of air bases in southeast China would provoke retaliating Japanese offensives, but Chennault insisted that Chinese ground troops aided by air support could protect such bases adequately. Even without Stilwell's wholehearted support, the achievements of the Fourteenth Air Force were without precedent. After three years' fighting it had lost, from all operational causes, 500 aircraft and had destroyed 2,600 Japanese aircraft and scored 1,500 "probables." It had sunk or damaged 2,500,000 tons of Japanese shipping, plus 44 naval vessels and 13,000 river boats under 100 tons. The Fourteenth Air Force may not have enjoyed Stilwell's unqualified support, but it was supported and revered by every Chinese from the generalissimo down to the humblest coolie who worked on the air fields. Chiang was increasingly insistent in his requests that the United States increase the Hump tonnage for the better equipment of the Chinese army and for the encouragement of Chennault's continued direct assault on Japanese positions—a plan which the British also favored.[29]

Stilwell's belief, however, was that the showdown would best come on the mainland of China, where a well-equipped, American-trained Chinese army under his personal direction could meet and defeat the bulk of the Japanese army. Such a plan, of course, called for a fantastic amount of heavy equipment—equipment that could come to China only via land route. It was upon this basis that he constructed the Stilwell Road from Ledo.

There has been much speculation that had Chennault really received the comparatively meager support he requested (and which, indeed, he was on more than one occasion promised); his strengthened air force, in cooperation with American-trained and equipped Chinese forces, might, pitted against the Japanese in southeast China, have sufficed to recapture Hong Kong and a strip of coast before the

[29] Grimsdale, G. E., British army, one-time Britain's military attaché at Chungking, "The War against Japan in China," *The Journal of the Royal United Service Institution*, xcv, 578 (May, 1950), pp. 260-267.

end of 1944. The Chinese forces, having been supplied and equipped by the allies, might then have consolidated their hold on the south and east sections of the country, providing far less chance for the "power vacuum" which prevailed shortly after V-J Day, the disastrous vacuum which fostered postwar confusion and facilitated the activities of the Chinese communists.

IV

While the Chinese armies were waging victorious campaigns in Burma, a struggle in which more than 200,000 of China's best troops were committed (the Japanese estimate of the total strength of China's effective strategic reserve for that year was 250,000 men), in China herself inflation and misgovernment had caused morale to hit a new low. The Japanese, well aware of this, chose this time to launch a gigantic trans-continental offensive, employing some 620,000 first-line troops for an all-out operation under the code name Operation Ichi-gō. The Imperial General Headquarters gave the objective of this offensive as follows:

"1. To forestall the bombing of the Japanese homeland by American B-29s from [the Chinese] bases at Kweilin and Liuchow;

"2. To secure the Kweilin-Liuchow area in anticipation of allied counteroffensive from India and [China's] Yunnan province and directed against [the Japanese forces in] south China area;

"3. In view of the increasingly insecure sea communication, the north-south trans-continental railroad network has to be restored to operation for the purpose of reestablishing land communication with the [Japanese] armies on the southern front;

"4. To destroy the backbone of the Chinese army and force increased deterioration to the political regime at Chungking."[30]

In the initial phase of this offensive, which was code-named Operation Ko-Gō, the Japanese struck in central China and in Honan, seeking to destroy the Chinese forces there and to capture the entire Peiping-Hankow railway. By June 1944 they had achieved this last objective with a powerful striking force comprised of one tank and three infantry divisions, together with a large number of mixed brigades. In the assault the Japanese killed several Chinese divisional commanders,

[30] "Strategic Direction from Imperial General Headquarters to the Commander-in-chief of the Japanese Expeditionary Army in China," Hattori, *op.cit.*, III, p. 247.

one group army commander, and a large number of men in the thirty divisions commanded by General T'ang En-po. Chinese resistance had been bitter, but a decisive factor in T'ang's defeat was the lack of support from the populace of Honan, where the National Government had persisted in trying to wring taxes out of a people who were undergoing a devastating famine, and had then bungled aid at every turn. When the Japanese came, the people of Honan did not actively aid the Chinese government troops but, in some cases, helped the enemy. Within three weeks the Japanese had broken up a Chinese force of 300,000 men and captured the railway to the south. The ancient capital of Loyang also fell into Japanese hands.

Having secured the Peiping-Hankow railway, General Shunroku Hada, the Japanese commander-in-chief in China, moved his field headquarters to Hankow. Under the veil of strict secrecy, his already powerful attacking armies were further reinforced by fresh units from the crack Kwantung army in Manchuria. In a surprise strategic move Hada threw 400,000 troops into pincer drives from the north and south in May 1944 (Operation To-Gō). His attacking armies—the largest ever assembled by the Japanese army for a single campaign during the entire Pacific war—consisted of 25 divisions, 1 tank division, 11 mixed brigades, 1 cavalry brigade, 1 air division, and 12,000 motor vehicles as well as 70,000 horses.[31] Devoid of the support of a strong strategical reserve, the depleted Chinese force yielded at Changsha, thrice before the site of Japanese defeat. Continuing their drive southward, the Japanese marched from Changsha to Henyang, an important railway center in southern Hunan. There, to the surprise of the Japanese, the 16,275 Chinese defenders staved off three fierce Japanese attacks by a total of six divisions and, assisted by the Fourteenth Air Force, held the battered city for forty-seven days—a feat which American observers, subsequently joined even by the opposing Japanese commanders, have attributed to Chinese courage. On June 28 the Japanese began to drive forward from Canton and, after a prolonged struggle, they eventually gained possession of the entire Canton-Hankow railway by the beginning of 1945.[32]

[31] Hattori, *op.cit.*, IV, p. 72, listing the order of battle of the campaign, also, *ibid.*, III, pp. 247-255.
[32] Hattori, *op.cit.*, III, pp. 262-265.

V

In October 1944 General Stilwell clashed with Generalissimo Chiang over the issue of his assuming command of all the Chinese ground forces. This proved the breaking point of their long-strained relationship, and Stilwell was recalled from China. Finding China at her lowest ebb both militarily and internationally, Japan strove through every propaganda device to widen the gulf between the United States and China by magnifying the Stilwell incident and offering peace terms to end her war against China. Failing to get results by these methods, Japan intensified her offensive toward the heart of Free China.

Further reinforced by fresh units, the Japanese pursued their drive westward along the Hunan-Kiangsi railway. Some 16 divisions out of a total of 20 were employed initially in the operations against Kweilin, and the force was soon increased to a total of about 400,000 men—the largest concentration of troops since the battle of Wuhan in 1938. China was in great difficulties, with ebbing strength and poorly equipped units left to face this offensive while many of her best troops were tied up in the Burma and Salween campaigns and in blockading the communists.[33] Kweilin fell on November 10, and the Japanese pressed on toward Kweiyang and Chungking. By the first part of December the Japanese had taken Tuyun and Kweiyang, and the situation in Chungking was tense.

It was to this uneasy city, on October 31, 1944, that Lieutenant General Albert C. Wedemeyer came as Stilwell's successor. From the beginning he exercised diplomacy and tact—the qualities which Stilwell never could command—and won the Chinese to his side. He set up machinery to facilitate closer understanding and cooperation between the Americans and the Chinese, and he won admiration from the generalissimo for his decisive action in flying some 23,000 fresh troops from the northwest to stem the onrushing Japanese tide near Kweichow. Other troops marched from the northwest to reinforce the airlift force. Meanwhile Wedemeyer ordered the hard-fighting General Fu Tso-yi to engage the Japanese in northern China in order to prevent enemy reinforcement in the Kweiyang area.

Having checked the pressing Japanese attack around Kweiyang, Wedemeyer turned to more general matters. At his request, some

---

[33] Tsao and Shu, op.cit., "Period June 15, 1944 to Dec. 1944."

500,000 unfit soldiers were withdrawn from the front lines and sent to the rear for medical treatment or other duties. The defenses of vital positions were strengthened, and air power was directed against enemy supply lines. A Chinese war production board was established with the assistance of Donald Nelson and a group of American experts.

By March 1945 things began to look brighter. Chinese forces under General Li Tsung-jen's over-all direction beat back a Japanese offensive in the Honan-Hupeh area, inflicting heavy casualties and regaining all American air bases captured in the initial Japanese assault. Equally successful were the Chinese in the western Hunan campaign to recover the strategic air base at Chihkiang. The Japanese had thrown 60,000 men into the battle along a 248-mile front, but the Chinese counteroffensive decimated their ranks. The Chinese now had the initiative and, when V-J Day came so suddenly, were massing for a projected offensive in the Canton-Hong Kong-Fukien area—an offensive which was designed to capture that section of the southern coast where American forces proposed to land in China.

SUMMARY

China's war of resistance during the years 1937 to 1945 had set a unique example of military unconventionality and national courage. The vastness of China and the iron will of her people in resisting aggression had successfully defied the technological superiority of Imperial Japan, the Chinese emerging victorious after years of suffering and numerous defeats. Chinese troops, recruited from the huge unlettered masses of a great nation, had fought with bravery and resourcefulness; behind the Japanese lines, the great masses of Chinese civilians had persistently refused to accept what many times appeared to be indubitable Japanese victory.

China had withstood foreign aggression even though she was a nation divided against herself. The generalissimo's own party enjoyed at best a precarious unity, composed as it was of many factions led by ambitious and independent generals. Against this party stood the communist organization, a group by now thoroughly Sinized but with ideals and aims at great variance with those of their non-communist countrymen. Fierce struggles went on as it became increasingly obvious that the communists were willing to fight China's battles only when winning them appeared to be advantageous to the grand communist design. Considerable strength which should have been at the disposal of the National Government in combating the external enemy was tied up in keeping the communists within check. Only a fraction of the nation's might could be employed against Japan; the rest was diverted to hold the shaky National Government in delicate balance and to keep watch over the threat from the Reds within the country.

Such strength as could be used against the enemy was incompetently managed. Befuddled in the beginning by the fallacious concept of military control, the administration robbed itself of the talents of top civilians capable of mobilizing China's national resources to the fullest. A cumbersome and corrupt organization, riddled with patronage and bureaucracy, ran the government, and was incapable of learning from the communists, who excelled in organizing the people down to the village levels, how to utilize all available talent in the national interest. With their single goal a tight control—a control they were never able completely to achieve—the administration stifled initiative and discouraged resourcefulness. As a consequence, there was an incredible waste of the nation's fighting power. A shortsighted economic and industrial approach crippled the armies on the battlefield and threatened the livelihood of the populace behind the lines. Scarcely a quarter of the nation's available manpower in arms was devoted to the actual shooting war, and no more than half the nation's available material resources were effectively exploited.

At the helm in China stood Chiang, the generalissimo, leading with selfless determination a struggle to the death for national independence. As for his government, perhaps the words of one of the great military minds of World War II, German Field Marshal von Rundstedt, offer us a keen insight into the Chinese situation when he describes his own country's wartime organizational confusions, rigid control, and the inherent weaknesses of such an autocratic or dictatorial rule, pointing out that such a pattern preceded the downfall of even so great a general as Napoleon.[34]

The Chinese wartime diplomacy which the generalissimo administered was a curious mixture of traditional Chinese passivity and startling candor; it was based less upon the consideration of international power politics than upon a kind of moral and philosophical attitude typical of the Middle Kingdom. China's wartime friends were that

[34] Blumentritt, Guenther, *Von Rundstedt, The Soldier and the Man* (London: Odham Press, 1952), Chs. 8, 9.

strange collection of bed fellows which adversity always makes, and her steadfast allies were few. Germany had contributed to the growth of her armed might, but China broke with Germany, unwilling to trade her national integrity for political expediency. Soviet Russia aided China, finding it to her own interests. China leaned heavily in her direction in the beginning: she refused to ally herself with the anti-comintern bloc led by Germany, signed a Sino-Soviet non-aggression pact in 1937, which was, more than any other single international factor, instrumental in effecting China's entry into a full-scale war against Nippon. The Chinese were often suspicious of Soviet intentions to dominate China, fearful that the Chinese communists claimed an allegiance with precedence over China's own interests, but they tagged along, becoming a willing instrument of Soviet policy in the Far East. The Russians were well aware of the Chinese and Japanese penchant for fighting to the finish, aware too of the truth in the significant Chinese proverb that when two tigers fight there must be one wounded tiger. Soviet Russia could not but benefit from the weakening of either or both of her dangerous neighbors. From the Kremlin the long-range planners watched the events in the Far East and saw how they furthered their grand strategy for world domination, a strategy which only they fully comprehended.

Britain was never more than lukewarm to the Kuomintang during and after the war, and China strangely, considering Britain's eminent position and her vast influence in world councils, failed to court her full cooperation. The conspicuous necessity for reform within the Chinese government—and its equally conspicuous absence—prompted many unsophisticated Americans to hold an exaggeratedly favorable opinion of the Chinese communists, extolling them as "agrarian reformers" and labeling the Kuomintang as a dangerous and decadent crew of medieval warlords and unprincipled opportunists bent on self-aggrandizement. Despite American determination to hold China as a strategic outpost, as the base from which to bomb Japan and as the battlefield on which they supposed the final confronting and defeat of the Japanese forces would come, and despite China's gratitude for the staggering quantities of supplies which the United States poured into her war, the Stilwell crisis served as sufficient cause to alienate two of the most faithful allies of the war. "A spark," said the Chinese, "can burn an entire plain," and the comparatively minor difference of opinion over Stilwell was spark enough to ignite many fires of mutual distrust and dislike.

Looking at the record of Chinese diplomacy during World War II, one is led to the inevitable conclusion that no case can be made for the existence of any single, clear, consistent diplomatic course on the part of Chiang's government. China's divergent approaches cannot be said to have failed, but it surely may be asserted with some degree of confidence that they did not succeed in maximizing her war effort. In the same way, it is true that China could claim no definite and devastating victory over the Japanese. She simply proved that she could not be defeated by them, that she could withstand—and occasionally trounce —a first-class military power in a war which lasted eight years, a war she entered only half prepared and fought with half her strength, a war against the same caliber of Japanese troops who faced the Americans in the Philippines, on Iwo Jima, on Okinawa, and who were present in far greater numbers on the mainland of China. For a long time she fought alone for international justice and later she made her invaluable contribution to the cause of the whole Free World.

I. THE JAPANESE SURRENDER AND ITS AFTERMATH.
II. REORGANIZATION TOWARD CHAOS. III. THE FAILURE
OF THE MARSHALL PLAN FOR CHINA.

I

FOUR days after an atomic bomb dropped from an American super-fortress devastated Hiroshima, Radio Tokyo, on August 10, 1945, announced Japan's readiness to accept the Potsdam declaration. Eleven days later Japanese emissaries of General Yasutsugu Okamura waited upon the Chinese at Chikiang to receive the terms of surrender in the Pacific theater. Following the signing of the instrument of surrender aboard the *U.S.S. Missouri* in Tokyo Bay, the Japanese commander-in-chief in China formally surrendered at Nanking on September 9 to Chiang's deputy, General Ho Ying-ch'in. The ceremony took place, by Chiang's express desire, in the auditorium of the Central Military Academy—the symbol of Whampoa's military might. The articles stated, in part:

"The Emperor of Japan, the Japanese Government and the Japanese Imperial General Headquarters, having recognized the complete military defeat of the Japanese military forces by the Allied forces and having surrendered unconditionally to the Supreme Commander of the Allied Powers, and the Supreme Commander for the Allied Powers having directed by his General Order No. 1 that the senior commanders and all ground, sea, air and auxiliary forces within China (excluding Manchuria), Formosa and French Indochina north of the sixteenth degree of latitude shall surrender to Generalissimo Chiang Kai-shek,

"We, the Japanese commanders of all Japanese forces and auxiliaries named above, also recognizing the complete military defeat of the Japanese military forces by the Allied forces, hereby surrender unconditionally all of the forces under our command to Generalissimo Chiang Kai-shek."[1]

---

[1] "Nanking Surrender Document, September 9, 1945," released officially for publication in *China at War*, xv, 3-4 (Sept.-Oct. 1945), p. 17.

In such a formal statement, couched in the precise phrases of cold legality, did the Japanese end the eight bitter years of war and turn over to Chiang Nipponese land and sea forces in the area totaling 1,313,240 men.[2]

Chiang thus came into technical control of the Japanese forces within his theater of war, but he was to encounter difficulties in his attempt to exercise control over some of the Chinese forces. In his victory message to the nation, he gave particular emphasis to this point: "The most important condition for national unity is the nationalization of all the armed forces in the country. There should be no private army within the country's boundary, nor should armed forces be kept by any political party. Only when armed forces are no longer directed by personal interests or individuals, no longer guided by the private wishes of a political party, can national unity be secured."[3] He was, of course, referring to the contest by the Chinese communists, even then begun, for the control of areas formerly held by the Japanese.

The forces of the National Government which had borne the brunt of the Japanese offensive were concentrated in central and southern China. The Chinese communists, organized as guerrilla units, were widely dispersed throughout central and northern China and scattered along the coast. When the Japanese surrender came, despite the government's efforts to ensure that all Japanese forces surrendered directly and only to the generalissimo, the Chinese communists were able to disarm many enemy troops and accept local surrenders in compliance with the order issued by their commander-in-chief, Chu Teh, under the authorization of the Yenan Army Headquarters. "Our armies," announced Chu, "have the full power to receive, occupy, carry out military control, maintain order, and appoint special commissioners to take charge of all administrative matters. . . . Any sabotage and resistance against the above measures will be treated as treason."[4]

The chief hope of the Chinese Red Army was to rely upon the Soviet dominance in Manchuria to effect the surrender of the Japanese Kwantung Army to the Chinese communists. Lin Piao, one of the ablest generals of the Chinese Reds, descended upon Manchuria with some 100,000 unarmed soldiers from Shangtung and northern China,

[2] Ho Ying-chin, "Report on Accepting the Surrender and Taking-over Conditions," *China Handbook, 1937-1945* (N.Y.: Macmillan, 1947), p. 765.
[3] Chiang Kai-shek, "V-J Day Message to the Nation, Sept. 3, 1945," *China at War*, xv, 3-4 (Sept.-Oct. 1945), p. 1.
[4] *Ta-kung-pao* Editorial, Sept. 4, 1945, Chungking edition.

80,000 of whom were placed under Lin's control by their former commander, Communist General Ch'en Yi of the New Fourth Army (later the Third Field Army).[5] In a most mysterious manner huge quantities of surrendered equipment belonging to 594,000 Japanese troops reappeared in the hands of the Chinese communists. The 300,-000 rifles, 138,000 machine guns, and 2,700 pieces of field artillery formerly belonging to the Japanese were never properly accounted for.[6] Many thousands of former Manchukuo regular soldiers were also released from their Russian captivity. With these additions, Lin Piao organized 8 columns, 7 cavalry divisions, 1 artillery division, and 3 other independent divisions. Suddenly Lin Piao's People's Army acquired a strength never enjoyed during the war by any comparable body of government troops. Indeed the Red forces had more equipment than manpower and, posing as the liberators of Manchuria, launched a vast recruiting program there in order to enlist enough men to handle the plethora of arms.

In order to check these communist moves if possible, three nationalist armies were airlifted to key sectors of northern and eastern China and about a half million more men were given sea transport to such areas by American vessels. At the request of the Chinese government, 50,000 U.S. Marines landed in northern China to defend vital points from the communists and to aid in the repatriation of Japanese nationals. But the communists on the spot had already achieved a great deal by speedy and decisive action, and the government's efforts to centralize control of all military power, native and defeated, in the hands of the Whampoa clique were greatly hampered. Nevertheless the government strove to realize that end, even when it meant short-changing many high officers who had served valiantly during the war but who were not within Whampoa's inner circle—generals like Li Tsung-jen, Pai Chung-hsi, Sun Lien-Chung, and Sun Li-jen. So determined was the Whampoa group to run the show that it subordinated the entire air arm to its command and, on January 1, 1946, announced that the Chinese navy thereafter would be managed as an adjunct to the army!

A lack of tact towards the puppet troops—Chinese who had served the Japanese during the late conflict—lost to the nationalists many a

[5] The 100,000 figure comes from Rigg, R. B., *Red China's Fighting Hordes* (Harrisburg, 1952), p. 252.
[6] Tsiang, T. F., "Statement before the First Committee of the United Nations' General Assembly, Art. 5," *China Handbook, 1952-1953* (Taipeh, 1953), p. 391.

valuable force such as the Manchukuo army. Subjected to unnecessary harshness at the hands of the victorious nationalists—a fault which communist propaganda skillfully stressed—many of these puppet troops, equipment and all, fled to the welcoming arms of the Chinese Reds. An American observer, Colonel R. B. Rigg, estimated that the Reds gained at least 75,000 such converts in Manchuria during 1945-1946.[7]

Another ill-advised policy on the part of the National Government was that concerning postwar demobilization. Without close scrutiny of many pertinent factors, demobilization was carried out on a sweeping scale, throwing thousands of career soldiers out of the nation's forces without any provision whatsoever for their reabsorption into civilian life. Jobless and disgruntled, many of these men swelled the ranks of the Chinese communists. Somewhat confident over the Sino-Soviet pact of 1945 and expecting that Russia would honor her pledge to aid the National Government rather than the Chinese communists, the nationalists decided to disband over 1.5 million troops and to retain only 39 divisions which had been modernized by the United States plus a selected section of the 180 provincial and central army divisions led by the more trusted generals. Some 200,000 officers alone were released from the service. Such a hasty and ill-considered action was to have far-reaching ramifications for subsequent developments in China.

Thus, immediately following V-J Day, the government's military policy reflected a strong suspicion of the non-central armies and was alienating, or at least losing the effective cooperation of, men who by every test had been loyal to the government and to the national cause. For instance, soon after the Yenan Army Headquarters announced its intention of receiving the Japanese surrender, Generals Li-Tsung-jen and Pai Chung-hsi suggested to the generalissimo that the government armies nearest the north China front should be immediately dispatched to north China in order to stabilize the confused situation there.[8] Instead, the government airlifted, or shipped by sea at considerable cost and after long delay, only Central Army units from Burma and Indochina to that faraway north China area, giving the communists a good headstart in seizing control of that vital area. Discriminatory policies then aroused a widespread anti-government senti-

[7] Rigg, op.cit., p. 249f.
[8] Yin shi, *The Chiang-Lee Relationship and China*, in Chinese (Hongkong: Freedom Press, 1954), p. 84.

ment which crystallized in defections and treacheries within provincial forces. In one single case, a commander-in-chief of a group army deserted with his units to the communist side and treacherously destroyed almost four army corps of the famous northern general Sun Lien-chung. This was the first government military disaster after V-J Day.

II

Meanwhile, a political consultative conference meeting in January 1946 was drafting plans which, at least in theory, would solve China's military administrative problems and eliminate some of the causes of the many serious errors then being made. The consensus of the conference on the fundamental principles concerning the creation of a National Army was this: "The Army belongs to the state. It shall be established in response to the necessities of national defense. Its quality and equipment shall be improved in light of the progress made in general education, science, and industry. The military system shall be reformed in the light of democratic institutions and the actual conditions prevailing at the time. The system of conscription shall be reformed and applied fairly and universally. Some form of volunteer system shall be preserved and reforms shall be introduced in order to meet the requirements of a fully equipped army."[9]

On the subject of the reorganization of the army, the conference stressed the necessity of separating army and party, and divorcing civil and military authorities:

"All political parties shall be forbidden to carry on party activities, whether open or secret, in the army. So shall be all cliques based on personal relations or of a territorial nature. All military personnel on active service who owe allegiance to any political party may not take part in the party activities of the district in which they are stationed, when they are on duty. No party or individual may make use of the army as an instrument of political rivalry. No illegal organizations and activities may be allowed in the army.

"No military personnel on active service may serve concurrently as a civil official. The army shall be strictly forbidden to interfere with political affairs. The country shall be divided into military districts which shall be made not to coincide with administrative districts as far as possible."[10]

[9] Chinese Ministry of Information, *China Handbook, 1937-1945*, p. 745.
[10] *Ibid.*

The conference stated its views on the advisability of civilian control of the army in these words: "The National Military Council shall be reorganized into a Ministry of National Defense under the [civilian] Executive Yuan. The Defense Minister shall not necessarily be a military man. The number of troops and military expenditure shall be decided upon by the Defense Ministry and passed by the Executive Yuan. All troops shall be under the unified control of the Ministry of National Defense in which a committee shall be established to be charged with the double duty of planning for a national army and of seeing to it that the plans are faithfully carried out. Members of the committee shall be drawn from the various circles."[11]

When the conference convened in the first month of 1946, the nation was yearning for the peace which the surrender of the Japanese enemy promised but did not bring. A number of minor parties, including the Democratic League, a leftist group operating under the colors of a moderate liberalism, were particularly outspoken in urging a military reorganization which would facilitate an amalgamation of the then opposing nationalist and communist armies. Moreover, the League members were canny enough to see that the newly important portfolio of defense minister might fall into the hands of one of their party when the nationalists and the communists, each unwilling that the other should capture this key post, deadlocked on the issue. The leaders of the Kuomintang were secretly unwilling to support this new organizational scheme, lest it put the armed forces, the heart of the party's power, in the hands of a non-party minister of defense, but they were sufficiently aware of the weight of public sentiment in favor of civilian control of the military not to come out openly against it. They contented themselves with forcing an arrangement whereby the chief of the supreme staff was empowered to ignore or even counteract the directives of the ministry of defense. Then they rested secure that no matter which party controlled the ministry, the Kuomintang retained its old power. Such were the "reforms" that could be effected. "The army belongs to the state," said the conference. "*We* are the state," said the Kuomintang, "and the army is ours."

In June a drastic military reorganization began, purporting to implement the decision to return military power to the nation and to place it under civilian administration. Pai Chung-hsi, the first defense minister under the new organization, stated to the press that, since

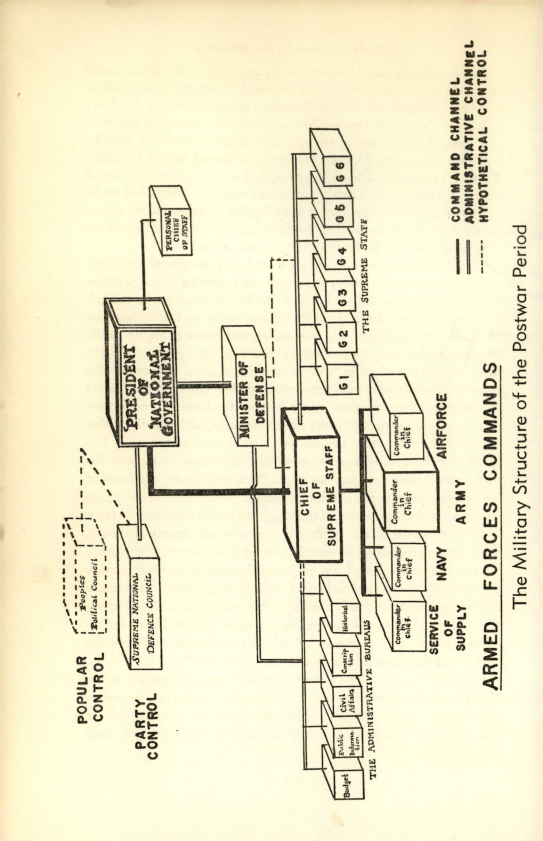

POPULAR CONTROL

PARTY CONTROL

Peoples Political Council

SUPREME NATIONAL DEFENCE COUNCIL

PRESIDENT OF NATIONAL GOVERNMENT

PERSONAL CHIEF OF STAFF

MINISTER OF DEFENSE

CHIEF OF SUPREME STAFF

G1 G2 G3 G4 G5 G6

THE SUPREME STAFF

Budget   Public Information   Civil Affairs   Conscription   Historical

THE ADMINISTRATIVE BUREAUS

Commander in Chief   Commander in Chief   Commander in Chief   Commander in Chief

SERVICE OF SUPPLY   NAVY   ARMY   AIRFORCE

ARMED FORCES COMMANDS

COMMAND CHANNEL
ADMINISTRATIVE CHANNEL
HYPOTHETICAL CONTROL

The Military Structure of the Postwar Period

China had entered into the constitutional stage, the national military council which was previously independent of the Executive Yuan would have to be abolished. Its functions were to be taken over by the new ministry, operating under the Executive Yuan, and a greater attempt was to be made to achieve close coordination between political policy and military strategy, and to integrate the command and administrative function of the armed forces.[12]

Under the Chinese constitution the president of the National Government "shall have the command of the armed forces." The new defense ministry, therefore, was subject to the president's control, as well as to the president of the Executive Yuan, of which the ministry was, in a sense, a subcommittee. The president of the National Government exercised his control through his deputy, the chief of the supreme staff, who commanded the six departments of the defense ministry which the Chinese had set up on the basis of American general staff structure: G-1, personnel; G-2, intelligence; G-3, war plans; G-4, operations; G-5, supply; and G-6, organization and training.[13] The minister of defense, though theoretically in charge of the whole, lost control of the above departments to the chief of the supreme staff and was left with actual control of only the following bureaus of the ministry: public relations and publicity, civil affairs, local security, budget, military history, inspection, and conscription.

The subordination of the defense ministry to the civilian Executive Yuan was in theory designed to achieve civilian control of the military. This control, though clear in law, was largely non-existent in fact, for though the civilian minister of defense had the duty of passing on the military budget submitted by the chief of the supreme staff and was empowered to determine (subject to ratification by the civilian Executive Yuan) the utilization of the manpower and resources of the nation and questions of general mobilization, he became the tool of the military and the president-generalissimo whenever a strong chief of the supreme staff decided to act. The defense minister and his three deputy ministers were no match, for example, for the first chief of the supreme staff appointed under the new arrangement, General Ch'en Ch'eng, a man of great personal integrity, a severe field commander, and a ranking member of the Whampoa clique. Ch'en's direct access to the presi-

[12] "Official Statement of the Ministry of National Defense," *Kuo-fang-yueh-pao*, I, 1 (Dec. 1946), pp. 103-104.
[13] "Organic Law of the Ministry of National Defense, Mar. 31, 1946," *Kuo-fang-yueh-pao, op.cit.*, p. 103.

dent gave him an inestimable advantage over Defense Minister Pai Chung-hsi, who had to act through the Executive Yuan.

The following table offers a comparison between the Chinese and the Anglo-American administrative hierarchy:

Anglo-American	Chinese
Commander-in-chief	Generalissimo
(head of state civilian status)	(president with military status)
Prime minister	Premier, Executive Yuan
(civilian)	(civilian)
Defense minister or secretary	Minister of national defense
(civilian)	(military)
Chief of staff	Chief of supreme staff
(military)	(military)

The important difference between the two command structures was this: in the Anglo-American system, the military chief of staff had to go through two civilian offices to reach his commander-in-chief; in the Chinese system, his counterpart (the chief of supreme staff) was granted direct access to the generalissimo whenever he cared to bypass the two officials above him.

Under the immediate direction of the chief of the supreme staff were the commanders-in-chief of the four services: army, navy, air force, and supply. These commanders were responsible for implementing the over-all plans formulated by the chief of the supreme staff. The Chinese structure incorporated many American organizational features of the 1942 reorganization of the United States War Department, but the Chinese supreme staff was closer to the German Wehrmacht's "OKW" (Oberkommando der Wehrmacht) in conception than to the American "Joint Staffs."[14] Indeed it resembled the older Kriegsministerium (war ministry) with the addition of the "OKW" of the Hitler period, although General Ch'en Ch'eng stated that the salient features of the Chinese reorganization had been suggested by General Wedemeyer's headquarters.[15]

The Chinese reorganization of 1946 placed the army in a dominant position, for the federation of forces was commanded by an army man and the separate services were each run by commanders-in-chief who were basically army men with army loyalties. The naval and air forces had inadequate representation on the supreme staff; proper

[14] Nelson, Otto, National Security and the General Staff (Washington: Infantry Journal Press, 1946), p. 373.
[15] Kuo-fang-yueh-pao, op.cit., pp. 103-104.

organization would have demanded a small supreme staff with equal representation in rank and numbers, except for one over-all director from the principal service, in this case the Chinese army.[16] As the case was, army commanders without sufficient knowledge of their specialized problems were dictating the operation of the highly technical naval and air forces.

The new organizational chart showed several marked improvements, at least on paper: it was more tightly knit and streamlined; it embodied the concept of singleness of control; and it eliminated many overlapping functions. It was considered adaptable to both wartime and peacetime requirements, thereby precluding the necessity of extensive changes in the event of sudden emergency. On the other hand, the idea of civilian rule was not being realized; with all key posts in the hands of army generals, the country was in the grip of an army monopoly. As for the political function of the ministry of national defense, a well-known political scientist, Professor Chien Tuan-sheng, later firmly identified with the communist cause, had the following comment: "In itself it is not a bad device, provided the minister is both a capable and powerful political leader and provided the chief of staff limits his authority to purely military matters and does not encroach upon the political sphere of the minister."[17]

Something more of the nature and extent of the 1946 reorganization may be gathered from these remarks of General Wedemeyer: "There must be a streamlined organization and clear-cut enunciation in the duties of all the ministries and bureaus of the government. In April a year ago I discovered that there were well over sixty sections in the National Military Council with duplicating functions and conflicting authorities. There was very little coordination between various groups and sections. Actually there were some groups within the National Military Council that were handling matters which had nothing whatsoever to do with national defense matters. Today in the Ministry of Defense we have grouped sixty sections under six general heads and reduced the personnel about fifty percent. Actually over 75,000 individuals were eliminated."[18]

[16] Smith, Bedell, "Problems at an Integrated Headquarters," *Journal of the Royal United Service Institution*, xc (Nov. 1945). Thompson, W. G. S., "Supreme Command," *Journal of the Royal United Service Institution*, xci (Feb.-Nov. 1946), pp. 196-203.
[17] Chien Tuan-sheng, "The Role of the Military in the Chinese Government," *Pacific Affairs*, xxi, 3 (Sept. 1948), pp. 239-251.
[18] "Summary Remarks Made by Lt. Gen. Albert C. Wedemeyer before Joint Meet-

The wholesale reorganization of the Chinese military machinery, from the cumbersome national military council to the streamlined ministry of defense, did not produce the amelioration expected. Rather that outright changeover severed all organizational continuity at a peculiarly inauspicious time. The prevailing sentiment among government leaders was that if such radical alterations of the entire machinery had been avoided at a period when American advisory assistance was virtually unobtainable, they might not have found themselves so disorganized in the face of imminent danger from the communists. From the autumn of 1945 until March 1948 the hands of MAGIC (the Military Advisory Group in China) were effectively tied by an American directive which prevented them from rendering the National Government the kind of assistance it required.

The reorganization caused confusion and dislocation throughout the entire Chinese forces. The inexperience of the infant ministry, coupled with the residue of incompetence in the old military bureaucracy, led to numerous reverses in the field. The enforcement of the truce agreement, for instance, demanded an effective control of the field forces from the ministry of national defense, which did not yet have such control, for the metamorphosis from the old military council to the new organization was neither speedy nor smooth. During the interim, for example, Chinese military representatives abroad were not only deprived of fast contact with their government but received no remittance for as long as three or four months. Even at that, they fared better than the average field commander, for communication between the central command and field units was inconceivably inefficient. Many combat units were cut off, for all practical purposes, from the new supreme staff and received little ammunition, funds, or replacements for several months. In this deplorable situation disquieting local incidents combined to produce in some areas large-scale conflicts about which Nanking could do nothing. The truce terms the government had guaranteed to General Marshall were violated in the field.

The Americans, who had a total of 60,000 military personnel in China on V-J Day, encouraged and indeed pressed for Chinese reorganization but were, due to the prevailing U.S. policy toward China at the time, largely unable to assist in that theoretically lauda-

ing of State Council and All Ministers of the National Government Aug. 22, 1947," *U.S. Relations with China, op.cit.*, p. 76.

[236]

ble aim.[19] Without their aid the job was so bungled that two years later an American White Paper conceded: "In view of the conflicting line of authority which had existed under the duplicating divisions of the old National War Council, the Chinese Minister of Defense faced a difficult problem in establishing clearly defined operating procedures."[20]

Even the dominance of powerful military men in important posts could not impose order. In the winter of 1948 General Ch'en Ch'eng, then chief of staff, went to Manchuria to assume command of the northeastern theater. Failing in both of his tasks, he was replaced as chief of staff by General Ku Chu-t'ung. By logical choice General Pai Chung-hsi should have been appointed to that vital post. However, because of his political differences with Chiang, Pai was given a major field command in Central China. The new chief of staff, certainly never a strategist of Pai's caliber, was not the best choice. Moreover, he no longer had the same amount of power as his predecessor, General Ch'en Ch'eng, for there was another reorganization: General Ho Ying-ch'in, recently appointed the new minister of defense, had now a greater amount of authority—not because of any statutory change, but because of seniority in the nationalist military hierarchy.

On April 22, 1949, when the peace talks had failed and tragic disunity of command threatened the government's forces, Li Tsung-jen, then acting president of China, met with Generalissimo Chiang at Hangchow. One of their decisions was that, to promote greater unity of command, the minister of defense should be permitted greater authority and should be vested with the direct command of the armed forces. The chief of the supreme staff was to be simply the principal staff officer, and in no way entitled to impinge upon the prerogatives of the defense minister through his hitherto direct access to the president, who wielded the highest authority in military command.[21]

The continuing organizational changes indicated that the Chinese had acted too hastily to have built upon firm foundations. As General Hans von Seeckt advised the generalissimo: "The hypothesis of every reorganization of an army is, first of all, peace on the outer

---

[19] *U.S. Relations with China*, p. 939.　　[20] *Ibid.*, pp. 341f.
[21] Yin Shi, *op.cit.*, p. 128. Liang Sheng-chuen, *Chiang-Li tòu-tsēng nèi-mou* (The Inside Struggle of Chiang Kai-shek with Lee Chong-yean), in Chinese (Hongkong: Union Asia Press, 1954), p. 120.

borders. That means several years of external peace and a state of political calm. . . . Before these conditions are achieved, a successful military reorganization cannot be attained in a short time.[22]

It was not enough that the new structure was in principle palpably superior to the old. It was ill-timed and ill-planned, and therefore ill-advised. Originally intended as a prelude to military unification, it disrupted the armed forces, confused the government, lost all the confidence of the communists, and even failed to achieve the unqualified support of the very American advisory mission which had advocated it and which later, because of U.S. policy toward China, could not assist it.

III

In November 1945 President Truman sent General of the Army George C. Marshall to China as his special envoy with the task of bringing about the "unification of China by peaceful, democratic methods" and the cessation of nationalist-communist hostilities as quickly as possible.[23]

Marshall hoped to achieve these goals partly through adhering to the principle of "the separation of the army from politics" by creating a national, non-political military force along the lines of Western tradition.[24] To reconcile and amalgamate the two opposing armies, the new ministry of national defense was established within the civilian Executive Yuan in lieu of the divided and irresponsible national military council.

In the American view, the two armies, nationalist and communist, had to be fused into one national army. American policy stated that "with the institution of a broadly representative government, autonomous armies should be eliminated as such and all armed forces in China integrated effectively in the Chinese National Army."[25] The Americans, moreover, intended to play their ace—promised assistance —to foster that goal. As President Truman's instructions to Marshall stated with surprising candor: "In your conversation to Chiang Kaishek and other Chinese leaders you are authorized to speak with the utmost frankness. Particularly you may state, in connection with the

[22] von Seeckt, Hans, *Denkschrift, op.cit.,* p. 1.
[23] *U.S. Relations with China,* pp. 605-606.   [24] *Ibid.*
[25] "Statement by President Truman on U.S. Policy towards China, Dec. 15, 1945," *Department of State Bulletin,* Dec. 16, 1945.

Chinese desire for credits, technical assistance in the economic field, and military assistance (I have in mind the proposed U.S. Military Advisory Group which I have approved in principle), that a China disunited and torn by civil strife could not be considered realistically as a proper place for American assistance along the lines enumerated."[26]

American policy in China had transcended the purely military sphere and now sought a politico-military alliance between China's two unconciliatory parties. To review the over-all American part in this Chinese picture, it will be necessary to harken back to General Wedemeyer's functions before and after V-J Day.

Prior to victory over the Japanese, the primary problem facing Wedemeyer was incontestably military. His political view was straightforward and succinctly stated on February 15, 1945: "My policy is this, that we will not give any assistance to any individual, to any activity, to any organization within the China Theater . . . but I am ordered to support the Central Government and I am going to do that to the best of my ability."[27]

Wedemeyer's assistance to the Central Government was indeed invaluable. In 1945, when he realized that the communists were massed on the Manchurian border, suspecting their aims and knowing that the nationalists were tied up with the Japanese conflict in southern and southwestern China, he petitioned the Joint Chiefs of Staff for authority to dispatch seven American divisions to Manchuria to assist in the acceptance of the Japanese surrender there. Wedemeyer was turned down by Washington. He had had the interests of the Central Government at heart, for his proposal would have given the government time to reoccupy Manchuria and to save it from the communists. Although Wedemeyer's plan to salvage Manchuria was rejected, he earned the gratitude of the Chinese nationalists by his bold airlift of government forces to Shanghai, Peiping, and Nanking; without this aid, the area as far south as the Yangtze River would have fallen into waiting communist hands when the Japanese surrendered. In recognition of his great contribution to the Chinese war effort, Wedemeyer was awarded the highest military honor in the gift of China—the Order of the Blue Sky and White Sun.

Two months after the Japanese surrender, Major General Robert

[26] "President Truman to the Special Representative of the President to China, Dec. 15, 1945," *U.S. Relations with China*, pp. 605-606.
[27] U.S. General Staff, *The Chinese Communist Movement*, *op.cit.*, p. 2395.

McClure was assigned the mission of maintaining liaison between the Americans and the Chinese headquarters command and of giving advice on staff procedure and training. Cognizant of the value of continued American assistance, the Chinese government asked the United States to create a five-year military mission which would train and develop the Chinese forces. Following President Truman's statement on September 14, 1945 regarding assistance to China, the Military Advisory Group in China (MAGIC) was formed and General McClure appointed its first commander.

On December 15, 1945, Truman couched the policy toward China in these words: "A strong, united, and democratic China is of the utmost importance to the success of this United Nation Organization for world peace. As China moves forward toward peace and unity along the lines described here, the United States would be prepared to assist the National Government in every reasonable way to rehabilitate the country, improve the agrarian and industrial economy, and establish a military organization capable of discharging China's national and international responsibilities for the maintenance of peace and order."[28]

In creating MAGIC to implement one phase of this policy, the United States joint chiefs of staff approved the sending to China of an advisory group of army and navy personnel not to exceed, 1,000 officers and men. Later an air advisory contingent was added. The advisory group was not authorized to make recommendations concerning the organization and equipment of the Chinese army units, nor to carry on advisory activities directly involved in the training and combat of Chinese units.[29] These reservations were dictated by the American policy of attempting to establish a nationalist-communist coalition government and by the parallel determination not to involve the employment of American assistance for the purposes of waging a nationalist-communist civil war. The joint chiefs were influenced in their decision by the policy pronouncements of the State Department, which in turn based its decision on the on-the-spot judgments of its foreign service men, although in many cases State Department decisions ran contrary to the best judgments of the military.[30]

Chinese leaders were not in accord regarding their own most press-

[28] *U.S. Relations with China*, pp. 607-609.   [29] *Ibid.*
[30] "Memorandum by Secretary J. Byrnes for the War Department, Dec. 9, 1945," *U.S. Relations with China*, Annex 61, pp. 606-607.

ing problems. One school proposed resolute action against the communists and, had it not been for the almost assured loss of American support which would have resulted, those of that mind might have succeeded in convincing the government to launch an immediate offensive. This strategy would at least have been better than suffering defeat as a result of inaction and, especially if the government had put forth a determined effort to follow up the communist rout at Szepingkai in May and June 1946, such a plan might have proved successful. Time was of the essence in this plan, for the communists were growing in strength while the government was deteriorating in force from its 1945-1946 peak in economic conditions, supplies, and troop morale.

Fully a year elapsed while the government and the communists engaged in the futility of negotiating some kind of entente. Certain hopes for a peaceful solution were being entertained by General Marshall, although they were based more upon optimism than upon observation. It was, however, in the happy conviction of complete success that Marshall left Chungking on March 13, 1946, to present to his president a report that plans had been made for the integration of the 50 government and 10 communist divisions in a single national army.

Three days later, while Marshall was in the United States, the Chinese communists attacked Szepingkai, a strategic Manchurian town, shrewdly timing their assault to coincide with the withdrawal of Russian troops. Marshall hurried back to China, arriving on April 16, just one day before Changchun, the capital of Manchuria, fell to the communists.

General Marshall was firmly opposed to the attitude of many government leaders of pursuing a settlement by force. Both sides jockeyed for position, bargained for a truce, and, as the truce collapsed, resumed fighting. The Chinese were unable to stop the fighting either by military victory or political concession and, about this time, the communists launched a bitter attack on American interference, protesting against United States assistance to the National Government. The nationalists also blamed America for the criticism that they had received and pointed to the communist violation of the agreement and to the Reds' clear intention of overthrowing the government.

Criticized from both sides, General Marshall strove to be both impartial and, at the same time, the instrument of American foreign policy. His government announced that in an effort to preserve Marshall's mediating role it had ordered a ten-month embargo on the shipment of American arms to China.[31] On August 10, 1946, the president warned Chiang Kai-shek that the United States might "redefine and explain"—diplomatic phraseology for some vague change —its policy toward China.[32]

While the nationalists were complaining against what they considered to be one-sided pressure against them from the Americans, the communist propaganda campaign attacked Marshall's personal integrity and questioned his honesty of purpose. These attacks, combined with undeviating refusal on the part of the communists to entertain any overture of peace the Americans could persuade the nationalists to make, made Marshall's position untenable. He withdrew as mediator.

Prior to his departure from China, General Marshall held conversations with several high-ranking government officials. He stressed the necessity of removing from the government the dominant and entrenched military clique and the reactionaries. He contended that he had exerted every effort to create an opportunity for the better elements in China to rise to the top, and that he considered a respectable opposition party composed of patriotic liberals a strong force in providing an effective check on the dictatorial control of the military leaders.[33]

It was, however, too late for reforms. War was inevitable. If Thomas Hardy was correct when he wrote in *The Dynasts* "My argument is that War makes rattling good history; but Peace is poor reading," then our narrative should hold interest, for we now have to chronicle and examine a civil war the devastation of which— even in this age of bigger and better mass annihilation—is awe-inspiring, and the ramifications of which may in time amount to no less than the global showdown between East and West, communism and democracy.

[31] "House Committee on Foreign Affairs, Testimony of General Marshall, Feb. 20, 1948," quoted in *U.S. Relations with China*, p. 355.
[32] *Ibid.*, p. 652.   [33] *Ibid.*, pp. 217-218.

19 · THE COMMUNIST TRIUMPH
ON THE MAINLAND

I. THE SEEDS OF DEFEAT. II. THE WIDENING GULF. III. THE
COMMUNIST STRATEGY. IV. THE LOSS OF MANCHURIA:
THE BEGINNING OF THE END. V. THE DECISIVE HUAI-HAI
CAMPAIGN: THE FALL OF HSUCHOW. VI. THE CROSSING
OF THE YANGTZE. THE EXILE TO FORMOSA.

"A family must first destroy itself before others can destroy it. A kingdom must first smite itself before others can smite it."—Confucius.

I

THE nationalists, more from fear of losing American support than as a reflection of Chinese national sentiment, went along with the United States attempt to negotiate a Kuomintang-Communist coalition. The communists had no intention of incorporating their armies in the national forces and in July 1946 boldly announced from Yenan the creation of a "people's liberation army," formed from the amalgamation of the Eighth Route Army, the New Fourth Army, and the newly formed Red forces in Manchuria. They were to prove a far more difficult foe than the Japanese had been. The nationalists had long feared that such would be the case.[1]

The communists in Manchuria clashed with the Kuomintang forces at Szepingkai and, facing a capable strategist like General Pai Chung-hsi, who flew to Manchuria to direct the over-all operation, saved themselves from destruction only by a rapid retreat across the Sungari River into Harbin, a city under the shadow of Soviet military power across the border. The government forces were the crack American-trained armies under the command of Generals Sun Li-jen and Ch'en Ming-jen, but the field command in the area was unfortunately en-

[1] Even during the Sino-Japanese war the nationalists had a premonition of this, and the people were saying, "The Japanese are only lice on the body of China, but communism is a disease of the heart."

trusted to the incompetent hands of General Tu Yü-ming, who failed to press his advantage at Szepingkai and permitted the communists to flee to refuge in Harbin. Then, on the sixth of June 1946, the Americans imposed a truce in Manchuria, and this intervention permitted the communists a breathing spell in which to recover and consolidate.

While the "truce" lasted the communists prepared for future tests of Mao Tse-tung's policy, which stressed the concentration of overwhelmingly superior forces designed to meet fractions of the enemy's hosts and to dispose of them one by one. The political strategy which accompanied this plan featured movements toward greater unity between the officers and men within the communist ranks, the improvement and extension of public relations with the masses of the people, techniques to demoralize the enemy, and elaborate programs for the indoctrination and conversion of prisoners of war.

The government forces initially envisioned a large-scale, all-out campaign against the Reds, but soon modified their plans to stress concentrated offensives in Shangtung and northern Shensi, the two spearheads of the communist front. The sheer inertia of a war-weary populace and the rapid deterioration of military morale contributed to the ever-decreasing momentum of the nationalist effort. Meanwhile, behind the scenes, competent generals like Li Tsung-jen, Pai Chung-hsi, and Hsueh Yueh were being given a fast shuffle by the Whampoa clique, which, considering that it had won the war, was engaged in dividing the spoils. The much-needed unity of command waned and there was an increasing reluctance on the part of various commanders to render that unswerving loyalty which the leaders could no longer compel.

By 1947 the government's military leadership was in incredible confusion, and the rate of turnover in the important field commands soared to a new high. Famous fighting generals like Sun Lien-chung, Hsueh Yueh, and Wu Chi-wei were relieved of their commands. The capable military strategist General Pai Chung-hsi was pigeonholed in an office without power, while the chief of the supreme staff was removed to Mukden and the commanding general of the new First Army relegated to a post of secondary importance. The ministry of defense and the supreme staff were disrupted, there was no continuity in the field commands, and everywhere there was uncertainty, confusion, and stalemate. Many of the generals who were not from the Central Army took the reshuffling as evidence of distrust and discrimination and were even further alienated from the Whampoa group.

With no sure hand on the helm, the entire Nationalist Army was rendered incapable of aggressive and coordinated offensives against the communists. Dissatisfaction at the top filtered down to the lowest levels of the troops. Those commanders who were not sure of themselves kept their troops behind city walls or, if compelled to venture forth, dug in elaborately at every halt on the march, tiring the men unnecessarily and giving rise to a hesitant, indecisive defensive psychology highly harmful to their fighting morale. Foremost among the many causes of indecisiveness was Generalissimo Chiang's policy of conserving the strength of his direct units rather than employing them in aggressive operations against the communists.

In wartime an army not constantly put under the test of battle is bound to lose its offensive spirit, and with it, the war. Prolonged garrison duties and the absence of a rotation plan caused the average soldier to despair of ever being discharged. Meanwhile, life in the army went on in a country where inflation had so devaluated the soldier's low pay that his salary would hardly permit him to feed himself adequately. In the less disciplined units the soldiers wrung an occasional decent meal out of the farmers by force, by such action losing popular support for their government which, although constantly claiming to be winning battles, had in effect begun to lose the war.

The communists, on the other hand, were assiduous in their efforts to maintain good relations with the populace. They avoided some of the problems of inflation by issuing food and small luxuries directly to the troops rather than paying them in cash. At the same time the communists were able to aggravate the government's economic plight by cutting lines of communication and preventing foodstuffs from reaching urban areas, thus sending city prices higher and forcing the government to pay ruinous prices to maintain troops in the cities.

Continuity in command structure was another strength of the Reds. Battle-tested generals were placed at the highest levels without favoritism, and merit won promotions for deserving junior officers. From top to bottom, the communist forces were well indoctrinated with the party's political and military objectives and unified by party loyalties.

The Chinese nationalists had built their fighting power around a core of 31 divisions equipped with American assistance during the latter part of the war, though not all of them were trained to combat readiness by V-J Day. Perhaps the fittest troops were those who had fought under Stilwell in Burma, and these were the core of the forces sent to Manchuria to face the communists. Other fine units, though they lacked American training and equipment, were the crack Kwangsi Armies, the efficient northern troops under Generals Fu Tso-yi and Sun Lien-chung, and the hard-fighting Moslem cavalry and other northwestern armies. Early in 1948, forced by the exigency of the situation, the government set up several military commands: the north China command was put under the direction of General Fu Tso-yi; the central China command, under General Pai-Chung-hsi; the northwest command, under the Moslem general, Ma Pu-fang. Although these tested soldiers were honored with the commission of major commands, none of them was entrusted with important authority in the central military establishment.

Against the government forces, the communists launched their divide-and-conquer tactics in the north, dispersing them and then devastating them through successive offensives against Kuomintang troops weakened and demoralized by mismanaged allotment of supplies and material. Such generals as Pai Chung-hsi and Fu Tso-yi were given a low priority in obtaining supplies and virtually left to fend for themselves. About two years later China's acting president, Li Tsung-jen, wrote to President Truman on May 5, 1949 decrying the ill effects that this policy engendered: "It is regrettable that, owing to the failure of our Government to make judicious use of this aid [American supplies in the campaigns mentioned above] and to bring about appropriate political, economic, and military reforms, your assistance has not produced the desired effect. To this failure is attributable the present predicament in which our country finds itself."[2]

One cannot, however, lay the entire blame of the material situation to injudicious distribution. The government often did not have enough to distribute, for instance, even to supply its direct army units in Manchuria. Failure to maintain marked material superiority to the Reds in the north was evidenced by the fifty-day summer offensive in May 1947 in which the communists made extensive use of heavy

[2] "Ltr. Acting President Li Tsung-jen to President Truman, May 5, 1949," *U.S. Relations with China*, p. 409.

artillery power against the best-equipped government units and claimed 89,000 government losses.

Meanwhile government supplies dwindled—in mid-1947 they had 16,000 motor vehicles inoperative because of lack of parts—as the Kuomintang hoarded material for the Central Army and as the communist forces grew.[3]

II

Amid the recurring crises, China's first constitutional assembly met in Nanking in March 1948 to elect a president and vice-president of the nation. Generalissimo Chiang announced that he would not accept a nomination for the presidency, though he expressed his willingness to serve his country in any other capacity. The powerful Whampoa group refused to cooperate with the government under any president other than Chiang, and the generalissimo was drafted for the job— evidence not only of his popularity but also of the overwhelming influence of the solid Whampoa machine.

Of the leading candidates for the vice-presidency, two were military men: Generals Li Tsung-jen and Cheng Ch'ien. Li was one of the greatest nationalist generals and was regarded as both the champion of a popular movement for reform and as the foremost spokesman of the non-Central Army group, but Chiang opposed his candidacy and advised both Li and Cheng not to run. It was reported that the Generalissimo summoned General Pai Chung-hsi, then minister of defense and a close friend of Li, and under threat of dire punitive action, directed him to withdraw his support of Li. Chiang advocated a civilian as vice-president and suggested Dr. Sun Fo. In spite of intimidation from the extremists, Li managed to rally around him most of the liberal elements of the assembly who were seeking reform in the government and to carry both the vice-presidential nomination and election. His victory angered Chiang's group, widened the gulf between the Central Army and the Kwangsi Army party, and led to Chiang's dismissal of Defense Minister Pai.

For more effective prosecution of the civil war, Li and Pai had long proposed a unified command for the government forces in the five provinces between the Yellow and Yangtze Rivers. Subsequently Pai was tendered command of troops in the central China area, with head-

[3] "General Albert C. Wedemeyer's Report to President Truman, 19 Sept. 1947," *U.S. Relations with China*, p. 851.

quarters at Hankow, only to learn that another headquarters was to be established at Hsuchow—a development which he considered as a dismemberment of the unity in command—and that he would not be permitted to organize local militia in his proposed areas. Thereupon he withdrew his acceptance and left for Shanghai in disgust. Later, at President Chiang's request, he was reappointed the commander-in-chief of the Central China command. The aggressive operations he conducted against the communists during the early part of 1948 once more confirmed his reputation as a celebrated strategist. Had he been offered a unified command with unhindered authority, the outcome of the later Huai-Hai campaign, which eventually led to the destruction of the main force of the Central Army, could have been drastically different.

Pai's experience was but one more instance of the lack of trust that the government had in leaders who were not from the Central Army. Two of China's best senior field commanders, Hsueh Yueh and Sun Lien-chung, had learned the difficulties of being awarded positions of responsibility without being permitted either sufficient troops or authority to perform the tasks allotted to them. Fu Tso-yi, the able northern commander, had been unable to conduct an all-out campaign against the communists in the north because of lack of wholehearted cooperation from Nanking, and the government refused to arm the 100,000-man local militia that Fu had raised and partially trained in north China.[4] Their attempt to enlist popular support for the government cause met with no cooperation on the part of the party leaders, although the communists were doing all in their power to win popular support for their forces. Of that propaganda campaign, arch-communist Mao Tse-tung declared:

"These methods have been worked out by the People's Liberation Army in the cause of a prolonged war with the internal and external enemies, and they are entirely compatible with the situation now facing us. . . . The Chiang Kai-shek group and the military personnel of American imperialism in China are well acquainted with these military methods of ours. On several occasions Chiang Kai-shek summoned his generals and other high-ranking officers to special lectures at which copies of our military textbooks and other documents seized in the war were distributed for discussion and study with a view toward devising counter-measures. American military personnel suggested

[4] *U.S. Relations with China*, p. 255.

that Chiang Kai-shek adopt this or that sort of strategy and tactics designed to wipe out the People's Liberation Army. In addition, Americans personally took part in training troops for Chiang Kai-shek and furnished them with military supplies. But all this failed to save the Chiang Kai-shek group from defeat. This is because our strategy and tactics are built upon the basis of the people's war and no anti-popular army can hope to employ our strategy and tactics. . . ."[5]

Mao's point was simply this: although the nationalists had studied the communist *modus operandi*, they did not learn the essential fact that all communist successes, military and political, were due in significant part to the support of the people, a support they constantly strove to ensure. Neither the nationalists nor the communists would have been able to enlist enthusiastic support from the people, for the people were tired of war and, of course, less inclined to fight fellow-Chinese than they had been to repel the Japanese invader, but the communists saw the necessity of winning whatever support could be achieved and they expended much more energy on the effort than did the nationalists. The communists unified their forces with the "party line," which gave them a common goal. They called for solidarity between officers and men in what they termed the "military democracy" of the army and stressed their political equality. Finally, the communists established the doctrine that "the people is the sea, and the soldiers are fish; without the water the fish can never survive," stressing the necessity for army discipline to guarantee cordial relations between the soldiery and the populace.

III

The civil war in China, spreading over thousands of square miles and involving millions of men on both sides, was in many respects an aggregation of small battles. The inefficiency of the government leadership led to many weaknesses on the nationalist side, and throughout the civil strife the communists held the initiative, seizing every opportunity to capitalize on these weaknesses and subjecting the government forces to a continuous series of ambushes, skirmishes, and attacks on isolated garrisons. This accumulation of minor successes inflated Red morale, demoralized the nationalists, and contributed to

[5] Mao Tse-tung, *On the Problems of Strategy in China's Revolutionary War*, (Harbin, 1948), in Chinese. "The Current Situation and Our Tasks," *Report to the Central Committee of the Chinese Communist Party, Dec. 5, 1947.*

the success of the communist plan: the achievement of local tactical successes rather than any grand strategy. In this manner the communists harassed the nationalists and avoided all government attempts to involve them in a major offensive or engage a large part of their forces in a decisive battle.

The nationalists, defending a large area and holding many critical lines of communication, were particularly susceptible to these hit-and-run tactics. Large portions of the nationalist force were rendered relatively immobile as defenders of this or that strategic point and vulnerable to the free-ranging Reds. Of course the communist tactics required a well-defined over-all plan and constant, speedy, high-level decisions, but the Reds were fortunate in enjoying a shrewd military leadership and relative freedom from that confusion which predominated at top nationalist levels. The strategic principles in the prosecution of the civil war were laid down by the astute Mao Tse-tung. These were the ten commandments of the communists:

"1. First strike scattered and isolated groups of the enemy, and later strike concentrated, powerful groups.

"2. First take small and middle-sized towns and cities and the broad countryside, and later take big cities.

"3. The major objective is the annihilation of the enemy fighting strength, and not the holding or taking of cities and places. The holding or taking of cities and places is the result of the annihilation of the enemy's fighting strength, which often has to be repeated many times before they can be finally held or taken.

"4. In every battle, concentrate absolutely superior forces—double, triple, quadruple, and sometimes even five or six times those of the enemy—to encircle the enemy on all sides, and strive for his annihilation, with none escaping from the net. Under specific conditions, adopt the method of dealing the enemy smashing blows, that is, the concentration of all forces to strike the enemy's center and one or both of the enemy's flanks, aiming at the destruction of a part of the enemy and the routing of another part so that our troops can swiftly transfer forces to smash another enemy group. Avoid battle of attrition in which gains are not sufficient to make up for the losses, or in which the gains merely balance the losses. Thus we are inferior taken as a whole—numerically speaking—but our absolute superiority in every section and in every specific campaign guarantees the victory of each campaign. As time goes by we will become superior, taken as a whole, until the enemy is totally destroyed.

"5. Fight no unprepared engagements; fight no engagements in which there is no assurance of victory. Strive for victory in every engagement; be sure of the relative conditions of our forces and those of the enemy.

"6. Promote and exemplify valor in combat; fear no sacrifice or fatigue nor continuous action—that is, fighting several engagements in succession within a short period without respite.

"7. Strive to destroy the enemy while in movement. At the same time emphasize the tactics of attacking positions, wresting strong points and bases from the enemy.

"8. With regard to assaults on cities, resolutely wrest from the enemy all strong points and cities which are weakly defended. At favorable opportunities, wrest all enemy strong points and cities which are defended to a medium degree and where the circumstances permit. Wait until the conditions mature, and then wrest all enemy strong points and cities which are powerfully defended.

"9. Replenish ourselves by the capture of all enemy arms and most of his personnel. The source of men and material for our army is mainly at the front.

"10. Skillfully utilize the intervals between two campaigns for resting, regrouping and training troops. The period of rest and regrouping should be in general not too long. As far as possible do not let the enemy have breathing space."[6]

But Mao Tse-tung's most vicious and most successful strategy was an unwritten one: the "divisive" strategy, aiming at dividing the strength of the government armies by exploiting rivalry and difference between the government's Central and non-Central armies, and even between different units of the same Central Army. Thus, the communist forces concentrated their strength and fought specifically those well-equipped units of the Central Army, ignoring such forces as those from Kwangtung, Szechuan, and Yunnan provinces. They purposely avoided, until the very last stage, major clashes with the hard-fighting and well-led armies from Kwangsi, or with the northern troops under General Fu Tso-yi.

Throughout 1946 and 1947 communist policy was one of avoiding decisive battles and of building up fighting strength with troops and equipment captured from small segments of the nationalist armies. During this stage guerrilla warfare was pursued on all fronts, and

---

[6] Mao Tse-tung, *Turning Point in China*, in English translation (N.Y.: New Century, 1948), p. 3.

gradually the Reds were enabled to merge into a war of maneuver involving larger bodies of troops. In March 1947 the communist forces under Chen Yi, after suffering a serious defeat in the hands of a Kwangsite army column (consisting of the Seventh and Forty-Eighth Corps), seized the opportunity to destroy one of the best U.S.-equipped army corps (the Seventy-Fourth) of the Central Army at Meng-liang-k'an in southern Shantung, killing its commander, General Chang Ning-fu, and capturing considerable heavy equipment. By then the downward trend of nationalist strength had become apparent, while the military power of the communists climbed steadily upward. In December 1947 Mao Tse-tung could declare with confidence that the Red Army's war against the government had taken a decided turn—the nationalists were on the run.[7]

The communists, who had hitherto specialized in hit-and-run tactics, could now afford another aspect of the "short attack" in a protracted war—the annihilating "human sea strategy" as they called it. In essence it meant nothing more than the concentration of vastly superior masses for a succession of resolute attacks aiming, without respite, at a breakthrough or complete destruction of the enemy. The communist strategy was a downright denial of the characteristic nationalist tactic of permitting an avenue of escape for defeated enemy forces in order to avoid the losses due to the desperate resistance of a cornered enemy after a victory.

This tactic needed not only large reserves of manpower but also heavy backing in equipment. By 1948 the Red forces were trained to the degree that they could employ the heavier ex-Japanese weapons acquired in Manchuria, and they were constantly adding to their supplies and firepower by victories over government units. As their firepower increased, the acquisition of new strength became easier.

The chief source of communist manpower was, as their commander Chu Teh had announced more than once, at the front.[8] The skillful indoctrination of prisoners of war and the shrewd management of former nationalists who defected to the Red forces—and brought their arms with them—swelled the communist ranks. The losses of the nationalists were doubly advantageous to the Reds, for each man the government lost as a result of communist propaganda was not only one less enemy but also one more comrade.

[7] *Ibid.*

[8] Chu Teh, Commander-in-Chief of the Chinese Red Army, *China's Revolutionary Wars* (Peking, 1951), p. 8.

The numerical strength of the Red armies continued to increase. According to their official account, at the end of the war against Japan, the communists had a regular army of 930,000 men and an organized militia of some 2,200,000.[9] By the end of 1946, an American military source estimated, the Red army numbered 1,150,000 men.[10] A year later, the figure had reached 1,622,000, and it was reported that the Reds had 6,000 guns of all kinds.[11]

Much of the rapid growth of the communist forces after V-J day may be attributed to the success of their plan to take over in Manchuria after the Japanese surrender. Generalissimo Chiang asserted, on March 18, 1946: "During the Japanese occupation, there were no Communist troops in the Northeast [Manchuria]. They appeared only after the Japanese surrender. Communist troops entered the Northeast by land through Jehol and they carried only a handful of arms with them in their trek into the Northeast. Other Communist troops crossed the Yellow Sea from Chefoo, carrying no arms with them. They now formed the so-called 'United Democratic Army.' They only work to obstruct the Government's taking over work and demanded special political rights in the Northeast."[12]

Having the political sympathy of the occupying Soviet forces, the sanctuary of North Korea and Dairen, and the protection of a "truce," the communists were able to build up a tremendous stock of arms upon which Mao could found his plan to conquer China.

In mid-1946 the government troops, some 3,000,000 men, outnumbered the communists almost three to one. Demobilization cut government forces to 2,600,000 by the end of the same year, while the communist forces grew. There was considerable evidence that substantial portions of the demobilized nationalists, as well as the disbanded Manchukuo and other puppet armies, were absorbed by the communist forces. As civil war became inevitable, the government resorted to conscription and, by late 1947, had built its strength back up to 2,700,000 men.[13] The hope to train 200,000 of these men by the end of 1948 in American-aided military training centers, however, was not fulfilled. Throughout 1948 the nationalists maintained an estimated strength of 2,730,000 men, but by February of the next

---

[9] *Ibid.*, p. 10.   [10] *U.S. Relations with China*, p. 314.
[11] *Asashi Year Book 1949*, in Japanese (Tokyo, 1949), p. 38.
[12] Chiang Kai-shek, "Address to the Kuomintang's Second Plenary Session Mar. 1-8, 1946," quoted in *China Handbook, 1937-1945*, p. 762.
[13] *U.S. Relations with China*, p. 317.

year heavy losses had reduced their strength to 1,500,000[14]—a reduction of 45 per cent of the government's total troop strength in a mere four and a half months. The National Government's official estimate of the relative strengths was as follows:[15]

	SEPTEMBER 1945		JUNE 1948	
	Government Forces	Communist Forces	Government Forces	Communist Forces
Men	3,700,000	320,000	2,180,000	2,600,000
Rifles	1,600,000	160,000	980,000	970,000
Artillery	6,000	600	2,100	2,280

The communist statistics on the same account are:[16]

	Government Forces	Communist Forces	Ratio
July 1946	4,300,000	1,200,000	3.58:1
June 1947	3,730,000	1,950,000	1.9:1
June 1948	3,650,000	2,800,000	1.3:1
June 1949	1,490,000	4,000,000	0.3:1

With the strength of the communist armies steadily on the increase, the government was now committed more and more to positional warfare, and it became overextended and, for reasons of prestige, debarred from withdrawal or consolidation. Viewing these facts, and the government's losses in men and equipment, the communists became more aggressive. By late 1947 the Red general Liu Po-ch'eng was harassing central China so effectively, and moving so elusively, that only a major offensive—which the nationalists could not afford—would have dislodged him. The communist Fourth Field Army, under General Lin Piao, was growing in strength in Manchuria while there was little prospect of the reinforcement of government troops in that area. In the east, Red general Ch'en Yi's Third Field Army in Shantung not only eluded a nationalist plan to encircle it but was able to destroy an entire U.S.-equipped corps of the Nationalist Army and to reinforce itself with trained men and material sent across the gulf of the Yellow Sea from the Russian-occupied Liaotung peninsula. In the northwest the Red First Field Army, under General Peng Teh-huai, and the forces under the direct com-

---

[14] Ibid.

[15] Source: Report of the Defense Minister, General Ho Ying-chin, to the Secret Session of the Legislative Yuan, Sept. 24, 1948.

[16] Ernburg, G. B., Ocherki Natsional'no-osvoboditel'noi Bor'by Kitaiskogo Narada (Moscow, 1951), p. 227.

mand of the commander-in-chief, General Chu Teh, avoided battle with the nationalists and permitted the occupation of their capital, Yenan, but the forces of Ch'en Yi and Liu Po-ch'eng were driving relentlessly southward across the vital east-west Lunghai railway and toward the Yangtze.

By October 1948 the Reds reported that the Kuomintang was confined to four points in Manchuria: Changchun, Mukden, Chengteh, and Chinchow. In addition the government held the railway between Tientsin and Chinchow. In north China they controlled the Tientsin-Peiping-Kalgan-Kweisui line and a few isolated strongholds, such as Tatung, Taiyuan, Paoting, and Tsingtao. Between the Yangtze and the Lunghai railway the Kuomintang regarded Hsuchow as their offensive base. Hankow as their defensive base, and Sian as a flanking position.

IV

Of all the critical decisions of the postwar period, none seem to be of greater historical significance than the National Government's resolve to reoccupy Manchuria. Although such overextension of its forces was perilous militarily, politically the government had no alternative but to commit itself to the arduous task of reasserting its sovereignty over an area for which China had fought her long war against Japan. She could not long remain passive while the communists seized that territory, despite the rights granted to the Soviet Union in the Yalta Agreement and despite the fact that the Russians were firmly entrenched in Manchuria. Soviet sympathy for the Chinese Reds prompted them to deny to the nationalists the use of port facilities, thereby making expeditious entry into Manchuria impossible and giving the communists time to organize in the area, to consolidate their local control, and to equip a military force with former Japanese weapons.

China was determined to reoccupy Manchuria even though General Wedemeyer hastened to point out the dangers of such an occupation in view of the logistical difficulties of supporting operations there while at the same time controlling China proper. In Washington, General Eisenhower viewed the nationalist effort as a gross overextension of forces. But Chinese political considerations outweighed military logic.

The communists in Manchuria had grown into no mean force.

Early in 1947, employing their strategy of "offensive defence," they were strong enough to present a considerable threat. For the first time in the history of Chinese communist warfare, the Reds had graduated from guerrilla tactics to the use of tanks and artillery. Their first offensive was deftly turned back by government forces under General Sun Li-jen, but soon afterwards Sun was relieved of his command and assigned to direct a training program at Nanking. His departure gave freer reign to the incompetence of his superior, General Tu Yü-ming, one of the most influential of Whampoa's generals and field commander of northeast China. There was little cooperation between him and his superior, General Hsiung Shih-hui, director of the generalissimo's headquarters in Manchuria. It was common knowledge that the Whampoa I-ch'i (the graduates of that military academy's first class) were so arrogant that they considered themselves obliged to deal independently with the generalissimo himself and not answerable for cooperation to their fellow generals. Two such were Tu and Hsiung, and the lines of responsibility in the command structure became unclear and the leadership confused.

Following their unsuccessful first offensive, which Sun had stopped, the communists unleashed three successive drives, wearing down the government defenders of the key cities. The communist strategy was aimed at forcing the government troops to disperse their forces and then decimating them through successive counter-blows. By the autumn of 1947 the situation had become so urgent that the government recalled Hsiung Shih-hui and replaced him as Manchurian commander with the capable Ch'en Ch'eng. Ch'en's immediate purge of the army not only disposed of a number of corrupt officers but unfortunately, in the disbanding of large numbers of ex-Manchukuo troops, also sent over to the communist side many disgruntled men whom the government could ill afford to lose. The consequent indignation of the Manchurian representatives at Nanking was one of the contributing factors causing the recall of General Ch'en.

The fifth communist offensive, in May 1947, which covered most of Manchuria, began to show the communist superiority in artillery power as well as in the number and technical proficiency of their troops: an indication that the communist training program had reaped results. The communist forces surrounded the government forces in Kirin, Changchun, and Szepingkai. Almost an entire government army was cut off from the rest of China, and the problems of maintaining some 700,000 government personnel (of which only about 250,000 men were effective combat troops) became almost insurmountable.[17] The lines of communication from China proper were long and tenuous, and the communists effectively eradicated them. It became a question of fight or starve. Despite this situation, and repeated demands from the generalissimo for aggressive action, the new commander in Manchuria, General Wei Li-huang, persisted in sitting tight, awaiting a further clarification of communist intentions.[18]

Meanwhile, a communist offensive launched late in the autumn of 1947 severed all railway connections into Mukden and isolated all the major nationalist garrisons in Manchuria. The winter brought a communist offensive in 40° sub-zero weather which resulted in the capture of a number of the government's fortified strongholds. The defeats forced the replacement of Ch'en Ch'eng by General Wei Li-huang as commander in Manchuria. To supply the 150,000 to 200,-000 troops in the immediate Mukden sector, the government resorted to a costly airlift, but the combined capacity of civilian and military air transports could barely deliver a third of the enormous tonnage requirements. In terms of financial drain, in September 1948, General Ho Ying-ch'in, then defense minister, reported to a secret session of the Legislative Yuan that the whole allotment of the military budget for the latter half of 1948 had been completely spent on air-supplying a single city, Changchun, for two months and four days.[19]

At the height of the crisis two of the most vital military posts— chief of the supreme staff and commander of the ground forces—were conferred upon men of no conspicuous abilities. The new appointees, Generals Ku Chu-t'ung and Yü Han-mou, were stanch supporters of the generalissimo. That is about all that could be said for them.

In central and eastern China, the key cities of Kaifeng and Tsinan fell in July and September 1948, respectively. The generalissimo ordered his forces to fight to the last to hold the two walled fortresses, but defeatism was growing among the troops and many defected to the communist attackers. The loss of these two points convinced the generalissimo at last that the old strategy of holding key points or strongholds at all costs would have to go, and that a reexamination of nationalist errors in strategy, tactics, training, and organization of

[17] Rigg, *op.cit.*, p. 268.
[18] "Report of Major General David Barr," *U.S. Relations with China*, p. 317.
[19] Ho Ying-ch'in, "The Report of the Defense Minister to the Secret Session of the Legislative Yuan, Sept. 24, 1948," *Original Document*.

field units would have to be made.[20] By then, however, it was too late.

Considering the confusion at planning levels it was surprising that even greater errors in strategy had not been committed. There was no efficient leadership to integrate plans, to implement them, and to direct their execution. The supreme general staff—the nerve center of the armed forces—had been hastily patched up after the 1946 reorganization and had failed to become a strategic directorate. It was simply a tactical command organ. The armed forces operated on a "six months' plan"! The confusion prompted the generalissimo himself to take over certain phases of the direction of military operations, which merely added to the chaos by having certain operational orders issued directly without the knowledge of the supreme staff and the minister of defense. He personally conducted regular operational briefings in the map room of his residence, issuing directives for field operations which were often transmitted directly to the combat units in the forms of *shou-ch'i* (personal instruction) or *shih-ts'an* (directives from the president's personal military staff). Usually only a few persons participated, including his personal chief of staff, the deputy chief of supreme staff, and the director of G-3. The defense minister was not always invited for the conference. If the briefing was held at 9 P.M., Chiang's personal directive would perhaps reach the front-line unit concerned by the next morning—already impractical for execution (although it had to be obeyed under threat of punishment) since the fast-moving communist force would be many miles away after a night of forced marching. In one such case three conflicting orders (from the generalissimo, the chief of the supreme staff, and his immediate superior) were given to the commander of an army group who was just about to administer the *coup de grâce* to an encircled enemy. Under threat of severe punitive action he was forced to abandon his attack and to relieve some other government forces of no importance to the entire military outcome and, worse still, the besieging communist force had already left the scene by the time his force rushed to the designated spot!

In October 1948, during the crucial stage of the Manchurian campaign, Generalissimo Chiang himself went to Peiping, whence he directed the entire operation alone without reference to the minister of defense or to the supreme staff to which he had previously promised to delegate all power of military command and administra-

---

[20] "Barr's Report," *U.S. Relations with China*, p. 332.

tion. But Chiang's earlier interference had muddled the command structure and now, despite the basic soundness of his order for simultaneous attacks from Mukden and Changchun in order to effectuate the breakout of government force from Changchun, his commands were not obeyed in full. General Wei Li-huang's force did not lash out from Mukden in full strength. In despair, one of the garrison units, the 60th Army (Yunnanese), revolted and turned its guns on the loyal New Seventh Army. The latter, a partly American-trained force, was the backbone of the city's defense forces. On the twentieth of the month Changchun and its starving defenders fell into communist hands.

In war, defeat engenders defeat. Within a few days Chinchow, a city between Mukden and Peiping, was surrounded. Chinchow, supply base for government forces in Manchuria, held some 70,000 nationalist troops, including crack units of the recently arrived Eighth Army under General Fan Han-chieh, reputedly one of Whampoa's ablest commanders. Wei Li-huang, 120 miles distant in Mukden, was ordered to bring his 150,000-man force (composed of 12 divisions and 3 cavalry brigades) to the relief of the Chinchow siege, but he delayed and then moved out hesitantly with only a fraction of his strength. To the south of Chinchow, meanwhile, strong government reinforcements (9 divisions) were landed at the port of Hulutao, but only a portion of them moved to the aid of besieged Chinchow. The whole situation was a tangle of discoordinated effort. Under the communists' incessant and terrifying artillery bombardment, certain government units within the city deserted to the communists and Chinchow fell.

News of the loss of Chinchow reached the headquarters of General Wei Li-huang. Wei's army had been largely recruited from South China, and there was among them a strong feeling in favor of a southward march toward the Great Wall, a march which would recapture Chinchow and take the army away from the bleak northern bastion of Mukden, where they had long been virtually exiled.

Wei instantly saw the opportunity. (He saw another opportunity in 1955—and went over to the communists.) He prepared to transmute his army's homesickness into an indomitable fighting spirit that would sweep all before it and regain Chinchow. Before his plan could be translated into action, however, curt orders arrived from the highest echelon ordering Wei's forces back to the Mukden they had

learned to hate. Morale dropped to a new low, and the entire disgruntled army seethed with rebellion. Thus one of the government's
finest units, one which might have been inspired with that fierce dedication which arises solely out of the happy coincidence of lofty principles and personal interests, lost the will to fight.

Lin Piao, himself a shrewd opportunist, cleverly timed his attack
on the government forces precisely when the disruptive and demoral-
izing influence of these unpopular orders was at its height. There
was also some conflict in the command picture. The generalissimo
placed Tu Yü-ming in charge of field operations, but Tu fought the
battle from Mukden and placed the burden of actual command in
the field on Liao Yao-hsiang, one of the Chinese heroes of the northern Burma campaign. Considering Tu's incompetence, this action
might have produced a better result than the generalissimo's plan,
but Liao was reported captured early in the action. In the confusion
that followed, the communists, yelling that "Chinese should not fight
Chinese," charged resolutely in human waves under terrific fire support from their artillery division. The attackers were finally able to
divide the nationalist forces and to destroy them piecemeal.

Not only was there bungling in the command in Manchuria, but
the general strategy was also all wrong. The government ought to
have capitalized upon its indisputable advantages: greater mobility
along the seacoast and control of the air. As it was, the Chinese air
force played but a small part even during the most critical of the
battles in Manchuria. It came into prominence only after the humiliating fall of Mukden—bombing the communists who had occupied the
city from such altitude that the operation was considered a complete
waste. It is incredible that inter-service cooperation could have been
so slight, especially since the air forces at the time were being commanded by an army general.

V

The loss of Manchuria and some 300,000 of its best troops spelled
the beginning of the end for the nationalists. Nearly 360,000 communist troops from Manchuria were now free to move against China
proper.

In well-coordinated actions, 550,000 men of the communist Third
and Second Field Armies, commanded by Ch'en Yi and Liu Po-ch'eng,

immediately marched on Hsuchow,[21] where the government had initially maintained 20-odd divisions, later increased to 7 army groups.

Hsuchow, an important strategic point and the chief railway link between east and central China, was exposed to enemy assaults on three sides, having long lines of supply in its rear area highly vulnerable to communist hit-and-run attacks. Two of the government's most experienced generals, Li Tsung-jen, who won the victory of Tai-erh-chuang against the Japanese in that area, and Pai Chung-hsi, the celebrated Chinese strategist, had repeatedly cautioned Chiang against making a stand in that city.[22] They suggested that the government forces should move southward, concentrating for the offensive defense of Pengpu and the Huai River, and, with a system of shortened inner lines of defense and communication, seize an opportunity to destroy the communist forces.[23] Their suggestions, however, were not adopted. The government intended to defend Hsuchow with 66 divisions.

The struggle for Hsuchow, generally referred to as the Huai-hai (Huai River-Haichow) campaign, was clearly going to be a battle of great moment, one in which the nationalists would need a strategist of great and proved ability. The generalissimo did not choose General Pai Chung-hsi, the best of the nationalist strategists, for the job in an earlier appointment. Pai was thoroughly familiar with the terrain around Hsuchow and was a logical choice.[24] Instead the generalissimo appointed General Liu Chih, a man of no particular ability, to the command. He was to be assisted by General Tu Yü-ming, fresh from defeats in Manchuria and famous, like Gilbert and Sullivan's Duke of Plaza-Torro, for "leading his regiment from behind" at Mukden. From the start the nationalists were in a bad way.

The two communist field armies which they had to face were supported by hundreds of thousands of farmers conscripted in the rear, and had been preparing for this gigantic operation for months. By night and day the communists harassed government troops, taking full advantage of their mobility. The inept nationalist command could not

[21] *China Handbook, 1950.* This estimate of communist strength was given from a ministry of defense source.

[22] Yin Shi, *The Chiang-Lee Relationship and China, op.cit.,* p. 101.

[23] Author's interview with former Acting President Li Tsung-jen.

[24] Chiang was reported to have offered Pai the "concurrent" command of the armies around Hsuchow at the eleventh hour. Pai, however, declined the offer on the ground of differences over strategy and of his inability to remedy the situation at that late hour.

decide where and when to concentrate its technically superior forces for a decisive engagement. Without any major tactical victory, and plagued with continuous communist harassment, the morale of the government forces rapidly deteriorated, bringing a considerable number of turncoats over to the Reds. The nationalist air force, unopposed in the air, could have become a decisive factor in the entire outcome, but was hoarded by its incompetent air commanders instead of being employed effectively to support land operations. The government, unable to maneuver an attack for some time, became increasingly incapable of stabilizing its defense. On top of all this, the nationalist field commanders—Generals Li Mi, Chiu Ching-chuan, and Huang Po-tao —hesitated to render each other full cooperation. Even this all-Whampoa team was not free from personal rivalries.

The communist gambit was a fierce "human-sea" attack on the weaker section of the government forces in the Hsuchow-Pengpu area and, circling Hsuchow, General Ch'en Yi succeeded both in threatening Hsuchow and in destroying ten nationalist divisions at Nien-chuang, east of Hsuchow, in the sector commanded by General Huang Po-tao. Ch'en's forces then evaded the strong government forces under Chiu Ching-Chuan and joined with Red general Liu Po-ch'eng's group south of Hsuchow. This action ended what amounted to the first stage of the campaign. The communists claimed about 178,000 nationalist casualties during this phase.[25]

The second phase of the campaign began on November 23, 1948. In a pincer movement the joint communist forces converged on Pengpu, while a group of Liu Po-ch'eng's Reds impeded General Huang Wei's Twelfth Army Group marching eastward from southern Honan and northern Hupeh. The government position in and around Hsuchow was now untenable. Huang Po-tao's army group on the eastern flank was destroyed. At the last moment, Generalissimo Chiang decided to withdraw his troops from Hsuchow, then hesitated: four of the nine nationalist armies at Hsuchow were not being employed in the attack to the south.[26] Under the command of Tu Yü-ming, three army groups moved westward in a desperate effort both to rescue Huang Wei's army group and to retreat to a more defensible

[25] Consult a series of articles written by the Chinese communist war correspondents on the Huai-Hai campaign in *Liberation Daily* and any other official communist papers during the period from December 1948 to February 1949. Also see *China's Revolutionary Wars, op.cit.*, articles on the campaign.
[26] "Barr's Report," *U.S. Relations with China*, p. 335.

position. Huang's army, ordered by Generalissimo Chiang to converge upon Hsuchow and consisting of five army corps, one division and a mechanized column, was taken away from Pai Chung-hsi's central China command.[27] With its marching order ill-coordinated with the general strategic situation around Hsuchow, and with snow and mud hampering the rapid movement of this heavily equipped force, it soon ran into communist encirclement southwest of Suhsien. The supreme command at Nanking ordered Huang to stay there and fight defensively, waiting for the arrival of a rescuing force. Stripped of his initiative to fight as he saw fit, Huang obeyed the order only to find that the communist troops had surrounded his army with several rings of trenches, defense works, and mine fields. The desperate efforts of Tu Yü-ming's three army groups to relieve the besieged army of Huang Wei were repulsed and these forces fled in a southwesterly direction. They were trapped by the communists at Yung-cheng in the province of Honan. The communist armies, moving with incredible speed, again surrounded this large nationalist force which was again being ordered to *Chien-shou tai-yüan* (tighten up defense and wait for rescuing forces).[28] The Sixth and Eighth armies (under Generals Li Yen-nien and Liu Ju-ming) also attempted to relieve Huang Wei from Pengpu, but were driven back. All attempts to relieve them having failed, Huang Wei's beleaguered forces were at last completely annihilated, with the exception of one division, which went over to the Reds. Under Tu Yü-ming's incompetent generalship, four army groups were destroyed and General Huang Po-tao, one of his army group commanders, was killed in action. The Hsuchow forces and the intended reinforcements both met with the same fate. From November to December 1948, the nationalists lost about 400,000 men, including most of Chiang's mechanized forces, in the Huai-Hai campaign. By now the only remaining forces of the once powerful Central Army were those commanded by General Hu Tsung-nan in the northwest and by General T'ang En-po in the southeast.

The communists poured into north China from Manchuria. The nationalist commander of north China, General Fu Tso-yi, concentrated his main force in the Peiping-Tientsin area for a decisive battle,

[27] "Ltr. General Pai Chung-hsi to Pan Kung-chang on the Hsuchow-Pengpu Campaign, Mar. 20, 1954," *Lien-ho-jih-pao*, New York City, April 12, 1954, p. 3.
[28] Information from a senior staff officer who escaped from the communist siege, but who preferred to remain anonymous.

counting upon a communist regrouping period of at least one and a half months before Red general Lin Piao could move his army into the Great Wall. To his surprise, Lin Piao's force appeared in his area barely twenty days after the fall of Mukden and, unfortunately, Fu's war plans and his troop dispositions became known to the communists through internal treachery.[29] Lin Piao's force and the Red Army commanded by General Nieh Jung-cheng now converged upon Fu's left flank, knocking out two nationalist army corps at Hsin-pao-an and Huai-lai along the strategic Peiping-Suiyuan railway. Striking northward, the Red force captured Kalgan and decimated 40,000 of Fu's forces around that strategic base. In the south, Tientsin fell on January 15, 1949, and the strategic gateway of Chü-yung-kwan was also taken by the communists. Peiping was surrounded by Red forces. One week later, General Fu Tso-yi, only recently appointed commander of the northern forces designated to defend Tientsin and Peiping, surrendered the city of Peiping and his 100,000 men to Red general Yeh Chien-ying, chief of staff of the People's Liberation Army. All of China north of the Yangtze River was in the hands of the communists.

VI

With the nation in turmoil and all China north of the Yangtze in communist control, the generalissimo yielded to pressures from within and without the government and announced his decision to retire. He left Nanking for Fenghua, his birthplace and a beautiful coastal town in the province of Chekiang, on January 22, 1949. In accordance with Article 49 of the Chinese constitution, Vice- president Li Tsung-jen assumed the acting presidency.

Li's first steps in office included an investigation seeking any reasonable grounds for peace with the communists and the issuance of a platform of governmental reforms. In the meantime, measures were formulated for the defense of the Yangtze River line in the event of a breakdown of negotiations for a peaceful settlement with the Reds. The communists continued the deployment of troops along the northern banks of the Yangtze and replied to government peace bids that communist forces would have to cross the Yangtze River.

Meanwhile Generalissimo Chiang prepared to make Taiwan (For-

[29] DeJaegher, R. J., and Kuhn, I. C., *The Enemy Within* (Garden City, 1952), p. 303.

mosa) a fortified redoubt against the communists. To the island
fortress went almost the entire government gold reserve, much of
the equipment shipped from the United States, and large concentrations of trusted troops, the navy, and the air force. Though outwardly
cooperating with the acting president, the generalissimo was in effect
maintaining independent political and military authority. Li had no
unified control of nationalist China. An able general, Li did not even
control the larger portion of the army. The generalissimo's power
continued to be felt in military affairs. What Li needed—the money,
the troops, the naval and air support, unity of command—all was
denied him. The largest single force that the acting president could
rely on were the 350,000 troops under General Pai Chung-hsi, whose
headquarters in central China command was at Hankow. Altogether
the government had at that time about 1,800,000 regular army troops;
of these Chiang still maintained firm control of two major army
groupings under the command of T'ang En-po and Hu Tsung-nan.[30]
The acting president was in dire need of time—three months to reequip the forces under Generals Pai Chung-hsi and Chang Fa-kuei;
to integrate the defense of Hunan, Hupeh, and Kiangsi; and to
carry out on a large scale a military training and organization program
in the provinces of Kwangtung, Kwangsi, Hunan, Yunnan, Szechuan,
and Kweichow. He and Pai thought that with this done southwest
China could be defended for at least a year, during which the international situation might turn to their favor. But time was not with
Li. There were ample stores in Taiwan, but these were not made
available to him even to reequip the forces of Pai and Chang, nor
could the government persuade the American ambassador to divert
the last consignment of American arms to Hong Kong or to Canton
for that purpose. In America, despite the advice of Senator Vandenberg, U.S. aid to nationalist China was gradually being cut off.[31]

Li struggled to obtain the full and unhindered authority constitu-
tionally given to the head of state and to effectuate the unity of military command over the government area. But Li was unwilling to
wrest authority drastically from Chiang and his generals; he still
wished to maintain some semblance of unity before the eyes of the
communists. And, as the White Paper pointed out, "He has increased

[30] Liang, *The Inside Struggle of Chiang Kai-shek with Lee Chong-yean, op.cit.,*
pp. 105-106.
[31] Vandenberg, Arthur, *The Private Papers of Senator Vandenberg*, A. H. Vandenberg, Jr. ed. (Cambridge, 1952), pp. 521, 531f, 534.

tremendously in stature; has greatly increased in his following, yet the centripetal forces in free China remain too strong for him to over-come."[32] Emissary after emissary was sent by Li to Chiang at Feng-hua in an attempt to secure a clear-cut division of authority and re-sponsibility between Li, as the president, and Chiang, as the titular head of the Kuomintang. All such efforts were of no avail.

Chiang had already begun the flight to Formosa. The move toward establishing a Free Chinese citadel on Formosa was contrary to the basic policy of the government to contain the communists north of the Yangtze and retain the mainland. The move was being debated during the lull in peace negotiations at Peiping. To make a success of this plan, the acting president quite obviously required the maximum cooperation of every element remaining of the nationalist forces. A successful defense of the Yangtze demanded the full support of the navy and air force. Chiang and not the acting president controlled these forces. Along the south bank of the Yangtze River, there were five army corps—about 120,000 men—available to defend the lower river valley. But General T'ang En-po, who commanded a large force, refused, upon Chiang's secret order, to move his troops up river from Shanghai to defend those sections where the communists would most likely attempt crossing, and to coordinate closely with the forces under General Pai Chung-hsi's command.[33] Chiang was still interfering in military affairs and, as the American ambassador reported on February 20, 1949, hampering rather than helping the Yangtze defense.[34] His desire was executed through the incompetent chief of supreme staff, General Ku Chu-t'ung, whose only contribution to the defense was to entrust the command of the strategic Kiangyin fortress area, the narrowest part of the Yangtze River, to one of his own protégés—the man who deserted to the communists at the critical hour and pointed the fortress guns at the government warships defending the Lower Yangtze.[35]

At midnight on April 20, 1949, the communists crossed the Yangtze at several strategic points, with their main concentrations at Kiangyin and south Anhwei. General Tai Yung-kwan, the bribed commander

[32] *U.S. Relations with China*, p. 301.
[33] Ltr., former Acting President Li Tsung-jen to President Eisenhower, March 19, 1954.
[34] "Ambassador Leighton Stuart's Report to the State Department," *U.S. Relations with China*, p. 295.
[35] Ltr. Former Acting President Li Tsung-jen to former Premier Chang Chun, March 1, 1954.

of the key Yangtze fortress at Kiangyin, protected the communist crossing and shelled the nationalist naval units. Another one-time aide of Chiang, Commodore Lin Tsun, went over to the communist side with his naval squadron at Nanking. The remaining naval and air forces failed to provide effective support for the defending forces on shore. By the secret order of General T'ang En-po, the Central Army units which had been assigned to resist any communist crossing into the lower Yangtze area were *withdrawn*. They were reassigned to defend the city of Shanghai by the secret order of the generalissimo in retirement. The battle was lost, first of all, because of no unity in command.

At the eleventh hour Chiang and Li had a serious difference over the grand strategy. The heart of the matter lay in Li's desire to mobilize and concentrate all available forces to hold China south of the Yangtze, his belief that the provinces of Kwangtung and Kwangsi and the southwest should be regarded as the stronghold from which there would be no retreat. Chiang, while ostensibly concurring in principle, was basically unwilling to commit his forces to a last-ditch stand on the mainland. Formosa was, in his view, to be the refuge and the last bastion of nationalist arms.

Chiang secretly withdrew T'ang En-po's army to Shanghai, not only to prepare for an eventual flight to Formosa but also in some vain hope that the main Red forces could be brought to fight around that strongly defended city where the Chinese might possibly be able to defeat them. Li and General Pai Chung-hsi's plan would have been to concentrate T'ang's army for the defense of the strategic Chekiang-Kiangsi railroad line, there to fight in coordination with Pai's central China armies.[36]

The Reds occupied Nanking on April 24. In a vain gesture T'ang En-po spoke of making Shanghai a "second Stalingrad" only to lose it a month later after a tepid defense. T'ang's forces were now out of the battle and Pai was stuck in central China. General Hsia Wei's army group, a unit under Pai's command, chalked up the only nationalist victory, at Anking, while communist General Lin Piao (the victor of Manchuria) moved down from the north to meet the main body of Pai's troops. Meanwhile, his forces threatened from the east by the communist capture of the Chekiang-Kiangsi railway, Pai with-

[36] Yin Shi, *op.cit.*, p. 131; Liang, *op.cit.*, p. 157.

drew from central China and retreated in good order along the Hankow-Canton railway toward Kwangtung and Kwangsi.

Around Hengyang Pai seized an opportunity to stand and counter-attack in force. He redeployed his troops to trap a Red column of 50,000 men, which he destroyed. His powerful thrust sent the whole communist army under Lin Piao reeling back into Changsha. At Tsin-shu-ping Lin's Reds, estimated at over 100,000 strong and reputedly the best of the communist troops, were thrown off balance. Pai's force then regrouped and cleared the front.[37] His next objective: the defense of Kwangtung, Kwangsi, and the southwest.

On August 3, 1949, an important conference at Canton brought together Acting President Li and Generalissimo Chiang. Li proposed a change in the nationalist defense strategy. The old defensive policy of holding specific positions and lines would have to be scrapped, he said, in favor of an offensive "on all fronts and all planes." Gaining Chiang's agreement on that point, Li went on to advocate that the Chiang forces then holding seacoast points be concentrated along the Ta-yi mountain range in northern Kwangtung and there, in close alliance with Pai's forces on the west, wage a war of movement to defend south China.[38]

Chiang countered that he must insist upon the defense of certain "vital points"—a liberal translation of the Chinese phrase originally derived from the German *Schwerpunkt*—and that he favored the concentration of all available strength for the defense of Canton as a "strong base point." Only if a surplus of troops were available could the government consider further offensive operations such as Li proposed, he said.[39] Indeed the forces that he had earlier assigned to the defense of Kwangtung province Chiang now withdrew, leaving Pai's forces weakened on the right and left and incapacitated for strong aggressive action.[40] Whether Chiang was prompted in this move by purely military motives, or whether he was unwilling to back Li's plan and support Pai for political reasons, will have to be determined at some future time, when all the smoke of the political battle between Chiang's and Li's supporters has cleared and the full facts can be ascertained.

[37] Grimsdale, G. E. (British Army), "The War against Japan in China," *The Journal of the Royal United Service Institution*, xcv, 578 (May, 1950), 265-266. Liang, *op.cit.*, pp. 149-150.
[38] Yin Shi, *op.cit.*, pp. 133-134.   [39] *Ibid.*
[40] Ltr. Li to President Eisenhower, *op.cit.*

In any case, Pai's hopes of aggressive action in the south and southwest were dashed. Meanwhile, in the northwest, there were instances of bravery and a strength which was, unfortunately, too little and too late. In June the 125,000-man communist force under General Peng Teh-huai was driving General Hu Tsung-nan's government force westward before it toward Szechuan. Twenty thousand cavalrymen commanded by the Moslem general Ma Chi-yuan daringly assailed Peng's flank. Seventy miles beyond Sian, Hu Tsung-nan's force turned and counterattacked in conjunction with the cavalry attacks. The communists sustained a serious reverse, for Ma pushed Peng's force back and drove into his new capital, Lanchow.[41] Ma's father, General Ma Pu-fang, was appointed commander-in-chief of China's northwest, presumably in token of the government's gratitude for the son's victories. The generalissimo's gratitude did not extend, however, to the point of rushing supplies to the younger Ma to enable him to exploit his victory. When two fast-moving communist armies under General Nieh Jung-cheng rushed to the scene, Ma's ammunition had been expended and he was forced to beat a hasty retreat through the mountains with Peng and Nieh in hot pursuit.

By August, Canton and all of south China were directly imperiled. The generalissimo strove vainly to regain the presidency, but, checked by constitutional considerations, was unable to do so. According to critics, Chiang seemed to have directed much of his effort toward preventing Li from gaining any tighter hold on power by ensuring as far as possible that Li's war against the Reds in south China should not be too successful. As the nationalists struggled among themselves, Canton fell on October 16, and in November the Red flag fluttered over Chungking and Chengtu. Chiang's forces under Generals Hu Tsung-nan and Sung Hsi-nien collapsed in a week. The government force of General Pai originally intended to protect Kwangtung, Kwangsi, and Yunnan provinces was stunned by the news that Yunnan had gone communist.

Pai himself was caught between the dictates of his own best judgment and the desire to compromise with Chiang if possible. His position had been weakened considerably by Chiang's withdrawal of troops from both his flanks; his own troops, by reason of supporting Chiang's defense of the Szechuan-Kweichow region, were now thinly dispersed over a large area. When Szechuan fell after a feeble de-

[41] Grimsdale, *op.cit.*, pp. 265-267.

fense, Pai decided to draw his troops into the Luichow peninsula and prepare for possible eventual evacuation to Hainan Island, dispersing parts of his forces in the mountainous regions of southwest China to wage future guerrilla warfare. Lin Piao's fast-moving columns swiftly took the decision out of Pai's hands, however, by launching an attack. In the ensuing confusion, the five army groups commanded by Pai were partly destroyed and partly dispersed in the mountains of Kwangtung and Kwangsi.[42] Forces loyal to Chiang were driven by Lin Piao's might to Formosa or to smaller islands out of the reach of the communists.

Is it Chiang's vision or his deliberate policy of conserving his own basic forces at all costs that led this titanic figure of China, the one-time leader of the revolution and the successor of Sun, to determine to continue the nationalist struggle from Formosa, when armies on the mainland of China were not given the opportunity to make their best stand against the onrushing Red tide? History will eventually provide the answer to the question and indicate whether Chiang's policy of the Formosan bastion or Li's policy of a concerted stand in south China was the better strategy. Meanwhile, the Red banners of communism have been hoisted all over the mainland of China.

In eleven months the communist banners of Mao Tse-tung and Chu Teh had advanced 2,000 miles from Mukden to Chengtu, averaging well over six miles a day. Theirs was a fine fighting force, but historians must nevertheless conclude that in the communist conquest of the vast mainland of China much of their success must be attributed to the default of the Chinese nationalist military power—a great military force taxed by eight years of supreme effort against Imperial Japan and betrayed from within by corruption, maladministration, and dissension in high places.

[42] Liang, *op.cit.*, pp. 196-197.

EPILOGUE · PORTAL TO THE FUTURE

I. THE PAST REVIEWED. II. THE FUTURE SUGGESTED.

> *"I shall be content if those shall pronounce my history useful who desire to give a view of events as they really did happen, and as they are very likely, in accordance with human nature, to repeat themselves at some future time,—if not exactly the same, yet very similar."*

So in ancient times wrote Thucydides,[1] who gave the world the concept of a cyclic design in history, who contended that as man remained unchanged in his nature his acts would tend to be similar. History for him was, therefore, not merely the accurate record of past events for the delectation of the curious, but a great teacher who could not only explain the past but, in some degree, foretell the future.

We hold today no firm belief that history must repeat itself, especially in modern warfare, where the tremendous technological advances of the past few decades have rendered obsolete many of the long-established "rules" of war and have presented modern man with horrendous weapons (and problems) undreamed of by his grandfather. And yet, as we study the turbulent years of war and revolution which shaped the greatest question mark in Asia—China—we perceive certain patterns which ought to be clearly defined, not "a tissue of disconnected accidents," as Tolstoy would insist, but, in a sense, a design for China's destiny. There are certain tendencies which have shaped her history in the past and which presumably cannot be without effect on her future. Let us examine some of these in a brief critical summary of the past, and attempt also to see how some of them are operating in the present.

I

China, to reduce the truth to a sweeping generalization, for a century and more has been passing through a period of transition, a transition which may be partially labeled modernization. Essentially this process has been one of adopting Western *methods* rather than *values*, and so the modernization of China has been in many respects,

[1] *History*, 1.1.2.

superficial. This fact is nowhere more true than in the realm of military affairs.

Every Chinese scholar begins with a thorough knowledge of, and profound reverence for, the Chinese classics handed down from Confucius, Mencius, and Sun Tzu. The age-old principles remain: in government, the necessity for civilian control of the military; in economics and defense, the unity between the soldiery and peasantry; the careful examination systems laid down as the basis for furnishing personnel in civil and military offices, and so on. The ancient writings on the strategies and tactics for success in peace and war remain for the Chinese fresh and vital. Wisdom for them has no age—all that is true is always timely. The Chinese will adopt modern methods if they have to for the good of their sons and their sons' sons, but they will always hold to the wisdom of their fathers and their fathers' fathers. They are often surprisingly quick to learn to use a modern system or a new machine, but are equally quick to sense or discover that the tactics used in a battle in which a new weapon is employed are essentially those of Sun Tzu and five centuries older than Christianity.

There exist, therefore, side by side, the traditions of China and her willingness to combine these traditions with new ideas. Unfortunately, a sense of past glory had blinded the Chinese mandarins of the nineteenth century. With a sanctimonious air and a false sense of confidence, they scoffed at Westerners as "barbarians." The "barbarians" simply replied to their arrogance with firearms and spoke through the mouths of their cannons. China's reception of Western ideas, then, became a matter of necessity. She adopted the methods of her enemies in self-defense, and acquired only a superficial knowledge of the West. The British brought, not the ideas of Shakespeare, Locke, Newton, and her other great thinkers, but the impressive warships and guns which protected their opium shipments to Canton. The French *colonisateur* and the Dutch trader were interested in lucrative trade in materials, not in ideas. Only a few Catholic and Protestant missionaries (and they were repressed by the Manchu government) could be regarded as anything like ambassadors of Western culture in China's first meeting with the West. The Chinese wanted technological information solely.

In 1863 Li Hung-chang, then China's leading advocate for military modernization, granted only this much in writing to the ministry of foreign affairs: "Everything in China's civil and military system is far superior to that in the West. Only in firearms is it absolutely impossible to catch up with them."[2] Under the Manchus, China erroneously supposed that if she could somehow simply acquire the weapons used by her enemies she could easily crush the "foreign devils." The Chinese gave no thought to the long history of scientific and technological progress in the West. They put control into the hands of their military leaders—or permitted them to seize it—and attempted to purchase from abroad the marvelous Western weapons of war. The money that should have been expended at home for the development of China's resources, agriculture, and industrialization, was spent abroad for those things which the Chinese could not, at that time, manufacture themselves. The investment was in war, not in peace or culture. Money that ought to have gone for rice went for guns.

Impressed by the power of the West, China turned from the traditions of her homeland, temporarily in awe of the great Western nations. The first schools were established, and they were military schools. For a time, instead of continuing their usual practice of integrating whatever was tested and found good in the new in the traditional body of the old, the Chinese grasped without question or complete understanding at the glittering promise of power through Western methods, through "modernization." Those who attempted to conserve the best of Chinese traditions were replaced by those who would have nothing that was not both new and foreign. The traditional civil service system of examination and promotion on the basis of merit was scrapped. The new leaders of China emerged, justified only by the strength of their personal followers and the number of guns they commanded. Traditional China fell, not to Westerners, but to Chinese warlords.

From 1850 until 1910 China was militarily weak. From 1911 to 1928 she was in the hands of the militarists. From 1929 to 1948 she went through a period of military nationalism.

Smarting in the second half of the nineteenth century from feelings of inferiority and weakness, China developed a reaction both anti-traditional and militaristic. In the crumbling of the old socio-political system under the Manchus, the militarists pushed themselves to the front. The traditional attitude of *chung-wen ch'ing-wu* (civilian con-

[2] Li Hung-chang, "Letter to Tsungli Yamen Urging the Study of Western Arms," *Ch'ou-pan-i-wu shih-mo* (T'ung-chi Period, 1862-1873), XXV, 4-10.

trol over the military) waned before the glowing promises that with strong men at the helm China would benefit, that with soldiers as leaders humiliating military defeats would never happen again.

The Chinese revolution of 1911, inspired by Sun Yat-sen's doctrine of nationalism, grew out of a military uprising. It soon got out of the hands of the political idealists. Into the vacuum left by the dissolution of imperial rule stepped the ambitious militarists, led by the chief warlord, Yuan Shi-k'ai, backed by the powerful army of Peiyang. In the name of Brutus he "clasped the diadem of the caesars," but his attempt to assume the imperial seat himself lost him the support of the people, and he went down to defeat.

Yuan Shi-k'ai's death plunged China into turmoil. The unifying force among the warlords was gone, and they fell to bickering among themselves, rending China with the distress of civil war. The Kuomintang arose to put down these warring factions and personal feuds and to unify China, but the harm done in the period of lawless warlordism was to have long-lasting ramifications.

The Kuomintang was at first a party without an army, but it soon became evident that a group of political zealots and idealists would be no match for ambitious militarists. The events of 1911 had taught that lesson. The Chinese of the party were well aware of the need for assistance, and the Soviet Union was willing to supply it. With Russian guns and Russian organizational methods, the Kuomintang built up a party army, the National Revolutionary Army, around a nucleus of expeditiously trained and indoctrinated Whampoa cadets. They provided themselves with, or permitted themselves to acknowledge, a strong military leader, Chiang Kai-shek, who was loyal to the aim of the party and capable of crushing the ambitious warlords and all other obstacles in the way of a united China. The participation of the Chinese communists broadened the party's membership, made its political tactics more aggressive (particularly in relation to securing popular support), and led to increased control of this Chinese party by the Kremlin. Bitter lessons taught the Kuomintang's nationalists that a party army, to back the political struggle with force, was indispensable.

At first, due to Sun Yat-sen's leadership, the Soviet influence, the strength of the political and civilian influence, and the smallness of the armed forces, the party army was distinctly under political control— the secular arm of the party as it were, the party militant. But the

National Government formed in July 1925 was erected on the foundations laid by Chiang Kai-shek's military victories. It owed its existence to the army's strength. Greater military influence was being felt in the government, and a military council took its place with the political council and the government committee as one of the three organs of government. Political control could still be exerted over military affairs, but the soldier-patriot Chiang and Whampoa's spreading power were in the ascendance.

The new unity was soon threatened from within for, during the Canton period, the Kuomintang and the Chinese communists, while ostensibly on amicable terms, were engaged in hidden struggles for political and military control. All sorts of infiltration and propaganda techniques were employed by the communists to wrest power from Chiang and the Whampoa group. Chiang first thwarted the military plans of the Reds and then began a systematic rooting out of the more treacherous Soviet advisers. His success was grudgingly admitted by one communist in this report to the Communist International: "After the March 1925 coup a 'military dictatorship' of the center was established, while the political power remained, as before, in the hands of the Right Wing. The political power, which should properly belong to the Left Wing, is finally lost."[3] By June of the same year the determination of Chiang and his supporters to defy the domination of the Soviets, as represented by their advisers, became clear in the quashing of their objections and the decision to initiate the northern expedition.

The phenomenal success of the northern expedition boosted the prestige of Chiang and the military to new heights. The communist effort to check this mounting influence resulted in the great split between Nanking and Hankow. Chiang's decisive action, the unswerving loyalty of his supporters, and a few tactical errors on the part of the communists culminated in a settlement of the inter-party struggle in favor of the generalissimo.

China was becoming an important participant in the international game. Even before 1928 it was clear that Japanese aggression and Soviet domination were two problems facing the Chinese government. Stalin, vulnerable because of the unreliability of his agents in China, lost to Chiang Kai-shek in 1927-1928; his defeat in China established Chiang even more securely and bolstered the spread of

[3] Tang Ping-shan's Statement to the Seventh International (E.C.C.I.) quoted in Trotsky, Leon, *Problems of the Chinese Revolution* (New York, 1932), pp. 35-37.

Chinese nationalism. The Chinese, with a growing awareness of their importance in the international picture and some confidence in the new-found strength which unity had brought, began to assert their desire for a place in the sun.

This place was to be achieved and justified and maintained by strength, and strength to the Kuomintang meant military power. A military-minded government dominated the civil authorities. Military thinking determined the policies of the government, military needs the expenditure of the treasury. The party, having begun as a political movement, had become a military movement as well.

After 1927 the omnipotence of the military was a *fait accompli*. The National Government assumed authority over all of China, although in fact the nation was not ruled by so single a force as that might suggest. Power rested in a tripartite administration: the army, the party, and the Executive Yuan. And the greatest of these was the army. The original structure of the government as conceived by Dr. Sun, with a harmonious balance between the civil authority and its servant the army, gave way to a basically military structure adapted from the Prussians and the Japanese. Bismarck and Ito had conceived of military power as a counterweight to the parliamentary body; the Chinese permitted it to dominate and to control the civil authority.

What honest intellectual opposition there was to the predominance of military power in government was not sufficient to effect a division within the party, and the Japanese invasion of Manchuria convinced even the hardiest Chinese pacifists that strengthening that nation's military defenses was the paramount concern of all loyal Chinese. Nationalism and the fear of foreign aggression stifled the voices that had formerly protested the dangers of military dictatorship.

Meanwhile civil war and communist campaigns raged within the nation's borders, and the military forces reigned supreme in all the troubled areas. The very fact that the communists were maintaining a separate Red army to challenge the authority of the government justified the dominant role of the military group in the government. The armed forces, if any power could, would assure the independence of China, and Chiang Kai-shek's leadership was the nation's sole hope for survival.

With the arrival of war, the Chinese pupils of Ludendorff firmly espoused his theory of total war and the all-out military control of the government on which it was based. For some time Chinese affairs in all branches of government were directed completely, or controlled indirectly, by military men until their own recognition of their inability to manage all the complex political and economic problems compelled them to request that they be relieved of excessive non-military responsibilities. There was, of course, still another reorganization of the government as a result. These reorganizations were frequent in recent Chinese history, and not always fruitful. The Chinese had forgotten the warning against constant reorganization which that venerable gentleman, Lao Tzu, had voiced centuries before: "The best ruler of a great kingdom governs it as you would boil a tiny fish: meddle with either and it falls to pieces."[4]

The conclusion of the war saw a resurgence of demands for civilian rule, backed by China's intellectuals. But because of the serious Kuomintang-Communist struggle civilian control was again circumvented by organizational arrangements designed to pay lip service to civilian administration without depriving the military of any of the power they needed to continue their struggle with the dangerous communist elements.

Several conclusions may be drawn. The lack of effective opposition to the military within the one-party structure, together with the impotence of the legislative branch, deprived the government of both the healthy effects of vigorous party politics and the means to check military dominance. Party measures alone, however, could not have silenced all opposition to military control. The military men had grown in numbers and prestige to the point where it was generally felt that their defense of China in the recent past had earned them not only the right to continue their efforts but also to determine the policies by which these efforts could be made most effective in the future. The situation had reached that stage where neither the traditional policies of civilian control, nor political opposition, nor a stable and capable civil service, could prevail against them.

There can be no doubt that the military dominance characteristic of the nationalist period was inextricably linked with the personal prestige of Generalissimo Chiang Kai-shek. The nation, grateful for the services of this leader in a time of dire need, was not disposed to criticize him for whatever measures he had taken to secure for himself sufficient power to direct China's battles with efficiency and dispatch. The death of Sun Yat-sen had left the country without any

[4] Lao Tsu, *Tao-teh-chin*, v.

civilian of sufficient prestige to claim the mantle of national leadership and Chiang, supported by a solid block of military men, had taken unto himself unopposed the nation's leadership, with undisputed sway in all matters, political as well as military. It was not that the German influence had led to military control in the Chinese government. The Generalstab was indeed very influential in the formulation of German national policy, but in domestic matters it had always permitted the Beamten (civil service) to carry out its proper functions. In China military men poached on the concerns of the civil government and Chiang himself reached a position of power far exceeding that of even Reichspräsident von Hindenburg.

In the early days the Chinese had tried many forms of military organization, some constructed upon careful theories and some as a result of sheer expediency. The various forms fell before the inherent limitations of men, bureaucracy, and foreign conquests. The usual procedure was to place reliance upon wise civilians at the highest levels who, unlike most professional soldiers, were well aware that military administration, while a key to national security, had to be complemented by domestic harmony and progress. Such men were Li Hung-chang, Chang Chih-tung, and Tso Tsung-t'ang of the late Manchu period. Like Alexander Hamilton they recognized that in the power of common defense "the circumstances which endanger the safety of the nation are infinite" and that the power to which the care of the nation's defense is committed must "be coextensive with all the possible combinations of such circumstances." The American way was to make the legislature the depository of military power, while the Chinese tradition decreed that the same goal could be effected by having "a wise and learned civilian" run military affairs.

The location of military power—whether in the hands of a parliamentary body, a dominant political party, or a single powerful leader —profoundly affects its nature. History provides us with many instances where military power can and may become a tool for the preservation and perpetuation of the regime. On the other hand, the democratic concept presupposes that military power is and should remain the servant of the people, not its master or even the strong right arm of its masters.

In the American and the British views, the legislative or parliamentary bodies are responsible for the military strength of the nation. Accountability to the people and vigorous party politics provide checks on military dominance. Military power is distinctly the servant of the civil government in these nations not, as in Germany prior to World War II, which Treitschke called a *militärstaat* (military state), founded upon the concept of the "unity of army and state." In the Soviet Union a highly political army carries out the policies and protects the existence of a single party. Military power is an instrument of communist party rule. In pre-war Japan the reverse was true: so strong were the military men that they reduced the power of the Diet to a very negligible one and even formed the so-called Niju Naikaku (a dual cabinet) in the government. They formulated and forced through their own foreign policy. A few military leaders could make or break a cabinet. The Japanese had once again imitated; in this case they had indiscriminately copied the German system and, as General Ian Hamilton put it, "the army was made [on the German pattern], and the policy inevitably followed the type of army." History has borne out the truth of the assertion that the German and Japanese type of militarism can lead only to ruin.

A military organization cannot, any more than a state, function healthfully under the tight control of a single individual. Centuries of military experience in China as well as in the Western world bear witness to the fact that a well-coordinated team is more efficient and more certain of lasting success than a single individual, no matter how determined and how gifted he may be. A general staff, well constituted and soundly trained, can handle more effectively the complex problems of war than any Caesar who attempts to bestride the narrow world like a Colossus and, as Cassius complained, "bear the palm alone." Such a staff can not only bring the varied experience and special knowledge of a number of experts to bear on all problems but, as Jomini shrewdly observed: "A good staff has the advantage of being more lasting than the genius of a single man."[5]

The time has passed when, in war or in any other great venture, a man can take all knowledge to be his province. Leadership at the highest level, despite the continuing value of bold field commanders and men who can think for themselves, must rest with a balanced, trained, and smoothly functioning group composed of experts from all the vital armed services. The danger is undeniable that such a group may potentially enlarge its sphere of activities to the detriment of the state it was originally created to serve. But that the general

[5] Jomini, A. H., *Précis de l'art de la guerre* (Paris, 1838), I.

staff is the solution to the direction of the intricate machinery of modern war has been proven in the classic writings of von Moltke, Schlieffen, Billot, De Philip, Wilkinson, and the works of such modern experts as Hamilton, Rosinski, Liddell-Hart, Otto Nelson, and Hittle.

China had evolved an armed force, then, as an expedient means to counter foreign encroachment, copying from the enemy a superficial modernity but retaining many of the defects of the mandarins and the warlords who plagued its infancy. It grew up ill-provided with effective organization or firm industrial backing and hampered by a malfunctioning general staff system. Under the firm leadership of Generalissimo Chiang Kai-shek the armed forces increased in power despite these flaws, became the instrument of the Kuomintang, and withstood both the forces of disruption within itself and the test of an eight-year clash with the forces of Imperial Japan. It emerged victorious from that conflict and, in that moment of triumph and weariness, was immediately confronted with the communist force which, having broken away from it earlier and after largely sitting out the war that had exhausted the nationalist strength, was determined to defeat it. It was to be the showdown for which the communists had planned ever since, long ago, it had become obvious to them that they could not conquer that force from within. The communist goal was no less than the subjugation of all of China. Their conquest of Manchuria but whetted their appetite, and no appeasement was possible. They were like the conquerors of the Ch'in dynasty in the third century before Christ of whom it was written: "To give away land to appease the Ch'in's is like putting out a fire by piling wood on it. The greedy fire will not die down till the last piece of wood has burned."[6]

Disunity and weakness within the nationalist ranks had piled fuel on the communist fire, and the flames were to devour all of the mainland of China, for the five dragons of Chinese legend did not arise to defend Cathay from the Reds.

II

Even after a succession of failures China has approached the stature of a great military force. The essentials of this power have always been there. They are deeply rooted in the strength of her people, in

[6] *Chan-Kuo Tse*, a dialogue on strategy.

the soil, in her ancient traditions. Her country is simply too large to be conquered by force. Her culture is too lasting to be eradicated or easily altered. Her people are too numerous, too resourceful, too perseverant to be enslaved by an enemy power or long captivated by foreign ideologies. Pride and confidence in the nation is found even in the most illiterate soldiers and the poorest peasants. In the essential Chinese values lies the peculiar innate military strength of that nation, the nature of which is often underestimated by and incomprehensible to many Occidentals.

The Chinese have never been a martial race, yet they will fight courageously and almost indefatigably for their own soil and in their own country. Their strength is greatest in a war in defense of their homeland against an alien aggressor. Traditionally, aggressive war has never appeared honorable to the Chinese, but defense has always been praised. The Chinese hold that aggressive war can ultimately bring a nation nothing but misfortune, that no prize can justify an aggressive attempt to seize it. Therefore, they will not fight whole-heartedly for simple material gain, though the ideal of "recovering the lost and restoring the vanquished" is deeply imbedded in the Chinese mind. The Chinese people can never be led against their will by any dictatorial power, no matter how powerful or firmly estab-lished, to engage in an aggressive war for material aggrandizement.

The Chinese are philosophical in war and extol moral righteous-ness, justice, and the spirit of sacrifice. Often the emphasis placed on these values has led the Chinese to a dangerous underestimation of material and technological factors. They have tended to rely upon fighting spirit—the "divine power" of the Boxers, the "revolutionary spirit" of the nationalists, the dogmatic "ideological strength" of the communists—even in the face of overwhelmingly superior arms. In a nation with smaller resources of manpower, this attitude would have proved disastrous, but, on the other hand, when skillfully and not recklessly employed, it can be a crucial factor in any war.

An obstinate defensive mentality is a notable characteristic of Chinese strategy. It may be attributed to two principal causes: tradi-tional concepts and, in our modern period, the consideration of China's material and technological weaknesses. The traditional concept is en-shrined in the strategical doctrine of *chien-pi ch'ing-yeh* (strengthen the wall, scorch the field). China long depended on the protection of the Great Wall. Her weakness in firearms is another factor which contributes to her reliance upon strong fortification and defensive wars. The lack of strong naval and air forces, when viewed in the light of China's geographical and topographical features, has also placed the army in a situation of strategic defense.

Protracted war as a means of achieving military and political aims has been repeatedly resorted to in Chinese history. The Chinese always tend to think in terms of long periods of time. They have great patience, persistence, and a capacity for enduring long humiliations *if* the prospect of eventual retaliation remains. These qualities of mind, in conjunction with great resources of manpower and vast geographical areas of difficult terrain, have made possible the Chinese prosecution of wars of long duration.

One notable Chinese strategical feature is the tendency to concentrate upon the exploitation of the enemy's weak point. The famous Chinese strategist Sun Tzu laid down the principle that "when the enemy is strong, avoid it; when the enemy is angry, stir it." The Chinese exhibit no predilection to clash head-on with an opponent in order to force a swift decision. They prefer to wear down the enemy by harassment, by non-resistance, by guerrilla warfare. They yield, they retreat, they maneuver the enemy into a position where they can do battle in their own good time and under their terms. It was on such a principle that Chiang Kai-shek resisted the Japanese, and it was the extension of the same basic concept that Mao Tse-tung used to formulate his strategy to defeat the nationalists. The Chinese have a traditional concept of overcoming hardness with elasticity (*i-jou k'e-kang*), which most Occidentals would find it hard to understand, but the very ignorance or disregard of which, as the Japanese have found to their sorrow, will invite eventual disaster.

The Chinese have a greater fondness for stratagems and tricks of war, for *ruses de guerre*, than for head-on battle. They prefer to win by strategy rather than by sheer force. They believe that the shrewd can always dominate the strong—a creed seen operative in almost all Chinese wars and especially exemplified by the recent communist triumphs on the mainland of China. The best-known Chinese strategist, Sun Tzu, centuries ago devoted a whole chapter (in his book *Chi-shih*) to stratagems and their limitations, and one of China's most popular classical novels, *The Three Kingdoms* (*San-kuo Chi*), treats war throughout in terms of a discussion of stratagems. War to the Chinese is, as Bismarck said of politics, more an art than a science. Ancient Chinese rules stress surprise, trickery, unpredictableness, and the avoidance of battle if possible. Mao Tse-tung was once quoted as summarizing his tactics in this way:

> "When the enemy comes forward, I withdraw;
> When the enemy withdraws, I go forward;
> When the enemy settles down, I disturb him;
> When the enemy is exhausted, I fight him."[7]

The Chinese creed was shared and succinctly stated by Julius Caesar: "Why stake your fortune on the risk of battle, especially as a victory by strategy is as much a part of good generalship as a victory by the sword?"[8]

Skill in psychological warfare and emphasis on the art of propaganda are other Chinese traits. The Chinese were some of the earliest users of psychological tools in war. They were often dexterous in exploiting the moral and psychological weaknesses of the enemy. During World War II Japanese commanders were subjected to constant anxiety over the psychological state of their troops in China, and the effectiveness with which the communists waged psychological war against the nationalists is well known. On the other hand, Chinese soldiers are themselves especially vulnerable to psychological offensives launched by an opponent if an appeal can successfully be made to their inner sense of justice.

Despite China's vast population, her traditional military doctrine has never placed undue emphasis on a mass army. Every Chinese strategical thinker has invariably stressed the principle of *chin-ping* (the elite army). The Chinese believe that true military strength and vast numbers of troops are two different things and that "to force the people to fight without training them is murder." Chinese historians and statesmen have also left no doubt that the maintenance of huge standing armies has been a basic cause of the fall of many a dynasty. On the other hand, the Chinese would never abandon numerical superiority in order to rely solely upon a small elite army for defense. They understand, like Napoleon, that "numbers annihilate." In compromise they are likely to maintain a small and highly trained professional standing army backed by a massive reserve which, in times of emergency, will share the military burden, a system in

[7] Military-political Institute (communist), *Textbook on Military Strategy* (Shue-chin, 1935), Chapter 3.
[8] *De Bello Civili* I, 72.

harmony with the oft-stated concept of "unity between soldiery and peasantry."

In modern times a nation's power to wage war has come to depend increasingly on an efficient mobilization of her economic resources. A nation's economic potential furthermore imposes limitations which her military power cannot exceed. In this era of material civilization and power politics, China is basically well endowed with many essentials of respectable military power. These include her huge manpower, her geographical vastness, her strategic and advantageous location, her diversified if none too abundant mineral wealth, and her agriculturally productive climate. She also has her limitations. Her manpower is largely untrained for modern technological war. Her industries are small and backward. Minerals are present in comparatively modest amounts. Her agricultural production is quantitatively impressive but so inadequate in terms of her vast population that there is little room for industrial crops or export surplus. The country is sorely in need of adequate and well-integrated communication systems. Perhaps the most serious lack of all is the absence of an effective and stable government dedicated to the exploitation of China's natural wealth for the advantage of the Chinese and for continuous progress, particularly in the economic sphere amid internal peace and stability. Except for this last great handicap, no other nation in eastern Asia is so possessed of the potential to become a first-class economic and military power.

To speculate upon the final outcome of the present situation in China and on Formosa is not the province of this book, although it is of course believed that a thorough understanding of the basic Chinese military principles and the events which led up to the communist triumph on the mainland as well as the subsequent nationalist resurrection in Taiwan (Formosa), is essential to any correct evaluation of current conditions or any enlightened guesses which may be hazarded as to the pattern that China's future may take. The aim of the present work is to examine the impact of various wars in China, and to emphasize the central role that military affairs have played in her history, economics, and politics.

In speaking of the Chinese people today, we deal with the greatest question mark in Asia. China has emerged in the east to become a highly significant factor in the world balance of power in this age of global conflict.

History, like nature, however, makes no leap. The reemergence of China under the Red regime, dramatic as it may appear, is largely the result of historical momentum, not wholly attributable to communist statecraft, nor certainly to any infallibility of Marx-Leninism. The danger in the East lies not in the non-existent hostility of the millions upon millions of Chinese peasants nor the full weight of that manpower; it exists in the over-exaggeration of communist invincibility, whereby self-conceited Red rulers may become so overconfident as to plunge a hungry people into war for the vaunted hope of communist empires. Meanwhile one can surely not entirely discount the new and old nationalists across the Formosan Strait, whose ambition to regain their fatherland finds its most characteristic expression in the words of one of China's greatest generals, Yueh Fei (A.D. 1103-1141): "It is intolerable to behold our brocade-like rivers and mountains falling into the hands of the barbarian enemy. I hereby rise up and, with the patriots of *Chung-yuan* (the Middle Lands) cry: Return to us our rivers and our mountains!"[9]

The armies of China will not long tolerate tyranny, especially if they suspect that they are being used as the tools of some alien power and not primarily for the economic benefit of their homeland. Once they become convinced that the cause for which they are fighting is not a righteous one, even the most eloquent political preaching will be of no avail. In 1934, when the Chinese communists in Kiangsi were in the depth of despair due to an economic and military blockade enforced by government troops, they lost faith in the vaunted Red ideals. A communist leader, Lo Min, declared publicly: "Even if our best leaders were to come, or to bring Stalin himself, or even resurrect Lenin, and were to speak all together to the masses, I do not think it would change their mood." Even the ruthless dictatorships of the Chin and Mongol Yuan powers fell when the people decided to exercise their right of revolution to remove oppressors. Even a victorious leader like Chiang Kai-shek could not arrest the tide of criticism from a people made weary by wars and misgovernment. No ruler in China could ever command an army and a police system huge enough to keep every square mile of the nation under surveillance. In time of oppression, as history has amply shown, the Chinese

[9] "Yueh Fei lieh-chuan," *Sung Shih*, Ch. 365, 124.

always rise in the ancient pattern in the mountain fastnesses and the remote villages, gaining strength, winning the gradual support of the government troops, growing finally into vast armies capable of crushing any opposition, and sweeping down to bring destruction upon the despot and whatever troops have still remained loyal to him. This is indeed an indisputable historical pattern of China.

In the world struggle of today, China is a major factor. One out of every four people in the world is Chinese. What role those 600 millions will play in the struggle, this book will not hazard to prophesy. There are a great many factors to be taken into account, and the prophet remains without honor since, if he guesses right, no one remembers, and, if he should guess wrong, no one will forget. This book attempts to present, however, the pattern of China's recent history, the basis upon which all enlightened guesses must be made. It is hoped that this brief analysis of China's turbulent modern period will contribute toward understanding, and it would be doubly wise to remember, as Theodore Roosevelt once told us, that the essence of wisdom is to be wise in time.

SELECTED BIBLIOGRAPHY *

I. EARLIER CHINESE HISTORY AND CULTURE, GENERAL AND MILITARY

Chang Chi-yuen, *Chung-kuo chün-shih shih-lueh* (A Brief History of Chinese Military Affairs), Shanghai, 1944. A comprehensive study of the history of Chinese military affairs by a prominent scholar. Part I of the book is a historical survey of the military system of earlier China.

Chen Fu-liang, *Lì-tài pǐng-chih* (The Records on the Military Affairs of Various Dynasties), 8 vols. (about 1200), Gest Collection, Princeton University.

Ch'ien Han Shu, Ch. 30.

Ch'ien Wên-tsǔ (grad. 1192), *Pu Han-pǐng-chih* (The Supplementary History of the Han Dynasty), Gest Collection, Princeton University. Part of *Erh-shih wu-shih pu-pien*.

Confucius, *Lu Yü* (Analect), a basic Chinese classic.

Dubs, H. H., "The Reliability of Chinese Histories," *Far Eastern Quarterly* 6 (1946), pp. 23-43.

Duyvendak, J. J. L., "The True Dates of the Chinese Maritime Expeditions in the Early Fifteenth Century," *T'oung Pao, 34* (1939), pp. 341-412.

Escarra, Jean, *Le Droit Chinois*, Paris, 1936.

Fitzgerald, C. P., *China, A Short Cultural History*, New York, 1938.

Franke, Otto, *Geschichte des Chinesischen Reiches*, 3 vols., Berlin and Leipzig, 1930, 1936, 1937.

Goodrich, L. C. and Feng, C. S., "Firearms," *The Early Development of Firearms in China, Isis*, XXXVI, pt. 2, 104.

Hsü Tsung-hao, *Chung-kuo ch'eng-ch'ih kai-yao* (A Brief Treatise of Chinese Administrative Institutions), Shanghai, 1946. A concise study of the Chinese governmental structures by a high Chinese official.

Ku-chin t'u-shu chi-ch'eng (1726), Section XXX, esp. Chs. 81-90.

Lai Chin-yuan, *Tang che-ch'ung-fu k'ao* (Research on the Che-ch'ung-fu Military System of the T'ang Dynasty), 1841. Part of *Erh-shih-wu-shih pu-pien*.

Lai K'an, "The Han Military System and the Han Military System Seen on Wooden Documents," *Bulletin of the Institute of History and Philology, Academia Sinica*, X, 1 (1942), pp. 23-54.

* In some cases there is no exact English translation of the Chinese title, and therefore only the Chinese (or Japanese) title is given. Where the title can be translated into English, it is given in parentheses after the Chinese (or Japanese) title. In some cases, particularly for the ancient works, date and place of publication are not available.

Latourette, K. S., *The Chinese: Their History and Culture*, 2 vols., New York, 1946.

Li Hung-chang, *Li Wen-chung-kung ch'uan chi* (The Collected Works of Li Hung-chang), Gest Collection, Princeton University. Contains many original documents dealing with the military affairs of China during its earlier period of modernization.

Liang Chi-chao, "Chung-kuo kǔ kuān-ch'ih pien" (A Chapter on Ancient China's Official System), *Hsin-ming Tsung-k'an pien*, Shanghai, 1920 ed. A penetrating study of ancient China's administrative system by one of the greatest literary figures of contemporary China.

Liang Chi-chao, *History of Chinese Political Thought: During the Early Tsin Period*, L. T. Chen, trans., New York, 1930. A highly important work by a great Chinese scholar on the background and evolution of Chinese philosophy.

Liu Hsien-chow, *History of Mechanical Engineering in China*, Peiping, Tsinhua.

Ma Kuei-yü, *Wen-hsien t'oung-kao*, 1300. Vol. XVI, Ch. 221. This volume contains an important study on the military systems of China by one of the most celebrated scholars and encyclopedists of classical China.

Ma Pei-lo, *Chung-kuo chün-sse chieh hsueh ti fa-ch'an* (The Development of Chinese Military Philosophy), Hongkong, 1954.

Mao Yuan-yi, *Wu-pei chih* (Records on Military Preparedness), Gest Collection, Princeton University, 1621.

Mencius, *Meng Tzu* (The Teaching of Mencius), a basic Chinese classic.

Mo Ti, *Mo Tzu* (The Collected works of Motzu), a Chinese classic.

Needham, J., *Science and Civilization in China*, Cambridge, 1954, Volume I. This work gives a comprehensive survey of China's hitherto unrecognized contribution to science, technology, and scientific thought.

Rotour, R. D., *Traite des Fonctionnaires et Traite de L'armee, traduit de la Nouvelle Histoire des T'ang*, 2 vols., Leyden, 1947.

Shih Chiu-kuan, *Chung-kuo kuo-fan shih* (History of China's Defense).

Ssu-ma T'an and Ssu-ma Ch'ien, *Shih chi*, 130 chs. (B.C. 180?-110).

Sui shu. The Books of the Sui Dynasty, Chs. 32-35.

Sun Tzu, *Ping-fa shih-san-pien* (Thirteen Chapters on Military Strategy), a Chinese military classic.

Swann, N. L., trans., *Food and Money in Ancient China*, Princeton, 1950.

T'ai P'ing Yü-lan (A Chinese encyclopedia), Chs. 270-359 (953).

Tanaka, Hisashi, *Shina senso-shi gairon* (A Treatise of China's History of War), Osaka, 1942. Written by a Japanese military officer, this book contains many misinterpretations, yet is a useful reference.

Tseng Kung-liang, *Wu-ching tsung-yao* (Collected Works on Essential Military Classics), in 40 chs. This collection comprises the important military classics of China, including all the edited or authenticated versions of such great works as *Sun Tzu*, *Wu Tzu*, *Ssu-ma Fa*, *Wei-liao Tzu*, *San lueh*, *Lu tao* and *Li-wei-kung wen tui*, which constitute the seven principal military classics.

Tsui chi, *A Short History of Chinese Civilization*, London, 1942

T'ung chih (circa 1150), Ch. 68.

T'ung Tien (circa A.D. 880), Chs. 148-162.

Vinacke, H. M., *A History of the Far East in Modern Times*, rev. ed., New York, 1942.

Voltaire, F. M. A., *Essai sur l'histoire et sur les moeurs*, Paris, 1756.

Wittfogel, K. A. and Feng, C. S., *History of Chinese Society, Liao*, New York, 1949.

Wu Chi, *Wu Tzu* (Six Chapters on War), a Chinese military classic.

Yang Sung and Teng Li-chün, *Chung-kuo chin-tai-shih chih-liao hsuan-chï* (A Source Book of Contemporary Chinese History), rev. by Yung Meng-yuan, Peking, 1954. A Chinese Communist version of contemporary Chinese history.

II. MILITARY ART AND STRATEGY: NON-CHINESE WORKS

Amiot, P., *Art militaire des Chinois, Memoir sur les Chinois*, Paris, 1778, 1782. This well-known French work contains many mistakes in translation and in interpretation. It includes a great deal that the original Chinese texts did not contain.

Anonyme, *État actual de l'art et de la science militaire à la Chine*, Paris, 1773.

Calthrop, E. F., *Sonshi*, Tokyo, 1905.

Cholei, E., *L'Art militaire dans l'antiquité chinoise*, 1 vol., Paris, 1922.

Fujichuku, T. and Mori, S., *Sonsi sin-syaku*, Tokyo, 1943.

Giles, Lionel, *Sun Tzu on Art of War*, London, Luzac & Co. 1910. This is about the most faithful translation of the book of *Sun Tzu* in English, although, strictly speaking, it still contains many misinterpretations. The Introduction of this book is a scholarly piece of work.

Kitamura, K., *Sonsi kaisetzu*, Tokyo, n.d.

Konrad, N. I., *Sun Tsz'i: Traktat o Voennon Iskusstre* (Sun Tsz'i: Treatise of Military Classics), Moscow, The Academy of Science of the U.S.S.R., 1950. A most thorough study of the Chinese military classics.

Nachin, L., ed., *Sun Tse et les Anciens Chinois Ou Tse et Se Ma Fa*, Paris, 1948. A recent and thoroughly revised French translation of two of China's military classics. The *Avant-propos* is a scholarly piece of work.

Oba, Y. and Koda, R., *Sonsi no Heicho*, in Japanese, Tokyo, 1935. One of the best expositions of *Sun Tzu* in Japanese by a noted Japanese military expert.

Philipps, T. R., *Roots of Strategy: Sun Tzu (500 B.C.) The Art of War*, London, 1917.

III. CONTEMPORARY CHINA BEFORE
WORLD WAR II

ASPECTS OF HER POLITICAL, MILITARY, AND GENERAL HISTORIES

Beloff, M., *The Foreign Policy of Soviet Russia*, London, 1943.

Bloch, Kurt, *German Interests and Policies in the Far East*, New York, 1939.

Borkenau, F., *The Communist International*, London, 1938.

Carlson, E. F., *The Chinese Army, Its Organization and Military Efficiency*, New York, 1940.

Casserville, Henri, *De Chiang Kai Shek a Mao Tse Tung*, Paris, 1950.

Chang Chi-yuan, *Chung-kuo chün-shih shih-lueh* (A Brief History of Chinese Military Affairs), Shanghai, 1946.

————, *Tang-shih kai-yao* (The Vital Historical Events of the Kuomintang Party), 3 vols., Taipeh, 1950. The above work, written by a scholar personally close to Chiang Kai-shek, contains many quotations from official documents and from Chiang's personal papers.

Chang Chih-tung, *China's Only Hope*, trans. by S. I. Woodridge, New York, 1900.

Chang Tze-sheng, "The War History of the Northern Expedition of the National Revolutionary Army," *The Eastern Miscellancy*, xxv, 15, 16, 17 (Aug.-Sept. 1928), in Chinese.

Chao Feng-t'ien, "Economic Thought during the Last Fifty Years of the Ching Period," Harvard-Yenching Institute Monogram.

Chassin, L.-M., *L'ascension de Mao Tse-tung, 1921-1945*, Paris, 1950.

Chen Chih-mai, *Chung-kuo Cheng-fu* (The Government of China), Shanghai, 1946.

Chen Kung-fu, *Chung-kuo Ke-ming-shih* (The History of Chinese Revolution), Shanghai, 1930.

Chen Po-ta, *Mao Tse-tung on the Chinese Revolution*, Peking, 1953.

————, *Stalin and the Chinese Revolution*, Peking, 1953.

The above books and pamphlets written by Chen Po-ta, vice-president of the Communist government's Academia Sinica, are Communist versions of Chinese historical events.

Chiang Fan-cheng, "Military Development of China during the Last Fifty Years," *Sheng-pao nien-chien*, Shanghai, 1933, in Chinese.

Chiang Kai-shek, *Chiang Kai-shek ti ke-ming küng-tso* (The Revolutionary Works of Chiang Kai-shek), Shanghai, 1930. A collection of Chiang's earlier speeches, writings, proclamations, official papers, etc.

————, *China's Destiny*, trans. by Wang Chung-hui, New York, 1947.

————, *Min-kuo i-t'ung chih* (Historical Records on the Unification of China), Shanghai, 1929.

————, *Lu-shan hsün-lien-chih*, National Military Council, 1937.

————, *Whampoa hsün-lien-chih*, National Military Council, 1943.

The above two works contain the collections of speeches which

Chiang Kai-shek delivered to the political and military training programs which he conducted at Lushan, Lo-chia-shan, Oumei, and Fu-hsin-kuan. There were many editions of these collected works, mostly issued by organizations affiliated with the National Military Council.

Chiang Kai-shek, *Sān-nien-lai ti Kuo-min-ke-ming-chün* (Three Years of the National Revolutionary Army), Shanghai, 1929.

"The Chinese Army," *The Far Eastern Review*, VI, 5 (Oct. 1909), pp. 171, 175-193.

Chinese Ministry of Navy, *Hai-chün ta-shih-chi* (Notable Events of the Navy), Peking, 1918.

Chow Mu-chia, *Sin-chung-kuo fa-chan-shih* (A New History of Chinese Development), Shanghai, 1929.

Condliffe, J. B., *China Today: Economic*, Boston, 1932.

Dallin, D. J., *The Rise of Soviet Russia in Asia*, New Haven, 1949.

Elmquist, P. O., "The Sino-Japanese Undeclared War of 1932," *Harvard Regional Study Program, Paper on China*, V, 1951.

Ennis, T. E. and Langsam, W. C., ed. *Eastern Asia*, Chicago, 1948.

Epstein, Julius von, "Seeckt und Tschiang-Kai-Schek," *Wehrwissenschaftliche Rundschau*, Nov. 1953, p. 534.

Fairbank, J. K., *The United States and China*, Cambridge, 1948.

Feng Yü-hsiang, *Wo-ti-sheng-ho* (My Life, in Chinese), Chungking, 1944.

Fischer, Louis, *The Soviets in World Affairs*, 2 vols, Princeton, 1951. Fischer's chapters on China were largely written from his conversation with Borodin.

Frey, H., *L'armée Chinoise*, Paris, 1904.

Fromentin, Pierre, *Mao Tse Tung, Le Dragon Rouge*, Paris, Editions Médicis, 1949.

Hedin, Sven, *Chiang Kai-shek*, New York, 1940.

Holcome, A. N., *The Chinese Revolution*, Cambridge, 1930.

Hsieh Pao-chao, *The Government of China (1644-1911)*, Baltimore, 1925.

Hu Shih, "China in Stalin's Grand Strategy," *Foreign Affairs*, Oct. 1950. Contains the view of China's leading scholar on Stalin's role in the Communist conspiracy.

Japanese General Staff, *History of the War between Japan and China*, trans. by Jikemura and Lloyd, Tokyo, 1904.

Kita, Ikki, *Shina kokumei gai shi* (China's history of revolution), Tokyo, 1930.

Kotenev, Anatol, *The Chinese Soldiers*, Shanghai, 1933.

Li Chien-nung, *Tsui-chin san-shih nien Chung-kuo cheng-chi-shih* (The Political History of the Last Thirty Years), Shanghai, 1932.

Li Tsung-jen, *Li tsung-ssu-ling yen-lun-chih* (The Speeches and Writings of Commander-in-Chief Li), Kweilin, 1934.

Lin, P. W., "A Statistical Study of the Personnel of the Chinese National Government," *XIXᵉ Session de Institut International de Statistique*, Shanghai, 1930.

Linebarger, P. M., *The China of Chiang Kai-shek*, Boston, 1943.

MacNair, H. F. (ed.), *China*, Berkeley, 1946.

Mao Tse-tung, *Selected Work of Mao Tse-tung*, particularly Vol. II, London, 1954.

North, R. C., *Moscow and Chinese Communists*, Stanford, 1953.

Peking Metropolitan Police Headquarters, *Soviet Plot in China*, Peking, 1927. Contains English translation of Soviet documents seized from Soviet Embassy in Peking during a raid ordered by General Chang Tso-ling.

Pick, E., *China in the Grip of the Red*, Shanghai, 1927.

Pictorial Review from Sino-Japanese Conflict in Shanghai, Shanghai, Wen-hua, 1932, in Chinese.

Powell, R. L., *The Rise of Chinese Military Power, 1895-1912*, Princeton, 1955.

Roy, M. N., *My Experience in China*, Calcutta, 1938.

————, *Revolution and Counter-Revolution in China*, Calcutta, 1946.

Sah Shih-chiung and Chien Tuan-shen, *Min-kuo cheng-chin-shih* (History of Political Institutions under the Republic), Vols. I and II, Chung-king, 1945.

Selle, E. A., *Donald of China*, New York, 1948.

Shen Chien, "The Army and Its Finance on the Eve of Revolution, 1911," *She-hui k'o-hsueh*, Vol. 2, No. 2 (Jan. 1937), in Chinese.

Shen, T. H., *Agricultural Resources of China*, Ithaca, 1951.

Seeckt, H. von, "*Denkschrift für Marschall Chiang Kai-shek*" (a carbon copy of the original memorandum contained in German army's documental file), *Heersarchiv, Potsdam, Sg. 60, Lager-No. 1864, Karten 15, Stück 205*.

Stalin, J. V., *Sochnenya*, Vol. VIII, Moscow, 1946.

————, "The Prospects of the Revolution in China," *International Press Correspondence*, Dec. 23, 1926.

Strong, A. L., *China's Million*, New York, 1935.

Sun Yat-sen, *Tsun-li yi-chiao*, Nanking, 1928.

Tanaka's Secret Memorial to the Japanese Emperor, Nanking, n.d.

Tang Liang-li, *The Inner History of the Chinese Revolution*, London, 1930.

Teng, S. Y. and Fairbank, J. K., *China's Response to the West, A Documentary Survey, 1839-1933*, Cambridge, 1954.

Tewksbury, D. G., *Sourcebook on Far Eastern Political Ideologies*, in mimeographed form.

Tong, H. K., *Chiang Kai-shek, An Authorized Biography*, Shanghai, 1937.

Trotsky, Leon, *Problems of the Chinese Revolution*, New York, 1932.

Tsou Lu, *Chung-kuo kuo-ming-tang kai-shih* (A General History of the Kuomintang of China), Chungking, 1944.

Upton, Gen. E., *The Armies of Asia and Europe*, New York, 1878.

Volpicelli, Z. (Vladimir pseud.), *The China-Japan War*, New York, 1896.

Wang Pei-ling, Ho Ying-chin, Chen Chih-cheng, *et al.*, *Whampoa chiēn-chün shih-hua* (Historical Notes on Whampoa and Its Founding of the Army), Chungking, 1943.

Wang Shih-chieh and Chien Tuan-sheng, *Pi-chiao hsien-fa* (Comparative Constitutional Law), rev. ed., Chungking, 1942.

Weng Kung-chih, *Tsui-ching san-shih-nien chün-ssu-shih* (The Military History of the Last Thirty Years), Shanghai, 1932. This is a useful reference book for the study of Chinese military history.

Yin Shi (pseudonym of Cheng Ssu-yuan), *Li-Chiang kuan-hsi yü Chung-kuo* (The Chiang-Lee Relationship and China), Hongkong, 1954.

Yüan Shi-k'ai, compiler, *Hsin-chien lu-chün ping-lüeh lu-ts'un* (Record of the Military Plans of the Newly Created Army), 8 vols., Peking, 1898.

IV. WORLD WAR II AND THE SINO-JAPANESE WAR

Abegg, Lily, *China's Erneurung*, Frankfurt, 1940.

Army Staff College of China, *Draft Campaign Histories of the Sino-Japanese War. The Attack and Siege of Sungshan by the Chinese Eighth Army. A Study of the Kaolikung Mountain, Tenchung Campaigns in West Yunnan. An Evaluation of the Campaign Experience of the Battles of Lungling, Manshih, and Wanting. Lu-ta chi-kan* (The Quarterly Journal of the Army Staff College), 1937-1945.
   The above publications of the Chinese Army Staff College are serious technical and strategic studies of the campaigns. They are objective research works of a non-partisan nature.

Baldwin, Hanson W., *Great Mistakes of the War*, New York, 1950.

Belden, J., *Retreat with Stilwell*, New York, 1943.

Bisson, T. A., *The Origins of the Sino-Japanese Hostilities*, New York, 1938.

Carlson, E. F., *The Chinese Army*, New York, 1940.

Chang Chi-yuan, *Tang-shih kai-yao*, *op.cit.*, Vol. II.

Chassin, L.-M., *Histoire militaire de la seconde guerre mondiale*, Paris, 1950.

Chennault, C. L., *Way of a Fighter*, New York, 1949.

Chiang Kai-shek, *The Collected Wartime Messages of Generalissimo Chiang Kai-shek*, 2 vols., New York, 1946.

Chinese Communist Eighteenth Group Army, Political Bureau, *K'an-chan pa-nien-lai ti pa-lu-chün yü hsin-sse-chün* (The Eighth Route Army and the New Fourth Army; After Eight Years of the War of Resistance), Yenan, 1946.

Chinese Ministry of National Defense, *Wei-ta-ti Chiang-chu-hsi* (The Great President Chiang), Nanking, 1946. This volume, though an official publication of the Chinese government, contains much original information, documents, and articles written by some of the leading military figures of China. It has a great many photographs of the generalissimo.

Chu Teh, The Commander-in-Chief of the Chinese Red Army, *Lun chieh-fang-chü ch'an-ch'ang* (On the Wars in the Liberated Areas), Yennan, 1945.

Churchill, Winston, *The Second World War*, 6 vols., Boston, 1948-1953. These six volumes are acknowledged as one of the several most important works on World War II.

Commager, H. S., *The Story of the Second World War*, New York, 1945.

Conn, Stetson and Morton, L., "The Military Threat to the United States, 1939-1941," paper presented to the American Historical Association's 1953 convention.

Eisenhower, D. D., *Crusade in Europe*, New York, 1943.

Eldridge, F., *Wrath in Burma*, New York, 1946.

Fall, Cyril, *The Second World War, A Short History*, London, 1950.

Feis, Herbert, *The China Tangle*, Princeton, 1953. This is one of the most authoritative and scholarly works dealing with Sino-U.S. relations during World War II.

Fuji, S., *Piru Daitoa Zenshi* (Confidential Notes on the War for Greater East Asia), 3 vols., Tokyo, 1950.

Fu Jun-hua, *Kan-chān-chien-kuo ta-hua-shih* (A Pictorial History of the Great War of Resistance and National Reconstruction), Shanghai, 1947.

Fuller, I. F., *The Second World War*, London, 1948.

Gaimusho (Japanese Foreign Ministry) *Shūsen Shiroku* (Historical Notes on the End of the War), Tokyo, 1949. This is a highly important Japanese account of World War II and how it was ended, including a number of excerpts from writings by Japanese authors and high officials.

Goerlitz, Walter, *Der Zweite Weltkrieg 1939-1945*, Stuttgart, 1950.

Hagiwara, Tôru, *Taisen no Kaibô* (An Anatomy of the War), Tokyo, 1950.

Han Ch'i-tung, *An Estimate of Chinese Losses during the Chinese War against Japan 1937-1945*, Nanking, 1946. In Chinese. A highly important statistical study of the economics of the Sino-Japanese war.

Hattori, Takushiro, *Daitōa Senso Zenshi* (A Complete History of the War for Greater East Asia), 4 vols. Tokyo, 1953. This is perhaps one of the most important Japanese works on World War II, written by a former responsible Japanese general staff officer. It is less biased than many other Japanese works.

Hayashi, Saburo, *Taihayo senso rikusen gaishi*, Tokyo, 1950?

Ho Yung-chi, *The Big Circle*, New York, 1948. This is one of the very few Chinese accounts of the Burma campaigns.

Huang, Jen-yü, *Mien-pei chih chan* (The Campaign of Northern Burma), Shanghai.

Japan Year Book 1940-1941, Tokyo, 1941.

Japanese *Rīkusho* (War Ministry), *Dairiku senshi*, Tokyo, 1941.

Japanese Military Files. After World War II, a large number of Japanese military documents and files of the Japanese military organization were captured; most of these were stored in the National Archives at Washington, D.C. The study of the Japanese war in China as contained in this book has been greatly facilitated through the cooperation of the members of the National Archives, who made available to the author many pertinent Japanese documents.

Kodama, Yoshio, *I Was Defeated*, Tokyo, 1951.

Levitsky, K. (pseudonym of a Soviet general), "Japan's Sedan Tactics in the China War," originally an article in Moscow's *Izvestia*; an English translation was made in *Pacific Digest*, II, 4 (April 1938).

Li Tsung-jen, *Tai-erh-chuang kan-chang hui-i-lu*, Hongkong, 1954.

Liu Fei, *Ti-wo chang-lueh chang-shu chi yen-chiu* (A Study of the Strategies of Our Forces and of the Enemy), Chungking, 1944.

———, "Military Campaigns," *The Chinese Year Book 1944-1945*. General Liu Fei was China's vice-chief of military operation during the Sino-Japanese War. In 1949 he defected to the Chinese Communist side during a peace negotiation conference at Peiping shortly before the Communist forces crossed the Yangtze.

Lo Ku, *In-mien chih cheng-chān* (The Expeditionary Campaigns in India and Burma), Nanking, 1945.

Mao Tse-tung, *On Protracted War*, Yennan, 1939 ed. *The Situation and Tasks in the Anti-Japanese War after the Fall of Shanghai and Taiyuan*, Yennan, 1938. *Strategical Problems of China's Revolutionary War*, Harbin, 1948 ed. *Problems of Independence and Autonomy within the United Front. Problems of Tactics in the Present Anti-Japanese United Front.*

A source containing almost all the above essays and articles is *Mao Tse-tung chuan chi* (Complete Works of Mao Tse-tung), Peking, 1952.

Marshall, George C., *Biennial Reports of the Chief of Staff of the United States Army, July 1943-June 30, 1945, and Oct. 1945*, published as pamphlets by the *United States News*, Washington, D.C. and by the Government Printing Office, 1945. A most important U.S. army official report, indispensable to any study of World War II events.

McNair, H. F., ed., *Voices from Unoccupied China*, Chicago, 1944.

Mori, Shozo, *Sempoo Niju-nen* (Twenty Years of Whirlwind), Tokyo, 1946.

National Military Council of China, *Kuo-chün Tien-mien chien-ti chih* (The Destruction of the Enemy Force in Yunnan and Burma), Nanking, 1946.

Ninth War Area Headquarters, China, *Ti-san-tze Changsha hui-chān chi-shih* (An Actual Account of the Third Battle of Changsha), Changsha, 1944.

Ploetz, *Geschichte des Zweiten Weltkrieg*, Bielefeld, 1951.

Romanus, C. F. and Sunderland, R., *United Army in World War II, China-Burma-India Theater, Stilwell Mission to China*, Washington,

1953. As an official account, this is a most accurate and scholarly work on Sino-American military relations during the war; admirably written and edited.

Schenke, Wolf, *Reise an der Gelbenfront*, Berlin, 1941.

Seagrave, G. S., *Burma Surgeon*, New York, 1943.

Sherwood, Robert, *Roosevelt and Hopkins*, New York, 1948. Acknowledged to be a most important work of its kind. Contains much information on the high-level dealings between China and the U.S. during the war.

Shugg, R. W. and DeWeerd, H. A., *World War II, A Concise History*, Washington, 1946.

Snow, E., *The Battle for Asia*, New York, 1941.

Stilwell, J. S., *The Stilwell Papers*, T. H. White, ed., New York, 1948. Strongly opinionated, with omission of pertinent facts, yet a frank and almost indispensable source book.

Stimson, H. L. and Bundy, M., *On Active Service in Peace and War*, New York, 1948.

Tan, P. Y., *The Building of the Burma Road*, New York, 1945.

Tan Tzu-chan, *Kan-chang ti Kuo-fan-lun* (The National Defence of the War of Resistance), Chungking, 1940.

Tanaka, Masasaku, *Miao-ping jin-ken* (The Miao Ping Affairs), Tokyo, 1953.

Tippelskirch, K. von, *Geschichte des Zweiten Weltkrieg*, Bonn, 1951.

To-a Ken-kiu-sha, *Saishin To-a Yoran*, Tokyo, 1941.

Tsao Chu-jen and Shu Tsung-chiao, *Kan-chan hua-shih* (Pictorial History of China's War of Resistance), Shanghai, 1946. Although this is written as a popular pictorial history, the authors have done a scholarly and fairly accurate work on the war history. It is one of the best war accounts in Chinese put out by Chinese authors, and a highly useful sourcebook on the Sino-Japanese war.

U.S. Coordinator of Information, *American Aid to China*, Memorandum No. B.R.T. 32, published as mimeographed pamphlet.

U.S. Strategic Bombing Survey, *Interrogation of Japanese Officials*, Washington: GPO, 1946.

———, *Japan's Struggle to End the War*, Washington: GPO, 1946.

———, *Summary Report, Pacific War*, Washington: GPO, 1946.

Utley, Freda, *China at War*, London, Faber, 1939.

Uyehara, Ye'tsujiro, *Naze Sensoho o koshita-ka* (Why the War and Why the Defeat), Tokyo, 1947.

Wang Chün, *Chung-kuo lu-chün chiao-yu kai-kuan* (The General Condition of China's Military Education), Chungking, 1943.

Whitney, C., *MacArthur, His Rendezvous with History*, New York, 1956.

Yang Hsien-kai, *Hsiang-pai ta-tsieh chi sh'ih* (An Actual Record of the Victory in Northern Hunnan), Chungking, 1940.

Yin Shi (pseudonym of Cheng Ssu-yuan), *Li-Chiang kuan-hsi yü Chung-kuo, op.cit.*

V. MILITARY AND GENERAL HISTORICAL
EVENTS OF CHINA AFTER WORLD WAR II

Casseville, Henri, *De Chiang Kai Shek a Mao Tse Tung*, Paris, 1950.
Chassin, L.-M., *L'ascension de Mao Tse-tung, 1921-1945*, Paris, 1950.
————, *La conquête de la Chine par Mao Tse Tung*, Paris, 1951.
China Handbook 1952.
Chu Teh, *On the Battle Fronts of the Liberated Areas*, Peking, 1952.
————, Nieh Jung-chen *et al.*, *China's Revolutionary Wars*, Peking, 1951.
  The above two books represent the Chinese Communists' view of their military achievements.
Ernburg, G. B., *Ocherki Natsional'no-osvobitel'noi Bor'by Kitaiskogo Naroda* (in Russian), Moscow, 1951.
Feis, Herbert, *The China Tangle*, op.cit.
Finogenov, K., *V Novom Kitae* (in Russian), Moscow, 1950.
Fitzgerald, C. P., *Revolution in China*, New York, 1952.
Forrestal, James, *The Forrestal Diaries*, New York, 1951. Ed. by W. S. Millis and E. S. Duffield.
Huang Tung-chou, *Wo-kuo tsin-hwa shih ti tou-ssu* (A Penetrating View of Soviet Russia's Aggression against China), Hongkong, 1953.
Kusano, Fumio, *Koku-kyo Ron* (On the Nationalists and Communists), Tokyo, 1946.
Liang Shen-chün, *Chiang Li tòu-tseng nèi-mou* (The Inside Struggle of Chiang Kai-shek with Lee Chong-yean), Hongkong, 1954. This book is an important work of its kind on postwar events in China, written by a member of the confidential staff of Acting President Marshal Li Tsung-jen. Contains much information based upon documentary research. It is well written, though somewhat partisan in view.
Lu Ke-nan, *Lun Chung-kuo ti cheng-tang* (On China's Political Parties), *Ta-kung-pao*, November 9, 1947. This is a very thoughtful and penetrating study of postwar political parties in China and their struggles, written by a trained political scientist.
Mao Tse-tung, *Hsin-min-chu chu-i* (New Democracy), Harbin, 1947. *On Coalition Government. Strategical Problems of China's Revolutionary Wars. The Present Situation and Our Tasks.* A number of the above works can be obtained in English translation, selected and compiled by Tewksbury, D. G., in a mimeographed publication entitled *Maoism, Sourcebook on Far Eastern Political Ideologies*, and in *Selected Works of Mao Tse-tung*, London, 1954.
Martynov, A., "The Present Situation in China," *Bolshevik*, No. 1, Jan. 15, 1949.
Pai Chung-hsi, "Lecture delivered at the Army Staff College," Shanghai, 1946.

Rigg, R. B., "How the Chinese Communists Wage War," *Infantry Journal*, LXIV, 2 (Feb. 1949), p. 4.
————, *Red China's Fighting Hordes*, Harrisburg, 1952.
Truman, H. S., *The Truman Memoirs*, Vol. II, New York, 1956.
U.S. General Staff, Intelligence Division, *The Chinese Communist Movement*, an Army report dated July 5, 1945, submitted as a Senate document, Washington, 1952.
U.S. Department of State, *United States Relations with China*, Washington: GPO, 1949. This China White Paper is an indispensable sourcebook for research work on postwar events in China.
Utley, F., *Last Chance for China*, New York, 1948.
Wang Tao, *Lun chiao kung ch'an chen* (On Communist Suppression), Taiwan, 1949.
White, T. H. and Jacoby, A., *Thunder Out of China*, New York, 1946.
Yeh Hu-shêng, *Hsien tai chung-kuo ke-ming shih-hua* (Historical Notes and Essays on Modern China's Revolution).
Yevgenyev, K., "The Victory of the Democratic Forces of China over Kuomintang Reaction," *Bolshevik*, trans. in *Soviet Press Translation*, 4, 1949.
Yin Shi (pseudonym Cheng Ssu-yuan), *Li Chiang kuan-hsi yü Chung-kuo* (The Lee-Chiang Relationship and China), Hongkong, 1954. This is a very important work on postwar events in China, written by a high official close to Acting President Li Tsung-jen. The description of activities within the government are generally considered to be accurate, although the interpretation may be partisan.
Young, A. N., *China's Economic and Financial Reconstruction*, New York, 1947. Contains an authoritative study of China's postwar economic situation, depicting the serious inflationary trend in one of the better postwar years under the Nationalist Government. It points out the effect of China's postwar military program on the national economy.

Reliable works on the postwar period are relatively few. In preparing Chapters 20 and 21 of this book, the author depended upon a large number of newspaper articles and official statements made by both government and Communist sources. These were checked and rechecked point by point through correspondence and direct interviews with the responsible National Government high officials concerned. Although these informants were helpful in most cases, they generally preferred anonymity.

VI. WORKS USEFUL AS BACKGROUND MATERIAL
DIPLOMACY, ECONOMICS, GEOGRAPHY AND INTERNATIONAL POLITICS

Chang Chung-fu, *Chung-hua min-kuo wai-chiao shih* (History of Foreign Relations of the Republic of China), Peiping, 1936.

Chao Chi-ming, "A Study of the Chinese Population, "*Milbank Memorial Fund Quarterly Bulletin*, XI, 4, Oct. 1933.

Chen Chang-hung, "Land Classification in China," *Geographic Magazine*, Vol. II, No. 4.

Chen Ta, *Population in Modern China*, Chicago, 1946.

Chiao-yü ta-tzu-tien (The Encyclopedia on Education), Shanghai, 1930.

Chien Tuan-sheng, *et al., Min-kuo cheng-chih shih* (History of the Political Institution under the Republic), Changsha, 1939.

Chow, Ting-zu and Hwang Kuo-chang, "Geography," *The Chinese Year Book, 1944-1945.*

Cressey, G. B., *Asia's Land and People*, New York, 1944.

Ennis, T. E., and Langsam, W. A. (ed.), *Eastern Asia*, New York, 1948.

Fang Hsien-t'ing, *Chung-kuo ching-chi yen-chiu* (Research in Chinese Economics), Nankai Institute of Economics, Changsha, 1938.

Griswold, A. W., *The Far Eastern Policy of the United States*, New York, 1938.

Haushofer, Karl, *Geopolitik des pazifischen Ozeans*, Berlin, 1939.

———, Obst, E., Lautehsach, H., and Maull, O., *Bausteine zur Geopolitik*, Berlin-Grünwald, 1928.

Hu Huan-yung, *Wo-men ti ch'iang-to* (Our Territory), Shanghai, 1947.

Huang Ching-peh, *Chung-kuo jen-shih sing-lun* (A New Study of China's Personnel Problems), Shanghai, 1946.

Kennan, George F., *American Diplomacy 1900-1950*, Chicago, 1951.

———, *Realities of American Foregin Policy*, Princeton, 1954.

Li Hsi-mei, *Chung-hua-min-kuo k'e-hsueh chih* (China's Scientific Development), 3 vols., Taipeh, 1955.

Li Hsueh-tseng, *Ya-chow Ch'ung-tsu ti-li* (Asia's Ethnological Geography), Shanghai, 1948.

Liu Ta-chun, *Chung-kuo kung-yeh tiao-ch'a pao-kao* (National Military Council's Report on Chinese Industries), Nanking, 1937.

Liu Ta-chung, *China's National Income 1931-1936*, Washington, 1946.

Mackinder, J., *Democratic Idea and Reality*, New York, 1919.

MacNair, H. F. (ed.), *China*, Berkeley, 1946.

Ministry of Commerce and Industry, *Chung-kuo ching-chi nien-chien* (Economic Year Book of China), Shanghai, 1934.

Moore, H. L., *Soviet Far Eastern Policy, 1931-1946*, Princeton, 1945.

Sprout, Harold and Margaret (eds.), *Foundations of National Power*, Princeton, 1949.

Wang Wei-ping, *Chung-kuo kang chan ti-li* (China's Geography in the War of Resistance), Shanghai, 1937.

Weng Wen-hao, *Wong's Essays*, Shanghai, 1937.

———, Ting, V. K., and Tseng Shih-ying, *Chung-hua min-kuo hsin ti-t'u* (New Atlas of Republic of China), Shun Pao, Shanghai, 1934.

Wu, Aitchen K., *China and the Soviet Union*, New York, 1950.

Yen, James Y. C., *The Mass Education Movement in China*, Shanghai, 1925.

Yang chüan, "China's Industrial Enterprises for the Past 50 Years," in *Tsui-chin chih wu-shih-nien* (The Past Fifty Years, in Commemoration of the Shun Pao's Golden Jubilee, 1872-1922), Shanghai, 1923.

Young, A. N., *China's Economic and Financial Reconstruction*, New York, 1947.

VII. COMPARATIVE MILITARY INSTITUTIONS

The following selected bibliographical list deals only with pertinent works on military affairs by Occidental and Japanese authors. For the Chinese works on military institutions, see Sections I and II of the bibliography.

Aston, Sir George, ed., *The Study of War for Statesmen and Citizens*, London, 1927.

Baldwin, Hansen W., *Great Mistakes of the War*, New York, 1950.

Baruch, Bernard M., *American Industry in the War*, New York, 1941.

Bliss, T. H., "The Unified Command," *Foreign Affairs*, I (December 1922), pp. 1-30.

Blumentritt, G., *Von Rundstedt, the Soldier and the Man*, London, 1952.

Bol'shaya Sovetskaya Entsiklopediya (Great Soviet Encyclopedia), XLIII, Moscow, 178-182.

Bugnet, Charles, *Rue St. Dominique et G. Q. H.*, Paris, 1937.

Bush, Vannevar, *Modern Arms and Free Men*, New York, 1949.

Clarkson, Grosvenor, *Industrial America in the World War; the Strategy behind the Line*, New York, 1923.

Clarkson, J. D. and Cochran, T. C., *War as a Social Institution*, New York, 1941.

Clausewitz, Carl von, *Vom Kriege*, Berlin, 1867, also trans. by J. J. Graham, London, 1911.

Davis, S. C., *The French War Machine*, London and New York, 1937.

Dawson, R. M., "The Cabinet Minister and Administration: Winston S. Churchill at the Admiralty, 1911-1915," *Canadian Journal of Economics and Science*, VI (Aug. 1940), pp. 325-358.

Delbrück, Hans, *Geschichte der Kriegskunst im Rahmen der politischen Geschichte*, Berlin, 1936.

Dunlop, Col. J. K., *The Development of the British Army*, London, 1938.

Earle, Edward M., ed., *Makers of Modern Strategy*, Princeton, 1944.

Foch, Marshal M., *Des Principes de la Guerre*, 3rd ed., Paris, 1917.

Fomicenko (ed.), *The Red Army*, London, 1946.

Fuller, J. F. C., *A Military History of the Western World: From the Earliest Times to the Battle of Lepanto*, New York, 1954.

———, *The Foundation of the Science of War*, London, 1926.

———, *The Army in My Time*, London, 1935.

Garthoff, R. L., *Soviet Military Doctrine*, Glencoe, Illinois, 1953.

Giles, Lionel (trans.) *Sun Tzu on Art of War*, op.cit., Introduction.

Goerlitz, Walter, *Der Deutsche Generalstab, Geschichte und Gestalt*, Frankfurt am Main, 1951.

BIBLIOGRAPHY

Graham, Frank D. and Scanlon, J. J., *Economic Preparation and Conduct of War under the Nazi Regime*, Historical Division, War Department Special Staff, 1946. Printed in mimeographed form.

Guillaume, A., *Soviet Arms and Soviet Power*, Washington, 1949.

Hamilton, Ian, *The Soul and Body of the Army*, New York, 1921.

Jaures, Jean L., *L'armee nouvelle*, Paris, 1915.

Jomini, Antoine H., *Précis de l'art de la guerre*, 2 vols., Paris, 1838.

Kingston-McCloughry, E. J., *The Direction of War: A Critique of the Political Direction and High Command in War*, New York, 1955.

Koji, Izuka, *Nihon no Guntai* (Japan's Military Forces), Tokyo, 1940.

Konrad, N. I., *Sun Tsz'i; Traktat o Voennom Iskusstre*, Moscow, 1952.

Koyama, Koken, *Nihon hagaku no ka-she* (The Development of the Japanese Military Concept), Tokyo, 1940.

Leeb, Ritter Wilhelm von, *Die Abwehr*, Leipzig, 1933.

Liddell-Hart, B. H., *The German Generals Talk*, New York, 1948.

———, *The Remaking of Modern Armies*, London, 1927.

———, *Why Don't We Learn From History?* London, 1954.

Luddendorff, Erich, *Der totale Krieg*, München, 1935.

Mahan, A. T., *The Influence of Sea Power upon History, 1660-1783*, Boston, 1890.

Maki, J. M., *Japanese Militarism; Its Cause and Cure*, New York, 1945.

Maurice, F. K., *Government and War: A Study of the Conduct of War*, London, 1936.

Meincke, Friedrich, *Die Deutsche Katastrophe*, Wiesbaden, 1946.

Mises, Ludwig von, *Omnipotent Government, The Rise of the Total State and Total War*, New Haven, 1944.

Mumford, Lewis, *Technics and Civilization*, New York, 1934.

Nelson, Otto, *National Security and the General Staff*, Washington, 1946.

Nokano, Tomio, *Tosuiken no dokuritsu* (The Independence of the Prerogative of the Military Command), Tokyo, 1934.

Palmer, J. M., *America in Arms: The Experience of the United States with Military Organization*, New Haven, 1941.

Rabenau, F., *Seeckt, aus seinem Leben 1918-1936*, Leipzig, 1940.

Rosinski, Herbert, *The German Army*, Washington, 1944.

Schellendorf, Bronsart von, *Der Dienst des Generalstab*, 2 vols. Berlin, 1876.

Seeckt, Hans von, *Gedanken eines Soldaten*, Leipzig, 1935.

Sheppard, E. W., *A Short History of the British Army*, London, 1940.

Stalin, J. V., *Über die Rote Armee* (keine Bucherei des Marxismus-Leninismus), Berlin, 1950.

Taylor, Telford, *Sword and Swastika*, New York, 1952.

Treitschke, H. G., "The Organization of the Army," *Politik II*, trans. by A. L. Gowan, London, 1914.

Upton, E., *The Armies of Asia and Europe*, New York, 1878.

U.S. Bureau of Budget, *The United States at War*, Washington: GPO, 1946.

Wavell, A., *Generals and Generalship*, New York, 1943.

Week, R. M., *Organization and Equipment for War*, Cambridge, 1950.

Wheeler-Bennett, John W., *The Nemesis of Power: The German Army in Politics, 1918-1945*, New York, 1952.

White, D. Fedotoff, *The Growth of the Red Army*, Princeton, 1944.

White, H., *Executive Influence in Determining Military Policy in the United States*, Urbana, Illinois, 1925.

Yamagata, Aritomo, "Rikugun shi" *Kaikoku Eogunen Shi* (The History of the Army, in Fifty Years of Founding the Empire), Tokyo, n.d.

VIII. PERIODICALS AND NEWSPAPERS

Bulletin of the Institute of History and Philology, Academia Sinica, Shanghai and Taipeh. Quarterly.

Cheng-chih ching-chi hsueh-puo (Journal of Politics and Economics), published by Nankai, Tientsin. Monthly.

China at War, published by China Information Committee, Chungking and printed in New York.

China Magazine, published by Chinese News Service, New York, 1946—. Monthly.

Command and General Staff School Quarterly, published at Fort Leavenworth, Kansas. Quarterly.

Chün-ssu tsa-chih (Journal of Military Affairs), edited and published by *Chün-ssu tsa-chih she*, Nanking and Chungking, 1929—. Monthly. One of the longest-established modern military journals in China, which emphasizes military science, military technology, and international affairs.

Eastern Miscellancy, edited by Commercial Press, Shanghai. In Chinese. Monthly.

Foreign Affairs, published by Foreign Policy Association, New York. Quarterly.

Hsin ching-chi (The New Economics), published by the *Hsin ching-chi pan-yueh-k'an she*, Chungking, 1938—. Bimonthly. One of the best-known intellectual periodicals in the wartime capital of China. Contributors included many responsible government officials and well-known scholars of China.

The Infantry Journal, published by Infantry Journal Press, Washington, D.C.

Journal of the Royal United Service Institution, published by the Royal United Service Institution, London.

Kaikosha kiji (The Journal of Kaiko sha), Tokyo. Monthly. This was an important Japanese military periodical, often containing information about Chinese military matters.

Kuo-fang yueh-kan (Journal of National Defense), published by *Kuo-fang yueh-kan she*, Nanking, 1946—. Monthly. A post-World War II military periodical; contains military articles written by distinguished military leaders and civilian experts.

Kuo-li chung-yang yen-chiu-yuan she-hui k'o-hsüeh yen-chiu-so chi-k'an
(Monographs of the Institute of Social Sciences, Academia Sinica),
published by the Academia Sinica, Shanghai and Taipeh.

Lu-ta chi-k'an, edited and published by the Chinese Army Staff College,
Nanking and Chungking, 1932—. Quarterly. A publication of the
Chinese Army Staff College, the highest educational institution of
the Chinese Army. Emphasizes research on tactics, grand strategy,
and translation of important foreign military works. Very small and
guarded circulation.

The above mentioned military periodicals were the most important
learned journals published by the Chinese military establishments. A number of technical-military periodicals were also published by the Chinese
infantry school, artillery school, ordnance school, etc. The Chinese Navy
Ministry published the well-edited *Hai-chün tsa-chih*; and the Air Force,
Chung-kuo ti kung-chün (China's Air Force). Both the War and Navy
Ministries periodically published their official *kung-pao* (public reports) or
gazettes containing laws, ordinances, and correspondence.

Militärwissenschaftliche Rundschau, in German, particularly the issues between 1932 and 1939, Berlin. Monthly.

Military Review, published by the U.S. Command and General Staff
School, Fort Leavenworth, Kansas. Monthly. The issues of the war
and postwar periods contained a number of articles on the China
theater.

Pacific Affairs, published by the Institute of Pacific Relations, New York.
Quarterly.

Pacific Historical Review, Vols. 1 to 18. Monthly.

Ti-li-hsueh-pao (Journal of the Geographical Society of China), edited
and published by the Chinese Geographical Society, Nanking, 1934—.

Tu-li p'ing-lun (The Independent Critic), edited by *Tu-li p'ing-lun she*,
Peiping, 1932-1937. Weekly. A highly respected liberal weekly of
prewar days. Often carried articles on problems of the Chinese government, constitution, and important national events.

Voyennaia Mysl, "Military Thought," Moscow. Monthly. The Chinese
Lu-ta chi-k'an, like a number of other foreign military periodicals,
carries regular translations of important articles from this Soviet
military journal.

Wei-chiao p'ing-lun (Review of Foreign Affairs), edited and published by
Wai-chiao ping-lun she, Nanking and later Shanghai, 1932—.

INDEX

advisers, *see* foreign advisers and instructors

Alexander, Harold R. L. G., 179, 211-212

Alpha program, 130, 195

American aid, influence on army, 130; medical, 140-141; to air force, 174-175; military mission to China (AMMISCA), 175; directive for, 192; in Burma, 184-191, 216-217; air force, 214; marines in North China, 228. *See also* Sino-American relations

Andrews, J. A., 186

anti-comintern pact, 98

armies, Soviet influence, 18-24; military politicians, 49; nepotism in, 55-56; personnel system, 94; financial reform, 94-95; three-year plan of rearmament, 99; Kwangsi Army, 111-112; troop disbandment, 111; basic reorganization, 115, 126-128; manpower, 131-136; strength, 135; casualties, 136, 145, 147-148; desertion and suicide, 137-138; diseases, 138-141; illiteracy, 141-143; "do or die" philosophy, 56-58, 143-145; women's corps, 143; educational background of officers, 146-147; compulsory military training, 148-150; commanders characterized, 150-152; airlift achievement, 157-158; attempted reorganization of 1946, 230-238

training programs: 136-138; centers, 189-191; Ramgarh, 141, 148, 183-189, 191, 215

units by name: Central army, 111-113; Chekiang army, 19; army of Hunan, 19; Kuominchun, 36, 111; Kwangsi armies, 19, 26, 38, 47, 68, 111-112, 123, 204, 246, 264; Kwantung (Japanese) army, 114, 171, 204, 214, 220; Manchurian army, 111; National defense army, 73; "The Party Army," 15-16; Peoples' army (*see* Kuominchun army); Red army, 35-36; Shansi army, 110; Szechuanese army, 137; Yunnan army, 19

units by number: First Army Corps, 22, 26, 37, 42, 47; new First Army, 215; Second Army, 51; Third Army, 51; Fourth Army Corps, 26-27, 34, 46, 49; new (communist) Fourth Army (later Third Field Army), 206, 228; Fifth Army Corps, 45, 92; Fifth, Sixth, and Sixty-sixth armies, in Burma, 210, 213; new Sixth Army, 215; Seventh Army Corps, 26, 34 47, 50; new Seventh Army, 259; Eighth Army, 259; Eighth Route Army (Red Army), 200-201; Twelfth Army, 262; Fourteenth Air Force, 214, 217-220; Nineteenth Route Army, 113; 22nd and 38th Divisions, 215; 22nd and 36th Divisions, nucleus of Ramgarh program, 184; 38th and 200th Divisions, in Burma campaign, 212

See also Central Army; communists and communism, armies; medical services; military organizations; Nationalist Army; National Revolutionary Army; schools, military

armored forces, 100

Arms, Thomas S., 189, 190-191

Arnold, Henry H., 217

arsenals, 27, 37-38, 101, 153-156; consolidation, 159-160

artillery, 84, 100, 155, 186, 254

Baldwin, Hanson W., 177-178

battles and campaigns, object of revolutionary war, 32; campaign against Wuhan, 36-39; creation of war areas, 128-129; "do or die" philosophy, 56-59; 143-145; Lungt'an, 50, 57-58; Honan, 50; Wuchang, 56-57; Pailing-miao, capture of, 114; Hengyang, defense of, 151, 220; Tai-erh-chuang-Hsuchow, 198, 200-201; Wuchang-Hankow, 202; Tsaoyang, 203; Changsha, 209; Salween campaign, 191, 215-216, 221; Hunan campaign, 222; fall of Loyang, 220; fall of Kweilin, 221; Szepingkai, 243-244; civil war, 249-264; Nationalist campaign in Manchuria, 254-260; Huai-hai campaign, 260-264; Hsuchow, 262-263. *See also* Sino-Japanese war, Burma campaigns, Northern expedition

Bauer, Max, 61-63, 68, 74, 91

Benson, C. C., 184

Bergin, W. E., 184

Bismarck, Otto von, 64, 66

Kai-shek as president, 9-24; faculty, 9, 14; curriculum, 11; policy and training, 11-12, 43; Japanese influence on, 13-14; Soviet influence on, 14-15; nucleus of National Revolutionary Army, 25; of Kuomintang, 53-58; heroism of cadets, 56-57; the "Whampoa mind," 59; the Whampoa group, 73, 228, 244; becomes Central Military Academy, 81-84, 112
Wu Chi-wei, General, 244
Wu Péi-fu, 27, 30, 36-37
Wuhan, regime, 42, 48-50; campaign against, 37-39; collapse, 49-52

Yalta agreement, 173, 255

Yang Chieh, 168-169
Yangtze, 58; failure of defense, 266-267
Yegorov, A. I., 4-6
Yeh Chien-ying, 14, 34
Yeh T'ing, 33, 34, 49, 206
Yen Hsi-shan, 51, 68, 74, 76
Yen, James, 142
Young, D. A., 184
Yü Han-mou, 257
Yü Ta-wei, 101
Yuan Shih-k'ai, 3, 69, 274
yuans, defined, 63
Yueh Fei, 285
Yunnan, *see* armies, training programs

Zhukov, Georgi K., 6, 20, 167

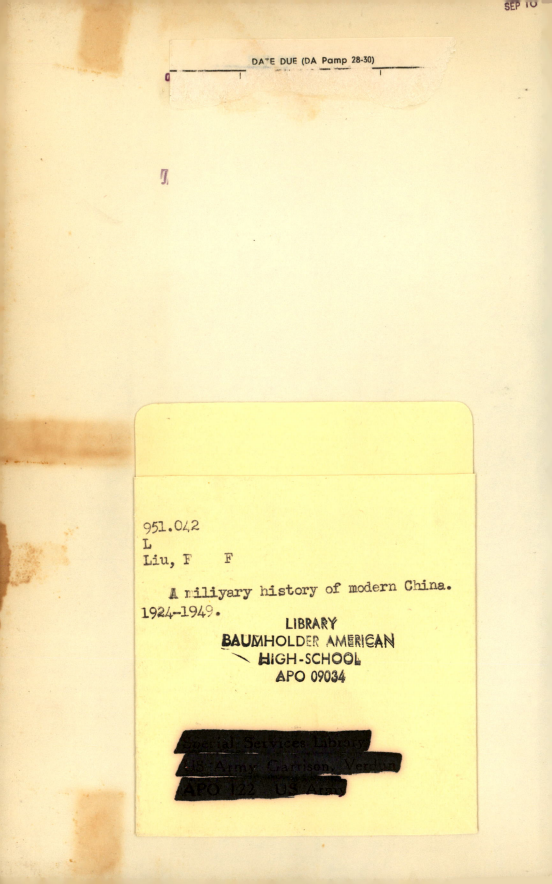